INTERPRETING AGRICULTURE AT MUSEUMS AND HISTORIC SITES

INTERPRETING HISTORY

SERIES EDITOR
Russell Lewis, Chicago History Museum

EDITORIAL ADVISORY BOARD
Anne W. Ackerson, Leading by Design
William Bomar, University of Alabama Museums
Jessica Dorman, The Historic New Orleans Collection
W. Eric Emerson, South Carolina Department of Archives and History
Tim Grove, National Air and Space Museum
Ann E. McCleary, University of West Georgia
Laurie Ossman, Preservation Society of Newport County
Laura Roberts, Roberts Consulting
Sandra Smith, Heinz History Center
Kimberly Springle, Charles Sumner School Museum and Archives
Elizabeth Joan Van Allen, Kentucky Historical Society
William S. Walker, Cooperstown Graduate Program, SUNY Oneonta

STAFF
Bob Beatty, AASLH
Charles Harmon, Rowman & Littlefield Publishers

About the Series
The American Association for State and Local History publishes the *Interpreting History* series in order to provide expert, in-depth guidance in interpretation for history professionals at museums and historic sites. The books are intended to help practitioners expand their interpretation to be more inclusive of the range of American history.

Books in this series help readers:

- quickly learn about the questions surrounding a specific topic,
- introduce them to the challenges of interpreting this part of history, and
- highlight best-practice examples of how interpretation has been done by different organizations.

They enable institutions to place their interpretative efforts into a larger context, despite each having a specific and often localized mission. These books serve as quick references to practical considerations, further research, and historical information.

Titles in the Series

INTERPRETING AGRICULTURE AT MUSEUMS AND HISTORIC SITES

DEBRA A. REID

ROWMAN & LITTLEFIELD
Lanham • Boulder • New York • London

Published by Rowman & Littlefield
A wholly owned subsidary of The Rowman & Littlefield Publishing Group, Inc.
4501 Forbes Boulevard, Suite 200, Lanham, Maryland 20706
www.rowman.com

Unit A, Whitacre Mews, 26-34 Stannary Street, London SE11 4AB

British Library Cataloguing in Publication Information Available

Library of Congress Cataloging-in-Publication Data
Names: Reid, Debra Ann, 1960– author.
Title: Interpreting agriculture at museums and historic sites / Debra A. Reid.
Description: Lanham : Rowman & Littlefield, [2017] | Series: Interpreting history ; 12 | Includes
bibliographical references and index.
Identifiers: LCCN 2016043889 (print) | LCCN 2016044469 (ebook) | ISBN 9781442230101
(cloth : alkaline paper) | ISBN 9781442230118 (paperback : alkaline paper) | ISBN 9781442230125
(Electronic)
Subjects: LCSH: Agricultural museums—United States—Planning. | Historic farms—United
States—Planning. | Agriculture—United States—History—Sources. | Agriculture—Study and
teaching—United States. | Museums—Educational aspects—United States. | Museum exhibits—
United States. | Historic sites—Interpretive programs—United States.
Classification: LCC S549.U5 R45 2017 (print) | LCC S549.U5 (ebook) | DDC 630.74—dc23
LC record available at https://lccn.loc.gov/2016043889

∞™ The paper used in this publication meets the minimum requirements of American National
Standard for Information Sciences—Permanence of Paper for Printed Library Materials, ANSI/
NISO Z39.48-1992.

Printed in the United States of America

CONTENTS

PART 4: DEVELOPING INTERPRETATION

FOREWORD

Tom Kelleher

WITHOUT AGRICULTURE there would be no civilization. You would not be reading these words, or any written language for that matter, were it not for farmers. Our ancient hunter-gatherer forebears lived in dispersed, roaming bands in an often-desperate effort to find enough food to survive. They had no need for writing, or the leisure to conceive it. It was the domestication of animals and the growing of crops that developed in the late Stone Age—in a word, agriculture; in a phrase the Neolithic Revolution—that allowed for settled living. Villages grew into cities, and with them civilization with all its fruits and curses.

Agriculture is not the antithesis of urban living, but its parent: what made and makes it possible. Farms not only feed the vast majority of the world's population, but they also furnish raw materials for clothing and countless other necessities of life, and luxuries now perceived of as necessities. In many countries today, even city dwellers still keep a pig or a few chickens, and tend kitchen gardens not as a hobby, but out of necessity. That was the case in early America as well, where pigs freely roamed the streets of most colonial cities. When urban farming happens today, however, it is remarkable enough to appear on the local evening news.

Thanks to the evolution of agriculture, food in Western culture has become so plentiful and so ubiquitous that threat of starvation is a distant cultural memory. Indeed, plenty has grown into its own threat to human health and longevity, namely in the epidemic of obesity and its related morbidities. Food ennui drives most of us not to hope for enough food, but to crave ever greater variety, luxury, and gastronomic novelty. Eating has gone well beyond survival and become recreational. Witness the continued proliferation of restaurants, cooking shows, cookbooks, and culinary websites. While kings and nobles have dined recreationally for centuries, it was not until 1830 that the Delmonico brothers, Swiss immigrants to New York City, introduced dining for pleasure to the middle class when they converted their confectionary shop into a restaurant. For a fee, colonial inns invited travelers to share the simple family table; restaurants today sell a dining experience, feeding not just the body but the soul, as well.

Yet while everyone eats (often too much), and agriculture is still a large part of the United States' economy, today fewer and fewer Americans play a direct role in food production. Big agribusiness continues to squeeze out traditional family farms, and force them to either "go big" themselves, or seek out niche markets in order to survive. Despite a modest proliferation of "locavores," almost a thousand acres of fertile American farm fields disappear every day under asphalt and lawns as housing developments and retail shops multiply. While an increasingly commercial "field to table" trend appeals to a relatively select few who can afford it, farms are often alien territory to most modern Americans. Few of us are more than a couple of generations removed from our farming ancestors, but the details of their lives are easily, and often purposefully, forgotten. A few tomato plants in a backyard garden do not an authentic farming experience make.

They took all the trees
And put them in a tree museum
Then they charged the people
A dollar and a half just to see 'em.
Don't it always seem to go
That you don't know what you've got
Till it's gone?
They paved paradise
And put up a parking lot.[1]

Today one might be inclined to alter Joni Mitchell's 1970 hit song "Big Yellow Taxi," by substituting "farms" for "trees." Of course, farms certainly still exist today, but most of us have no contact with them beyond as end consumers of their produce. While the American farm still tugs romantically at our collective heartstrings with powerful nostalgia for a past only vaguely understood, for many of us agriculture is a curiosity to be viewed at and explained by a museum.

The proliferation of agricultural museums is, therefore, something to be lauded, not lamented. Those who want to know more about where their food and fibers originate need not entirely change their way of living or undertake a timely investigation. Museums do that for us. An afternoon's visit to a farm museum typically provides a good summary introduction to the subject for the curious and their children. Surveys repeatedly tell us that Americans trust museums more than they do the Internet, news media, academia, or just about any other source of information. Perhaps the unrelenting toil, drudgery, uncertainty, and risk of farming cannot be fully conveyed by a visit to a museum, but people nonetheless experience firsthand some of the authenticity they expect to find there. In our increasingly virtual world, visitors to farm museums see real chickens laying real eggs, real cows giving real milk, and real crops being sown, cultivated, and harvested.

Some agricultural museums explore the science behind farming. Some provide hands-on opportunities, from incidental sampling to immersive weekends. (I still fondly recall milking a cow at a farm museum when I was six, and how her swishing tail felt hitting my face.) Some demonstrate once-common household tasks, like making butter, cheese, or candles, or even that increasingly rare household phenomenon, routinely cooking from scratch. Some provide historical perspective, showing us how we got to where we are by showing us where we as a people have been. All museums combine scholarship with a variety of educational techniques to help us better appreciate and make sense of our world. Just as farms feed our bodies, museums feed our minds and souls. Arguably, farm museums do both.

Tom Kelleher
Sturbridge, Massachusetts
June 1, 2016

Note

1. From "Big Yellow Taxi," words and music by Joni Mitchell. © 1970 (renewed) Crazy Crow Music. All rights (excluding print) administered by Sony/ATV Tunes, LLC. Exclusive print rights administered by Alfred Music. All rights reserved. Used by permission of Alfred Music.

PREFACE

Debra A. Reid

THIS BOOK has taken much longer than it should have. If only it could have been a piglet, gestated in three months, three weeks, and three days. Or a calf, gestated in 285 days (approximately nine-and-one-half months). Even elephants take only twenty-two months to gestate, the longest of any land mammal. Why did this book take three years?

I could blame Bob Beatty, who told me in June 2013 that authors could set their own schedules. Instead, I will be honest. The quantity of information that warranted inclusion proved overwhelming. Furthermore, I set a high bar—pledging to make this book provocative in the ways that Freeman Tilden made us all think about interpretation. His six principles, rationalized in *Interpreting Our Heritage*, originally published in 1957 and continually in print, stand as a compelling call to action. I equate the need to interpret agriculture to the need to interpret, period. The future of humanity on the planet depends on it.

I took Bob Beatty's directions to heart. *Interpreting Agriculture at Museums and Historic Sites* is designed to help local history museums use their stories and their collections to make a difference. Chapters define agriculture and identify themes that museums, historic houses, and historic sites can use as a basis for interpretation. Chapters explain how to document agriculture at the local level, and use the archival and artefactual evidence as the basis for expanding local relevance to regional, state, national, and international contexts. Examples provide models of how local history takes on new meaning when informed by agricultural topics, and how agricultural history requires the human dimension to be most complete.

Transforming local stories and objects into excellent exhibits and public programming requires dedication, concentration, and investment of resources. This involves a self-conscious effort to avoid presentism, to avoid transplanting our modern suburban worldview onto the historic agricultural past. This warrants careful thought at all stages of interpretive planning, and at all levels of source analysis and program development.

Bob Beatty asked me to survey the history of agriculture. Other books provide a chronological survey, and the bibliographic essay online identifies a few studies to consult.

Instead, I identified critical themes in agriculture that shaped America historically. I emphasize themes that remain relevant today because they affect the consuming public and modern farmers daily, though rhetoric may trivialize them or cause the public and farmers alike to discount them. Revealing the meanings and interrelationships of themes such as national policy, labor laws, and the world's food supply can launch conversations about agricultural practices at any place and time in the past, though the details will vary based on location and chronological coverage.

I appealed to friends to help me get this book done. The contributions that they provided should help "spur" thinking about interpreting agriculture. I learned by working with the authors not to settle for good information about agriculture, but to take that information and turn it on its head to prompt additional thought. Furthermore, no matter how much you think and rethink a topic, a person with different experiences can help you see it differently. For example, Pete Watson, Howell Living History Farm, Lambertville, New Jersey, explained how a friend, Horseman Halsey, helped Pete see "places where the Valley Road leveled off, climbed, leveled off, climbed, etc." as tools that farmers used to get loaded wagons up and down hills without stressing the horses by having them hold back the load with their britchen, or stressing the equipment by applying the brakes excessively. Remembering Halsey's point of view can help us all see hills differently, whether we go up them or down them.

Many museums and historic sites have artifacts to document agriculture. They have walking plows, feed sacks, and banknotes with agricultural artwork. They have embroidered samplers with pastoral scenes, tablecloths and curtains printed with fruits and vegetables, and artwork featuring prize racehorses. They have archives full of diaries, letters, and photographs that document family farming. Putting the pieces together can help us see the stories in three dimensions, and this can help us recognize the complicated relationships that drove human life for centuries, and that still affects the life of farm families and living history farm interpreters.

None of us knows all we need to know about agriculture. It takes a team to make the most of interpreting an interdisciplinary topic. I am not a machinery expert. But I have friends who see an image and can recall the make, model, years of production, and geographic range of influence. They constantly remind me of the value of adopting a technology and science focus, and I share my humanist point of view with them. Together, we can document a more complete past.

The farmers today have a lot to share, too. All farmers. They may be crop farmers or hog farmers who model production agriculture. They may work at modern agribusinesses transformed into tourist destination spots to diversify their income, as does Farmer John's CSA—Angelic Organics—in Caledonia, Illinois, near Chicago; dairy farm attractions such as Fair Oaks Farms, complete with a robotic milker that holds seventy-two cows—in Fair Oaks, Indiana; and market orchard agribusinesses such as Eckert's near Belleville, Illinois. They may be advocates of alternative agriculture who work with traditional practices—draft horses or draft oxen—as part of a larger goal to model sustainable and organic production practices, as do staff at Tillers International near Kalamazoo, Michigan. They may work at living history farms and open-air museums, where they maintain crop and stock varieties of their time period but also translate historical research into public programming respectful of modern environmental and animal welfare standards.

The process of interpreting agriculture requires knowledge of several disciplines—biology, botany, zoology, history, geography, mathematics, politics, economics, and geology. It requires an understanding of modern guidelines for animal husbandry in an educational setting, as well as an historic perspective that helps you see what artwork and photographs can tell you about people and their animals in the past. It depends on asking questions that generate conversations.

Documenting agriculture takes time, and truth be told, the documentation should never end. Sharing the findings as research-in-progress can help you generate interest. The public can participate. The institutional mission should guide the process. Do not be afraid to generate dialogue, but do be prepared to engage in conflict resolution. Agriculture can be polarizing, but we all owe our lives to farmers, so the conversation warrants the risk.

Debra A. Reid
Charleston, Illinois
June 2016

ACKNOWLEDGMENTS

I T TAKES A community to sustain those who work in museums and historic sites, a community that involves family, faculty mentors, and fellow travelers. My parents and aunts and uncles raised me up on farms in Rockwood, Illinois, just north of the Randolph-Jackson County line. They have my unconditional love because of the ways they supported my interest in agriculture and history throughout my life. Several amazing professors at SEMO guided me as I learned about historic preservation. These included Dr. Frank Nickell and Mr. Bob White, but especially Dr. Arthur Mattingly, the director of the new Historic Preservation Program. I spent two idyllic months as a summer Fellow at Historic Deerfield in Deerfield, Massachusetts. The residents and the staff at Historic Deerfield, especially J. Ritchie Garrison, helped me envision a career in public history. He told me I should consider applying to the Cooperstown Graduate Program in History Museum Studies. I followed that advice. In the meantime, I worked for two years at the Washburn-Norlands Living History Center near Livermore Falls, Maine (1983 and 1984), and for a season at Old World, Wisconsin (1985).

For thirty years, between the 1980s and 2010s, I encountered many people with many perspectives on agriculture. I have tried to listen to them because I believe that provocation comes from the classic debate strategy: know the counter argument as thoroughly as you know the argument. We all should look for something that jostles us from our preconceived ideas about the subject. Then the book has done its job.

Several members of the Rowman & Littlefield staff deserve special thanks for shepherding the pages through production—especially Charles Harmon, Kathleen O'Brien, and Karen Ackermann. Jacqueline Wehrle wrestled the material into an index that should help readers find what they need to support their efforts.

I have benefited from the thoughtful comments of students and faculty at Eastern Illinois University and of friends and colleagues, including Becky Crabb, Cliff Jones, Bob Powell, Todd Price, Wayne Randolph, Ed Schultz, Jim Slining, Todd Stockwell, and Pete Watson. I wish I could have written this book by committee, but I found that the more I talked about the possibilities, the more paralyzed I became. I had to isolate myself to put words on paper. For those eager to get involved in the important work, turn to the Association for Living History, Farm and Agricultural Museums, the Agricultural History Society, and the American Association for State and Local History. I hope that this book, and the personal and professional connections that you can build, help to sustain your efforts.

PART 1

DEVELOPING INTERPRETATION WITH AN AGRICULTURAL PERSPECTIVE

CHAPTER 1

INTERPRETING AGRICULTURE

Introduction to Terms and Themes

Introduction

The Institute of Museum and Library Services (IMLS) identified 35,144 museums in the United States in 2014. Many items in these thousands of collections can help interpret a topic as pervasive as agriculture, not just those collections in history museums or historical societies. Masterpieces in art museums feature succulent fruit, food and drink, and farm fields at harvesttime. Domesticated animals and plants attract attention at zoos.[1] Much remains to be known, however, about what visitors think about agriculture, or what they might like to learn about it, as informed by a museum's unique resources. The National Museum of American History's exhibit *American Enterprise* features agriculture in its overview of business opportunity and exploitation.[2] The Museum of Science and Industry in Chicago hatches chicks as part of its educational programming. The Smithsonian Institution's National Museum of Natural History showcases soil, the basis of most agriculture, in an interdisciplinary exhibit, *Dig It: The Secrets of Soil.* Metro-parks and forest preserve districts operate living history farms with complete environments with heritage breeds of plants and animals and multisensory, interdisciplinary programming (Photo 1.1). In fact, all museums, historic sites, and park districts have resources to interpret agriculture.[3]

Many of these institutions embrace the challenge of interpreting agriculture. Those interested in trying can start by revisiting Freeman Tilden's definition of *interpretation*: "an educational activity which aims to reveal meanings and relationships through the use of original objects, by firsthand experience, and by illustrative media, rather than simply to communicate factual information."[4] The most effective interpretation will help the public connect agriculture as practiced in the past (and about which they know little), with agriculture as practiced in the present (about which they know little more).

Holmdel farmers grew a variety of crops and raised animals for local use. Bigger farms, like those owned by the Longstreets, raised large amounts of potatoes, apples and corn.
Some Holmdel farms specialized in raising dairy cows for fresh milk and milk products. Milk, meat, vegetables and fruit were either harvested in season for sale, or smoked, canned, dried, or preserved for later use.

Photo 1.1 The orientation exhibit at Historic Longstreet Farm, a living history farm operated by the Monmouth County [New Jersey] Park System, features the Handy Buncher, a machine to bind asparagus spears, patented in 1902, a historic photograph depicting the 1910 potato harvest, and a potato barrel used to transport spuds to market.

Source: Photograph by Debra A. Reid, March 2015

Gauging public interest can start with surveying the ways that local agribusinesses incorporate historic assets into their corporate brands. For instance, customers at a pick-your-own agritourism destination near Belleville, Illinois, carry their bakery purchases away in a box stamped: *Eckert's Bakery: A Tradition of Goodness. For over 170 years people from all over have found their way to Eckert's family farms to enjoy the freshest, sweetest fruits around. Thanks for enjoying Eckert's.*[5] Truth be told, the family farm began in Pennsylvania over 170 years ago, not in Illinois. Regardless, the sixth and seventh generations of family farmers operate two seasonal market-orchards in small communities along the Mississippi River, and the year-round headquarters in the southeastern suburban fringe of Belleville. Eckert's antique farm truck at the store entrance symbolizes the family commitment to the farm, and a tractor situated under the slogan, "Creating Family Memories," becomes the centerpiece of family portraits.

You will also find agricultural interpretation where you might least expect it. Travelers have to seek out the vertical aeroponics garden installed in the Rotunda Building in Terminal 3 at the Chicago O'Hare International Airport, but those who find it will learn about resource stewardship and green initiatives in the midst of concrete spaces (Photo 1.2).

Few people have direct experiences with agriculture today. Few understand the symbiotic relationship between crops, livestock, and humans or the ways that the cycles of domesticated crops and livestock affect human behavior. Few comprehend the entanglement of independent family farms and government policy. Interpretation can start by helping people recognize these things, either in modern agriculture or in historic settings. Doing this is not simple, because few staff can identify agricultural tools, implements, and machinery in their collections. Lacking basic visual literacy makes it difficult for curators to put implements into context. This makes it difficult to curate and interpret agricultural artifacts. *Interpreting Agriculture* will help us address these issues and face these challenges.

The good news: Everyone will learn something through the process that your museum or historic site undertakes. The process of developing an awareness of agriculture, documenting its relevance to your museum or historic site, managing collections to reflect that relevance, and developing interdisciplinary interpretation about agriculture can be transformative. It will take work. It will take dedication. It requires self-awareness and self-analysis. It requires hearing from people with different perspectives on the subject, and managing the conversations to allow all voices, past and present, to be heard. Breadth of coverage involves respecting the voices and hearing the perspectives of American Indians and enslaved people and wage laborers and sharecroppers as well as landowners and policy makers and processors.

Why is learning more about agriculture (its present and its past) important? The United States remains, in sheer acreage, remarkably rural and agricultural. The cities and the suburbs with their concentrated populations have a relatively small geospatial footprint on the national landscape. Regardless, urban and suburban populations rely on agriculture today, just as they did historically. Then, the average urban resident interacted with livestock constantly. The smell of draft animals and their manure permeated

Photo 1.2 Travelers visit the O'Hare Urban Garden, installed in 2011 to produce leafy vegetables and herbs for O'Hare restaurants. Interpretive panels line the walls in the seating area above the walkway to Concourse G in Terminal 3. They explain how the twenty-six vertical grow towers work, and how the aeroponics garden furthers the green agenda of the Chicago Department of Aviation.
Source: Photograph by Debra A. Reid, June 2013.

all spaces. The stockyards were where workers slaughtered livestock and processors cured hams, fabricated bristle brushes, and packaged natural fertilizers. Offal removal practices at the Union Stockyards in Chicago prompted the community of Hyde Park to take the Yards to court on the grounds that noxious smells disrupted town life. Upton Sinclair went undercover in the Yards and in the ethnic communities Back of the Yards, to collect data for his novel *The Jungle*. The moral of the story: Agriculture is about much more than plants and seeds, but processing and consuming plants and seeds relates to agriculture, and the connections warrant interpretation.

The learning curve for everyone involved will be high, because documenting, collecting, preserving, and interpreting agriculture becomes more complicated by the day. The variety of crops grown and stock raised over time offers limitless opportunities to explore topics from an agricultural point of view, whether or not your institution had any relationship to the production side of agriculture. Historic houses offer a perfect place to talk about agriculture: horsehair upholstery on furniture in the parlor, pastoral scenes on the table setting in the dining room, flower garden re-creations that feature arrangements advertised in a period-appropriate horticultural catalog, portraits of people with animals, photographs of children in carts pulled by goats. The evidence of agriculture can overwhelm, but the process of identifying resources, determining relevance, and planning interpretive programs will pay off. It takes an open mind, a basic understanding of agriculture, and some creative thinking to act on the potential.

What if your museum or historic site does not exist anywhere near farmers? In reality, farmers are closer than you think. Reaching out to them can enrich interpretive planning.[6] Potential partners abound, and include the local county Farm Bureau office or the Future Farmers of America chapter at your nearest high school. The coordinators and members of your local 4-H club likely will appreciate your goals and be able to help in various ways. You can find faculty who teach agricultural literacy by contacting your regional education service center, or by reaching out to charter schools that specialize in agricultural sciences. These schools are often in urban school districts, that is, Chicago High School for Agricultural Sciences. Go to your local farmers' market and talk to the vendors.

If your museum is in a food desert, be aware of the public health initiatives to increase the options available to residents in places with limited access to affordable healthy food choices. The Let's Move campaign, launched by First Lady Michelle Obama, began as an effort to reverse childhood obesity and has broadened its agenda to eradicate food deserts by 2017. Museums and historic sites have participated since its beginning. If your museum is in a foodie zone, reach out to locavore restaurants, brewpubs, and other farm-to-table businesses, such as community-supported-agriculture operations (CSAs). You will find kindred spirits, all partners in the uphill battle to engage customers.

You should not have to look far to find a farmer. It will take more effort to adapt to the farmer's limited availability, but just ask to meet. Shared interests provide a basis to build a dialogue with increasing public understanding about the business of farming at the center. Such partnerships can launch an exploration of modern agriculture.

Ideally, agricultural understanding will start with some fundamentals: identifying the type of fruit on a still life, or the vegetable on a piece of majolica. But the process cannot stop there. After mastering the basics, expand your horizons to learn more about agricultural processes and routines. You can visit local history museums and meet with curators who have mastered the identification of agricultural artifacts. You can learn from staff at living history farms about harnessing horses, yoking oxen, hitching plows, planting when the moon is growing, and castrating livestock when the moon is shrinking. Each skill adds depth that will lead to more thoughtful interpretation of topics as diverse as physics and traction, ecosystems, biological sciences, and all the humanities disciplines.

Layout of the Book

Interpreting Agriculture emphasizes the human perspective on a multidisciplinary subject—agriculture. The STEM (science, technology, engineering, and mathematics) and STEAM (add art) disciplines already enhance agricultural understanding, especially as formalized in the national Agriculture in the Classroom curriculum. A STEALTH approach puts art, literature, theater, and history (plus economics, the environment, and politics) onto an equal playing field with the STEM disciplines by focusing on the humans at the heart of the story. People passed the laws that created "public lands" that people bought and sold, and plowed, planted, and cultivated with machinery that other people designed and fabricated, using draft stock that people bred to do the work. These human-centric stories become the tools to reach members of the general public who are physically close to the historic fields and factories that fed and clothed them, but who cannot see those buried clues through the accretions overlaying the past.

A STEALTH approach can start with a conversation between farmers and the general public.[7] It can continue with an organized trip to a pick-your-own orchard or an open house at a local farm where visitors can talk with farmer–business owners on their own properties. Visitors could tour equipment sheds and learn about the costs of machinery and maintenance. A driving tour linked to a mobile app can orient the general public to the crops in the field, the routes from farm to market, and the storage and processing businesses that move it from farm to table. These relatively low-cost public programs take time, but they can motivate the public to learn more about what existed before modern agriculture. They can lay the foundation for interdisciplinary programming based on local research and proactive collecting.

Approaching agriculture from a humanist perspective provides focus without diminishing the potential of interpreting agriculture from other disciplinary points of view. This can help people be more informed about the landscapes through which they commute (be the travel time accomplished in seconds from their kitchen to the barn or hours from their garage to their high-rise office building). It can help people comprehend the mutual dependency between farm family members and the livestock that they husband and the crops that they cultivate. It can help people understand the relationships of daytime and night to the biological rhythms of human and domesticated animals.[8]

To accomplish these goals, *Interpreting Agriculture* is organized into four parts. The first includes chapters focused on developing an agricultural point of view, making humanities more central to agricultural education and interpretation, and using agriculture as the basis for exercises in historical thinking. The second part focuses on research methods and models to inform the process. The third part provides examples of local research as the basis for agricultural interpretation. The fourth part provides exercises that can help you become mentally engaged with agricultural sources, and that you can use in training. It also includes a case study about historic house interpretation and a case study about exhibit research and design.

An appendix lists organizations that offer skills-building conferences, how-to publications, and useful models to help you develop agricultural education and interpretation. The appendix also includes links to three digital resources: 1) a timeline focused on national policy and agrarian legislation that can help you locate your institution in the national context; 2) a bibliographic essay that summarizes major themes in agricultural history (i.e., labor, crop cultures, agricultural markets, government policy, national surveys, etc.) and scholarly book-length studies that you can use as a starting point to develop context for your site; and 3) the guidelines for "Livestock Care in Museums," prepared by the FARM Professional Interest Group of the Association for Living History, Farm and Agricultural Museums.

Terms Defined

The U.S. Census Bureau differentiated between rural and urban populations with the second population census, enumerated in 1800. The majority of the U.S. population lived in rural places before 1920. As of the 1920 U.S. Census, the majority of the population lived in communities of more than 2,500 people, the definition that the Census Bureau used to distinguish between *rural* and *urban*. Many associate the term *rural* with agriculture, but few people in rural America "farm." In fact, the 2010 decennial population census reported that 19.3 percent of the U.S. population (nearly 59.5 million people) lived in rural America.[9] The U.S. agricultural census of 2012 documented only 3.2 million farmers (only 1 percent of the U.S. population) operating 2.1 million farms.[10]

Some farmers do not live in rural America, but they farm in the city. For the first time in 2015, the National Agricultural Statistical Service of the U.S. Department of Agriculture conducted a pilot study of urban agriculture to collect data to document farmers living in "urban" areas. As agricultural land values and agricultural equipment costs escalate and exceed the reasonable mortgage rates extended to farmers seeking loans, the ideal of producing food where the majority of the population lives may be gaining traction. Early twenty-first-century agricultural census data should document this trend.[11]

What is agriculture?[12] The *Oxford English Dictionary* (*OED*) defines *agriculture* as "the practice of growing crops, rearing livestock, and producing animal products (as milk and eggs) regarded as a single sphere of activity; farming, husbandry;[13] (also) the theory of this." This definition allows for numerous scenarios to increase our understanding of what it took historically (and what it requires today) to raise crops and livestock and to produce milk, eggs, and other products using either free-range, organic, or confinement approaches.

What is farming? The *OED* explains it as the business of growing crops and rearing livestock.[14] Throughout *Interpreting Agriculture* the term *farming* will refer to the business of and *agriculture* to the practice of growing crops and rearing stock.

The other "sphere[s] of activity" mentioned in the *OED*'s definition of *agriculture* refers to businesses that existed, historically and today, to keep farmers in their fields. No study of agriculture is complete without this breadth of coverage. Farmers needed auction houses, agricultural newspapers and journals, country farm bureau offices, crop and liability insurance agents, market advisers, veterinarians, meteorologists, and fertilizer suppliers. Farmers also depended on agricultural equipment manufacturers and dealers for new combines, tractors, and other equipment, and on rural supply stores for barbed and woven wire, fence panels, watering troughs, and creep feeders. Other services included processing facilities that transformed agricultural commodities into marketable products (corn into high-fructose corn syrup, pigs into sausage, and milk into cheese and other dairy products).

The term *agribusiness*,[15] coined by agricultural and business professors at Harvard in 1957, refers to integrated industries that produce, process, and market agricultural commodities. Examples range from transnational corporations such as Monsanto or John Deere, cooperatives such as Ocean Spray, trans-state pig producers such as Maschhoffs, and even local pick-your-own market gardens. The term *agribusiness* carries negative connotations among critics of large-scale production agriculture. Family-owned and operated agribusinesses counter by using the word *family* strategically, and often linking sustainability and stewardship to their branding, too. The Maschhoffs tagline reads: "Progressive Farming, Family Style," and their homepage balances family history as well as impressive production statistics: "We're the Maschhoffs. In 1851, our ancestors came to Illinois and began a family farming tradition. Today, we are one of the largest family-owned hog farming networks in North America. With our family farm partners across the Midwest, we raise enough hogs for U.S. packers and processors to feed 16 million consumers annually."[16] Obviously, the term "family farming" has cachet in the competitive world of agribusiness.

What is family farming? The family unit provided a relatively stable foundation for farming historically. Today the term *family farm* can accurately describe a farm lived on and worked by one family or by multiple generations. The longer the family has farmed, the more the operators celebrate their longevity. Two pick-your-own orchards near Belleville, Illinois, indicate shared values but different marketing strategies. Sixth-generation farmers Pat Braeutigam Range, her husband, Tom, and their extended family members live on and operate Braeutigam Orchards. Pat's grandfather diversified the century-old family farm in 1935 by starting the orchard.[17] Nearby, Eckert's operates a year-round agritourism business, but emphasizes the family farm legacy: "Proud of their farming heritage and diligent stewards of the land, the Eckerts have cultivated and preserved their orchard business for seven generations."[18] A third example, Marcoot Jersey Creamery, reinforces the powerful connection between family tradition and high quality: "We are a seventh-generation family-owned Jersey dairy farm in Greenville, Illinois. We handcraft only the highest-quality artisan and farmstead cheeses. We are excited to bring our family's passion and tradition to your table!"[19]

A deeper understanding of the demands of agriculture historically can help explain the link between family and farm labor demands. It took a united herculean effort on the part of women, children, and men to keep up with the workload on family farms. Families often had to hire help during planting or harvest times, or contract with jobbers to break sod or thresh grain. The family unit helped sustain diversified agriculture. Several factors combined during the early twentieth century to change family farming practices. This included technological changes that reduced the demand for labor on farms, in combination with opportunities that drew youth away from the farms. Remaining in farming, as a family, became a source of honor and respect. As a consequence, rural culture, public policy, and even agribusiness celebrated the family farm, and still do so. The family farm played an important role in agriculture historically, and continues to influence public perceptions and actual practices today, but the family farm really represents just the tip of the barn's cupola when trying to understand agriculture on a local, state, regional, or national scale.

Today only a few of us can claim knowledge of farm life. The majority of us have little to zero direct experience with agriculture or its traditions, or with family members who may have lived it and who can still talk about it. This poses a significant but not insurmountable challenge to museums and historic sites interested in collecting, preserving, and interpreting agriculture. Getting started involves thought and action, but the time has come to take the steps that will allow your museum or historic site to identify relevant topics, and to research, collect, preserve and interpret them in engaging ways.

Agricultural Themes

Opinions about agriculture often reflect attitudes about moral values, political philosophies, economic theories, and attitudes about technology, human ingenuity, and American exceptionalism. Themes that warrant coverage include the myth of the independent farmer, the nostalgia for a "simpler" rural life, and the reality that land-owning farmers benefited from national policy, particularly land policy and market regulations, in ways that tenants and sharecroppers did not. Themes addressing less uplifting lessons include the treatment of Indians removed from their lands, people of color entrapped in slavery, and rural and agricultural laborers relegated to second-class citizenship. Topics worthy of interpretation, such as animal welfare, genetic modification, consumer health, and business regulation, become flash points for heated conversations. The debates reflect extremes: capitalism or communalism, democracy or socialism, individualism or kinship, and independence or mutual dependency. Interpreting agriculture must take into account the sorts of power that farmers wielded, as well as the influence that they lacked as they did their daily chores.

Popular perceptions of farmers often reflect nostalgic ideas of family farms as the backbone of America, and farmers as stewards of the environment. Furthermore, the American agrarian ideal associates land-owning farmers as morally superior and invaluable to the nation's success and undervalues farmers who did not own land, or who owned small acreages. These ideas originated during the early national period as influential politicians, specifically Thomas Jefferson, depicted the yeoman farmer as an independent, morally upright citizen whom the new United States needed to support to ensure national survival. As the numbers of farmers declined, their claims to a privileged status increased. Today, farmers, public policy makers, farm lobby groups, and even agribusiness operators perpetuate the agrarian ideals of the 1780s. Historical amnesia accounts for this emphasis on a national agricultural story based on technological innovation, bountiful fertile land, and free and independent yeomen. Such origin tales push other stories to the margins, stories about inequality, racism, labor activism, and Indian removal, to name just a few.

All-consuming physical labor more accurately symbolizes U.S. farming history. Farmers put blood, sweat, and tears into their business. Evidence confirms that farmers had to balance the demands of plowing, planting, cultivating, and harvesting crops and tending livestock with other duties. The farm routines reflected the characteristics of soils and sediments, the climate, animal and plant biology, and topography, all factors beyond the control of humans. Farmers managed these factors by being technologically savvy; or failed given these extenuating circumstances. They used technology to reduce labor needs, transform arid environments into fertile fields (irrigation), overcome short growing seasons (drought-resistant plant varieties), and standardize and maximize reproduction (artificial insemination).

Farmers almost always worked at more than one job, and self-identified as farmer-merchant or farmer–government agent or farmer–business owner. These dual responsibilities gave them added leverage that they used to exert political influence, stabilize processing and marketing networks, and ultimately sustain their own social and economic status and political influence. Sometimes the system fell apart. When farmers found their influence on money, markets, and processing slipping out of their reach, they organized the most successful third-party movement in the history of the United States—the People's Party (also known as the Populists).[20]

From colonization to the Civil War, crops that required physically demanding labor nearly year-round perpetuated enslavement. Other crops—grain crops, for instance—required less constant labor. Agricultural manufacturers further reduced labor needs by inventing machines like reapers and mowers. This reduced the dependency that farmers had on expensive wage laborers or the enslaved. Thus, the reaper represented freedom for farmers, no longer dependent on laborers, but the reaper represented a threat to wage laborers, who lost their income.

Agriculture drove national expansion from the colonial era, when English investors realized they could get rich from tobacco, or when families realized they could secure land. Until 1776, the agricultural commodities that farmers grew in North America either satisfied local demand or made their way into highly regulated markets in the Atlantic world. After the American Revolution, government policy remained influential in agriculture, even as laissez-faire economic theory opened markets and self-regulation replaced British mercantilism.

Legislation often protected farmers, an irony given the ways that the nation's economic philosophy, capitalism, and advocates of the free market, capitalists, preferred minimal regulation. Interpretation should address the entanglement of the government in agriculture. National and state policy made it possible for individuals to secure land, and created opportunities to capitalize land and speculate on it. Political cartoons often depicted agriculture as central to power grabs and unearned largesse (Photo 1.3).

Consistent agricultural market prices across eastern North America after the American Revolution marked the start of capitalism, according to economic historians. This did not stabilize farm income, however, and farmers sought greater control of markets, guaranteed access to low-interest, short-term loans, and a greater share of profits otherwise gobbled up by middlemen (transporters, processors, and traders). Farmers argued for these regulations to help them manage risk.

Managing risk involved futures contracts. These obligated buyers to purchase crops not even in the ground for a set price. Farmers benefited because they could hedge against falling prices. Corporate buyers, such as Quaker Oats or Del Monte, benefited because they had some guarantee that their supply of oats or peas would meet customer demand. Today, the farmer, while riding in a combine and harvesting soybeans, can talk to a broker about next year's crop sale, knowing that it will take a year to know whether his futures contract will pay off.

As rural places lost residents, rural places also lost political leverage. Farmers retained disproportionate political influence, however, for many reasons. They had effective lobbying organizations, such as the American Farm Bureau Federation. Their representatives argued for favorable policy because of the importance of agriculture to the national economy (a sector too big to fail), and the international trade and aid programs that U.S. production sustained. Ironically, many farmers still profess to favor small government and limited regulation.

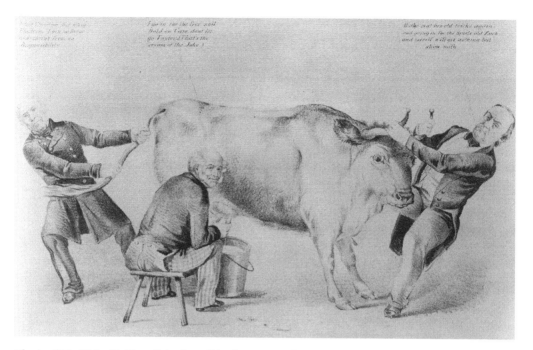

Photo 1.3 This 1848 satirical political cartoon featured Martin Van Buren, the "Barn-burner" or Free-Soil coalition candidate, seated on a milking stool and reaping the benefits of exclusive access to the cow's udder. His opponents, Zachary Taylor and Lewis Cass, ensured that Van Buren reaped the benefits of the cow's milk (and of the patronage and spoils of the nation). Taylor held on to the cow's tail while Cass pulled on the cow's horns, knowing that he would "get nothing but skim milk." Farmers understood that such pressure would keep the cow standing still for the milking.

Source: "The Strife, between an old hunker, a barnburner and a no party man," published by Henry R. Robinson, 1848. Library of Congress.

Since the early 1970s, the farm bills have been as concerned with delivering inexpensive food to consumers as subsidies to farmers. Consider that agricultural laborers and migrant workers were and still are excluded from Social Security or workmen's compensation benefits because strong lobby groups work for the economic interests of farm owners, not for the interests of laborers.

Since the early 1980s, the farm bills have been as concerned with delivering inexpensive food to consumers as subsidies to farmers who manage their production. This reflects a long-standing tension between competing agendas (affordability and profit). Furthermore, since the 1930s, farm policy has excluded agricultural laborers and migrant workers from Social Security or workmen's compensation benefits because strong pro-agriculture lobby groups work for the economic interests of farm owners who need short-term affordable labor, not for laborers. These two examples indicate the politics of agricultural policies that protected farm owners but that can put migrant laborers and consumers at a disadvantage.

Consider the fact that Monsanto, which created Roundup in 1974, promotes its "conventional and biotech" seeds and "crop protection products" as tools that help farmers become better stewards of their environment. The marketing strategy has not protected Monsanto from backlash, as it protects its patents by suing seed-saving farmers for patent infringement and wins hundreds of times. Some farmers respond by purchasing seeds and herbicides from other sources.[21]

Resistance to interpreting agriculture still arises because many people associate agriculture and farming with rural life. They do not believe that constituents care, and they do not see the relevance of the science and business of farming to their museum or site. To counter this perception, imagine the three essential elements of museums (collect, preserve/document, and interpret) as the three legs of the milking stool in the 1848 political cartoon (Photo 1.3). The legs provide stability, but just enough to get the job done. It takes practice to use the stool as a tool to accomplish the task of milking. It will take time to identify the human interest in agriculture and the resources that your site holds to flesh out those topics. It will take time to build the humanistic interpretation around those resources. It's time to get started.

Notes

1. Some examples of agriculture interpretation at zoos: The Lincoln Park Zoo in Chicago, Illinois, had a barn and domestic animals by the 1960s; the Woodland Park Zoological Gardens in Seattle, Washington, employed a keeper of domestic livestock during the 1980s; the Phoenix Zoo has heritage breeds and offers tractor rides at its Harmony Farm; the Wells Fargo Family Farm at the Minnesota Zoo interprets food sources and agricultural processes.

2. The Smithsonian Institution's permanent exhibition on business history, *American Enterprise*, incorporates agriculture in all four chronological eras featured (Merchant, Corporate, Consumer, Global). It urges visitors to "think about how Americans have mixed capitalism and democracy, in an effort to balance individual opportunity and the common good." See http://americanhistory.si.edu/american-enterprise-exhibition (accessed 20 February 2016).

3. Institute of Museum and Library Services, "Government Doubles Official Estimate: There Are 35,000 Active Museums in the U.S.," 19 May 2014, https://www.imls.gov/news-events/news-releases/government-doubles-official-estimate-there-are-35000-active-museums-us (accessed 14 August 2016). Nearly 56 percent are history museums (2,636; 7.5 percent) or historical societies and historic preservation organizations (16,880; 48 percent).

4. Freeman Tilden, *Interpreting Our Heritage*, 3rd ed. (Chapel Hill: University of North Carolina Press, 1977), 8.

5. You can get a sense of the scale of the family farm business and its products at www.eckerts.com (accessed 21 May 2016). "About Us" summarizes the family history and mentions Eckert who started the orchards at Turkey Hill Farm in 1890 and who opened the first roadside stand in 1910. Eckert descendants operate Eckert's Headquarters at Turkey Hill Farm today. They also operate two other seasonal farms (Eckert's Millstadt Fun Farm and Eckert's Grafton Farm) and a seasonal outlet in Missouri: St. Louis Farm Market (Sappington Store).

6. Marcella Wells, Barbara Butler, and Judith Koke, *Interpretive Planning for Museums: Integrating Visitor Perspectives in Decision Making* (Walnut Creek, CA: Left Coast Press, Inc., 2013).

7. Be sensitive to the demands on farmers' time. The weather dictates farm routines during spring planting, summer cultivating, and fall harvesting seasons, so schedule programs involving farmers accordingly.

8. Nora Pat Small, professor of history, Eastern Illinois University, deserves credit for the STEALTH idea. On 11 May 2016, in response to a history faculty e-mail thread prompted by Julia Brookins's article, "The Decline in History Majors: What Is to Be Done?" *Perspectives on History* (May 2016), Small wrote, "I suggest STEALTH—science, technology, engineering, art, literature, theater, history (or choose your favorite humanities). We can then ensure that those heading for STEM fields have fully integrated the absolutely essential knowledge and skills learned through studying the humanities." For the Brookins essay, see www.historians.org/publications-and-directories/perspectives-on-history/may-2016/the-decline-in-history-majors (accessed 21 May 2016). To Small's list, I add environment and economics, both critical to an understanding of agriculture. Politics should be the amoeba wending its way through and around all other disciplines.

9. 2010 Census Urban and Rural Classification and Urban Area Criteria, U.S. Census Bureau, (accessed 20 August 2016). "Rural America at a Glance, 2015," Economic Research Service, U.S. Department of Agriculture (accessed 20 August 2016).

10. Farm Demographics: U.S. Farmers by Gender, Age, Race, Ethnicity, and More, ACH12-3, May 2014 (accessed 20 August 2016).

11. 2015 Urban Agriculture Pilot Study, National Agricultural Statistics Service, U.S. Department of Agriculture (accessed 20 August 2016).

12. "agriculture, n." OED Online. March 2014. Oxford University Press (accessed 9 April 2014).

13. "husbandry, n." OED Online. December 2015. Oxford University Press (accessed 6 January 2016).

14. "farming, n." OED Online. December 2015. Oxford University Press (accessed 7 January 2016).

15. "agribusiness, n." OED Online. March 2014. Oxford University Press (accessed April 9, 2014). John H. Davis and Ray A. Goldberg, *A Concept of Agribusiness* (Boston: Division of Research, Graduate School of Business Administration, Harvard University, 1957).

16. The Maschhoffs, http://www.themaschhoffs.com/ (accessed 22 May 2016).

17. "Family History," Braeutigam Orchards, http://www.braeutigamorchards.com/ (accessed 14 August 2016).

18. "Eckert's History," http://www.eckerts.com/eckerts/eckerts_history/ (accessed 22 May 2016).

19. Marcoot Jersey Creamery—Artisan and Farmstead Cheeses, http://marcootjerseycreamery.com/ (accessed 22 May 2016).

20. Monographs about farmers and politics in states and regions convey details about farmer activism over time. For an overview, see survey texts by David B. Danbom, *Born in the Country: A History of Rural America*, 3rd edition (Baltimore: The Johns Hopkins University Press, 2017), and R. Douglas Hurt, *American Agriculture: A Brief History*, revised edition (West Lafayette, IN: Purdue University Press, 2002).

21. The Monsanto website homepage stresses the company's concern for sustainable agriculture and the people around the world who depend on the food produced with Monsanto-designed seeds (conventional and biotech) and chemicals (www.monsanto.com). For the quote about "crop protection products," see "Monsanto Comments on Recent Media Reports," regarding an unsolicited bid from Bayer AG to acquire Monsanto (Wednesday, 18 May 2016), available at: http://news.monsanto.com/press-release/corporate/monsanto-comments-recent-media-reports (accessed 22 May 2016). For a case decided by the Court of Appeals for the Federal Circuit that held that a farmer who saved and replanted Roundup Ready 2 soybean seeds infringed on Monsanto patents, see *Vernon H. Bowman v. Monsanto Company* (2013), https://www.law.cornell.edu/supct/cert/11-796 (accessed 22 May 2016). For the corporate explanation, see "Why Does Monsanto Sue Farmers Who Save Seeds?" http://www.monsanto.com/newsviews/pages/why-does-monsanto-sue-farmers-who-save-seeds.aspx (accessed 22 May 2016).

CHAPTER 2

ONCE A FIELD, NOW SUBURBIA

Interpreting Agriculture in Any Context

The Smell of Money: A Warm-Up

Let's take some inspiration from this oft-quoted passage from Shakespeare's tragedy *Romeo and Juliet*, based on a 1562 English translation of an Italian novella:

> What's in a name? That which we call a rose,
> By any other name would smell as sweet.
>
> —First Quarto (1597) [Act II, Scene II],
> Folger Shakespeare Library

These classic Shakespeare lines of Juliet's might not cause most of us to think about agriculture. Instead, we might associate the smell of a rose with pleasure, or the beauty of the rose with a lover's gift, or the name of a rose as symbolic. Most would not associate the sweet smell of the rose with the smell of fertilizer. In reality, horticulturalists invested time, talent, and money to improve the beauty if not the smell of the rose, and laborers spent their lives stooped over the prickly twigs to make it so. Domesticated roses needed more fertilizer than wild roses. Research into the chemical properties of soils and the benefits of manure or compounds of elements called "philosopher's soil" proceeded for three hundred years until the 1940s, when synthetic fertilizers became commercially available. Prior to the introduction of synthetic chemical fertilizers for roses, horticulturalists used manure to deliver nitrogen, phosphorus, and potassium (N-P-K) and other elements to their rose beds. Today consumers reach for organic products such as liquid manure or synthetics designed specifically for roses, such as Miracle-Gro water-soluble rose plant food with an N-P-K ratio of 18-24-16.

Synthetic chemicals have removed the smell of manure from the business of farming, and confinement operations have concentrated it in places distant from population centers. Thus the gap increases between the general public and the people who tend the plants, run the nursery businesses, document the horticulture industry, and plan interpretation strategies to convey that to the public. Agriculturalists perceive the odor of manure (and of other distinctly country smells such as freshly plowed dirt and freshly mown hay) very differently from those who do not make their living on the organisms that generate the smells. Interpreting agriculture can help put the relatively odorless nature of plant fertilization into the context of massive changes in the business of horticulture that delivers the rose to the consumer.

Thinking about something as ubiquitous as a rose can lay the foundation for a people-based approach to planning agricultural interpretation.[1] The process could start by reaching out to local Master Gardeners, or to the keeper of the roses at a local garden center or botanical garden. Ask them what they might find interesting about a history- or humanities-focused program on agriculture. Expand to formative evaluation of the general public—the customers at the garden center or botanical garden, with permission of the keepers. The topics in which the public expresses interest might include rose varieties, and from this you could launch a program about how changes in the plants required changes in care techniques, or about the history of a local nursery.[2]

The more refined the rose, the more it needed fertilizer, and this leads naturally to topics relevant to agriculture. Histories of intensive animal husbandry can enlighten us about manure and its use in crop fertilization over time. Studies of "shit" include Steven Stoll's *Larding the Lean Earth*[3] or Richard Jones's edited collection, *Manure Matters*.[4] Neither focuses on the nursery business, but both draw on archival evidence to document the commitment that farmers had to make to control animal manure and to deploy it in ways that sustained plants in a pre-synthetic-fertilizer world. The crops that resulted fed animals and their stewards, and the circle of intensive animal husbandry began anew each spring. No wonder farm families associated the smell of manure with money (and those few who still keep livestock still do!). We have to work hard to regain the historical mind-set that valued manure. Once we gather evidence, then we can document the nuances of the culture, science, and business of farming and discern the mind-set of those who appreciated the smell of manure even though they did not like it. Museums might not be able to capture the smell of manure, but they can collect the stories of those who value the smell.

Collectively, these museums equate to tens of thousands of agricultural history classrooms, scattered across the country. They offer collections of tools and equipment and complete environments with the potential to help increase agricultural literacy.

Many have histories that reinforce agricultural determinism, that is, changes in agricultural technology that improved on past practices. Many feature the accomplishments of wealthy white men and their creature comforts, displayed in the form of an impressive historic house. They do not address the smelly aspects of agricultural history. This means that most of these museums and historic sites can do more to interpret their unique agricultural history. We have our work cut out for us.

First Lady Michelle Obama's Let's Move campaign made agriculture a popular thing to do. Let's Move, an antiobesity campaign, brought attention to agriculture by involving children in growing healthy foods. The program provided a reason for urban museums and historic sites to research and interpret agriculture. Children got moving by gardening. The Institute of Museums and Library Services (IMLS) helped spread the word by featuring *Let's Move: Museums & Gardens*. Social media provided a mechanism for museums and historic sites to sign up and get involved. Getting out and getting physical with dirt and seeds, and rakes and hoes, helped museums reach visitors of all ages on new levels. Success stories abounded, and the IMLS featured those in the *Let's Move Museums & Gardens Newsletter*. The Spring 2016 issue included a description of the Hawaii Children's Discovery Center's gardening program designed to:

- Instill in children a strong sense of environmental stewardship,
- Connect children with nature and the outdoors as a vital part of their healthy development and well-being,
- Provide children with direct experience with nature through active play,
- Give children the opportunity to grow food, maintain a garden, and eat what they grow, and
- Encourage families to appreciate and enjoy active outdoor activities and learning through exploration.[5]

The L. C. Bates Museum in Hinckley, Maine, took the Let's Move initiative a step further, developing *Animals Eat Smart* for rural children to learn about the food chain for nondomesticated animals in natural environments. This program built on other routine offerings at the Bates Museum, such as vigorous hikes to the pond and personal encounters with wetland plants and animals. Deborah Staber explained that children imitate the activities and food chains of pond life that they have observed in a charade game. "These pond investigations get kids moving and understanding healthy pond food webs and how the pond 'Animals Eat Smart.' The children often choose to discuss and compare the diets of the birds eating at the local fast food dumpster compared with those living and eating in a healthy pond habitat. This leads to the children evaluating how they also can eat smart like the pond animals."[6] Transferring lessons learned during the exploration of the natural environment to their own cultural context represents a higher level of thinking; the students do not just recall, but they synthesize information and compare and contrast situations. A slight modification could help rural children see their own environment as an agricultural biosphere, much as they see the fish and plant life in the pond as part of a whole. They could also investigate the factors that throw either the natural or the human spheres out of balance.

Interpreting agriculture must start somewhere. Gardening (if not growing roses) provides as good a place as any, as do walks through environments with an eye toward the plants and animals and grass and foodstuffs that visitors see. Children (and adults) who have never had the opportunity to dig in the dirt and plant vegetables will learn a lot about the process of gardening, just as students who have never taken a close look at a natural environment will learn from the process of observing. The education in agriculture increases if the visitors return to weed, harvest, and transform the garden from productive to dormant, or to watch the changes that occur seasonally in a natural environment.

It can be overwhelming to tackle a huge topic such as agriculture. Betsy McCabe asked experienced advocates employed at living history sites the question: "Interpreting agriculture in an ever-changing environment: What do you do?" She found that farmers at living history sites tended to answer the question by talking about the changing natural environment while "consultants . . . took a more philosophical look at the big picture of living history, and the [interpreters] . . . talked about the changing cultural environment."[7] Such differences of opinion indicate the potential. You can reach out to constituents, visitors and non-visitors alike, who can tell you what interests them about agriculture. This could be accomplished through *Topic Talks*, my term for brainstorming sessions that get constituents in your community talking. The same people could return for more detailed conversations as you identify topics that fit your mission and that have potential for new lines of research in your community. With that information you can begin to put the pieces together.

The process of finding evidence and collecting stories can involve partners. A partnership between Writers Block Ink and Connecticut Landmarks earned an Award of Merit from the American Association for State and Local History in 2013 for a program that employed youth to research and write about local history topics. Specifically, the partnership "create[d] a summer youth employment program to explore the history of slavery in New London and to develop an exhibition and theatrical production inspired by the life of Adam Jackson, who was enslaved at the Hempsted House from 1727 to 1758, and by others living and working without the full benefit of citizenship in the New London area from 1646 to the era of civil rights." The entanglement of agriculture and New London might not have received attention, because other profound lessons provided focus in keeping with Writers Block Ink's mission: to "arm young voices with the power of pen and prose, reinforcing teamwork, accountability and responsibility to ignite social change on the page and stage."[8] Another program at Hampton National Historic Site in Towson, Maryland, researched and developed by the Sophomore Acting Ensemble of the Baltimore School for the Arts, resulted in the production *Finding the Story: Confronting the Past*. The topics of three short plays—"Historic Preservation," "Voices," and "The Gardens"—engaged the audience through well-acted vignettes in the Hampton mansion's hallway. The "Historic Preservation" act featured a young African American woman interested in the stories of enslaved women and men whom she met as she toured the house, but whom the tour guide could not see and did not want to stop and talk about.[9] Interjecting agriculture into these stories would offer additional opportunities to explore the systems—almost all based on some form of agricultural commodity—that people created to profit from the forced labor of others.

Shifting the perspective on historic evidence can change the entire message of a program. For example, a description of "huts of the Blacks" at Mount Vernon, written by a Polish visitor to George Washington in June 1798, made disparaging comments about living conditions, but then praised the garden and poultry: "We entered one of the huts of the Blacks, for one can not call them by the name of houses. They are more miserable than the most miserable of the cottages of our peasants. The husband and wife sleep on a mean pallet, the children on the ground; a very bad fireplace, some utensils for cooking, but in the middle of this poverty some cups and a teapot. . . . A very small garden planted with vegetables was close by, with 5 or 6 hens, each one leading ten to fifteen chickens. It is the only comfort that is permitted them; for they may not keep ducks, geese, or pigs. They sell the poultry in Alexandria and procure for themselves a few amenities." Living conditions reflected injustice and inequality, but the other message relates to what people created despite the discrimination.[10]

Finding historical evidence to support new interpretation takes time, but it warrants the investment. It involves the process outlined by Julie Rose in *Interpreting Difficult History*, because the different approach to interpreting the evidence challenges assumptions.[11] Martha Katz-Hyman explains this in her essay, "Furnishing Slave Quarters and Free Black Homes," in *Interpreting African American History and Culture at Museums and Historic Sites*: "For the most part, the legal status of slavery and the amount and quality of goods owned by enslaved people were independent of each other. . . . Enslaved people slept in beds, lived in houses with wood floors, cooked with a variety of equipment, wore . . . coarse fieldwork shirts and trousers . . . dresses of printed cottons . . . suits of fine livery." Interpreting everything that enslaved people encountered presents the most comprehensive impression of "the world of a slave." This should include "the houses they lived in and worked in as well as the landscape in which they were situated, the clothing they wore and how they wore it, their food and how they prepared it."[12]

Visitors and staff may perceive the process of rethinking and reinterpreting evidence as threatening. Tools exist to make it less so. Identifying clear goals and planning for implementation over the long term will make the process less overwhelming. Involving as many constituents in the process as practical will help convey the information and increase the perspectives on the process. Group work can make it less onerous and more collegial. Reaching out to new partners helps make your institution more relevant. For example, you could partner with Master Gardeners, trained volunteers who share gardening tips and techniques with anyone seeking the information. Master Gardeners operates out of county agricultural or cooperative extension offices, administered through land-grant universities across the nation, and within reach of all museums everywhere.[13]

Agriculture Everywhere

Thinking about how to incorporate agriculture into interpretive themes can be overwhelming. Manage the process by identifying a clear goal. You might pledge to do the following: *I will think about one common discussion that I have daily with visitors. I will ask them about their interests in agriculture. I will incorporate a new way of thinking about a topic relevant to their interests. I will test the process over one week of interpretation. I will take note of visitor responses to it, and refine over the course of the week. Then I will share the challenges and the potential with peers and identify a new common discussion topic, and repeat the process.*

One place to start might be expanding the "process" focus of interpretation by using it as a prompt to collect information about what visitors think about "agriculture." Process has a place; it plays a critical role in establishing a basis for understanding. For example, it is important to see how wool gets processed, spun, and woven, but the interpretation often stops there. Visitor interest may wane when they see a process through; they have little time to dawdle. Expanding the process to discuss what the process causes them to think about could yield useful information. With some evidence of visitor interests in hand, you could develop some basic information about sheep farming in your area. You could develop an interpretive handout or a visual prop to help make the process of spinning a conduit to learn more about agriculture.

Intentional connections between process stations can stretch connections between themes. Mutton becomes important in the context of food interpretation, but doing this will require rethinking a traditional historic house tour that features a kitchen tool tour. Expanding the discussion of the cooking process to include the fields and the livestock from which the food originally came can help visitors learn more about agriculture. This can be difficult for visitors to envision when concrete and asphalt have paved the orchards, grapevines, and farm fields that once surrounded museums and historic sites. Reproductions of historic maps with the house and outbuildings, on roadways and within fields can help visitors envision this. Sometimes those maps have such detail that they show breweries, and agricultural implement manufacturers, horse-drawn trollies, and people plowing. These details add additional layers to site interpretation.

The plow in the field in a historic map that includes lands on which a historic house stands can become the place to either start or end, or continue, interpretation about agriculture. Consider the wordless books of Istvan Banyai as an example. Banyai's book *Zoom* starts with a detail of a rooster's comb, but each page turn takes the reader into a different context, from the rooster's comb to the farm and beyond. Readers end up in outer space. Banyai's artwork plays with the concept of the visual effect of the "zoom," or telephoto, lens on a camera. For the purposes of interpreting agriculture, *Zoom* can help us envision connections between some specific thing and the larger context in which it exists, and which relates more directly to visitors' lives.[14]

Living plants and artistic depictions of plants can be the catalyst of agricultural interpretation. So, too, can artifacts and photographs prompt conversations about agriculture. What about the plow? Jonathan Kuester, farm manager at Volkening Heritage Farm, considers the plow an iconic farm implement—"the most recognizable and least understood farm implement. With the exception of the modern chemical sprayer it is possibly the most polarizing farm implement encompassing all that is good and bad about western agriculture, and it dates back to the origins of farming so it is good for any place or time period."[15] The plow warrants more thought, and historical thinking provides ways to consider the walking plow as a tool of a time, and of a culture, and of an environment, and within a crop culture. A display puts a plow on a pedestal with a label, but more engaging interpretation can add video and oral histories, made available to the public via phone apps or in an audio loop embedded into the exhibit. It can include cross-cultural perceptions of the plow, as relevant to your institutional mission. Educational programs might ask children to draw a plow, or photographers to take pictures of plows, or international aid organizations to explain the role of the plow to their work. Farmers and agricultural scientists can deliver a public program that explains the need for cultivation to crop cultures, and the new research in soil science that affects current practice.[16]

Agriculture and Creative Activity

Audiences can explore the art of agriculture through a variety of creative works ranging from literature, poetry, and radio programming, to quilts, portraits, and other individual expressions. Institutions can engage the public through reading circles, film series, and even original productions or art installations that result from public creativity. Imagine a "look at the pig" exhibit that features the work of local schoolchildren who participated in Agriculture in the Classroom. Children would consolidate their understanding of the science of raising pigs, the ubiquitous farm animal, into creative expression. A public program and exhibit could feature their work. This would provide the basis for thought-provoking public engagement but would not require manure shoveling.

The greater the depth of understanding, the easier it becomes to link objects in the collection that might not be catalogued as agricultural artifacts, to the agricultural interpretation. For instance, a radio takes on new meaning if it historically furnished a farm home during the 1920s. It means that the farm family had a generating plant and produced their own electricity to power low-voltage equipment. This allowed the farm family to tune in to weather and market reports and to programs such as the *National Barn Dance*, broadcast over the Sears Roebuck radio station's WLS-AM starting in 1924, or the *WSM Barn Dance*, which became the *Grand Ole Opry* broadcast on WSM-AM starting in 1925.

Popular artwork, such as the mass-produced Currier & Ives prints, featured bucolic scenes. The mass-produced prints could become a vehicle to launch a conversation about why the printmakers produced the work that they did. Why did they put livestock front and center, and not the farmhouse, in the image *American Farm Yard: Evening*? (Photo 2.1). Use this image as a catalyst for learning about how to care for different farm animals historically, and today, about different housing choices, and about different breeds and feeds. It could also launch an activity in drawing your barnyard today. This might require students to engage in a FarmVille type of experience, collecting the animals they would have in the place where they live, given local conditions, markets, and food choices. For older students, this could incorporate a discussion of the theory that farms should mimic the environment/ecosystem in which they exist, a philosophy advocated by Wes Jackson, an advocate for sustainable agriculture who cofounded the Land Institute in 1976.[17]

Reading circles offer low-cost opportunities to launch discussions. Short stories and novels convey contemporary mind-sets. The provocative short story, "A Jury of Her Peers" (1917) asks the question—did the farm wife kill the farm husband? The reader observes clues that the male investigators do not recognize but that the female observers see all too well. It can provide the basis for discussions about the level of comfort in a farmhouse, the work routines expected of farm women, and the conflicts that existed in

Photo 2.1 *American Farm Yard: Evening.* Currier & Ives

Source: Library of Congress

one farm family. With the details established, it could be put in the context of depictions of urban life, *The Jungle* (1906) perhaps. These would provide good contrasts to discuss objectives of the Country Life Movement and the mind-set that favored country life over city life at a time when the majority of the nation's population lived in urban rather than rural locations. Collections of rural literature, such as Rural Lit R.A.L.L.Y., and synopses of rural melodrama films of the early twentieth century offer opportunities for public programming.[18]

A museum or historic site that documents 1920s life might feature the novel *So Big*, by Edna Ferber, published in 1924, and could screen the three feature-length films based on *So Big*, one released during the 1920s, one during the 1930s, and the last during the 1950s. Ferber won the Pulitzer prize for *So Big*. It featured Selina Peake DeJong, a character based on Antje Paarlberg, a resident of South Holland, Illinois. Peake left the city of Chicago and married a Dutch farmer. Her son (Dirk "So Big" DeJong) left the farm for life in the city and work in investment banking. Another farmer's son left the country to become an international artist. Peake DeJong stayed in the country and operated her farm as a model market garden. Urban residents depended on the vegetables that farmers near the city sold to green grocers and market stands.

Reading circles focused on literature depicting rural black experiences could include *The Known World* by Edward P. Jones, which starts with Moses bending down, taking a pinch of soil, and eating it, because "the eating of it tied him to the only thing in his small world that meant almost as much as his own life." It includes the perspective of black farmers during the time of slavery.[19] The novel won the Pulitzer prize in 2004, and the National Book Critics Circle Award. Studies such as Scott Casper's *Sarah Johnson's Mount Vernon* can be read in conjunction with the novel to provide another Virginia family perspective on the subject of freedom during slavery, and the business of farming in both contexts.

Studies by award-winning author Ernest J. Gaines could address race relations in rural Louisiana and put the civil rights movement into the context of rural and farm life. Gaines has written eight novels, including *The Autobiography of Miss Jane Pittman* (1970), *A Gathering of Old Men* (1983), and *A Lesson before Dying* (1993). Each features memorable characters, black and white and Creole. Gaines's minimalist descriptions help readers focus on the characters and the choices available to them in the segregated South. History and contemporary struggles in the region speak loudly through all of Gaines's novels. *A Gathering of Old Men*, set during the 1970s, portrayed elderly black men in the post–civil rights era as gun-toters, not nonviolent protestors. The men unite and stand ready to share the blame for the murder of a white brute, Beau Boutan, but symbolically they seek redemption for not protecting their kin from earlier racist attacks. Gaines tells the story through first-person accounts of several participants, including a white newspaper reporter, a white Louisiana State University football player, and several of the black men involved in the resistance movement. This tactic helps the readers understand the construct of race and the ways that it obscures shared human emotions, goals, and fears.

Places matter in Gaines's work. He develops all of his narratives around plantation quarters near the town of Bayonne, Louisiana, a fictional community of six thousand residents patterned after New Roads, Louisiana, a town near the River Lake Plantation on which Gaines was born and raised, just northwest of Baton Rouge. Only two of the more than thirty cabins that remained in Cherie Quarters at the time of Earnest Gaines's birth still survive. A preservation effort launched by The Friends of Cherie Quarters during the mid-1990s sought to preserve these and other key landmarks associated with Gaines's youth, including the building in which he was born, the 1930s church in which he attended school, and the graveyard where his friends and relatives are buried. The preservationists planned a museum to interpret the community's relationship to Gaines. Through it and the preserved landmarks, the public could explore buildings once ubiquitous on the Southern landscape, but now nearly extinct. The Louisiana Division of Historic Preservation estimates that only forty to fifty slave quarters exist where once thousands stood. Most of the homes housed families throughout the twentieth century, until abandonment and land consolidation led to their destruction, a fate that befell all but two of the Cherie Quarters homes.

Even vintage baseball can provide an opportunity for interpreting rural and farm life. To consider the potential, read David Vaught's *The Farmers' Game: Baseball in Rural America*.[20] Baseball history aficionados might be frustrated by the context that Vaught provides about the game. One reviewer cautioned that readers looking for "pastoral baseball stories reminiscent of the films *The Natural* (1984) or *Field of Dreams* (1989) might have a tough time slogging through lengthy discussions of agriculture history." Those who read on gained a "refreshing and thoughtful addition to the history of baseball."[21] The teams that formed in rural black communities represented another statement of autonomy earned through independence. As Vaught summarizes, "The freedom to play baseball stemmed directly from the freedom of farming, the freedom of landownership, and the freedom from white authority. The game reinforced black farmers' burning desire for autonomy, rewarded their persistence along strong family lines, and restored their sense of whimsy and innocence."[22] An exhibit on baseball could convey the relationship between the experiences of many players formed in farm fields and the urban game that has dominated much of baseball interpretation. Additional opportunities for making baseball history an agricultural story involves the brewing industries and other business sponsors and their role in agricultural processing.

Last, a discussion of the nature of rural out-migration might start with a broadside or collection of "farm for sale" advertisements focused on your location and incorporating evidence from the earliest printed record to the present. Replicas printed on museum presses allow the public to handle the broadside, feel the impressed printing, and read the text in detail. They could compare the language in advertisements published in local newspapers, and those posted on the Internet. They could consider the role of urban investment in farmland, and the shift in farmland to recreational land use for hunters. This could contribute to conversations about those who stayed and those who left, and about measuring the costs of declining numbers of farmers.

What does the public lose when museums and historic sites do not interpret agriculture? Only the opportunity to contribute their version of a national story, warts and all. Agriculture provided the common experience around which most families functioned—be that family indigenous or enslaved, the colonized or the colonizer, the landowner or the squatter. Fixing interpretation on the places people farmed lays a foundation for exploring relationships that evolved between humans in those places over time. Telling the stories about how people controlled the land and how they commodified it and manipulated it over time helps explain the most common experiences of Americans before 1890. Stories must take into account the stamina required to work the land; the backbreaking labor required to create a farm; and the risk that farmers managed so they could stay in business. The most compelling stories add the modern context to reach a public very distant from the fields that feed and clothe them. These stories help the public understand earlier practices, but can also engage them in the process of learning more about today's agricultural industry.

Notes

1. Lisa Brochu, *Interpretive Planning: The 5-M Model for Successful Planning Projects* (Fort Collins, CO: National Association for Interpretation, 2003). Brochu summarizes market-based planning, an approach she describes as "driven to a large extent by the consumer. . . [based on] an awareness of consumer desires" (15; 16). An objective-based planning format develops best when visitor expectations and needs drive the process. Brochu describes resource-based planning, however, as "often overlooked . . . visitor motivations and interests" (18). Thus, "it can be difficult to

establish relevancy" (18). Marcella Wells, Barbara Butler, and Judith Koke, *Interpretive Planning for Museums: Integrating Visitor Perspectives in Decision Making* (Walnut Creek, CA: Left Coast Press, 2013) puts the visitor perspective central to the planning process.

2. Formal curriculum materials, including those produced by Agriculture in the Classroom, as well as products focused on horticulture history, provide good models to follow; that is, Cheryl Lyon-Jenness, "Planting the Prairies: John Kennicott and Horticultural Advocacy in Nineteenth-Century Illinois," *Illinois History Teacher* 13, no. 1 (2006), 2–16, available at http://www.lib.niu.edu/2006/iht1310602.html (accessed 11 June 2016).

3. Steven Stoll, *Larding the Lean Earth: Soil and Society in Nineteenth-Century America* (New York: Hill & Wang, 2002).

4. Richard Jones, ed. *Manure Matters: Historical, Archaeological and Ethnographic Perspectives* (Farnham, UK: Ashgate Publishing, 2012).

5. Loreta Yajima, "The Wonder of Gardening," *Let's Move Museums & Gardens* (Spring 2016).

6. Deborah Straber, "Animals Eat Smart," *Let's Move Museums & Gardens* (Spring 2016).

7. Betsy McCabe, "Portraying Historical Agriculture through Public History: A Work in Progress," *Proceedings of the 2015 ALHFAM Conference and Annual Meeting* (North Bloomfield, OH: Association for Living History, Farm and Agricultural Museums, 2016), 16.

8. Richard M. Potvin, "The Power of History and Words," *History News* 69, no. 3 (Summer 2014), 29.

9. The author observed only the "Historic Preservation" play, presented to attendees on an optional field trip during the National Council on Public History conference, April 2016. The "Gardens" might have featured more information about agriculture. The tour of the quarters that followed the play introduced attendees to the community of the enslaved but did not elaborate on agriculture as practiced on the plantation, or the role of the enslaved as experts in the fields, stables, barnyards, or farmyards.

10. Martha B. Katz-Hyman, "Furnishing Slave Quarters and Free Black Homes: Adding a Powerful Tool to Interpreting African American Life," *Interpreting African American History and Culture at Museums and Historic Sites* (Lanham, MD: Rowman & Littlefield, 2015), 105–14, quote 106, quoted from Julian Ursyn Niemcewicz, "Under Their Vine and Fig Tree: Travels through America in 1797–1799, 1805, with some further account of life in New Jersey," Metchie J. E. Budka, trans., ed., in *Collections of the New Jersey Historical Society at Newark*, 14 (1965): 100–01. For more on the African American community at Mount Vernon, see Scott E. Casper, *Sarah Johnson's Mount Vernon: The Forgotten History of an American Shrine* (New York: Hill and Wang, 2008), and for more about agriculture as practiced by members of this community, see Scott E. Casper, "Out of Mount Vernon's Shadow: Black Landowners in George Washington's Neighborhood, 1870–1930," *Beyond Forty Acres and a Mule: African American Landowning Families since Reconstruction* (Gainesville, FL: University Press of Florida, 2012).

11. Julie Rose, *Interpreting Difficult History at Museums and Historic Sites* (Lanham, MD: Rowman & Littlefield, 2016).

12. Katz-Hyman, "Furnishing Slave Quarters and Free Black Homes," 105–14, first quote 108–09, second quote 109. Kym S. Rice and Martha B. Katz-Hyman, eds., *World of a Slave: Encyclopedia of the Material Life of Slaves in the United States* (Westport, CT: Greenwood, 2010).

13. For information on Master Gardeners and contacts within all fifty states, consult the homepage of the American Horticultural Society.

14. Istvan Banyai, *Zoom* (New York: Puffin Books, reprint 1998).

15. E-mail, Jonathan Kuester to Debra A. Reid, 8 June 2016.

16. Sarah Anne Carter, "A Hand Plow: Plowshares and Sword," in *Tangible Things: Making History through Objects* (New York: Oxford University Press, 2015), 148–52.

17. Judy Soule and Jon Piper, with a foreword by Wes Jackson, *Farming in Nature's Image: An Ecological Approach to Agriculture* (Washington, D.C.: Island Press, 1992).

18. See Rural Lit R.A.L.L.Y. available at http://rurallitrally.org (accessed 10 June 2016). Hal Barron, Silent Film, *Agricultural History*.

19. Edward P. Jones, *The Known World: A Novel* (New York: HarperCollins, 2003), 3–4, quote 4.

20. David Vaught, *The Farmers' Game: Baseball in Rural America* (Baltimore, MD: The Johns Hopkins University Press, 2013).

21. George B. Kirsch, "Review, *The Farmers' Game*," *Journal of American History* (September 2013), 571–72, quote 572.

22. Vaught, 69.

CHAPTER 3

AGRICULTURE

Developing a Humanist Point of View

DEVELOPING an agricultural point of view will help you identify the human issues of agriculture, the conflict and contradictions of agriculture, and the ways to engage others in the process of discovery. Developing an agricultural point of view will also help you to see agriculture from other vantage points, the "plant's eye view" as Michael Pollan explored in *Botany of Desire*.[1]

Articulating point of view is relatively easy. A person involved in agriculture today becomes "I," the conveyor of the first-person point of view. They describe their experiences today. They have authority over this present. Few of these people exist. Contemporary collecting can help us capture their stories, and farm tours and in-museum conversations provide opportunities for them to interact with the general public. The first-person plural, "we," takes on additional meaning because the more people involved in this exploration of agriculture, present and past, the more rich the experience becomes. The people of the past used "I" and "we" when they described whatever they happened to be doing on their farms and in their fields in letters to family and friends. Today museums and historic sites can convey that first-person point of view through exhibits and educational programming. Instead of describing what they did in label copy, the people become the subjects and the verbs become active.

The second-person, "you," draws people into the process of exploration. You, the historic site interpreter, the museum docent, the historical consultant, the agricultural historian, have the power to convince "them," the audience you seek, of the value of your work. "You," the pronoun, becomes a tool that you, the reader, can use to convince them, the public, of the reasons to care. You drive past places with agricultural pasts obscured every day. You craft interpretive statements that have the potential to make this past matter. You can use this book to help you accomplish the task.

The third-person point of view serves a useful purpose as a tool to describe what he, she, or they did in the fields, the barnyards, the kitchens, and the markets. These pronouns indicate what someone else did. They work just fine to convey details about agriculture, but they imply a distance that might work against the overall goal of making agriculture something to think about. It is not just something that she or he or they do/did; it is something that we should think about to gain perspective on processes that affect us today, and that reflect centuries of human-animal-plant-environment relationships.

As we work on our agricultural point of view, we must be mindful of how our present affects our interpretations of her, his, and their pasts. The public has created the museums and historic sites to preserve places and things that the public wants to preserve. The early migrants who claimed land in an area and who built homes in the middle of their farms capture the attention of the public. Urban and suburban sprawl consumed the fields. The farmhouse seems out of place among ranch houses. But the public remained vested in the historic house preserved by well-meaning local historians. Museums of local history may face similar challenges, created to collect, preserve, and interpret the history of a county, or of a region, but full of things that people have given who wanted family heirlooms to have a home. In both situations, adopting a first-person point of view on the subject of agriculture can help staff think through questions such as: What would it take to put food on the table in 1624, in 1776, in 1836, in 1926, in 1956? What did [insert the name of the mother of a family] have to do to have bacon and eggs or porridge for breakfast? What livestock did a family in North Dakota have to have to survive a year (during these years)? Did a family in Texas, or California, or Florida have to have the same livestock? On what plants did the family depend for food, or what crops did the family grow to survive (during these years)? On what animals did the family depend for food and fiber? Questions such as these can prompt thought that will help people develop an agricultural point of view, even if they have never thought about agriculture before.

Starting with basic questions about crop cultivation and animal husbandry can establish safe parameters, ones that become the foundation for exploring the ways that people in the past met basic human needs. These basic questions may not be so easy to answer, but once documented, the answers can add new dimensions to interpretation, and can support comparison between the place and time interpreted at a museum, and the same place today.

Answers to basic questions about "where food comes from" can also lead to questions about more controversial topics, including the construction of gendered divisions of labor, of racial hierarchies, of class status, and of political ideology. Consider the question "Who owned the farm?" We might answer with "The farmer is the man!" Those who might come to that conclusion without first checking the deeds to the property express a centuries-long precedent based in English common-law practice. Married men had legal authority over their wives and over their wives' property. Spanish law granted married women some authority over their property, and this law affected some colonial and state legal systems, too. The married women's property laws protected the woman's and her family's interest in her calves, and in the natural increase of her calves, after she married. It protected her brand. It protected the people whom she owned, too. The evidence, on second look with a more informed agricultural point of view, will document men and women with power and influence, and unfree laborers who built, grew, managed, and trained for those with legal authority. Agriculture rests at the heart of almost all historical controversies.

Thinking about Agriculture

Learning about agriculture can start with documenting a range of philosophies and approaches to the business. Three not-for-profit organizations that emphasize sustainable agricultural practices use a variety of historic resources to accomplish their goals. The Center for Land-Based Learning, a not-for-profit organization in Winters, California, operates out of a 1920s farmhouse. The staff farms forty acres and partners with a new agri-hood, marketed as "California's first farm-to-table new home community."[2] The Food Literacy Project at Oxmoor Farms maintains a market garden on a former plantation now managed by the Filson Historical Society. The educational programs help children from Louisville, Kentucky, learn about growing vegetables and working on the land.[3] Tillers International, a Michigan-based not-for-profit, has operated on three different historic farm properties since 1981. Staff balance numerous duties, including operating a diversified farm, managing a museum of agricultural tools and equipment, and coordinating workshops focused on historic trades from blacksmithing to chair caning. They have also trained a generation of farmers to work with draft animals.[4]

Staff at these organizations do not lecture about the history of their sites. Instead, they translate the lessons learned from working in an environment modified by generations of farmers into life-changing public programming. The sites reach urban and suburban residents far removed from agriculture today, as well as farmers seeking new information about how to manage the risks of modern agriculture. They do their job in a place with a past. Farming lands that have a history of agricultural production does not automatically translate into appreciation for that agricultural past. But documenting and interpreting agricultural practices conducted in one place over time can help people grasp the relationships of crop culture, climate, and cultivation routines, the role of livestock in the practice, and the need for human labor at critical times. Comparing what happened then to what happens now helps the public grasp the ways in which agricultural practices have changed over time. Ultimately, all members of the general public, including farmers today, can learn about the ways that different agricultural approaches helped farmers manage risk in the past.

Much of the evidence exists in intangible cultural heritage—the traditions, beliefs, and practices that informed farmers historically. Farmers made their decisions about what to plant, when to plant it, and how to cultivate it based on accumulated knowledge. A recent example indicates the numerous factors that affect the variables that farmers have to consider when making decisions that can make or break their operations. Journalist Seamus McGraw documented the ways that Ethan Cox, a farmer from White Hall, Illinois, read the natural rhythms of the place where he had been born and that he and his daughters farmed in west-central Illinois. "Ethan was a guy who measured time by the sort of work he did and when he did it. . . . That previous winter had been an especially mild one, and all winter long Ethan had been thinking about the lessons his father had taught him—how in those years when the real deep freezes and the snows didn't come . . . were, as often as not, followed by drought. . . . And all winter long, the signs were pointing toward drought. . . . [Ethan] was sure that pretty much no rain would come. In fact, he was so sure, he was willing to bet the farm on it. . . . And so, on that unseasonably warm morning, March 13, 2012, weeks earlier than he had ever done it before, at precisely the moment that NOAA [National Oceanic and Atmospheric Administration] meteorologist [Martin] Hoerling would later say no farmer could have gone out into the fields and predicted a drought, Ethan Cox fired up his tractor and headed out to his fields to plant. Because he was sure a drought was coming."[5]

Mr. Cox did many things, but predicting the future was not one of them. He had to make an educated decision based on evidence at hand, but the stakes were high. If his gamble paid off, he would be harvesting his crops earlier than other farmers, and that could translate into higher market prices. But if it rained (especially if it rained too much) or if a cold snap froze his early corn crop, he risked losing his farm and his way of life.

The pressures to respond to factors beyond their control weigh heavily on farmers. We all should care about these pressures, because we all depend on farmers for everything that does not start as a petroleum product. Farmers even depend on other farmers for the food they eat and the fibers they wear (and increasingly for wood products, because woodlots are not considered agricultural production). Most of us, however, have much to learn about the decisions that farmers make every day of their lives that affect our own lives.

Popular Opinion

Despite the real drama of modern farming, many people still respond to the mention of "agriculture" by rolling their eyes, stifling a yawn, or sarcastically saying, "That'll be a page-turner!" Public opinion polls, however, indicate that strong opinions exist. For instance, 93 percent of Americans say the federal government should require labels saying whether a food product has or has not been genetically modified, or bioengineered—labels that would, for some, designate "safe" foods. An ABCNews.com report on these findings indicated that: "Such near unanimity in public opinion is rare."[6]

Consumer interest in foods has made a dent in the distance that exists between farmers' reality and consumers' awareness. That awareness, however, does not extend far beyond fresh-food procurement. Carnivores who purchase grass-fed, free-range, or antibiotic-free meat from the local butcher indicate their preference for freshness or for humane animal husbandry and butchering techniques. Restaurants may feature the farm families that supply locally sourced meat, meal, garden vegetables, eggs, butter, or fish. Many of these locavore producers may favor heritage breeds and seeds and commit to genetic diversity rather than genetically modified organisms (GMOs), but their sustainable practices may not qualify as certified-organic. If you grow a garden to put fresh vegetables on your table, do you apply MiracleGro? The "plant food plus calcium," popular among gardeners, contains nitrogen-phosphorus-potassium (N-P-K) ratios similar to the synthetic chemical fertilizers that many monoculture producers use on their corn, soybeans, and other row crops.[7]

Growing awareness for some has not changed the massive international infrastructure that exists to move crops planted and harvested in one place to the other places where they are processed and consumed. Understanding farmers' decisions requires moving beyond the personalized frame of reference that most consumers consider as they decide what to eat, drink, wear, and champion. Those decisions matter, but agriculture consists of much more than localized producers and consumers.

Scholars of public opinion help us make sense of this disconnect between our understanding of agriculture and our strong opinions about farming. They explain that "individuals are cognitive misers or at least satisficers, who collect only as much information about a topic as they think is necessary to reach a decision." They base their opinion on "shortcuts such as values and trust in combination with the interpretations of the issue most readily available from media coverage."[8]

Many factors other than knowledge of science affect opinion formation. An analysis of responses to a 2001 survey about agricultural biotechnology indicated that factors such as age, gender, and sociocultural identity, as well as economic status and political ideology, affected opinions about agricultural biotechnology. Well-educated, economically stable older male respondents tended to trust biotechnology experts, policy makers, and university scientists more and perceived less risk as a consequence of scientific agricultural innovation. They also equated innovation with progress and economic gain. In contrast, younger, female, or less well-educated and lower-class respondents trusted the experts less and perceived higher risks to health and the environment. Those who favored conservative economic and political ideologies (free-market capitalism and limited government regulation) tended to have a more favorable view of agricultural biotechnology.[9]

The electronic news and information explosion since 2001 has transformed the ways that individuals can learn about issues. Idealists might think that increased access to credible sources would allow "cognitive misers" to gather evidence more easily, and thus be better informed about divisive topics such as agricultural biology. As danah boyd argued in *It's Complicated*, "New communication media often inspire the hope that they can and will be used to bridge cultural divides. This hope gets projected onto new technologies in ways that suggest that the technology itself does the work of addressing cultural divisions."[10] New technologies might capture the attention of the people already trusting of science, but this will not affect the exogenous factors that inform opinion, too. As scholars Dominique Brossard and Matthew C. Nisbet have argued: "The more they knew about the science of agricultural biotechnology, the more supportive they were of the technology. Yet contrary to the still prevailing assumption of many scientists, journalists, and policy makers, science knowledge was not a stand-alone influence on citizen judgments, and was in fact relatively modest in its influence when compared to heuristics such as values, trust, and generalized feelings about the impacts of science."[11]

Because people form opinions based on values, trust, and feelings, as well as information about the science of agricultural biotechnology, those who support the science interpret criticism of the science as an affront to their values and their ideologies. And because agriculture is so intertwined with national identity, discussions about agricultural policies and practices sometimes escalate into caustic exchanges that question the critics' level of patriotism. Learning more about the history of pro-farm politics will help fill the void between the poles of public opinion. This so-called agrarian policy, that is, policy that secured land for the nation, established the process of selling that land to agriculturalists, and protected farmers as a class from paying minimum wage, overtime, and Federal Insurance Contributions Act payments for foreign agricultural laborers.[12]

Museums and historic sites offer untapped potential to inform the public about the historical context for modern agricultural decisions. Does the underwhelming public interest in the topic warrant the effort to add agriculture to collection, preservation, and interpretation plans? This book argues—YES—unequivocally. Museums and historic sites provide places for groups of people with differing opinions on the subject of agriculture to gather and explore historic tools and equipment and discuss competing concepts of technological determinism and the social construction of technology. Museums and historic sites have a lot of work to do to realize the potential of serving as three-dimensional learning laboratories where visitors can learn about agriculture, historically and today, and can interact with others who have different perspectives and opinions. Such cultural engagement can lead to exchanges that can create more enlightened understanding as a basis for decision-making. Historic sites with complete environments provide opportunities for an interdisciplinary study of landscapes. Others remain in operation as living history farms where process-based interpretation might provide opportunities for visitors to wield a hoe or shovel manure or slop the hogs. Visitors cannot engage in such activities elsewhere. The stakes are high—the general public needs to learn more about the sources of their food, fiber, and fuel, and they need to interact with the farmers who produce them.

Realizing the potential requires conversations about topics that divide people. Who originally occupied the land? Who first cultivated it? Any history that does not acknowledge indigenous people in the answers to these two questions does a disservice to the first people and to the overall understanding of land use in the North American continent. Does genetic diversity still exist? The answer to this question must take into account everything from virgin timber to the plants and animals raised in a place by different people over time. Why do people assume farmers are male? Why do people assume that farmers are white? Why do farm operators who never owned the land that they farm receive so little attention? What relationships exist between crops and livestock on productive farms? What philosophical issues arise when people anthropomorphize animals? What environmental characteristics and what crop-driven cultural practices caused farmers to do what they did historically?[13] How have farmers changed the environment over time? How have changes in the environment affected landscape use over time?

Finding the answers to these questions will take time and energy and a team of interested folk. The answers can go a long way toward addressing gaps in the historical understanding of a critical industry—agriculture.

Agricultural Literacy and History

Concern over the lack of knowledge about agriculture is not a new thing. During the late nineteenth century, a rapid decline in the rural population led philanthropists to collect, preserve, and interpret rural buildings and landscapes, and traditional agricultural practices. Visitors interacted with these collections in open-air museums and historic sites created by industrialists who got rich from the technologies that often pushed rural populations off the farms in the first place. During the early twentieth century, a new wave of worry over rural out-migration led President Theodore Roosevelt to create the Commission on Country Life. It consisted of intellectual progressives committed to improving the rural standard of living to reduce the attractiveness of non-rural alternatives. This worry coincided with the industrialization of wheat cultivation in the plains of the North American continent. Economic and environmental extremes during the 1930s pushed more people off of their farms, particularly in areas where the prairie grasses had been eliminated and where cattle ranges and wheat fields took their place. Then, between 1945 and 1972, yet another revolution in agricultural technology transformed farming in the Midwestern Corn Belt to the industrialized monoculture of corn and soybean fields that prevails today.

By 1981, stemming the tide of out-migration seemed futile. Instead, the U.S. Department of Agriculture (USDA) launched Agriculture in the Classroom (AIC), an interdisciplinary curriculum designed to help school-age children learn about food and fiber systems.[14] The USDA partnered with state departments of agriculture and state Farm Bureau offices to distribute AIC materials to local school districts. By 1988 the concept of agricultural literacy gained traction. The National Research Council's report, *Understanding Agriculture: New Directions in Education*, used "agricultural literacy" to distinguish education about agriculture from vocational training in agriculture. The agriculturally literate student, as the NRC report explained, would "understand" the "history and current economic, social, and environmental significance [of the food and fiber system] to all Americans."[15]

Does Agriculture in the Classroom accomplish its goal? Assessment conducted since 1988 measures student knowledge before and after instruction to determine changes in student comprehension of food and fiber systems. Educators refined themes in response, and the National Agriculture in the Classroom curriculum now addresses five themes: 1) Agriculture and the Environment; 2) Plants and Animals for Food, Fiber, & Energy; 3) Food, Health, & Lifestyle; 4) Science, Technology, Engineering, & Math; and 5) Culture, Society, Economy, & Geography. In 2014, the AIC published *National Agriculture Literacy Outcomes*, which itemized discipline-specific benchmarks (science, social studies, and health) for each theme. Social studies—especially sociology, anthropology, politics and policy, economics, and history—appear prominently in the benchmarks, but the lessons submitted by educators and posted on the AIC webpage [http://agclassroom.org/] do not incorporate the history of agriculture in any substantive way.[16] Other than history, humanities disciplines (art, literature, theater, philosophy) appear not at all.

Critics have argued that the information about the past that remains in the curriculum reflects stereotypes and politicized goals that attribute agricultural success to free-market capitalism and large-scale production. One analyst, Dr. Cori Brewster, an English professor at Eastern Oregon University, critiqued the AIC history lesson, "Growing a Nation: The Story of American Agriculture." She argued that the photographs of iconic figures (Abraham Lincoln, farmers plowing with horses, and George Washington Carver at work in his laboratory), along with other images of an anonymous woman scientist, a strand of DNA, and a single plant, each conveyed broad-based support for scientific "progress." Brewster claimed that the images of Carver and the woman reflected tokenism.[17] But you can take Brewster's argument even further, and to do so, Lincoln's opinions must be put into chronological context. Lincoln had strong opinions about the need for education for the agricultural classes, but he also had strong opinions about scale of production and about scientific "progress." In a speech to the Wisconsin Agricultural Society in 1859, he criticized large-scale production and technologies that exceeded the needs of a family-scale farm. His signature on three bills in 1862 that influenced agriculture then and now did not necessarily reflect a change in his opinion about scale of production or the value of family farming. But several things had changed. Lincoln was president of a nation at war. Representatives and senators seated in the U.S. Congress came from states that had not seceded from the Union. These congressmen supported national authority, not state sovereignty, and the three bills reflected that shift in political philosophy. One authorized the creation of the U.S. Department of Agriculture, another launched land-grant university education for agricultural and industrial classes, and the third—the Homestead Act—established the system for public land distribution west of the Mississippi. The curriculum tends to emphasize these positives, and not the controversy at the heart of the Civil War: Would the nation continue to protect the rights of owners to control their property—specifically unfree agricultural laborers—or not? Freeing the enslaved resulted in four million freed people who could, technically, reap the benefits of the legislation passed during Lincoln's administration to retain Northern commitment to the war. Freed people could theoretically have taken advantage of the promises of the Homestead Act and secured land west of the Mississippi River. Some did, and Freedom's Frontier National Heritage Area and the National Historic Landmark in Nicodemus, Kansas, documents part of the Exoduster movement of freed people to western lands during the 1870s. Agricultural literacy lessons should also address the ways that the Homestead Act affected American Indians, a consequence of agricultural expansion not usually included in the AIC curriculum.

The diverse U.S. population warrants a more comprehensive interpretation of agriculture, but the national story of agriculture remains largely white. Some might counter with the argument that the majority of the American story is white, and therefore, agricultural interpretation should tell the majority story. Doing so minimizes the issues that helped shape public policy, that exacerbated sectional tensions and led to the Civil War, that affected land distribution, and that ultimately caused agriculture to develop as "the whitest of occupations."[18] The AIC website available in early 2016 included numerous evocative photographs in a slide show that introduced the curriculum, "Growing a Nation: The Story of American Agriculture." Most of the images featured faces of white men along with white women and children going about their business. Shadows on faces made it difficult to identify people of color: one image of dark hands peeling potatoes, one of a young girl opening a refrigerator, one of several young people perhaps playing volleyball, and one of an educator with a visual aid. But the most identifiable image appeared in Lesson 3: Prosperity and Challenges, illustrating the subtheme: Food for Peace. Most viewers might interpret the image literally (two school-age children drinking milk); others might put it into the context of the civil rights movement of the early 1960s; and others might link it to an expansion of Cold War commodity programs during President John F. Kennedy's administration. Surplus agricultural production increased domestically and abroad as a result of the 1962 Food and Agriculture Act. This included school lunch and milk programs, which the image likely depicts. I drank milk in my parochial school's cafeteria, thanks to this expanded commodity distribution program. But some might interpret the image of African American students in a stereotypical way—African Americans receiving public aid (Photo 3.1).[19]

Brewster concluded her essay by calling for an expanded approach to teaching agricultural literacy. Her recommendations emphasized critical thinking to encourage students of all ages to move outside of their comfort zones and engage with perspectives and ideas with which they might be unfamiliar: "Helping students read and respond to the agricultural world requires that we pose problems about where our food comes from and why; and about how we continue to be raced, gendered, faithed, and classed

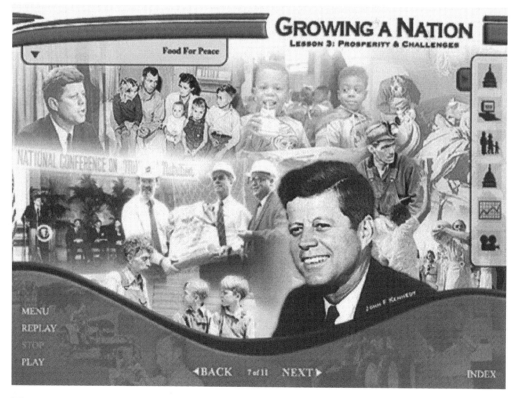

Photo 3.1 Screenshot of page on the Agriculture in the Classroom website (14 February 2016)

by agricultural policies, practices, and groups." Of course, the use of "continue" implies a history to the process by which agricultural policies, practices, and groups became "raced, gendered, faithed, and classed." History is an essential ingredient to a more comprehensive and balanced agricultural literacy curriculum.[20]

Agricultural history exists all around us in material form, including in places no longer rural or farm-focused. Learning to read this evidence increases visual literacy, a powerful tool that can add a whole new dimension to agricultural literacy. It is impossible to comprehend agriculture and farming historically, or today, by focusing only on the local or only within the family farm. Collection and interpretation must document the local, but must also move beyond the domestic and local and look outward, taking into account the roadways as well as the geopolitical and sociocultural milieu in which the farm operated. People and businesses in rural, urban, suburban, and industrial locations all interacted at different stages of agricultural processing, and each changed in different ways as farming changed. Living history farms and agricultural museums can inform this process. Visitors can learn a lot by visiting museums that provide complete environments with minds- and hands-on opportunities to learn about seasonal rhythms, work routines, farm ecosystems, and crop and livestock care. Most museums and sites cannot provide such experiences, but they have many other agricultural stories ripe for the picking.

Notes

1. Michael Pollan, *The Botany of Desire: A Plant's Eye View of the World* (New York: Random House, 2001).

2. The Center for Land-Based Learning: The Center began in 1993, and it operates out of the Farm at Putah Creek in Winters, California. Its mission is "to inspire and motivate people of all ages, especially youth, to promote a healthy interplay between agriculture, nature and society through their own actions and as leaders in their communities." The Farm at Putah Creek consists of a 1920s farmhouse and forty acres dedicated to Land-Based Learning programming. Land-Based Learning committed to managing the 7.4-acre farm at The Cannery, marketed as "one of California's first agri-hoods" and as "Davis, California's first farm-to-table new home community." "The Cannery Farm will serve as a state-of-the-art example of sustainable urban farming and as an agri-classroom for beginning farmers." See The Center for Land-Based Learning: http://landbasedlearning.org/, and The Cannery at Davis, California: http://livecannerydavis.com/ (accessed 9 January 2016).

3. The Food Literacy Project at Oxmoor Farm, Louisville, Kentucky, began as a not-for-profit educational organization in 2006 with the mission to "inspire a new generation of people to build relationships with healthy food, farming and the land." The Food Literacy Project grew out of the eight-acre market garden, Field Day Family Farm, operated by a tenant on Oxmoor Farm (a plantation site listed on the National Register of Historic Places and operated by the Filson Historical Society). The Food Literacy Project educates schoolchildren about urban agriculture by providing hands-on gardening experience. The Project constructed its Outdoor Teaching Kitchen in 2011 on the foundation of the historic creamery of Oxmoor Farm. See http://foodliteracyproject.org/ (accessed 9 January 2016).

4. Tillers International exists to "preserve, study, and exchange low-capital technologies that increase the sustainability and productivity of people in rural communities" in the United States

and internationally. "Our vision is to create an international learning community in which we seek an understanding of local conditions, inspire an attitude of experimentation, and give the promise of rural sustainability for generations to come." See Tillers International at http://tillersinternational .org/ (accessed 9 January 2016). Dick Roosenberg, founder of Tillers International, has partnered with historic properties since its founding in 1981, first with the Kalamazoo Nature Center in Michigan, and with local draft horse clubs and antique machinery and tractor clubs, and with farmers on properties in production since the early twentieth century. Tillers International has a historic implement museum and maintains a working farm with stock (six oxen, four draft horses, a fifty-cow breeding herd of milking shorthorns, and forty merino sheep) and crops (corn, oats, wheat, and clover) that mirror historic ratios for home use and market production.

5. Ethan Cox farmed in southwestern Illinois near White Hall in Greene County, northeast of St. Louis, Missouri. See Seamus McGraw, *Betting the Farm on a Drought: Stories from the Front Lines of Climate Change* (Austin, TX: University of Texas Press, 2015), quotes 108, 109, and 111.

6. ABCNews.com poll, June 2001, for more information, see http://iatp.org/news/american -public-opinion-polls-on-ge-foods (accessed 1 May 2016).

7. The Miracle-Gro ratio is 24-8-16. Miracle-Gro Water Soluble All Purpose Plant Food Material Safety Data Sheet (29 July 2005), http://eldoradochemical.com/MSDS_Sheets/EDC/ Third_Party_Products/MIRACLE_GRO_ALL_PURPOSE_PLANT_FOOD_24-8-16.pdf (accessed 19 January 2016).

8. Dominique Brossard and Matthew C. Nisbet analyzed responses to a 2001 survey mailed to New York State residents outside of the New York City metropolitan area. The survey asked for their opinions about agricultural biotechnology. Brossard and Nisbet cited selected studies of cognition, that is, S. T. Fiske and S. E. Taylor, *Social Cognition* (2nd ed.), (New York: McGraw-Hill, 1991), and S. Popkin, *The Reasoning Voter* (Chicago: University of Chicago Press, 1991). For the survey analysis, see Brossard and Nisbet, "Deference to Scientific Authority among a Low Information Public: Understanding U.S. Opinion on Agricultural Biotechnology, *International Journal of Public Opinion Research* 19, no. 1 (2006), 25–52; first quote 25; second quote 43.

9. J. C. Besley and J. Shanahan, "Media attention and exposure in relation to support for agricultural biotechnology," *Science Communication* 26, no. 2 (June 2005): 347–67, especially 350. Brossard and Nisbet, "Deference to Scientific Authority among a Low Information Public," 26–28, 38–40.

10. danah boyd, *It's Complicated: The Social Lives of Networked Teens* (New Haven, CT: Yale University Press, 2014), 156.

11. Brossard and Nisbet, "Deference to Scientific Authority among a Low Information Public," 43–44.

12. "Fact Sheet #12: Agricultural Employers under the Fair Labor Standards Act," U.S. Department of Labor, http://www.dol.gov/whd/regs/compliance/whdfs12.pdf (accessed 20 January 2016).

13. Pollan, *Botany of Desire*.

14. *Agriculture in the Classroom, 1981–2006* (Washington, D.C.: Agriculture in the Classroom Program, U.S. Department of Agriculture, Cooperative State and Research, Education and Extension Service, 2006), http://agclassroom.org/get/doc/25th_book.pdf (accessed 11 January 2016); M. J. Frick, A. A. Kahler, and W. W. Miller, "A Definition and the Concepts of Agricultural Literacy," *Journal of Agricultural Education* 32, no. 2 (1991), 49–57.

15. Committee on Agricultural Education in Secondary Schools, Board of Education, National Research Council, *Understanding Agriculture: New Directions for Education* (Washington, D.C.: National Academy Press, 1988), quote 8–9.

16. D. M. Spielmaker and J. G. Leising, *National Agricultural Literacy Outcomes: Benchmarks Related to Agricultural Literacy and Academic Achievement* (Logan: Utah State University, 2013), http://www.agclassroom.org/get/doc/NALObooklet.pdf (accessed 16 January 2016).

17. Cori Brewster, "Toward a Critical Agricultural Literacy," in *Reclaiming the Rural: Essays on Literacy, Rhetoric, and Pedagogy*, Kim Donehower, Charlotte Hogg, and Eileen E. Schell, eds. (Carbondale, IL: Southern Illinois University Press, 2012), 34–51, quote 41.

18. Calvin L. Beale described *agriculture* as the "whitest of occupations" in "The Negro in American Agriculture," in *The American Negro Reference Book*, John P. Davis, ed. (Englewood Cliffs, NJ: Prentice-Hall, 1966), 174; revised as "The Black American in Agriculture," in *The Black American Reference Book*, Mabel M. Smythe, ed. (Englewood Cliffs, NJ: Prentice-Hall, 1976), 292. John C. Hudson noted that "with a white population percentage of 97.5 in 1990, farming has become one of the whitest of occupations in the United States," quote from "The Other America: Changes in Rural America During the Twentieth Century," in *North America: The Historical Geography of a Changing Continent*, Thomas F. McIlwraith and Edward K. Muller, eds., 2nd ed. (Oxford, UK: Rowman & Littlefield, 2001): 409–21, quote 419. Greg Burns quotes Beale making the same statement in "Farms Run by African Americans in Illinois are 'Mighty Few' at 59," *Chicago Tribune* (12 June 2005), 1.

19. "Growing a Nation: The Story of American Agriculture," http://www.agclassroom.org/gan/index.htm (accessed 17 January 2016).

20. Brewster, "Toward a Critical Agricultural Literacy," quote 48.

CHAPTER 4

AGRICULTURE AND
HISTORICAL THINKING

D AVID LOWENTHAL starts his chapter, "Memory," in *The Past Is a Foreign Country*, with the following statement: "All awareness of the past is founded on memory. Through recollection we recover consciousness of former events, distinguish yesterday from today, and confirm that we have experienced a past." Remembering everything can stymy us, however, so to act effectively, we must be "highly selective" and must exercise "the ability to forget what no longer matters." Lowenthal claims that "the need . . . to forget as well as to recall, force[s] us to select, distil, distort, and transform the past, accommodating things remembered to the needs of the present."[1] The process requires prioritization, sequencing, and accurate recall of the distillations, and while the process can result in knowledge "about the past," it "convey[s] no *sense* of the past." Gaining a "sense" of the past requires higher levels of thinking that link the selected knowledge to other "aspects of history." Individual reverie, functional memory, self-conscious denial, and collective understanding represent distinct acts of remembering and forgetting, and the process creates a memory of a "past . . . recognizably different from yet not altogether unlike the present: different enough to know it as another time, similar enough to make us aware of our continuity with it."[2]

Lowenthal explains that understanding the past based on personal memory is fundamentally different from an historical understanding of that past. Why? Because "historical knowledge is, by its very nature, collectively produced and shared; historical awareness implies group activity."[3] The collective effort to vet evidence about the past results in a collection of "histories—oral, scribal, and printed" that we consider "stable and faithful records." In contrast, Lowenthal argues that "we expect memory . . . to mislead us." Furthermore, the ongoing process of vetting, analyzing, and contextualizing the "histories," the "stable and faithful records," is part of a self-conscious process of revision. "Memory . . . is seldom consciously revised, [whereas] historians deliberately reinterpret the past through the lenses of subsequent events and ideas. Both history and memory engender new knowledge, but only history intentionally sets out to do so."[4] This prods us to balance the knowledge of the ways that memory can inform but also distort, with the reality that the public can influence the history conveyed in museums and historic sites.

This chapter argues that agriculture provides a perfect topic to incorporate in an exercise that engages the public in rethinking history interpretation. Museums and historic sites provide an ideal location to do this important work, because these institutions exist to educate the public and because they preserve the variety of records essential to the process. Furthermore, fewer and fewer people have direct experience with agriculture. Therefore, fewer and fewer people can put current events, such as shopping at the grocery store or commuting along farm-to-market roads (or major thoroughfares), into a continuum that started when a majority population lived on farms. Regardless, people engage with agriculture indirectly on a daily basis, and they express strong and often contradictory opinions about agriculture and farming.

Curators and historians who work with and study farm and rural life can inform us about the history of agriculture. The Agricultural History Society (AHS) is the second-oldest professional history organization in the United States (started in 1919), and it championed public history from its beginning. By 1970, AHS members who advocated for careful collecting and interpretation of that past to public audiences started a new organization, the Association for Living History Farms and Agricultural Museums (ALHFAM). ALHFAM formed during an AHS meeting at Old Sturbridge Village in 1970. ALHFAM changed its name in 1996 to broaden the network of people dedicated to studying agricultural history and committed to living history programming.

Recognizing the ways that people in the past popularized, mythologized, collected, and reenacted the past establishes a firm foundation on which to build a more self-aware and objective study of agriculture. Lowenthal explains that "historians go beyond the actual record to 'explain' the past . . . to frame hypotheses in present-day modes of thought."[5] This has always been the case for both historians dedicated to the historical record, and the general public dedicated to memorialization and monument building. Historians have documented the ways that people create and perpetuate myths, and how these popular interpretations have influenced collective understanding of the past. Examples include *The Age of Homespun* by Laurel Thatcher Ulrich, and *Race and Reunion*, a study of the long process of reconciliation after the Civil War by David Blight.[6]

Historical thinking about agriculture starts with acknowledging the ways that romantic notions of a "simpler time" have captured the imagination of rural residents in different places at different times in the past. They saw opportunities to convey a moral lesson, as did the Reverend Horace Bushnell in August 1851. During a secular sermon that he delivered on the occasion of the centennial of Litchfield, Connecticut, he argued that "the sources of our distinction [are] the spinning-wheels [and not the doctors, judges, military men, politicians, and landed gentry]. . . . Enough that they are the King Lemuels and Queens of Homespun, out of whom we draw our royal lineage."[7] Bushnell described the reciprocal relationship between farming and rural domestic industry, a relationship that contrasted with the industrialization of rural New England at the time. He theorized that, "if clothing is to be manufactured in the house, then flax will be grown in the ploughed land, and sheep will be raised in the pasture, and the measure of the flax ground, and the number of the flock, will correspond with the measure of the house market—the number of the sons and daughters to be clothed—so that the agriculture out of doors will map the family in-doors."[8]

Historian Laurel Thatcher Ulrich describes Bushnell's speech as "a small masterpiece, a lyrical and cohesive rendering of one of the central myths in American history."[9] You can imagine how such a speech might cause some in the audience to take a second look at the domestic tools and trinkets in their attics. Ulrich argues that the interest inspired antiquarians to collect, preserve, replicate, and interpret domestic artifacts for the next fifty years. They emphasized independent and self-sufficiency yeoman farm families, ordinary people engaged in their daily routines. The story provided a compelling counternarrative to that of the great men and great events of mainstream U.S. history. The story had traction all across the nation, because the myth provided citizens a way to celebrate success without owning reality—that the United States resulted from successive waves of forced removal of American Indians, labor exploitation of Africans and their descendants, and capitalist policies that allowed power to accrue to the wealthy at the expense of the poor. An article about inventions over the first one hundred years of the United States, published in *Harper's New Monthly Magazine* in 1874, began with the "principal agricultural tool"—the plow. The author justified the choice because of the "respectability of the employment [of farming] and its ancient fame . . . and the precedence of the husbandman."[10] These popular perceptions of the rural and agricultural past must be taken into account as the context in which museums and their collections originated.[11]

Other romanticized notions of the past exist in the collections of decorative arts. During the nineteenth century, architects and artists co-opted past aesthetics, repackaging them in the form of artistic revivals. The chairs, tables, sideboards, and bedroom suites that farm families purchased to furnish their houses contained elements of classical, gothic, Renaissance, and Rococo aesthetics. Ironically, the products of the mid-nineteenth century's aesthetic revivals existed in counterpoint to the new horse-drawn farm equipment that farmers purchased during the first agricultural revolution of the early- to mid-nineteenth century to reduce dependency on expensive labor and increase production. The income generated through their state-of-the-art agricultural equipment funded their purchases of Greek Revival and French Restoration–style furniture that provided tangible evidence of an improved standard of living in their modern farm homes.

The vast majority of consumers, inventors, and revivalists had firsthand experience with agriculture and rural life, in the fields, at the udder of the milk cow, and with an ox goad or driving line in hand. Most of them also observed a lifestyle fast disappearing in the wake of changing agricultural technology and industrial-scale production. The Reverend Bushnell acted on his concerns in 1851 by mythologizing the pre-industrial processing of yarns and textiles. Others took different tactics, thinking about the potential of historic sites to preserve historic agricultural practices. In 1850, Charles Lyell, a British geologist, lawyer, and landed gentleman, believed that Mount Vernon would make the perfect place to preserve a representative plantation, complete with the main house, outbuildings, and "negro houses." The "time capsule" would "showcase 'the state of agriculture at the period when the Republic was founded and how the old Virginia planters and their slaves lived in the eighteenth century.'" The Mount Vernon Ladies Association, however, did not devote resources to documenting or re-creating past agricultural practices for the sake of a history lesson.[12]

A case study of a bar share plow in the collection of the General Artemas Ward House Museum indicates the potential for agricultural artifacts to stimulate historical thinking.[13] Sarah Ann Carter, in a chapter in *Tangible Things: Making History through Objects*, describes the plow as a common tool on New England farms into the early nineteenth century, when farmers began buying patent plows with cast-iron shares and moldboards to replace their plows with wooden moldboards and wrought-iron shares and coulters. General Ward's son purchased cast-iron plows during the 1820s, and Carter theorizes that the small wooden plow got hauled into the family's attic, where it took up residency with other relics, including an old chair, a bed warmer, a walking wheel for spinning yarn, snow shoes, a reflector oven used in hearth cooking, a spade, and other tools from the barn and farmhouse. A photograph from the 1890s shows these objects in the attic of the house that the descendants of the Revolutionary War general maintained as a memorial to their famous ancestor. Carter explains that the family members engaged in a self-conscious effort to convey their "material legacy. As artifacts of the colonial revival, these objects were part of a broader movement to remember and recreate stories and plausible fictions about America's past." Furthermore, for the family members, "American history was personal, national, and material. This small plow became a tool for shaping this history and their memories"[14] (Photo 4.1).

But what "plausible fictions" might the family have associated with that plow, even though they relegated it to the attic? Did they realize the origins or use of the bar share plow beyond central Massachusetts? George Washington noted in his diary on 27 June 1786, that he directed laborers to stop using the "Hoe Harrow . . . in the drilled Corn" and to use "the Bar share plow . . . till the common Corn was all crossed; after which to use it, when the ground was worked the other way."[15] A lightweight plow such as the Ward plow may have served as a cultivating tool as Washington described, rather than a plowing tool. Did the Ward family forget (or did they ever know) the variations that existed in the model? Thomas Jefferson provided step-by-step directions to construct a bar share plow with "the mould-board of least resistance [with] this great advantage, that it may be made by the coarsest workman, by a process so exact that its form shall never be varied by a single hair's breadth"[16]

Farmer journals of the era share few details about such common routines as plowing, so documenting contemporary thoughts about plows or confirming the form of a plow without illustrations or artifacts can be difficult. Yet, nuggets exist that convey farmers' opinions about their plows. Horace Clarke, a Connecticut farmer, documented his regret that a plow that he had used for years was "completely worn out," with an entry in his journal on 8 May 1837: "I have followed that plow . . . more miles than any one man ever did or ever will any plow whatever in my *opinion*."[17] Jack Larkin, author of *The Reshaping of Everyday Life*, interprets this as evidence of the farmer's "sense of the endless recurrence of the agricultural cycle on his Connecticut farm that generations of American men would have shared."[18] Clarke's memories might fit Lowenthal's description of the

Photo 4.1 Detail, Walking Plow bar share, locked coulter, and moldboard. Source: General Artemas Ward House Museum

Source: Courtesy of the President and Fellows of Harvard College

personal memory memento that allowed Clarke to revisit his earlier self.[19] The women who spearheaded the preservation of the General Artemas Ward historic house, and who may have documented the collection, likely did not share such personal memories, given gendered divisions of labor common on New England farms during the era. The women, however, might have associated the plow with other work routines on the farm, or they may have envisioned the plow as the tool that farmers used to plow the lands in which they planted the flax that they processed into linsey-woolsey. They created the assemblage in the attic in homage to the Age of Homespun popularized during their youth and reinforced by colonial revivalists. Others organized exhibitions around the theme of the Age of Homespun, thus making it a tangible thing, rather than myth. The Farmers' Museum, Inc., in Cooperstown, New York, which opened in 1944, featured a permanent exhibit in the Main Barn, the *Age of Homespun*. Visitors walked through a year in the life of a farm family, one season and one farm task after another. Similar exhibits featuring early agricultural implements and tools of domestic processing existed across the country, and popular literature such as Laura Ingalls Wilder's *Little House* book series primed the public's perceptions of these tools.

The users, collectors, and curators all leave their mark on artifacts as they use the objects to make meaning of the past. The meaning of artifacts becomes more and more complicated when neither we nor our visitors understand the object in its original historic context. This should not dissuade us. It behooves us to remember that the past is a foreign country with which we have no personal connection, regardless of cultural connections or disconnections. Remember that Lowenthal argued, "We remember the past only as a congeries of distinctive occasions, recognizably different from yet not altogether unlike the present: different enough to know it is another time, similar enough to make us aware of our continuity with it."[20] The artifacts give us something tangible to work with, using them to discern meaning about anonymous makers, long-dead users, and generations of people who have preserved and interpreted the object with various ends in mind. Distinguishing between original use and later accumulations of meaning prompts a healthy exercise in historical thinking.

Reading objects often starts with naming—and the process should preserve the folk taxonomy of the donor as well as the nomenclature essential for retrieval. Naming can hint at context, but without context, plows in collections lack their soul. In 1946, the collection amassed by industrialists Albert B. and J. Cheney Wells became part of a new, large open-air museum, Old Sturbridge Village (OSV). Over the next generation, staff documented a variety of plows. Examples in the collection included bar share plows with locked coulters similar to the General Artemas Ward House Museum example, and numerous other forms. The "Old Colony" locked coulter breaking plow resembled the Ward model, but the Old Colony plow was bigger, with more stout component parts. Another plow, identified as a "Dutch plow," differed in a fundamental way; it had a pyramidal share without a coulter, a totally different construction from the bar share.[21] The differences warranted attention because plow forms reflected their function, but the names also mattered, confirming a New England folk taxonomy during the early national era. Names referenced cultural origins of plows ("Dutch") and associations of artifacts with different eras ("Old Colony," the plow type used around Exeter, New Hampshire, a place settled by migrants from Plymouth Colony).[22] The names farmers used conveyed their culture, their farming practices, and their own historical thinking.

OSV staff also researched and wrote reports describing types of plows in use in central Massachusetts during the late 1700s and early 1800s. They identified manufacturers, including farmers, local mechanics and blacksmiths, and upstart foundries and factories.[23] With context, the plows became objects useful for telling a story about differences within regional farming cultures, about the variety of implements essential for farmers to do their jobs, and about the influence of the land topography and the soil types on plow selection. The plow varieties helped visitors explore form and function in agricultural production as well as economic aspirations of farmers and businessmen. Such interdisciplinary thinking about technologies can help us avoid a linear interpretation of progress when looking at technology.

Rows of plows, a common approach to exhibiting such implements, can help visitors see differences, but few visitors have the depth and breadth of knowledge needed to make sense of what they see. The plow made or used in one place at a particular time needs the social as well as the technological, environmental, economic, and political context of that place and time to be fully understood. As Jim Slining, museum director at Tillers International, reminds us, we have trouble with plow nomenclature "because the context they have been placed in is the social context, and not the technological one (disclaimer: that is not to imply that I am not concerned with what 'the people' called these objects, how pertinent they found them, or how they changed society). Many nuances within a 'type' reveal gobs of information about the object, but also the paradigm—the construct within which the style found usefulness (or the hope of usefulness); the failures as important as the designs which eventually have won out." The museum of historic tools and equipment allows the staff at Tillers to "put history to work in the contemporary world." They can explore artifacts to identify "various approaches to solving similar problems." Thus, Slining argues "'context' can have various parameters, various definitions [and] that having a great variety in front of our eyes encourages contemporary onlookers to understand how complex history is, cautioning to place the 'down-pat' homogenous narrative into context as well! It does require greater investment on the part of the student, however."[24]

Culturally, the plowshare may retain its Old Testament symbolism as the opposite of a sword (Isaiah 2:4: "He will judge between the nations . . . and they will beat their swords into plowshares and their spears into pruning hooks."). The plow looks different to the person holding its handles, to the person repairing the wrought-iron straps on the moldboard, to the person feeding the oxen that pulled it, to the person waiting supper for the plowman. The plow represented conflict and warfare to the people displaced by the plowman. As Carter explains in *Tangible Things*, the Nipmuc people inhabited the land that the Ward family eventually farmed in central Massachusetts. In 1728, representatives of the Massachusetts Bay Colony confined the Nipmuc Indians to a 7,500-acre land grant. Artemus Ward, a colonel in the Massachusetts militia at the time, became the guardian to the Hassanamisco Band of Nipmucs in 1762. The families used plows like the bar share walking plow to "transform Nipmuc land into settled farms." Over time settlers encroached on the reserve until only three and a half acres remained.[25]

The opinions of farmers active during the early national era indicate that the walking plows helped farmers get their work done. By the mid-nineteenth century, however, agricultural scientists labeled the plows old-fashioned and out of date. Charles L. Flint, a mid-nineteenth-century lawyer and agricultural reformer from Massachusetts, described "the old 'Carey plough' [with] a clumsy wrought iron share, a land-side and standard made of wood, a wooden mould-board, often plated over, in a rough manner, with pieces of old saw-plates, tin, or sheet iron."[26] Flint illustrated an old Carey plow with a pyramidal share in "Farming tools in use in 1790," a plate in his book, *Eighty Years' Progress in the United States*. By 1840, Carey plows with wrought-iron moldboards were marketed in Illinois, a state replete with fertile land and farmers needing tools to decrease their labor costs.[27] These new Carey plows were part of a most successful industrial revolution, to put it simply.[28] Flint celebrated the new patent plows and other implements and tools as nothing short of miraculous. Advocates of the older plows remained, however, so not all recognized technological changes as progress. In June 1870, O. Jones of Mineral Springs, Arkansas, informed the editors of the *Southern Cultivator* that the "old fashioned Carey plow so much in use out here" worked well in the stiff black lands, better than more recent patented plows. The plow had a wrought-iron share and a wooden "mould board" that turned the stiff black dirt. Jones said, "the Carey plow will last twenty years, if kept in repair, and then can be worked up into something else, which is not the case with cast plows."[29]

Flint and other agricultural scientists advanced the theory of technological determinism, that rapid and successful innovation in agriculture reflected wider social and cultural progress. This has a circular logic to it that historical evidence complicates. New technologies for some led to debt and foreclosure for others. Threshing machines displaced laborers. Laborers went to the cities to work in agricultural-implement manufacturing companies, or moved west with the intention of farming someone else's land until they could afford to purchase their own. Advocates for technological innovation countered by arguing that the technology ensured that the shrinking number of farmers could still feed the world. Conveying these nuances takes time and creativity, but exploring historical evidence can facilitate historical thinking in ways that technological determinism cannot.

Technological determinism truncated the complexity of change, but the theory also influenced the ways that people perceived the old tools that they saw in barns and farm outbuildings. The first collectors of agricultural implements intended to showcase the benefits of scientific agriculture rather than nostalgia or history. They did not invest in collecting the old-fashioned. Well-to-do farmers, lawyers, bankers, and public officials at the city and county levels formed agricultural institutes and collected and preserved agricultural artifacts and specimens to inform farmers about new techniques, breeds, and seeds that could help them improve operations. The educational exhibitions at local and state fairs, and stock shows featured the three-dimensional "how-to" lessons.

The effort to generate public interest in agricultural collections continued to no avail. At the national level, the U.S. Patent Office's national gallery displayed patent prototypes, also featuring modern rather than historic lessons. The first commissioner of the U.S. Department of Agriculture (USDA), in 1863, called for the creation of a museum that would "embrace models of all the most approved implements of husbandry" as well as soil specimens, grain samples, paintings of recognized breeds of livestock, and a variety of other garden, field, and forest products.[30] Townend Glover, the first USDA entomologist, became the first curator of the USDA's fledging national agricultural museum in 1864. In 1865, Glover toured European agricultural museums, which made him aware of the potential, yet unrealized, of a national agricultural collection in the United States.[31] Glover's enthusiasm sustained the national collection until his resignation in 1878, at which point lack of financial and intellectual support caused the collection to languish.

National agricultural museums began contemporaneously in Hungary, Poland, and Denmark during the 1870s and 1880s, but the international momentum did not sway U.S. lawmakers. Sporadic calls to revitalize the U.S. museum, as expressed by Secretary of Agriculture Jeremiah M. Rusk in 1889 and 1890, and by USDA botanist and applied plant pathologist Dr. Frank Lamson-Scribner, fell on deaf ears, though specimen collecting continued with practical issues driving the process.[32] Scientists turned to experts within and beyond the United States to secure the best collections, and they used these collections to teach farmers lessons that could help them solve real problems they encountered in their fields, lessons indispensable to furthering scientific agriculture.

The USDA hired Lamson-Scribner to curate the national agricultural museum in 1894. Between 1904 and 1922 he worked as a member of the Government Exhibit Board, charged with coordinating agricultural exhibits for world expositions. He already had extensive international experience before his appointment to the Exhibit Board. He continued his international travels, always attentive to new approaches to agricultural exhibitions. After World War I, Lamson-Scribner toured three museums he considered "the world's [best] museums in agriculture," in Buenos Aires, Berlin, and Budapest. He wanted a national museum of agriculture in the United States, and he could see the potential everywhere: "All outdoors is replete with agricultural subjects. Just common, every-day subjects that we like because they are common and the more we see them the more we appreciate their value and importance."[33] He knew, however, that the agricultural museum had to use new techniques to instruct and entertain the public. He believed that a variety of techniques, including static exhibits, habitat groups, and displays of fresh vegetables and fruits, could best convey information to the public. He explained these ideas to members of the American Association of Museums in his 1921 article, "Agricultural Museums," published in *Museum Work*.[34]

The circles in which nationally prominent curators and collectors moved sometimes overlapped, and farms provided a space for them to interact. Lamson-Scribner grew up on a prosperous farm in Maine. Wallace Nutting, a skillful promoter of the colonial revival, visited the family farm often as he collected images and information for his book, *Maine Beautiful*, published in 1924.[35] Nutting and other revivalists embraced the cultural preservation impulse at the heart of the Age of Homespun myth much more than agriculture curators did.[36] That momentum helped launch local and state historical societies, and filled them with agricultural artifacts and domestic artifacts of rural and farm life.

Two oft-told tales of museum building incorporated farm families and rural folk in the process. Arthur Hazelius created Skansen, the open-air museum in Stockholm, Sweden, as a private venture to tell a national story. Its opening in 1891 coincided with the rapid growth of industrial production and urban populations and a corresponding rapid decline in rural and farm populations. The threat to farm buildings and associated artifacts created a sense of urgency, and Hazelius capitalized on it, relocating farmsteads to his museum. He wanted his Skansen to be a "living museum," a place that engaged the public in the collecting and the reenactment of rural and farm life.[37] It attracted hundreds of thousands of visitors during its early years. Many donated to it; thus they had lived the "history" they encountered there. They had helped create it. After Hazelius died in 1901, administrators remained committed to collecting and preserving regional culture and rural traditions as documented in barns, outbuildings, homes, and typical livestock and crops.

The combination of nostalgia and nation-building proved potent. Open-air folk-life museums became popular destinations across Europe. One of the most documented examples in the United States, Henry Ford's Greenfield Village, resulted from a similar effort to tell a national story based on the stories of farmers and inventors, but it opened nearly forty years after Skansen, in 1929. Ford turned to his Ford dealers, asking them to solicit objects from patrons, assuring them that the objects would be kept in an institution that documented their history. The museum that Ford opened in Dearborn held their donations, and the village became a place where they could reinforce their perceptions of agricultural, rural, and small-town superiority in contrast to urban and suburban environments.[38]

Both Hazelius and Ford learned that collections built around a shared experience—agriculture and rural life—had the potential to attract crowds. Theoretically, the more common the experience, the more even the playing field for exploring the past. The strategy of turning to people with firsthand knowledge and experience in agriculture to document their experiences with agriculture sounds like an exercise in contemporary collecting. But the process solicited heirlooms more than life stories. Romantic and nostalgic notions of family farming affected choices that donors made. Thus, the interest in preserving farming and rural life at the time of the Industrial Revolution created museum collections that documented the preindustrial era, or the first agricultural revolution of the early- to mid-nineteenth century, not the real experiences of farmers adopting tractors with internal combustion engines during the Golden Age of the early twentieth century.

Historical Thinking

The evidence of the past (artifacts, family histories, landscapes, public records) in combination with historical context, become valuable educational tools. The plows become more than the repurposed sword of the Old Testament, or the tool of cultivators, or the relic of the colonial revival, or the artifact overlooked because of the lack of provenance associated with it. Thinking about the plow on the hillside, designed to turn the dirt to defy runoff, adds the environment and geography to the humanities-based analysis of the plow. Thinking about the plow in the wheat stubble might lead to conversations about wheat as a crop, and about harvests, markets, trade, and blight, and about food processing and preparation. Thinking historically about this requires discussions of scale of production. How much can a person plow in a day? It depends on the plow, the landscape, the experience of laborers and draft animals, and the length of the day. Agricultural historian Leo Rogin explained that laborers, "working through the plowing season" with a yoke of oxen or team of horses pulling a wooden bar share plow, could turn three-quarters to one acre per day on average. Plowmen could turn one to two acres per day with a wooden breaking plow or one-and-one-half to three acres per day with a steel breaking plow. Animals and people had to rest to keep up the pace. This evidence can jumpstart historical thinking by relating available labor, available draft power, and available technology to farm size. The family provided its own labor in the form of children, and hired additional seasonal labor when needed. These factors affected how much land a farm family could manage[39] (Photo 4.2).

Details about average workdays (ten hours) and rates of plowing, planting, cultivating, and harvesting indicate the heavy labor required on the farm. All shared in this labor, whether in the fields or farmyards, barnyards, or farmhouses. The production and processing consumed all labor available. A laborer could average one-half acre a day cradling grain, and others spent the day binding the sheaves and arranging them in stooks to cure.[40] A sense of urgency swirled around this work, because the grain crop had to be

Photo 4.2 Wayne Randolph, using a new Pennsylvania bar share plow set to turn the soil to the right (the normal setting). Randolph's experience, plus the steady team of Roy and Jake, and experienced driver Jonathan Failor, produced consistent furrows during an ALHFAM workshop held at Horne Creek Living History Farm, near Winston-Salem, North Carolina, June 2009.

Source: Photograph by Ron Westphal

at the right stage to prevent the grain from flying from the head during cradling, and summer storms could flatten a crop ready for harvest. All these factors affected what a farm family could manage. Understanding details such as labor routines and pace of work can help explain historical scales of production. Families might have cultivated only five acres of corn, fifteen acres of wheat, five acres in oats and barley, five acres in hay, and maintained other fields in fallow, and other unimproved lands in pasture or woodlots. These acres required constant labor, giving meaning to the adage that "men worked from sun to sun, but women's work was never done."

Work routines included animal care, too. This requirement continued, day in and day out, as stock in farmyards had to be fed, stock on pasture had to be checked, cows had to be milked after they freshened, and draft animals had to be trained and exercised. It is one thing to read about the routines of livestock care, and the criticisms of people who did not care for their stock as they should, and it is another to think about the depth of mutual dependency between humans and their animals. Some might argue that keeping pets today offers a comparable experience, and while pets can help teach responsibility, the similarity ends there. Animals provided food, companionship, and draft power, and they consumed food, which added to the long list of things that farm families had to do. Farmers had to account for the needs of their livestock. Acreage of a farm had to be devoted to the upkeep of the livestock. Farm families could not just go to the store and buy cat or dog food. Those who tended animals had to put the needs of their live-stock first; farm families fed the stock before the families ate their own breakfast, and after long days in the fields, the draft animals received their rations before laborers did. Perceiving of animal-human relationships in this way prompts historical thinking, a process that involves moving outside of preconceived ideas and beyond the confines of the present day.

Educator Sam Wineburg, in his book, *Historical Thinking and Other Unnatural Acts*, says that "Historical thinking requires us to reconcile two contradictory positions: first, that our established modes of thinking are an inheritance that cannot be sloughed off, and second, that if we make no attempt to slough them off, we are doomed to a mind-numbing presentism that reads the present into the past." The best history teachers (and history students) overcome presentism and replace it with a self-conscious effort to find the "other" rather than the familiar in the past.[41] Wineburg quotes Carlo Ginzburg, author of *The Cheese and the Worms*, to emphasize this point and indicate why this is so difficult to accomplish. Paraphrasing Ginzburg: The historian's task is just the opposite of what most of us were taught to believe. He must destroy our false sense of proximity to people of the past because they come from societies very different from our own. The more we discover about these people's mental universes, the more we should be shocked by the cultural distance that separates us from them.[42]

Few people today have a false sense of proximity to farmers, a cultural chasm exists between "us" and farmers, past or present. A very different societal and cultural milieu existed between the majority of the population then, and the majority culture today ("our own"). Yet, agriculture today and in the past should be just as comprehensible as any other history if we take to heart Ginzburg's and Wineburg's advice. The fact that agri-culture, past and present, is "foreign" to the majority of us provides an opportunity. The lack of understanding creates an even playing field of exploration, one full of the human dimension that we can explore one plowshare at a time. Staff have as much to learn from this exercise as does the general public.

A method developed by educators to get teachers and students to "think like a his-torian" can guide the process. Nikki Mandell and Bobbie Malone explain that "'doing history' is an active process of asking good questions about the past, finding and analyz-ing sources, and drawing conclusions supported by evidence." Mandell developed the "Thinking Like a Historian Chart" as a framework that teachers can use to keep them-selves, and their students, mindful of the need to think about evidence, not just mem-orize names, dates, and events. The chart provides a visual prompt by which staff can assess their interpretive hooks, their exhibit scripts, and their interpretive plans. Do ques-tions provoke thought? Does credible evidence exist to answer the questions? How do we incorporate the evidence? Do we let the people of the past speak through the evidence?

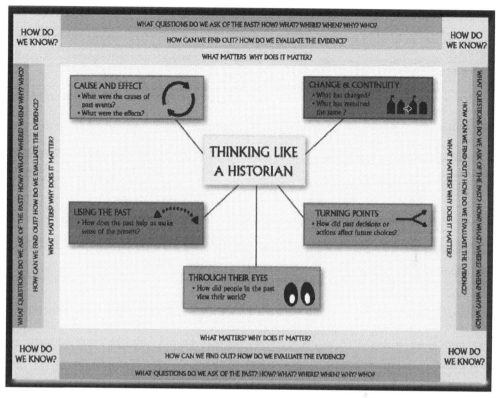

Photo 4.3   Thinking Like a Historian Chart

Source: Copyright Nikki Mandell. Reproduced with permission. For a full-color chart, please go to: http://wihist.org/TLaHposter.

Does the history help us understand the past time, but also the differences that defined the past worldview?[43] (Photo 4.3).

The process will involve careful selection of museum objects, historic records, and historical narratives that support the mission and convey multiple perspectives on the past. This process can encourage exploration of a topic that we need to know more about. This can be "history that does work in the world," as historian Carl Becker explained it in his 1931 presidential address to the American Historical Association: "The history that lies inert in unread books does no work in the world. The history that does work in the world, the history that influences the course of history, is living history, that pattern of remembered events, whether true or false, that enlarges and enriches [society's] collective specious present."[44] Learning more about the ways that different people remember their experiences with plows, those in the fields and in the sheds, in the attic and on exhibit, will add depth and breadth to agricultural interpretation.

Museums and historic sites can facilitate historical thinking in numerous ways, but they have to use historic evidence to engage the audiences. Any museum, from the farmhouse–turned–historic site to the business building–turned–history museum, contains valuable historical resources. The location of the farmhouse today should not matter. It can be landlocked in a suburb or city block, or situated on a vestige of a rural environment preserved in a metro-park complex or nature preserve. The historic records provide evidence, and the historic setting becomes a place to explore agriculture.

Notes

1. David Lowenthal, *The Past is a Foreign Country* (Oxford: Cambridge University Press, 1985), first quote 193; second quote 194.

2. Lowenthal, first quotes 201, italics in the original; second quote 201–02.

3. Lowenthal, 213.

4. Lowenthal, 214.

5. Lowenthal, 216.

6. Laurel Thatcher Ulrich, *The Age of Homespun: Objects and Stories in the Creation of an American Myth* (New York: Knopf, 2001); David W. Blight, *Race and Reunion: The Civil War in American Memory* (Cambridge, MA: Harvard University Press, 2001).

7. Ulrich, *Age of Homespun*, quotes 15, 17.

8. Ulrich, *Age of Homespun*, 17.

9. Ulrich, *Age of Homespun*, 17.

10. Edward H. Knight, "The First Century of the Republic: Agricultural Implements," *Harper's New Monthly Magazine*, 50, no. 295 (December 1874): 70–77, quote 70. I thank Jim Slining, Tillers International, for tracking down this source.

11. Ulrich, *Age of Homespun*.

12. Scott E. Casper, *Sarah Johnson's Mount Vernon: The Forgotten History of an American Shrine* (New York: Hill & Wang, 2008), 68, including quote. Casper notes that Mount Vernon began living history farm interpretation in 1990.

13. I thank Jim Slining, Tillers International, for identifying this plow and sharing resources documenting similar plows. He also reminded me of the efforts over several decades to replicate plows, including bar share models, and use them in open-air museums and living history farm settings to better understand cultivation practices.

14. [Sarah Ann Carter,] "A Hand Plow: Plowshares and Swords," in Laurel Thatcher Ulrich, Ivan Gaskell, Sara Schechner, Sarah Anne Carter, *Tangible Things: Making History Through Objects* (New York: Oxford University Press, 2015), 148–52, quotes 150–51. For an image of the plow, see Walking Plow, The Artemas Ward House and Its Collections, available at http://vc.lib .harvard.edu/vc/deliver/~ward/olvwork387843 (accessed 20 June 2016).

15. "[Diary entry: 27 June 1786]," Founders Online, National Archives, http://founders .archives.gov/documents/Washington/01-04-02-0003-0006-0027 (last update: 28 March 2016). Source: *The Diaries of George Washington*, vol. 4, *1 September 1784–30 June 1786*, eds. Donald Jackson and Dorothy Twohig (Charlottesville: University Press of Virginia, 1978), 353.

16. Thomas Jefferson, "The description of a mould-board of the least resistance, and of the easiest and most certain construction," *Transactions of the American Philosophical Society* 4 (1799), article no. 38, 313–22; quote 315. Jefferson's notations included the length, breadth, and thickness of the bar, exclusive of the wing; the dimensions of the wing length, exclusive of the coulter point, and the wing breadth, inclusive of the bar; the dimensions of the beam, the handles, and the moldboard. Wayne Randolph, "The Bar Share Plow in Virginia," *Proceedings of the 1988 ALHFAM Conference and Annual Meeting*, vol. 11 (Washington, D.C.: Smithsonian Institution, 1991), 20–23. Jim Slining, formerly a blacksmith at Colonial Williamsburg (CW), and now museum curator at Tillers International, indicated that while at CW, he and others on staff

replicated a bar share plow based on Jefferson's directions for use at Monticello. Another replica is in use at Great Hope Plantation, Colonial Williamsburg.

17. Jack Larkin, *The Reshaping of Everyday Life, 1790–1840* (New York: Harper & Row, 1988), 15, emphasis in original. I thank Jonathan Kuester for reminding me of this quote.

18. Larkin, quote 15.

19. Lowenthal, 194, 197.

20. Lowenthal, 201–02.

21. Two walking plows in the OSV digital collection resemble the Ward walking plow: 1) *Lock Colter or Bull Share Plow*, collection no. 1.57.12, dated c. 1780–1830; maker unknown; described as: "Small lock coulter plow with wooden mould board sheathed with iron strips. Iron coulter (knife) locks into flat triangular share and wooden beam. Landside is sheathed with iron; iron rod braces mould board against the beam. Iron loop on right side of beam for hitch; beam is flattened tear-drop shape with cross section. Left handle has odd repair with new curved grip scarfed and riveted on. Wooden elements are white oak. Unmarked." Materials: wood (white oak), iron/steel; Dimensions: Beam length 54 inches (137.2 cm), overall length 74 inches (188.0 cm) height mid handles 35 inches (88.9 cm). On exhibit in the Fitch Barn. Available at http://resources.osv.org/explore_learn/collection_viewer.php?N=1.57.12 (accessed 20 June 2016); 2) *Wooden Breaking Plow, Lock Colter Type*, collection no. 1.57.21, dated mid-eighteenth century; described as: "Large wooden 'breaking plow' of 'Old Colony' pattern. Flat, triangular share of hand-forged iron and lock coulter. Large, relatively well-formed moldboard is reinforced with a variety of strap iron, broken saw & hoe blades. Moldboard is pegged to standard and locked onto share by one of wear-plates. Wooden landside fits into socket at back of share. Wear plates on bottom and side of landside; also on side of standard and left handle. Beam has triangular cross-section. Hitch is on right side of beam. 2 extra iron bands on beam are of uncertain purpose. Traces of original (?) red paint on beam & handles. Diagonal brace between beam & back of standard. Marked on beam: 'H. RICE'." History: Said to have been once owned by Joseph Breck of East Pepperell (as of 1975 Willard Cousin's home); in possession of the Breck family for 150 years. From family of Luther (?) Breck. Joseph Breck was founder of Breck Seed Store in Boston in mid-nineteenth century; Dimensions: Beam 68 inches; height at standard 18½ inches; height of handles 37 inches; height of moldboard 13½ inches; point to tip of moldboard 41½ inches; point to tip of landside 30 inches. For information on the Old Colony pattern, see Item 10: "Old Colony Strong Plow, 1732. USNM 34769; 1899. In 1732 Peter Hardy of Raymond, New Hampshire, made this plow for Henry Lamprey of Kensington, New Hampshire. Gift of J. P. Lamprey, Kensington, New Hampshire," in John T. Schlebecker, *Agricultural Implements and Machines in the Collection of the National Museum of History and Technology*, Smithsonian Studies in History and Technology 17 (Washington, D.C.: Smithsonian Institution Press, 1972), quote 7; two images of the Old Colony Strong Plow, 8.

22. "Wood's Plough," *The Plough Boy, and Journal of the Board of Agriculture* (Albany, New York), vol. 2, no. 17 (23 September 1820): 133. A contributor to the *Rhode-Island American*, using the pen name the Plough and the Sickle, described the Old Colony plough: "They may be the same one our grand-father ploughed with, only repaired from generation to generation, with now and then a handle, a beam, or a mould-board. It is the true original plough of the Old Colony with about ten feet of beam, and four of mould-board." Another plough, a "dwarf" when compared to the Old Colony plough, the Sutton, he found lacking due to inadequate materials and construction. He claimed that "they are not fit to plough any land which has any kind of sod upon it; your furrows will stand up like the ribs of a lean horse in the month of March." The contributor compared the giant and the dwarf ploughs to make the point that "much of the success of every operation of art depends on the kind of tools used in the performance of it." Charles C. Coffin reduced the two plow descriptions into one line and replaced "mould-board" with "land-side"

(further misrepresenting the 1820 description) in "Argument of Mr. Coffin," *Arguments before the Committee on Patents, U.S. House of Representatives in February and March 1878* (Washington City, D.C.: Thomas McGill and Co., 1878), 42. A few years later, the *Delaware County Republican* included a summary of Charles C. Coffin's speech, "Machinery and Civilization," delivered in Lowell, Massachusetts, and associated both quotes and the term *land-side* with the Old Colony plough. See "Primitive Ploughs and Reapers," *Friends' Review: A Religious, Literary, and Miscellaneous Journal*, 35, no. 15 (19 November 1881): 229–30, quote 230. A comparable misquote appeared in the 1899 *Yearbook of Agriculture*, published by the U.S. Department of Agriculture, and J. B. Davidson repeated it in "Tillage Machinery," published in L. H. Bailey, ed., *Cyclopedia of American Agriculture: A Popular Survey of Agricultural Conditions, Practices, and Ideals in the United States and Canada*, vol. 1, *Farms* (New York: Macmillan, 1907), 387–97, quote 388: "The Old Colony plow, which was used in the eastern states in 1820, 'had a ten-foot beam and a four-foot landside' and that it made the 'furrows stand up like the ribs of a lean horse in the month of March'." I thank Jim Slining for bringing this last quote to my attention.

23. Andrew Baker and Frank G. White, "The Impact of Changing Plow Technology in Rural New England in the Early 19th Century," OSV Research Paper, January 1990, available at http://resources.osv.org/explore_learn/document_viewer.php?Action=View&DocID=715 (accessed 20 June 2016).

24. E-mails, Jim Slining to Debra A. Reid, 23 June 2016.

25. [Carter,] "A Hand Plow," 148–52, quotes 150–51, last quote 152.

26. Charles L. Flint, "Progress in Agriculture," *Eighty Years' Progress in the United States: A Family Record of American Industry, Energy and Enterprise showing the various channels of industry and education through which the people of the United States have arisen from a British colony to their present national importance . . . with a large amount of statistical information* (Hartford, CT: L. Stebbins, 1868), quote 27; illustrations of 1790 technology, 28; illustration of 1860 technology, 29. Available at https://archive.org/details/eightyyearsprogr00agenrich (accessed 20 June 2016).

27. Leo Landis, "Development of the Plow in the Midwest," *Midwest Open Air Museums Magazine*, 18, no. 2 (1997), 22–27, reprinted in a special issue of the *Midwest Open Air Museums Magazine*, 32, nos. 1 and 2 (2011), 14–18.

28. To learn more about the Industrial Revolution of the nineteenth century and the expansion of agricultural implement manufacturing, see surveys such as R. Douglas Hurt, *American farm tools: From hand-power to steam-power* (Manhattan, KS: Sunflower University Press, 1982), and Leo Rogin, *The Introduction of Farm Machinery in its Relation to the Productivity of Labor in the Agriculture of the United States During the 19th Century* (Berkeley: University of California Press, 1931). Other studies document economic factors and farmer attitudes toward technology as documented in manufacturers' records. For example, see Alan L. Olmstead and Paul W. Rhode, "Beyond the Threshold: An Analysis of the Characteristics and Behavior of Early Reaper Adopters," *Journal of Economic History*, 55, no. 1 (March 1995): 27–57.

29. O. Jones, "Carey Plow," *Southern Cultivator*, 28, no. 9 (September 1870), 310.

30. C. A. Browne, "A National Museum of Agriculture: The Story of a Lost Endeavor," *Agricultural History*, 13, no. 3 (July 1939): 137–48, quote 137.

31. Debra A. Reid, "Agricultural Artifacts: Early Curators, Their Philosophy and Their Collections," *ALHFAM Proceedings 2010*, vol. 33 (North Bloomfield, OH: Association for Living History, Farm and Agricultural Museums, 2011), 30–52, especially 33–34.

32. Browne, 139–40.

33. F. Lamson-Scribner, "Agriculture Museums," *Museum Work*, vol. 4 (1921): 125–35, especially 133. The entry for the tenth object accessioned to the collection of the National Museum

of History and Technology (NMHT), the old Colony plow, arrived in 1899. This likely involved Lamson-Scribner given the shifting nature of collections among national agencies to their ultimate destination at the NMHT. Schlebecker, *Agricultural Implements*, 8.

34. Lamson-Scribner, 134.

35. James W. Hilty and Paul D. Peterson Jr., "Frank Lamson-Scribner: Botanist and Pioneer Plant Pathologist in the United States," *Annual Review of Phytopathology*, 35 (1997): 17–26, especially 18 and 24.

36. Ulrich, *Age of Homespun*.

37. Sten Rentzhog, *Open Air Museums: The History and Future of a Visionary Idea*, Skans Victoria Airey, trans. (Sweden: Jamtli Förlag and Carlsson Bokförlag, 2007), 10–11. Rentzhog positioned Skansen at the center of the open-air vision. He argued that Hazelius outpaced his contemporaries because he involved Swedes in his contemporary collecting effort, and this generated unprecedented public interest and support. Hazelius, a trained educator, applied his knowledge of pedagogy to his open-air experiment and created a "living museum" that engaged visitors directly in the exercise. As Magdalena Hillström has argued, "The national narrative told and performed at Skansen is built up of different national symbols and is intertwined with discourses of modernity, civilization and gender. Metaphorically, Skansen is a large-scale *tableau vivant*, incorporating the visitors in the national spectacle." See Hillström, "Nordiska Museet and Skansen: Displays of Floating Nationalities," *Great Narratives of the Past. Traditions and Revisions in National Museums. Conference Proceedings from EuNaMus, European National Museums: Identity Politics, the Uses of the Past and the European Citizen*, Paris, 29 June–1 July and 25–26 November 2011. Dominique Poulot, Felicity Bodenstein, and José María Lanzarote Guiral, eds., *EuNaMus Report*, No. 4. (Linköping, Sweden: Linköping University Electronic Press), http://www.ep.liu.se/ecp_home/index.en.aspx?issue=078; for Hillström, http://www.ep.liu.se/ecp/078/004/ecp12078004.pdf (accessed 1 June 2014), 37.

38. Jessie Swinger, *"History Is Bunk": Assembling the Past at Henry Ford's Greenfield Village* (Amherst: University of Massachusetts Press, 2014).

39. Rogin, *Introduction of Farm Machinery*, 16 for the wooden plow; 51–52 for the breaking plows.

40. Rogin, *Introduction of Farm Machinery*, 234–35 for wheat cultivation, including hours estimated.

41. Sam Wineburg, *Historical Thinking and Other Unnatural Acts: Charting the Future of Teaching the Past* (Philadelphia: Temple University Press, 2001), 12.

42. Wineburg, 10.

43. Nikki Mandell and Bobbie Malone, *Thinking Like a Historian: Rethinking History Instruction* (Madison: Wisconsin Historical Society Press, 2007), quote 3, chart 115.

44. Carl Becker, "Everyman His Own Historian," *American Historical Review*, 37, no. 2 (January 1932): 223–35, quote 234–35.

PART 2

AGRICULTURE IN TIME AND PLACE

Research as the Foundation for Interpretation

CHAPTER 5

DOCUMENTING AGRICULTURE IN TWO DIMENSIONS

Background Research

RESEARCH INTO local history sources can inform you about details, but transforming them into provocative interpretation takes effort. Engaging audiences in the interpretive planning process can redirect the minutia of agricultural details into programming that can distinguish your museum and historic site from others. Details matter, but how many acres of corn, oats, and wheat a farm family grew or how many hogs ran in the woods matters less than the context in which those acts occurred. Reading secondary sources can help you develop context and prioritize your goals before leaping into original research. This takes time, but secondary sources can inform you about the agricultural past in general, and help you identify topics that relate to audience interests. Archival sources then help you fill in the details in your local context. The complexity of the subject—agriculture—warrants the investment.

Understanding agriculture over time and across disciplines starts with compiling a reading list that incorporates multiple disciplinary perspectives (history, anthropology and sociology, economics, environmental studies, political science, and gender and sexuality studies).[1] Surveys of agriculture and rural life synthesize information drawn from monographs, both book- and article-length studies, focused on either a place over time, or an issue or event and its broad influence. They provide a good starting point for gaining a broad overview of the subject and will help establish the parameters around which you can build a statement of agricultural significance for your site. Surveys by David Danbom (*Born in the Country*) and R. Douglas Hurt (*American Agriculture: A Brief History*) both provide long chronological overviews. Both begin with American Indian agriculture before contact, and Danbom describes European agriculture before contact, too. Both incorporate farmer politics and agricultural policy. Hurt focuses more on technological change than Danbom. Both attempt to move readers beyond the myths of self-sufficiency and technological progress by emphasizing how farmers participated in commercial markets from the beginning. Pamela Riney-Kehrberg's anthology, *The Routledge History of Rural America*, includes essays by experts in their fields that provide details about seven agricultural regions across the United States. The authors introduce you to topics not covered in depth in the broad surveys, topics such as rural masculinity, women and families in rural America, utopian and communal societies, historic structures and landscapes, international relations, agricultural labor, and race in rural context.[2]

With the broad parameters of the agricultural story most relevant to your site, you can begin to drill down into state and regional histories, and relevant monographs. WorldCat can help you find books to flesh out your story.[3] You can find articles in state history journals or in regional journals such as the *Western Historical Quarterly*, or in journals dedicated to the subject, such as *Agricultural History*. Consult with the reference librarian at your public library, or a nearby college or university. Call ahead; set up an appointment; ask questions. Librarians provide access, and they want to help you find what you need to do your job.[4]

Detailed reading in state and regional histories and in monographs can help you identify historical trends specific to your area. For instance, during the early national era, the market revolution affected local agricultural markets. In addition to books and articles about the market revolution, and about agriculture prior to 1860, you will find more details in state and county historical and biographical atlases and plat books. During the 1870s, county historical and biographical atlases became popular tools for local boosters to celebrate their origins and for economically and politically prominent families to reflect on their heritage and their contributions.[5] The Haithi Trust Digital Library and other state-level repositories, such as the Michigan County Histories and Atlases Digitization Project, or the Missouri Historical Maps and Atlases Project, provide PDF facsimiles available at no charge. These publications include detailed histories, not footnoted, and illustrations of farmsteads, businesses, and prominent people willing to pay for the service. The sources promoted county resources, so they contain bias, and no one vetted the contents. Regardless, the county histories provide contemporary perspectives available nowhere else. They provide an early secondary source about antebellum market history in your local area.

Monographs differ in their interpretation of agricultural topics. This becomes obvious as you become more familiar with the literature about the subject of your research. Selected studies of Midwestern agriculture indicate the range of interpretation possible. Each scholar, one trained in economics, one in sociology, and two in history, came to very different conclusions even as they analyzed similar materials. Carrie A. Meyer focused on diaries and ledgers kept by May Lyford Davis between 1896 and 1944 that documented the farm that she and her husband, Elmo M. Davis, operated in Winnebago County, Illinois, near the city of Rockford. Jane Adams analyzed census records, memoirs, and oral history interviews to document a century of change in rural and farm life in southern Illinois with a focus on Union County between 1890 and 1990. This region differed markedly from other areas of Illinois due to low land values and rural poverty, but also due to market options including truck farming, dairying, hog and beef production, and coal mining. Dennis S. Nordin and Roy V. Scott provide the geographically broadest survey, considering change across an area of intense corn and soybean production that spans 469 counties across eleven states from eastern Ohio into Kansas and the Dakotas. While all of the authors recount hard-fought struggles waged by farm families to manage the largess of the Golden Age, to weather the vagaries of volatile markets during the 1920s, and to manage the low commodity prices of the 1930s, they come to very different conclusions about the outcome of the struggles. Nordin and Scott explain that "painful as the tragedies of failure were for individuals, their net effect was the Midwest agricultural miracle, a blessing that continues to provide an ever-growing population of consumers with abundant food at low prices." Adams's findings counter that. She claims that farm families in Union County, Illinois, "did not resist change: the historical record shows that people actively positioned themselves in relation to changes they experienced and that they tried, with the material, cultural, and individual tools at hand, to fashion satisfying lives. They did not, however, necessarily agree with the direction that changes were taking." Adams explained that the diverse region lacked outlets to discuss what would be in their best interests, and what strategies could help them secure the future that they envisioned. Meyer likewise links community to farm family survival: "The well-being, the resilience, and often the survival of any one individual depended on strong family and community connections. Together farmers weathered all kinds of crises and learned to respond to change."[6]

Not all will agree that the "Midwest agricultural miracle" is "a blessing," as Nordin and Scott describe it. Studies of agricultural sustainability tend to emphasize the success of practices that suit landscapes rather than novel approaches that tax the environment and exploit the labor supply. Today, entrepreneurial approaches to farming include more than row-crop monoculture, confinement operations, and robotic milking parlors. Some farm entrepreneurs base their business plan on community-supported agriculture, low to no chemical dependency, and heritage breeds and seeds. Research that documents change in one place over time can discern trends and provide platforms for conversations about agriculture today, but those conversations depend on facts, not on opinion or myth. And those conversations offer the potential of building a community of consumers who want to engage with farmers and laborers in solving modern agricultural challenges.

You cannot interpret agriculture without researching the technology, not just the mechanical but the biological and chemical, available at any given time in the past. Peter H. Cousins, curator of agriculture at The Henry Ford from 1969 to 1995, informed ALHFAM members that "we must rigorously define the scope of our presentation—its boundaries in time and place, the entire sociocultural milieu of its inhabitants—before we can begin to discover what constitutes appropriate tool and implement systems."[7] Cousins explained that research should document the tools and implements that reflect "crop systems, cultural differences among farmers, and differential rates by which changing ideas were accepted, and differences in economic scale." Research gets even more complicated when documenting changing technologies that reflect larger sociocultural and economic transformations.

Research on internal combustion engines indicates how adoption of the engines decreased farm labor needs, increased employment opportunities in manufacturing industries, and eased farmers' workloads. Carrie A. Meyer's article-length study of early gasoline engines confirms that at least one million U.S. farmers had adopted the technology by 1915. This hastened the adoption of automobiles on farms, including the 1908 Model T, which Henry Ford marketed with add-ons to power other farm equipment. Farm family familiarity with engines and automobiles, in turn, facilitated early adoption of tractors, particularly the Fordson, launched in 1917.[8] Innovation in tractor design responded to farmers' needs. The McCormick-Deering Farmall, launched in 1924, included a power takeoff that farmers could use to run corn pickers, shellers, silage choppers and blowers, and numerous other implements that revolutionized labor demands on the farm. The income from stable prices during the Golden Age made these investments possible, but others mortgaged their farms, which put them in a precarious financial position.

Many questions remain about the changes facilitated by tractors. U.S. Department of Agriculture publications and compendia that summarize agricultural census data provide some answers. Economists Alan L. Olmstead and Paul W. Rhode indicated that farmers adopted tractors rapidly after 1910 and used tractors alongside horses for forty years, because each source of power suited a particular purpose on the farm. Farmers slowly transitioned pastures from use by horses or mules to dairy and beef cattle, and they shifted arable acreage from stock feed to commercial crop production. Olmstead and Rhode estimated that farmers who adopted tractors reduced man-labor hours by 1.74 billion annually between 1944 and 1959. The consequences of the transition extended beyond the business of farming. Tractor manufacturers hired more wage laborers, and competition increased to design products that farmers would buy.[9]

Farm families who adopted technology generated additional changes in rural business, education, and social and political organizations. Originally, farmers had to choose between four commercial liquid fuels classes, including alcohols, gasolines, common kerosenes, and the low-cost heavy-oil fuels for internal combustion engines.[10] Many farmers had no dependable supply. Farmers with tractors used their economic leverage. The Farm Bureau, a membership organization that includes farmers and businessmen and implement dealers, responded. County-level Farm Bureaus opened gasoline stations and mechanic shops to serve farmers' needs.[11] Farmers in New York, Illinois, and Iowa joined and remained Farm Bureau members because of services that suited farm family goals.[12] The offices did not have a consistent policy for retaining membership records, but Bureau publications at the county, state, and national levels provide evidence of rural and farm consumer culture, and indicate the stances that the Farm Bureau took over time.

Membership provided farm families access to the Bureau services, which included conduits of information about changing technology for farm and home. The changes did not threaten the gendered division of labor on farms, and in fact, the farm family came to symbolize the hope for the future. Nancy Berlage explains, "The farm bureau and 4-H combined newly emerging precepts of the modern family with older strategies of family labor. Rather than going out to work, as so many professional and industrial workers did, rural youth were to go home to work."[13] Other historians believe that the state more than the families and their membership organizations bore the bulk of the responsibility for implementing national agendas. Gabriel Rosenberg explains that 4-H provided a means for the government to manage life. The "4-H's iconic clover . . . inscribed on the chests of millions of youth around the world [symbolized] the American state insinuating itself into the intimate spaces of the rural world and connecting national projections of population and crop yields to the vigor and health of the individual bodies. . . . 4-H is a sophisticated biopolitical apparatus—a state infrastructure built out of youth instead of concrete."[14] These sorts of connections between technology and humanity and political agendas warrant study and debate.

With a well-honed understanding of the different ways that authors interpret major themes in agriculture, you can begin to synthesize your findings into your own narrative about agriculture at your museum or historic site. Your findings should incorporate information from the earliest published sources you can find, and continue to the most recent. Your bibliography can list all sources in alphabetical order by the author's last name. The narrative portion of your report should provide an overview of agriculture in the area, a synthesis of information contained in your sources. You should arrange it either topically or chronologically, bearing in mind the layers of occupation and distinct cultural practices that affected agriculture on your site. It should include an overview of how authors disagree, or how interpretation has changed over time. This is a natural outcome of detailed reading because it should generate an understanding of what some call the "meta-discourse" about the past. As we increase our depth of understanding based on information from multiple sources, the ways that the interpretation changed over time becomes clearer. You can determine the factors that affected the mind-sets conveyed in the interpretations by putting the authors into the context of their times. This will help you explain the reasons why the authors presented the information in the ways that they did. This exercise in expressing the meta-discourse will help you articulate the goals of those who came before you, and it will help you understand your own goals. Digging through the layers of meaning can make the history of agriculture and farming most meaningful, but such work takes time and patience to develop this depth of understanding.[15]

Synthesizing Published Sources: The Hog

Published sources that focus on the hog provide a case study in synthesizing information to understand the creature more.[16] Southern and Midwestern agricultural histories incorporate hogs into their studies more than do historians in other regions. In fact, you cannot write about Midwestern agricultural history without including hogs. Hogs and corn developed in tandem, and as an integral part of agriculture in the "Corn Belt." The well-respected agricultural historian Allan G. Bogue started a chapter in his classic, *From Prairie to Corn Belt*, with a quote from a 1938 novel, *American Years*, not an 1838 primary source. He quoted author Harold Sinclair's fictionalized account of a character based on hog drover and seed corn patriarch Isaac Funk, and his uncontrollable herd. Bogue explained that "the Yancy family . . . came upon an abandoned cabin. They counted themselves lucky to find shelter, but around midnight a horde of grunting, clattering animals poured through the door to contest their claim. These were Ike Frink's hogs."[17]

Bogue used few words, but he alerted readers to the distinction between the historic evidence about hogs on the Illinois and Iowa prairies, and the fictionalized account. Bogue explained that "the hog was as important on the farms . . . as the steer or milk cow. . . . The hog and the steer actually complemented each other. . . . For cattle-feeders the margin of profit was often represented by the nutriment that his hogs gleaned from the droppings of the steers. For dairymen the hog strained out the last bit of usefulness which remained in buttermilk or whey." Bogue continued: "None of the American farm animals can convert grain into meat of high quality with greater speed or efficiency than can the hog." The hog could have no less than two litters a year, and "one litter of pigs will produce as much or more meat than a steer in half the time." Furthermore, farmers needed "little capital" to raise pigs. "A litter of weanling pigs cost less than half the cost of one steer ready for the feedlot." Bogue concluded his explanation of the virtues of the hog by quoting an excerpt from a statement attributed to S. B. Ruggles, delivered in Chicago, and published in the *Atlantic Monthly*. The entire quote sensationalized the real relationship between the pig and the corn crop: "The corn crop is condensed and reduced in bulk by feeding it into an animal form, more portable. The hog eats the corn, and Europe eats the hog. Corn thus becomes incarnate; for what is a hog, but fifteen or twenty bushels of corn on four legs?"[18] The 300,000,000 pounds of pork exported to Europe in 1863 equaled "a million and a half of hogs marching across the ocean."[19] While the Confederacy sought European markets for cotton, pork from the North sailed across the ocean blue.

Published memoirs indicate the value of hogs on the hoof and in the frying pan. Rebecca Burlend, in *A True Picture of Emigration*, explained how the costs of provisioning a farm on the Illinois frontier during 1831 sometimes exceeded resources. The Burlends purchased "a cow and calf, for which we paid fourteen dollars, a young mare, which cost us twenty dollars, two pigs, and a shallow flat-bottomed iron pan, with cover to it, to bake in." The family turned the cow and calf onto a field only partially harvested and let them forage throughout the winter. They butchered the two pigs, because "we wanted them for our own use, and we wished to spare the small stock of Indian corn we had on hand." This left the Burlend family with little cash. "Five or six dollars were all the money we had, and we fully purposed to buy a pig or two with them, as we had been some weeks without any animal food, except a few fowls for which we had bartered one of our china tea-cups." Working with a neighbor led to the purchase of "three young pigs just taken in from the range; for which we paid him the small sum of three dollars. They were scarcely fat enough to kill; we therefore gave them a little unsaleable wheat which fed them very rapidly, so that in about a month's time they became nice pork, weighing between nine and ten stones each."[20]

The Burlend family settled on eighty acres of land that they purchased on a preemption—acquiring it from a squatter. They collected sap from a maple grove, processed it into sugar, and traded forty pounds of it "for a sow and a litter of pigs, which we kept near home till they knew the premises, and afterwards allowed them to run at large until autumn." By 1845 they owned 360 acres of land. They had plenty to eat, a new and comfortable house, and twenty head of cattle, seven horses and one or two foals, and "pigs, sheep, and poultry, the number of which I am not able to state as they keep continually breeding, and are never to be seen altogether."[21]

The prolific hogs on the Burlend farm represented productivity across the state. Comparing the number of hogs raised in one county, to those raised in another, can give you an idea of the relative investment of farm time in hog raising. Think of these as relative numbers rather than absolutes, given the difficulty of reporting the exact number of hogs a farm family owned. Rebecca Burlend indicated that she did not know how many hogs the family owned in 1845. The census enumerators visited around mid-June of the decennial census years. A sow's gestation cycle is short (three months, three weeks, three days), so the number of pigs on a farm could vary considerably over time.[22] Consider this justification to respond to the question, "How many hogs did the family own?" with an answer that addresses the biology of the hog, or the environment of the farm, or the fluctuations of the market.

Adding More Detail: Primary Sources

After expanding your understanding based on what others have written about agriculture, then start asking questions.

How did the farmers acquire the land?
Did it begin with confiscation from American Indian nations?
Did the family squat on public land or purchase acreage through public land sales?
What businesses catered to farm family needs?
Did family members do farm chores, or did the family own or hire laborers to perform most work on the farm?
How did the farmers secure laborers?
Did migrant laborers work on the property during harvest, and if so, who were they?
What roles and responsibilities did women and children have on the farms?
How did culture and ethnicity affect gender roles, work routines, and inheritance practices?

You can start your original research by determining the types of two-dimensional primary sources that could best answer what you need to know. Researchers have written about the steps to take and the primary sources to consider to answer these questions. Historian R. Douglas Hurt described the process in *American Farms: Exploring their History*. He recommended consulting land records, personal correspondence and diaries, ledgers and account books, oral histories, photographs, real and personal property tax rolls, and agricultural and population census data.[23] City directories and records of agricultural businesses such as seed companies, feed stores, gas stations, mechanic shops, and shoe factories may exist to extend the network that sustained farms historically. Archaeologist John S. Wilson urged researchers to start with local and regional published records; then continue with archival research utilizing personal papers and public records such as tax assessments and census returns; and then begin fieldwork at sites that fit certain criteria of significance. The work takes time, travel, and endurance, but from such work it is possible to focus energies on the most significant site, be it a historic house, a farmstead, or other structure critical to understanding the past.[24]

Staff can use the site-specific evidence to generate research reports. A historic landscape and building report should put the site into the larger context, drawing on agricultural and local histories. From these, staff can identify interpretive goals and develop an interpretive plan; house, barn, and landscape furnishing plans; a scope of collections statement; and ultimately plan for exhibitions and public programming. The primary sources (the historic records) become the basic building blocks for everything the museum or historic site will do. Such research can turn a historic farmhouse, or acreage in a forest or nature preserve or metro-park or county park district, into a place to launch civic dialogue about agriculture, past and present. Realize that the process can take months, if not years. Some evidence may prove particularly elusive. In that case, leave a research question for the time being, and move on to another topic. Do not get discouraged, but be realistic. Talk to others, share your findings, keep your nose to the scent, and the effort put into research will reap benefits of a well-documented site with confident staff ready to share the information.

Case Studies

Evidence of agriculture exists in numerous archival sources. Letters, diaries, journals, and ledgers may provide the only evidence of daily chores and once-common practices. Maps, drawings, paintings, and photographs document the buildings, fence rows, farmyards, creek bottoms, roads, and ridges once integral to the farm environment and now long gone from the landscape. Women and girls documented these things, as did men. The following examples indicate that archival collections not identified as agricultural, or historic sites not considered agricultural, can still tell you much about farming and rural life.

Ten miles south of Boston, in Quincy, Massachusetts, the Adams National Historic Park preserves houses constructed in 1663, 1681, and 1731. President John Adams's father, John, bought the 1681 house and six acres in 1720. He purchased an adjacent house in 1744. At the time of patriarch John's death in 1761, records indicate that he owned approximately 188 acres of land. The family grew grains (corn, rye, wheat, oats, and barley) and raised livestock (oxen, horses, sheep, hogs, and poultry), a fitting combination of crops for a family farming along the Old Coast Road from Boston to Plymouth. The family's political status in 1788 warranted purchase of another house near the family properties, the Old House at Peacefield, built in 1731. The property served as a gentleman's estate that included formal gardens and orchards. Structures on the property served agricultural purposes.[25]

Artistic renderings provide evidence of the site's agricultural vitality in the past. These visual cues help staff and visitors envision the agricultural past even though the farms operated by the Adams families now sit in the heart of a city. The Old House at Peacefield is better documented, visually, than the other Adams farms, perhaps because it captured the public's imagination during John Adams's term as the second president of the United

States (1797–1801). The illustrations indicate the home's location on a busy roadway. They also document the numerous outbuildings needed to sustain a gentleman's estate.

A watercolor done in 1798 featured a roadway with a team of horses pulling a phaeton with two passengers, a stone fence with wooden gates to admit vehicles, and a section of rails so pedestrians could climb over to access the house. The fence protected the house yard from the hogs and fowl that drovers herded from the country to the city markets in Boston. Stories of such drives and the remains of roadside holding pens add depth to stories about the reasons for fenced yards during the early national period.

The farmyard included barns, sheds, and stables, and a series of fences to keep travelers out and livestock in, all depicted in a sketch done by President John Adams's granddaughter, Abigail Smith Adams, in 1820. Different structures served different needs. Some stored grain, others hay and dairy cattle. Others stored farm equipment, carriages, and driving horses. The location of the estate on busy roadways increased its visibility. An 1828 drawing by Mrs. George Whitney leaves little to the imagination about the importance of access on the part of farmers and politicians to transportation networks (Photo 5.1). It added detail to the stone fences, and a wagon to imply the function of one of the hipped roof buildings as a hay barn. Whitney's illustration also showed the corn house, the structure next to the stable, behind the house, and between the stable

Photo 5.1 A drawing of the Adams Seat in Quincy by Mrs. George Whitney, 1828. The drawing shows the Old House at Peacefield during John Quincy Adams's term as the sixth president of the United States (1825–1829). This is the only illustration of the corn house. Courtesy of National Park Service, Adams National Historical Park

and the first of the two hipped roof barns. The corn house stored grains, likely cereal crops (the English called these "corn"), as well as ears of corn, or maize. These illustrations indicate that the gentleman's estate functioned as a working farm, not just as a showplace.

Personal papers hold clues to agriculture as practiced on properties associated with wealthy families in Indiana Territory. The Murrell Home, a state historic site in Oklahoma, is the only surviving example of a home occupied by the Cherokee elite that survived a period of intense conflict (1840s to 1860s). Minerva Ross, the niece of John Ross, principal chief of the Cherokee nation, married George Michael Murrell in 1834. George, his brother, and Minerva's father, Lewis Ross, operated a mercantile in Athens, Tennessee. The Cherokee families relocated to Indian Territory in 1839. Murrell established a stock farm and built Hunter's Home. After Minerva died in 1855, George married her sister, Amanda Ross, in 1857.

Many agricultural topics beg for attention. How different were Ross-Murrell family agricultural practices from the agriculture practiced in the area prior to their arrival? Did agriculture as practiced by the Ross-Murrell families reflect cultural identity? In what capacities did enslaved people of African descent affect work on the stock farm, or in the barns and outbuildings and agricultural fields at Hunter's Home? Did Cherokee matriarchs have authority over any parts of the plantation? What tasks did they perform? Did status, kinship, or talent determine who had responsibility for agricultural decisions about stock, gardens, or dairy processing?[26]

According to David Fowler, Murrell Home administrator, George Murrell reputedly imported the first Hereford cattle into Virginia, and he transferred his interest in purebred stock to Indian Territory, importing Durham cattle, Berkshire hogs, and merino sheep. The Cherokee National Agriculture Association formed by 1848, and members held annual meetings and fairs, documented in the Cherokee newspapers the *Advocate* and the *Sentinel*. The Cherokee published an almanac that borrowed from other almanacs and planting guides. George Murrell, the Virginian, and Lewis Ross, brother of Chief John Ross, supplied oxen to whites from Washington County, Arkansas, and Cherokee from the Territory who headed west in 1849 to California on the Cherokee Trail.[27]

George's niece, Emily L. Murrell, who lived in Madison County, Mississippi, described her uncle George's farm while visiting during the spring and early summer of 1850. She mentioned a gristmill with a large circular treadmill. Oxen walked on the canted platform, and powered the mill, which ground corn.[28]

During the Civil War, raiding parties pillaged the productive farms. Robert Morris Peck, a civilian teamster employed by the U.S. Army, recalled women, children, and "Negroes" "abandoning livestock, poultry, furniture, crops and everything; some going north, some going south, in whichever direction they have friends or their political sympathies lead them. Some families are still remaining and holding on to their homes and property, loath to abandon and lose what they cannot take away with them; but they have a rough time of it, being subjected to abuse and robbery by roving parties from either army."[29] Peck continued, "All horses, mules or other property captured from the rebels or taken from the families of rebels, are supposed to be confiscated for the use of the government and the livestock (cattle, sheep, hogs, etc.) is turned into a drove called the 'contraband herd.' The country is full of nice fat cattle and of these the army appropriates what it needs for beef." Peck described vegetable gardens and ducks, geese, turkeys, and chicken, all ripe for the picking by waves of Union and Confederate soldiers passing through.[30]

Emily Murrell and Teamster Peck both documented enslaved people in Indian Territory. During the Civil War, Peck explained that "those whose masters have gone into the rebel army usually help themselves to the best of their owner's horses and mules and ride away to Kansas or to the Union camps to seek freedom and employment. . . . Many of the women and girls eagerly accept service as cooks or to do any kind of work for the teamsters, soldiers or anyone who can afford to feed them, asking no other compensation." The fugitives quickly overcrowded the U.S. Army camps, so the commanding general ordered them "and their plunder" loaded into the empty mule trains for shipment back to Fort Scott, Kansas.[31]

Until the Civil War, enslaved residents on the plantation and Ross-Murrell family members and laborers used the springhouse, a smokehouse hidden from view, and the kitchen ell to process and preserve foodstuffs. George and Amanda Ross Murrell and their family relocated to Louisiana during the Civil War.[32] Farming continued on the property, even though the Murrell family never returned. Photographs by Jennie Ross Cobb, great-granddaughter of Chief John Ross, taken between 1896 and 1906, document outbuildings, livestock, riding horses, and house yards. Now interpretive signs orient Murrell Home visitors to agricultural features that have since disappeared, and Jennifer Frazee, historical interpreter, coordinates living history programming that uses the house yard and outbuildings to discuss agricultural processes.[33]

Men communicated with their wives about agriculture to keep them apprised of critical information such as market prices and feeding rations. On 28 November 1850, John Brown wrote his wife, Mary, about the price of wool, and that he elected to sell "our wool at about 60 cents per lb." He also told Mary that he might have told the boys "to feed out the potatoes too freely," and he urged her to be "very careful to have no hay or straw wasted, but I would have them use enough straw for bedding the cattle to keep them from lying in the mire." Then he shifted to a discussion of the Fugitive Slave Law and the ways it moved abolitionists. Brown concluded the letter with more references to agricultural markets. He "told Mr. Cutting of Westport he might have either of the yearling heifers for thirty dollars. I want Owen to get the largest bull in order, if he can do it by any means." This provides rare evidence of farming at a distance, and indicates the need to keep Mary, his wife, mother of five living children by 1850, and responsible for day-to-day farm management, informed of decisions made that affected her, but over which she had no legal leverage.[34]

Correspondence from different members of the same family includes enlightening comments on farm family routines. John W. Williams, and his wife, Elizabeth Dumville, and their children moved from west-central Illinois to Poweshiek County, Iowa, in 1854. John corresponded regularly with his wife's siblings back in Illinois. During the Civil War, he wrote about crop acreage, stock prices and debt, mixed in with concerns about how he would manage his affairs if he was drafted, and descriptions of the disruptive influence of peace Democrats (also known as Copperheads) in Iowa. One of his children, precocious Margaret Emily Williams, wrote her aunt Eppy on 11 August 1862, about how a move back to Illinois would mean that she could go to school, and her father hinted that he might come to Illinois in the fall and "get a small place that I can make a living." The last surviving letter from Margaret (20 July 1863) indicated that "Paw has got A reeper and he has not got time to rite." He apparently reaped for hire. Margaret reiterated her father's concerns about internal politics: "The Copperheads is Going by to there peas meeting in wagons and buggies and every other way. Tha [They] are gitting very strong and well armed. Tha [They] have shut up the school house against all republican preaching. . . . Maw sais she don't believe it will be long till the Copperheads and republicans has a fuss."[35]

Photographs: Potential for Interpreting Agriculture

Personal papers can document routines of farm life, describe features of farms not otherwise documented, and indicate the politicized contests that played out in farm communities. Cities depended on agriculture, too, and photographs confirm the dependency of urban businesses on farmers and their products. Brewers depended on farmers for three of the four raw ingredients used in beer—grain and hops—and brewers' yeast derived from malted grains. These, when combined with the fourth ingredient, water, matured into beer (Photo 5.2).

Horses and other livestock in the city needed hay and grain for feed. Remember Mrs. O'Leary's cow, blamed for kicking over the lantern that started the fire that burned much of the city of Chicago to the ground; the fire began on the eighth and ended on the tenth of October 1871. The media perpetuated the myth of Mrs. O'Leary's cow by publishing images of the barn interior with the milk cow standing at the hay manger. The jury remains out about the actual cause of the fire. Other cities burned; the tragedies occurred all too frequently given the preponderance of wooden building materials. That said, did agriculture play a role? Hay markets existed in every city (Photo 5.3). Farmers and consolidators hauled hay to city centers and sold it in bundles or by the wagonload. Livestock owners frequented the hay market to purchase hay for their stock. They went to the green grocer to purchase fruits and vegetables for their own consumption. Some speculate that green hay combusted in the O'Leary barn, causing the fire. Others argue no, that could not have happened because of the dry, hot weather. Uncured hay had the potential to combust, regardless of the aridity, as many a farmer who lost a barn could attest.

Photographs can deceive viewers. Inadequate provenance can lead curators astray. The moral of the story: Stick with the facts; do not speculate. The reality will defy imagination. For instance, the International Harvester Company offered garden plots to unemployed or underemployed laborers in company factories between 1932 and 1937. Only employees with a minimum of five years of service qualified for a plot. In Chicago, the McCormick Works "Garden Project" consisted of 440 acres of land near 95th Street and Crawford Avenue, divided into fifty-by-one-hundred-fifty-feet plots. More than

Photo 5.2 Wagon filled with Fauerbach Beer barrels, pulled by a two-horse hitch. The wagon is parked in front of the International Harvester Building on S. Blount Street near Williamson Street, Milwaukee, Wisconsin. The barrels' ends are stamped: *Fauerbach BRG CO, Madison, WIS.* The shield on the end of the driver's seat contains a stylized FBC. A sign hanging from the harness on the horse's loin reads *Fauerbach.* In the background on the left are railroad tracks and a sign that reads: *Look Out for the Cars.* ca. 1876

Source: Wisconsin Historical Society, Image ID: 115584

1,800 employees participated, an indication of the economic distress of the era, and the potential of gardening to relieve family need (Photo 5.4).

Photographs can help us overcome perceptions that secondary sources reinforce. For instance, studies of black farm operators tend to emphasize the powerlessness and poverty of farm laborers, particularly sharecroppers. A growing body of scholarship documents black landownership and farm owner activism, but only about one-fifth of all black farmers owned their acreage and had the freedom to make their own business decisions during the early twentieth century.[36] A tour for members of the Negro Farmers of America of the crawler tractor (TracTracTor) assembly line at the International Harvester's Tractor Works (2600 West 1st Boulevard, Chicago) indicates the interest of a class of black farmers in new technologies during the early years of the agricultural production revolution that followed World War II (Photo 5.5).

Photo 5.3 Hay Market, Milwaukee, Wisconsin. A building marked Froedtert Bros Grain & Malting Co. is visible in the upper left corner. No date.

Source: Wisconsin Historical Society, Image ID: 56410

Pick-your-own orchards and migrant labor activism might lead us to think that truck farmers and market gardeners never mechanized. That's flawed logic. Many perishable fruits and vegetables require careful picking, one peach or tomato at a time. Sweet corn, however, lends itself to mechanization. Dale Eisenman, a farmer in Jefferson, Oregon, field-tested the Model 24-SC corn picker prior to its production run, on the farm of Douglas Bradley (Photo 5.6).

Research and Public Engagement

Conveying historic evidence in different ways can engage a public that appears to be conflicted about the role of museums in educating them about the past. A cross-section of the non-digital-native public, interviewed during the 1990s, claimed that they trusted museums, "as much as their grandmothers," as a source of information about the past. Roy Rosenzweig and David Thelen based this conclusion on interviews conducted with 1,453 people about their perception of the trustworthiness of sources. Options included, in addition to grandparents and relatives (which public opinion ranked highest), movies and television, nonfiction books, high school history teachers, college history professors,

Photo 5.4 African American woman tending her plot in the McCormick Works Garden Project, 1932–1937.

Source: Wisconsin Historical Society, Image ID: 11633

and people who lived through events. The public differentiated between situations in which they constructed their own history and situations in which they consumed "histories constructed by others."[37] The findings that the public trusts family members and museums more than history purveyors does not mean that the general public dismisses the work of historians. Nor should we assume that digital natives, and non-digital-natives who tap in to the rich resources of digital databases, continue to vest the highest trust in relatives or museums. Does the distinction between personal memory and historical practice that David Lowenthal made in *The Past Is a Foreign Country* still apply to the digital age? He explained that reinforcing personal memories and opinions about the past is an individual undertaking. In contrast, historical practice involves communal processes of identifying, analyzing, and interpreting historic sources. The rapid growth of access to digitized primary sources has increased opportunities for communal reinforcement of personal memory as well as facilitating historical research, rather than diminishing it.[38] The question that remains is, how can public engagement in historical practice inform individuals about the past, and can it motivate them to personally invest in it?

Ongoing studies of the popular uses of history in American life vary in their conclusions. Sobering findings from a study in the United Kingdom indicated that the public

Photo 5.5 African American Farmers Touring Tractor Works, International Harvester Company, Chicago. 29 November 1948.

Source: Wisconsin Historical Society, Image ID: 7232

did not want the museum to mediate by interpreting the evidence. They did not want museums to take a stand in exhibitions, or attempt to persuade visitors of the rightness of an interpretation. In other words, the public opinion seems to reinforce the role of museums as repositories of information and not active analysts or interpreters of evidence that generates new understanding. These findings imply that the public wants access to evidence, but not the interpretation of it.[39]

Studies of the museum perspective indicate that credibility depends on research and interpretation. John Krugler, professor emeritus as Marquette University, argued that the need for accuracy in museums of early national history warranted the research effort: "Villages and towns, estates and plantations, historic houses and other sites—all rebuilt or restored according to the best available historical, archaeological, and architectural data—are the chief way many Americans learn their history and chiefly what they envision when they think of history."[40] More recent research by Alison Landsberg documents the numerous ways that mass culture affects historical knowledge. Her research incorporates mass culture engagement with technology not even envisioned when Rozensweig and

Photo 5.6 Dale Eisenman, a farmer in Jefferson, Oregon, field tests the Experimental 24-SC Corn Picker, a product manufactured by International Harvester, hitched to another IH product, a Farmall H tractor. 1949. The company distinguished the sweet corn picker from its field corn counterpoint with these details: "This Model 24-SC (sweet corn) picker is approximately the same as the regular No. 24 field corn picker with the husking rolls removed and stripper plates added alongside the snapping rolls. A newly designed star-type snapping roll and high-speed gear case are also utilized."

Source: Wisconsin Historical Society, Image ID: 22856

Thelen conducted their research. Electronic access to primary source material and crowd sourcing interaction have transformed the public's engagement with historic sources.[41] Commercial products such as Ancestry.com have revolutionized genealogical research, allowing individuals to engage in original research and source analysis, and to form virtual communities to assist them in the effort. The genealogy networks facilitate the objective vetting that Lowenthal described as essential to the analysis process. Finally, public engagement with the past, often aided and abetted by commemorations such as the U.S. Bicentennial of the 1970s or by visits to museums that help visitors suspend their disbelief, facilitate public construction of historical consciousness. This is a vibrant process that can be richer if the community includes the technical experts, that is, agricultural historians, representatives from history museums and historic sites, and others who teach source analysis and research techniques. The research process can be vibrant, indeed, with numerous perspectives engaged in a process that historic sources drive, that social media facilitates, and that museum spaces sustain.[42]

The research process becomes more communal than solitary as a consequence if we share what we find as we find it and release selected information in ways that presage formal exhibitions or new public programs. Early release offers opportunities for guided instruction that asks the public to search for certain things. For instance, an exhibit on Victory Gardens during the Great War will involve research in newspapers, public records, and archival and museum collections. Planned release might involve selecting one find each week, and posting it, with permission of the keeper of the document, in the museum's official public media outlets, with a statement that guides the public in their reading and analysis of the document.[43] This approach does not mean jettisoning the traditional narrative, or the interpretive plan, or exhibit script. Instead, it follows Freeman Tilden's recommendations about engaging the general public in the process of discovery, but starting that engagement during the research process, rather than with the public interpretation.[44]

Museums can issue summaries of secondary research and facsimiles of primary sources in ways that engage the public in interpretation rather than telling the public what they should think. The documents, released on schedule, can include annotations that convey the discovery process to the public and leading questions that walk them through sequential steps of source analysis. The approach could be game-like, with the ability to move on to the next level of analysis based on completion of the first. The public can learn techniques to discern the validity of evidence and identify bias and nuanced meaning in historical sources. They can learn to read between the lines to recognize the privileged and the powerless perspectives conveyed in the sources. They can remain attentive because of the provocative nature of the topics and the delivery that lures them in to learn more. The foreign nature of agriculture requires this intervention. It also provides the opportunities to get people to think about things they might not otherwise think about. Bear in mind that the community of researchers involved in the process includes museum staff (paid and unpaid) and the general public and other experts in agriculture topics invited to participate. The process needs to include opt-in buttons to confirm that the contributor realizes that their information will become part of the public record, not the ephemera of mass culture.

Research provides opportunities to practice what Cori Brewster called for in her critique of the agricultural literacy curriculum. Students should be encouraged to "read and respond critically to agricultural 'words'. . . , directing explicit attention to the powerful roles rhetoric plays in mediating our relationships to one another, farm owners, farm workers, farming communities, and food."[45] Everyone can learn from shared analysis of sources.

Evidence can also become the focus of an immersion experience in the process of research. The Washburn-Norlands Living History Center incorporated two research-focused programs into an intense four-day live-in experience, launched during the 1970s. Participants role-played characters assigned to them, based on family members who lived on neighboring farms. They found their graves in a nearby cemetery (or did not), and researched their character using primary sources and published county histories and family memoirs compiled by volunteers. This program allowed visitors to realize the thrill of the hunt as they conducted research. The program design inverts the normal course of interpretation, with visitors generating understanding rather than receiving information. The participants become the interpreters. An exercise in interpreting agricultural evidence can draw in more perspectives on the process and can yield new insights into the data. Guided instruction provided by museum and site staff can add to the educational value of the program, while the institution should realize benefits from the perspective of fresh eyes analyzing the data.

To review, thinking about interpretative potential should start with audience research. The research process can focus on topics identified through audience research, but increased depth of understanding about a time when people had more regular and personal relationships with domesticated animals, plants, and the natural environment will help you see additional connections. Pay attention to the narrative tracks—whether the authors focus on the society, culture, technology, economics, or politics of agriculture. Take note of the arguments that the authors make, that is, whether or not farmers succeeded because they mechanized or failed because they mechanized. Look for evidence of mutual dependency as well as conflict and discord in the past. Identify different agendas that farm families in your area pursued in the past. Draft a narrative that summarizes your findings. Look for your relationship to the agricultural past, not by emphasizing your proximity to it, but by identifying your distance from it, and your need to learn more about it. Then you can begin your own fact-finding mission by identifying primary sources, created by people directly involved in the history you want to document. Your research findings can inform many decisions, from helping you say "yes" to selected artifacts as well as "no" to donors offering something not directly related to your local story. The research process will help you develop intellectual control over collections. It should follow a plan that has a procedure systematic enough so paid and unpaid staff and members of the general public can participate in the process. The primary sources (two-dimensional and three-dimensional) become the basis for developing traditional exhibits and public programs, but can support more free-form platforms that can link public interest to the evidence that you hold in the public trust.

Notes

1. See Appendix, Part III: Selected Readings in Agricultural History, and Part IV: Timeline: National Policy and Agrarian Legislation, available at ALHFAM.org. These can help you position your institution's history in relation to major trends and national policy that affected farmers, processors, and consumers alike.

2. For complete citations, see Appendix, Part III: Selected Readings in Agricultural History, online at ALHFAM.org.

3. WorldCat is the catalog of libraries from around the world. You can find books and archival collections. The general public can search it, available at: http://www.worldcat.org/ (accessed 1 June 2016).

4. Sara E. Morris, "Sources for the Researcher," *The Routledge History of Rural America*, Pamela Riney-Kehrberg, ed. (New York: 2016), 349–64.

5. Walter Goffart, *Historical Atlases: The First Three Hundred Years, 1570–1870* (Chicago: University of Chicago Press, 2003). For an analysis of illustrations in U.S. publications, see Cheryl Lyon-Jenness, "Picturing Progress: Assessing the Nineteenth-Century Atlas-Map Bonanza," *The Michigan Historical Review*, 30, no. 2 (August 2004): 167–204. See also Michael P. Conzen, "Landownership Maps and County Atlases," *Agricultural History*, 58, no. 4 (Spring, 1984), 118–122; "North American County Maps and Atlases," in *From Sea Charts to Satellite Images: Interpreting North American History through Maps*, David Buisseret, ed. (Chicago: University of Chicago Press, 1990), 186–211; "The All-American County Atlas: Styles of Commercial Landownership Mapping and American Culture," in *Images of the World: The Atlas Through History*, John A. Wolter and Ronald E. Grim, eds. (Washington, D.C.: Library of Congress, 1997), 331–65.

6. Dennis S. Nordin and Roy V. Scott, *From Prairie Farmer to Entrepreneur: The Transformation of Midwestern Agriculture* (Bloomington: Indiana University Press, 2005), for the scope of the study, see 2–3; for the conclusion, see 205. Jane Adams, *The Transformation of Rural Life: Southern Illinois, 1890–1990* (Chapel Hill: University of North Carolina Press, 1994), 251. Carrie A. Meyer, *Days on the Family Farm: From the Golden Age through the Great Depression* (Minneapolis: University of Minnesota Press, 2007), 215. For alternative interpretations of agricultural "progress," see Gigi M. Berardi and Charles C. Geisler, eds., *Social Consequences and Challenges of New Agricultural Technology* (Boulder, CO: Westview Press, 1984).

7. Peter H. Cousins, "Defining the Typical: Documenting Tool and Implement Programs," *Proceedings of the 1974 ALHFAM Conference*, vol. 1 (Washington, D.C.: The Association for Living Historical Farms and Agricultural Museums, 1975), 15–20, quote 15.

8. Carrie A. Meyer, "The Farm Debut of the Gasoline Engine," *Agricultural History*, 87, no. 3 (Summer 2013): 287–313. Company archives provide invaluable evidence of manufacturer intentions. Few businesses, however, open their archives to the general public. A notable exception exists in the McCormick-International Harvester Collection at the Wisconsin Historical Society. The Society provides access to photographic and archival collections, including paint specifications and other primary sources to serve the needs of collectors. See Debra A. Reid, "McCormick-IHC Collection, Wisconsin Historical Society, Madison, Wisconsin," *The Public Historian*, 33, no. 4 (November 2011): 106–16.

9. For an overview of tractor, farm truck, and thresher adoption to 1930, see W. M. Hurst and L. M. Church, *Power and Machinery in Agriculture*, Misc. Pub. 157 (Washington, D.C.: U.S. Department of Agriculture, 1933). Hurst and Church include maps that show geographic distribution of gas tractors, stationary engines, farm trucks, electric plants, and threshers across the United States. Robert C. Williams, *Fordson, Farmall, and Poppin' Johnny: A History of the Farm Tractor and Its Impact on America* (Urbana, IL: University of Illinois Press, 1987). Robert E. Ankli, "Horses vs. Tractors on the Corn Belt," *Agricultural History*, 54 (1980): 134–48. Alan L. Olmstead and Paul W. Rhode, "Reshaping the Landscape: The Impact and Diffusion of the Tractor in American Agriculture, 1910–1960," *Journal of Economic History*, 61, no. 3 (September 2001): 663–98, for man-hour reduction based on tractor adoption, see 666; for combined savings based on adoption of tractors, automobiles, and trucks, see 667, n. 5.

10. John A. Secor, "Kerosene as a Tractor Fuel," *The Society of Automotive Engineers Technical Paper* (1920), 666–700, available at http://papers.sae.org/200078/ (accessed 30 June 2016). Nebraska Tractor Test Laboratory operates as the national testing center, one of twenty-five in the world. Since 1920 it has tested 2,035 tractors. The headquarters building, constructed in 1919, houses the Larson Tractor Test and Power Museum. For more information, see http://tractortestlab.unl.edu/ (accessed 30 June 2016). This structure is a designated American Society of

Mechanical Engineers (ASME) landmark. The ASME recognizes "Historic Mechanical Engineering Landmarks" through its History and Heritage Landmarks Program, with more than 250 designations since the program began in 1971. See https://www.asme.org/about-asme/engineering-history/landmarks (accessed 20 February 2016). The American Society of Agricultural and Biological Engineers (ASABE) has commemorated historic landmarks since 1926. See http://www.asabe.org/awards-landmarks/asabe-historic-landmarks.aspx (accessed 20 February 2016). For a timeline, see Carl W. Hall, "Timelines in the Development of Agricultural and Biological Engineering," ASABE (2011), available at http://www.asabe.org/about-us/history/timelines.aspx (accessed 20 February 2016).

11. Eric W. Mogren, *Native Soil: A History of the DeKalb County Farm Bureau* (DeKalb: Northern Illinois University Press, 2005).

12. Nancy K. Berlage, *Farmers Helping Farmers: The Rise of the Farm and Home Bureaus, 1914–1935* (Baton Rouge: Louisiana State University Press, 2016).

13. Berlage, *Farmers Helping Farmers*, 224.

14. Gabriel N. Rosenberg, *The 4-H Harvest: Sexuality and the State in Rural America* (Philadelphia: University of Pennsylvania Press, 2016), quote 3–4.

15. Agricultural historians might ally with you. For example, Carrie A. Meyer wrote an overview of agriculture in Northern Illinois for Midway Village and Museum Center: *Founding Farmers: Roots of agriculture and industry in Northern Illinois* (Rockford, IL: Midway Village and Museum Center, 2005). Other researchers have served as humanists on grant applications, on exhibit and interpretive plan development teams, and on collections committees and as coordinators of speaker series. If you respect the work of a researcher, ask them to partner with you on a specific task.

16. J. L. Anderson, *Pigs in America: A Narrative History* (DeKalb: Northern Illinois University Press, under contract).

17. Allan G. Bogue, *From Prairie to Corn Belt: Framing on the Illinois and Iowa Prairies in the Nineteenth Century* (Chicago: Quadrangle Books, 1963), 103. Bogue explains that "Frink's half-wild, ill-tempered, and nimble-footed hogs [resembled] Illinois swine of the time. Few of them ventured to attack people, but the behavior of many of them suggested that they would enjoy doing so" (103).

18. The *New York Times* published S.B. Ruggles's speeches or quoted his comments on topics as wide-ranging as the merits of the flax plant, relations of the church and state, and the value of metropolitan fairs. Bogue cited Ruggles as quoted in Howard C. Hill, "The Development of Chicago as a Center of the Meat Packing Industry," *Mississippi Valley Historical Review*, 10 (December 1923): 259–60. The original quote appeared in "Chicago," *Atlantic Monthly*, 19, no. 113 (March 1867): 331.

19. "Chicago," 332.

20. The Burlend family arrived in Pike County, Illinois, in 1831. The book appeared in print in London in 1848, anonymously. The 1936 publication was the first that attributed the book to Rebecca Burlend: *A True Picture of Emigration, or Fourteen Years in the Interior of North America*, Milo Milton Quaife, ed. (Chicago: Lakeside Classics, 1936), available at https://ia801408.us.archive.org/24/items/truepictureofemi00burle/truepictureofemi00burle_bw.pdf (accessed 1 January 2016), quote 59; in the quote about cattle foraging Burlend does not clarify the crop in the field, 63; 109; for the three little pigs, 110–11. Sam Bowers Hilliard, *Hog Meat and Hoe Cakes: Food Supply in the Old South, 1840–1860* (Carbondale: Southern Illinois University Press, 1972; reissued Athens: University of Georgia Press, 2014).

21. Burlend, quote 121; 150–52, quote 151. Burlend used the British measure of weight, the "stone," which equaled fourteen pounds avoirdupois. Laws regulated weights and measures, and local elected officials policed them. Steven Hahn, *The Roots of Southern Populism: Yeoman Farmers*

and the Transformation of the Georgia Upcountry, 1850–1890 (New York: Oxford University Press, 1983), addressed the importance of open-range hog raising in the South.

22. Manuscript agricultural census returns for 1870 and 1880 have become more easily available via Ancestry.com. Published compendia are digitized and available at the U.S. Department of Agriculture's census of agriculture website: https://www.agcensus.usda.gov/ (accessed 30 June 2016).

23. R. Douglas Hurt, *American Farms: Exploring their History* (Malabar, FL: Krieger Publishing Co., 1996). See also Tom Isern, "How to Read a Farm: Stories from the Material Culture of Bowman County, North Dakota," *Heritage of the Great Plains*, 38 (Fall–Winter 2005): 22–39.

24. John S. Wilson, "We've Got Thousands of These!: What Makes an Historic Farmstead Significant?" *Historical Archaeology*, 24, no. 2 (1990): 23–33; part of an issue dedicated to methodological assessment of the archaeological significance of historic sites.

25. Adams National Historical Park, NPS, Quincy, Massachusetts, https://www.nps.gov/adam/index.htm (accessed 2 January 2016).

26. Amanda Pritchett, *A Short History of the George M. Murrell Home Historic Site* (Tahlequah, OK: Friends of the Murrell Home, 2016).

27. Conversation between Fowler and Reid, 16 June 2016.

28. A facsimile of Emily L. Murrell's seventeen-page diary (1 April through 10 July 1850) is in special collections at Rutgers University. Emily married Milton Preston Jarnagin of Athens, Tennessee, on 3 December 1852. The finding aid indicates that Emily, not a Cherokee, made the ten-day journey from her Mississippi home to the Cherokee nation to visit relatives and friends, including the farm operated by her uncle, Major George Michael Murrell, and his wife, Minerva Ross (a Cherokee). Diary entries indicate that she may have traveled with a slave, and she visited with slave owners. The description is available at http://www.libraries.rutgers.edu/rul/libs/scua/womens_fa/wfa_h_k.shtml (accessed 17 June 2016). For a conjectural map of George's farm, "Hunters Home," see Amanda Burnett, comp., *Teacher's Curriculum and Activity Guide: George M. Murrell Home Historic Sites* (Pawnee, OK: Oklahoma Historical Society's Sites Service Center, 2007), 13, available at http://www.okhistory.org/sites/forms/mhguide.pdf (accessed 17 June 2016).

29. Thanks to David Fowler for recommending Peck's dispatches. For an overview of Peck, his service, and his writings, see Arnold W. Schofield, "Battlefield Dispatches 244: 'Wagon Boss and Mule Mechanic No. 1'," *Fort Scott Tribune* (Friday, 17 December 2010), including excerpts from Peck's dispatch, "Wagon-Boss and Mule-Mechanic: Incidents of My Experiences and Observations in the Late Civil War," *National Tribune* (21 July 1904). This was the first of Schofield's series that reprinted excerpts from Robert Morris Peck's Civil War experiences as published in the *National Tribune* (Washington, D.C.). For a list of all Schofield columns excerpting Peck's dispatches, see http://www.fstribune.com/columns/schofield (accessed 17 June 2016). Readers can access the *National Tribune*, page by page, through Chronicling America, a service of the Library of Congress [loc.gov]. See Peck, *National Tribune* (28 July 1904), quote 2, col. 2.

30. For all quotes, see Peck, *National Tribune* (28 July 1904), 2, col. 2.

31. For quote, see Peck, *National Tribune* (28 July 1904), 2, col. 2.

32. By 1857, George M. Murrell owned one-half of the Tally-Ho Sugar Plantation that his unmarried brother, John William Murrell, had owned. William D. Reeves, *From Tally-Ho to Forest Home: The History of Two Louisiana Plantations* (Bayou Galou, LA: D. Denis Murrell and David R. Denis, 2005), 88.

33. For information about the potential that backyards hold for interpreting the lives of the enslaved, and agricultural subjects, see John Michael Vlach, *Back of the Big House: The Architecture of Plantation Slavery* (Chapel Hill: University of North Carolina Press, 1993). For relevant historic photographs, see OHS, Image 20661, 10: George M. Murrell House—Pigs and cattle feeding

next to barn—Photo by Jennie Ross Cobb, c. 1896–1906; in the Jennie Ross Cobb Collection, Historical Societies—OHS—Sites—George M. Murrell House; and OHS Image 20661.5: George M. Murrell House—Robert Bruce Ross and Anne Ross Pilburn at the springhouse and pond—Photo by Jennie Ross Cobb, c. 1900, both in the Jennie Ross Cobb Collection, Oklahoma Historical Society.

34. John Brown to Mary Brown, 28 November 1850, in Franklin Sanborn, ed., *Life and Letters of John Brown* (1885), 106–07. Brown wrote this letter from Springfield, Massachusetts. Mary, the recipient, may have still resided at the Brown farm in North Elba, New York, but she returned to Ohio between 1851 and 1854. Brown had worked with Simon Perkins Jr. in the wool trade, starting in Richfield, Ohio, in 1844, and then in Akron, Ohio, but the business failed, and Brown was fired. Brown recalled "our log-cabin at the cent[er] of Richfield, with a supper of porridge and johnny-cake, as a place of far more interest to me. . . . But 'there's mercy in every place and encouraging thought.'" The John Brown Farm State Historic Site, near Lake Placid, New York, focuses interpretation on the legacy of John Brown more than on the farming that occurred there, or the ways that Mrs. Brown and her numerous children (she had thirteen before John Brown died, but only half lived to adulthood) survived. I thank Bonnie Laughlin-Schultz for sharing this letter with me.

35. Anne M. Heinz and John P. Heinz, eds., *Women, Work, and Worship in Lincoln's Country: The Dumville Family Letters* (Urbana: University of Illinois Press, 2016), moving to Poweshiek County, Iowa, 34; Margaret Emily Williams to Aunt Eppy, 11 August 1862, 151; Margaret, 20 July 1863, 157; and about her father's political concerns, 158.

36. See Debra A. Reid and Evan P. Bennett, eds. *Beyond Forty Acres and a Mule: African American Landowning Families since Reconstruction* (Tallahassee: University of Florida Press, 2012).

37. Roy Rosenzweig and David Thelen, *The Presence of the Past: Popular Uses of History in American Life* (New York: Columbia University Press, 1998), quote 195; Table 2, 23. For the questions used in the survey, see http://chnm.gmu.edu/survey/ (accessed 30 March 2016).

38. Amy M. Smith, *Tracing Family Lines: The Impact of Genealogy Research on Family Communication* (Lanham, MD: Lexington Books, 2012).

39. "Trust Me, I'm a Museum," Center for the Future of Museums Blog (Tuesday, 3 February 2015), available at http://futureofmuseums.blogspot.com/2015/02/trust-me-im-museum_3.html (accessed 30 March 2016).

40. John D. Krugler, "Behind the Public Presentations: Research and Scholarship at Living History Museums of Early America," *William and Mary Quarterly*, 48, no. 3 (July 1991): 347–86, quote 347.

41. Alison Landsberg, *Engaging the Past: Mass Culture and the Production of Historical Knowledge* (New York: Columbia University Press, 2015).

42. Malgorzata Rymsza-Pawlowska, *History Comes Alive: The Making of Postwar Historical Consciousness* (Chapel Hill: University of North Carolina, 2017). Alison Landsberg, *Prosthetic Memory: The Transformation of American Remembrance in the Age of Mass Culture* (New York: Columbia University Press, 2004).

43. Amy Bentley, *Eating for Victory: Food Rationing and the Politics of Domesticity* (Urbana: University of Illinois Press, 1998); Cecilia Gowdy-Wygant, *Cultivating Victory: The Women's Land Army and the Victory Garden Movement* (Pittsburgh: University of Pittsburgh Press, 2013).

44. Freeman Tilden, *Interpreting Our Heritage* (Chapel Hill: University of North Carolina Press: 2008).

45. Brewster, "Toward a Critical Agricultural Literacy," quote 48.

CHAPTER 6

DOCUMENTING AGRICULTURE IN THREE DIMENSIONS

Artifacts

Debra A. Reid and Cameron L. Saffell

NOTE: This chapter evolved from two articles published by the authors in the journal, *Agricultural History*, and at a panel session that each participated in during the 2015 Agricultural History Society conference. For the complete articles, see Debra A. Reid, "Tangible Agricultural History: An Artifact's-Eye View of the Field," *Agricultural History*, 86, no. 3 (Summer 2012): 57–76; and Cameron L. Saffell, "An Alternative Means of Field Research: Extending Material Culture Analysis to Farm Implements," *Agricultural History*, 88, no. 4 (Fall 2014): 517–37. Reid provides an overview of numerous approaches to reading material evidence, and walks readers through a multistep approach to analyzing three objects (a pitcher, a sorghum can, and a milk can). Saffell applies E. McClung Fleming's model for material cultural analysis to Deere and Company's No. 999 Two-Row Planter. The research creates a more complete understanding of cultural practices on farms in the West, drawing on collections from several museums in Texas and New Mexico.

WHAT IS AN *agricultural artifact*? For the purposes of this paper we'll use a sweeping definition: animal, vegetable, mineral . . . (and I don't mean the start of Twenty Questions or the second line of the lyrics from the 1879 Gilbert and Sullivan song: "I Am the Very Model of a Modern Major-General" [*Pirates of Penzance*].)

- Animal (paintings of animals, but also living heritage breeds, and DNA)
- Vegetable (horticultural catalogs depicting them, but also seed samples, pollen samples, heritage seeds, and living plants)
- Mineral (inert, but from the ground: marl; soil samples and cores; stone transformed by humans into fence posts)
- Archival (diaries, letters, catalogs, prints and photographs, maps, especially when the thing itself warrants analysis; the thing takes on a stature equal to that of the information that words or images may reveal)
- Structures/buildings (barns, farmhouses, sheds)
- Landscapes (fields, fences, hedgerows, plow marks, stock tanks, water troughs)
- Tools (manure forks, potato diggers) and equipment (plows, cultivators, reapers, hoes, and ox yokes)
- Transportation artifacts (wagons, buggies, surreys, ox carts); personal artifacts (clothing); furnishings (household accessories)
- Communication artifacts (advertising media; i.e., campaign buttons) and even recreational artifacts used on farms (bats, baseballs, frog gigs).

And this list barely touches the surface. Many things on this list can become the catalyst for engaging the public in provocative interpretation of agricultural topics.

Historian Marc Bloch, cofounder of the journal *Annales d'Histoire Economique et Sociale,* with Lucien Febvre, explained his philosophy simply: "The variety of historical evidence is nearly infinite. Everything that man says or writes, everything that he makes, everything he touches can and ought to teach us about him." Bloch believed that the best research drew on diverse sources, including paintings and sculpture, place names, maps, building ruins, and plant life in pasture and field, because "without all these . . . how could one pretend to describe the history of land use?" Christopher Witmore, an archaeologist of classical landscapes, more recently expressed similar advocacy for diversity of evidence. He explained the importance of documenting the "multiple lives" of objects, describing a terrace as "a collector of soil, a property boundary, a 2,000-year-old enclosure wall, or a useless pile of stones," depending on its circumstance at any given time. Yet, while some seek objects that make their rural and agricultural histories more detailed and complex, others adhere to texts and a disciplinary purity that seems strangely out of touch with the subject matter.[1]

This chapter tries to get us all to think outside the box—anyone studying agriculture can learn more by studying the artifacts that people used, and anyone trying to interpret agriculture in museums and historic sites can benefit from thinking about things in their collection in new ways. Several have explained what agricultural artifacts can help us know. John T. Schlebecker, curator of agriculture at the Smithsonian Institution (1965–1984) and president of the Agricultural History Society (1976–1977), opined that "objects are, of course, part of the historical record."[2] He chastised his peers for failing to recognize objects when they saw them. "One prominent agricultural historian" refused to acknowledge that ancient Romans used scythes even "while holding an authenticated Roman scythe . . . [because] a thing could not exist unless it had been written about."[3]

Objects, in combination with social and cultural history, can provide a more complete view of the past. Darwin Kelsey, the director of historical agriculture at Old Sturbridge Village, articulated in 1970 the potential for object-based history, not just the lowbrow agriculture, but the highbrow art history, as well. "The word 'museum' almost invariably brings to mind a collection or repository of physical things. If research is at all a part of that mental image, it is probably thought to be 'on' or to involve the study 'of' those objects. . . . [Yet] a historian [or living history farmer] interested in the size, color, and conformation of early nineteenth-century livestock may study the impact of romanticism on American art. Such studies, though not wholly related to items in the museum's collections, clearly can contribute to a fuller understanding of those objects."[4]

Schlebecker believed that "historians should be able to use artifacts and objects while employing only those skills which ordinary people have." He described a process that began with correct identification of the object then moved to physically examining and using the object, documenting its provenance, and critically analyzing it within its cohort and within its context.[5] That approach might have worked fine in 1977, when the majority of older Americans still could recall their experiences of life on the farm, but the approach does not work so well in the twenty-first century. Few people today comprehend the function of agricultural tools and equipment. This makes it difficult to identify objects, and identification is the basis of retrieval. Thus, identification holds the key to using objects in the process of building interpretation based on agriculture.

Nomenclature imposes standard names on things that perform the same function (because calling a manure fork a manure fork separates it from other things that might look similar to the uneducated, but that performed very different chores: a pitchfork, a frog gig, or a potato digger for instance). Robert G. Chenhall's system of nomenclature, originally published in 1978, is in its fourth edition and used at most history museums in North America (*Nomenclature 4.0*). Nomenclature incorporates agricultural artifacts in several categories, and agricultural artifacts can appear in other categories (i.e., Category 8: Communication Artifacts; Category 9: Recreational Artifacts).

- Agricultural Structures in Category 1: Built Environment
- Agricultural Tools & Equipment in Category 4: Tools & Equipment for Materials (and numerous other classifications in Category 4 apply, as well: Cultivation Equipment; Feed Processing Equipment; Harvesting Equipment; Planting Equipment; Animal Husbandry T & E; Animal Care Equipment; Breeding Equipment; Farrier Equipment; Veterinary Equipment; Fishing & Trapping; Food Processing & Preparation T & E).
- Animal-Powered Vehicles in Category 7: Distribution & Transportation Artifacts

Identifying the agricultural artifact by object name may prove challenging when you have no idea how people used the tool or equipment. *Interpreting Agriculture* is not designed to tell you how to identify objects. Instead, learn by doing. Acquire one of the numerous identification guides designed to help you identify objects. These include visual dictionaries with detailed drawings and numerous parts labeled with accurate terminology. Anyone curating agricultural tools and machinery should also consult identification guides, such as the encyclopedias on antique tools and machinery or farm implements compiled by C.H. [Charles] Wendel.[6] One of these identification books, *Identifying Horse-Drawn Farm Implements* by R.W. Runyan, had added value, as Cameron L. Saffell explains: "Runyan worked from the premise that his reader will not be able to tell a cultivator from a planter or a plow, so he laid out an identification system based on parts—runners, moldboards, shovels, handles, discs, wheels, and so forth."[7] Barbara Corson takes this approach, categorizing harness types and parts, and carriage types and parts, in her essay in *Interpreting Agriculture*. Other identification and how-to publications featuring agricultural equipment link the tool to the draft power of choice, as Lynn R. Miller does in *Work Horse Handbook* and in *Horsedrawn Plows and Plowing*.[8] The real work of accurate cataloging rests with the cataloger. As Saffell opined, "the biggest obstacle is the individual reluctance to 'learn the language' and to take advantage of the resources available."[9] What's at stake? Inaccurate identification that can undermine the usefulness of the agricultural artifacts to tell the stories we want to tell.

Bottom line: Access to agricultural artifacts depends on precision in the cataloging process. Accurate identification by object name, category, and classification based on function creates a rich collection database that can help researchers and museum curators find the proverbial needle in the haystack.

Visitor interests combined with institutional mission help define the focus and prioritize the research agenda. The tools and equipment can tell stories about relationships between humans and animals and plants in a place at any given time. Historic houses might emphasize domestic processing spaces or consider ways that leather harness under repair in the kitchen could tell stories about farm work spaces. A museum might decide how to make its clothing and decorative arts collections a tool to interpret labor needs on a farm. The interpretation could focus on seasonal rhythms of the product(s) (wool, linen, cotton). It could expand to include labor needed for processing to make the wool, linen, or cotton marketable. Finally, it could address the fact that income from the commodity might become the disposable income used to buy silk dresses. This can help readers wrestle with the reality that world trade in certain agricultural commodities clothed people historically, even as those same people processed their own wool (or cotton) for their socks, etc. So, a cotton frock or a butter paddle or even a cookstove can launch a story, not just about agricultural seasons or social customs of the time, but also about consumerism, international trade, the producer, and the consumer.

Agricultural artifacts have the potential to help us rethink the standard historical narrative. Edward C. Kendall, the Smithsonian Institution's associate curator of agriculture (1952–1965), validated the attribution of the John Deere plow in the Smithsonian collection as an early example, quite plausibly constructed in 1838 as donors claimed. Kendall also affirmed that "the successful prairie plow with a smooth one-piece moldboard and steel share was basically Deere's idea." Yet, Deere made his moldboards of wrought iron, not steel, until 1852. It took a sharp edge and highly polished moldboard to cultivate the sticky prairie soils. Thus, "the importance attached to the steel share led to [Deere's] plows being identified as steel plows" from their earliest permutation, even though Deere apparently did not construct steel share plows until around 1852. This indicates the influence of public opinion on historical understanding of iconic technological innovations. Schlebecker opined that "what is strange about this is that it took historians more than a century to make this fundamental discovery [about John Deere's plow]. Had they examined objects as carefully as they studied documents they would have written more accurate history."[10] Other scholars use numerous artifacts to understand agriculture. For example, Henry Glassie documented thousands of barns and rural houses to devise new understanding of cultural influences on folk structures, and Charles Orser analyzed archaeological assemblages and corroborated the information found with fragmentary textual evidence to interpret tenancy and sharecropping in Georgia.[11]

Agricultural artifacts can help us understand cultural practices and changes in animal conformation. John T. Schlebecker wrote about nineteenth-century yokes not fitting today's American oxen as evidence of differences between American and European farm implements.[12] The conformation of livestock changed over time, too, and historical artifacts can inform us about structural changes in animals, and about cultural differences in the ways that Europeans yoked oxen compared to the ways that Americans yoked oxen.

Given the potential for using agricultural artifacts to rethink historical assumptions and to illustrate historical details, how should museums and historical sites proceed? If we do not have artifacts, we can rely on memory and as much description as provided to get a sense of the artifacts. For example, Emanuel Vocale of Deming, New Mexico, spoke in an oral history of how he had convinced his father to switch from horse-drawn equipment to a tractor. His father was reluctant because he did not think he could afford it. Vocale said they could not afford not to because he was raising crops and caring for several mules, and the family was not getting ahead. He threatened to leave if they did not make the switch. Eventually, his father agreed to pay $1,800 for a new tractor and related equipment—two mules were worth only $500 at the time—but only if he kept two horses and a cultivator, "just in case." The next year he sold those and rented one hundred sixty more acres of land to use with their new equipment. This is a colorful anecdote, but we do not have the tractor, the livestock, or any of the farm implements to examine further. Did the Vocales use the equipment as purchased, or did they make modifications?[13]

More often there is a physical tool or farm implement available to be inspected and analyzed, but there are limits to what information we can learn beyond its physical parts. Sometimes there is information about who owned the piece—either who gave it to a museum or some general understanding of the previous owners of where the implement was found. In some cases in a museum setting there may be other implements from the same donor, but usually not of the same type—perhaps a plow and a planter that accompanied a cultivator. This gives some understanding of the farmer-operator of the implements, but lacking other details about the family or the farm, what historians can glean is more limited. But there is information there that can be used to create better understandings.

The moral of the story: Anyone planning to interpret agriculture should utilize the archive as well as the museum collections. The combination increases understanding about agricultural artifacts, and in turn, about the agricultural history of the people in the place.

The bigger problem in analyzing agricultural artifacts—including farm implements—relates to the level of basic understanding of the objects. Many agricultural historians have considered whether to go look at a reaper or a grain drill but stopped short because they did not know the parlance. An English-language historian has the same issue if s/he considers whether to examine a document written in French or Spanish. As for the language problem, the solution is to do some studying and find some guides. This is part of the reason museum curators exist. Not only do they conduct their own research and cataloging of their objects, they consult with and assist others with their research. If we had problems with something in a manuscript collection, we would likely consult the archivist; the museum curator serves the same function. Thus, the museum curator has a vested interest in learning about agriculture and has a vested interest in increasing the understanding that others have about agriculture.

Identification: Visual Literacy

Increasing understanding of historical artifacts can be accomplished by adopting any one of numerous approaches, or by combining steps in the process and devising your own.[14] Reid proposed a five-step process in "Tangible Agricultural History":

1. Mentally prepare so you can look for something in artifacts that can tell a story about agricultural history. In other words, conceptualize a philosophy that can help you value agricultural artifacts as evidence, but also see evidence of agriculture in non-agricultural objects.
2. Identify relevant artifacts/objects to study.
3. "Read" the objects; that is, study the object in detail. Numerous methods exist to walk you through this process.
4. Put the object into context; apply nomenclature (functional categories), but think about aesthetics, culture, and adaptive reuse. Think about the object in different contexts.
5. Interpret the object with the goal of gaining a new or a more nuanced understanding of the past.[15]

Reading an object, the third phase of object-based research, requires meticulous evaluation of the object's details. Text-centric analysts might look at the words on the objects and stop there. But it is critical to consider the object as a whole (its overall appearance and form) and then move to the details: materials (wood, stone, synthetic), techniques used in construction (forged, welded, hewn, soldered, riveted, stamped, woven), finishing techniques (planed, distressed, carved, plated), and decorative or ornamental features and patina (ornament, color, style). Ultimately, this detail allows the researcher to form an opinion about the condition of the object (its completeness or quality as a whole artifact). These attributes constitute ten of the fourteen "points of connoisseurship" most associated with analysis of high-quality decorative arts. The connoisseurship approach merits consideration by scholars of ordinary, factory-produced material culture, as well, because following the procedure forces novices to think about what they have in front of them.[16]

Ultimately, we have to accept that objects will tell us something we do not already know or will corroborate what other sources have indicated in ways that deepen understanding. Schlebecker may have appealed to historians to consider objects to spare themselves embarrassment, explaining that examining objects "often saves the historian from blunders," but saving face should not be our sole reason for learning about agricultural artifacts.[17]

Documentation: Provenance Required

An ordinary domestic artifact, a sorghum can, seems worthy of more analysis. The can is sheet metal plated with tin, with lapped and rolled seams. The tin plate has corroded and disappeared on the surface, except in the area protected by the label. The can manufacturer is not known, but the can is of standard size and, assuming Melvin Shaw practiced truth in advertising, it held approximately five pounds of sorghum, a syrupy natural sweetener rendered from the juice of the sorghum plant. The lid has a lip that, when pressed into the rim of the can, creates an airtight seal. A paper label identified the can's contents—sorghum—and advertised the business. The label is polychrome, with blue, black, and red lines framing a four-color illustration bracketed by an intricate pattern of red c-scrolls. The image depicts a sorghum field on the right hand, fenced with posts and rails, and a log house with stone chimney on the left hand. A rutted road separates the house from the field. A woman stands on the house porch, two men work in the yard, and a horse-drawn wagon moves out of view past the house and sorghum field. The label includes the footer: R. J. K. Co. 331. Some investigation indicates that the R. J. K. Company apparently operated out of Chicago. I have found no archives with papers documenting the company, but a cursory search using Google resulted in two labels produced by R. J. K. Co., including a label for a can that likely contained yellow string beans dated 1918 by the antique dealer and a label for a "Skysweep Broom," dated 1920s. The label probably dates from the mid-1950s when M. L. Shaw operated a sorghum mill near Steelville, Illinois. The mill went out of business in 1970[18] (Photo 6.1).

Melvin Shaw was the son of Ralph and Mary Welshans Shaw, who married in 1921 and started operating a sorghum mill during the 1930s in Cutler, Illinois. Mary had experience with sorghum production, having grown up in a family of sorghum makers with a pedigree stretching back four generations. Ralph and Mary relocated to Steeleville, Illinois, built a new building at a state highway intersection in 1955, and remained in business through Ralph's death in 1964. Melvin depended on his mother, Mary, to oversee the finishing process until 1970, when the processing equipment was sold.[19]

Context, of course, means more than function. Additional background research allows researchers to position the object relative to other evidence about the thing or the process or activity at a particular time or along a time continuum. A symbiotic relationship existed between the processor and the farm families. When a family near Rockwood stopped producing sorghum, families that grew sorghum cane had to go further afield

to have their cane processed. This involved driving to the mill Shaw operated, about fourteen miles from Rockwood when located in Cutler, and about equal distance but in a different direction when the Shaw family relocated their mill to Steeleville.

The sorghum can label indicates that the Shaw family adopted a different process for finishing their sorghum than that associated with the folk industry. Their "organically grown and made" sorghum fits the context of the organic food movement of the Green Revolution era, but it also continues a tradition among sorghum processors trying to distinguish themselves as exceptional. Textual evidence documents the movement during the late nineteenth century of sorghum growers responding to new technologies. They organized into state-level cane grower associations and held conferences to discuss improved varieties, chemical additives and resistance to them, and new technologies, including steam heat, to refine the sap into sorghum. The organic approach included sorghum grown without synthetic chemical fertilizers or pesticides, as evidence of an effort to retain tradition in opposition to production revolution trends of the 1950s and 1960s (in the case of the Shaw business).[20]

Objects play a critical role in the research required to understand agriculture. The goal should be to understand the objects as thoroughly as possible and, through that understanding, to gain a new perspective about a time period or a rural or farm process. The sorghum can, for example, documents that small-scale, labor-intensive agriculture persisted during the production revolution, as evidenced by the label on a sorghum can marketed by experienced sorghum processors trying to distinguish themselves from production revolution practices. While numerous models for reading material cultures exist, the key is to be as aware as possible of the potential for increasing understanding by incorporating objects as historic evidence.

Field Research: Documenting the Deere Model No. 999 Two-Row Corn Planter

Another case study of objects as evidence focuses on an object used in west Texas and eastern New Mexico during the early twentieth century and the ways that farmers modified the equipment to suit their business plans. The seasonal cycles of the farm year inform the types of artifacts analyzed. The first category, implements used to till or prepare the soil, includes plows, spades, chisels, harrows, and some types of discs. Then farmers used planting implements, regardless of size, from pouches to broadcast seed by hand all the way up to multi-row planters and grain drills. After plants came up, farmers used cultivation tools to kill weeds and keep the soil loose to help facilitate moisture retention and penetration.

Sorting out the tillage equipment from the cultivating equipment can be tricky, as both types will sometimes utilize the same kinds of shovels and discs; we have to look closely to determine the purpose of the attachments. There is a whole category of harvesting equipment used at the end of the growing season, from simple sickles to complex threshing machines and cotton harvesters. Of course, like most attempts to broadly categorize things, some equipment simply does not fall into the above groups—like a handmade broadcast pesticide dispenser to kill insects—so they get lumped into a miscellaneous group. While this can seem dismissive, those "miscellaneous" implements are critical to understanding the special issues or challenges facing a particular farm.[21]

An inventory with these broad classifications is a start to understanding the role of the machinery in a single farm's history or, if done on a wider scale, toward learning more about a region's agricultural practices. We have to study closely the artifacts themselves to learn more. So, how do we analyze physical artifacts? Drawing on material culture methodology, we can construct several suggestions specific to this example of examining farm implements.

While a number of material culture study models have been proposed in the post–World War II era, one of the strongest that has stood well against the test of time was first suggested by E. McClung Fleming in the mid-1970s. Fleming proposed that each object has five basic properties: history, material, construction, design, and function. He then applied a four-step analysis to each of these properties to better understand the object. Later writers have proposed adjustments or alternatives to either the properties or the analytical steps, but overall the model is very durable.[22]

Fleming's model focuses on the analysis of a single object. This is a critical step in utilizing material evidence, but it takes on broader significance when it is applied to many objects, and comparisons and contrasts can begin to be seen. One form of comparative analysis is to contrast what we see on a particular object and compare it to other objects of the same model and/or to the original as sold by the manufacturer. As a case study, let us take a look at several extant versions of the Deere and Company Model No. 999 Planter, one of the company's most popular farm implements produced from 1913 to the 1950s.

The No. 999 was a successor to the popular Deere and Mansur No. 9 Planter first introduced in 1901. The changes in design and model number are largely attributable to the 1911 acquisition of Deere and Mansur as a subsidiary of Deere and Company, a consolidation that gave Deere and Company a full line of farm equipment in almost every area of production for all major crops. We can often identify a No. 999 planter by its key features, even if the paint and decals have all worn away. The planter was a riding implement so the operator could manually raise and lower the machine in the field. It was a two-row implement with large, round seed hoppers or boxes sitting directly above flat blade openers with built-in chutes through which seeds dropped into the opened soil. A double-rim press-row wheel followed directly behind each opener/seed box to promptly press dirt back over the freshly dropped seed. So the farmer could be sure to have even spacing in his rows, most No. 999 planters had an automatic row marker. This is a long bar with a knife or a small disc that lowered on the unplanted side and created a parallel line in the dirt to show where to line up the planter on the next pass across the field. Primarily marketed as a corn planter, the seed box could accommodate several sizes of plates not only for different sizes of corn seed, but also for other types of crops like sorghum, peas, beans, and cotton. Over the years the No. 999 had no major design changes, though several small modifications or attachments became available. The Deere company magazine, the *Furrow*, said in the 1940s that "nearly every major improvement in planters has appeared first on the No. 999," improvements that included natural-drop seed plates, enclosed gears, the safety fertilizer attachment, and a tractor hitch and tractor-operator lever for raising and lowering the implement[23] (Photo 6.2).

A popular attachment for the No. 999 and many multi-row planters was a trip valve tied to a check-row system. The purpose of this was not only to produce perfectly aligned rows as a result of using the row marker device, but also to have the seeds dropped in perfect alignment across all the rows, thus creating a very precise grid of all the plants in the field. At the bottom of the tube or as part of the runner assembly, a check valve would sit closed until "tripped" by a mechanism. The farmer set up a long check wire with little knots across the field. As the planter ran along, a device on the implement ran along the check wire that "tripped" when it hit each knot, thus opening the valve and dropping the seed at a precise point.[24]

Of course, this detailed description could apply to International Harvester's No. 1 Planter, the P&O No. 71 Planter, or several other competing models to Deere's No. 999. A clincher is to closely examine an implement to find evidence of decals, stencils, casting marks, or faded paint colors. If we find several stamps of an *IH* inside a large *C* or a red color, it will not be a Deere implement, which probably has a *JD* logo stamp or a stencil of one of the company's "flying deer" logos. Finding only one of these markings may not mean anything—if it is the lid on the seed box, for example. The farmer may have lost the original and recycled a part from another machine. Instead we hope to find that faded Deere green color or the *JD* stamp on some of the individual parts.

Better yet, we can identify part numbers from each casting and match them up to a parts catalog or repair list to confirm the model designation. Today some of those catalogs are easier to find, compiled on CDs available on the Internet or at auction websites. Until

Photo 6.2 A Jasper County, Iowa, farmer checking a mechanism on his horse-drawn, two-row corn planter. John Vachon, photographer. May 1940. Image no. LC-USF33-001837-M5 [P&P] LOT 1181.

Source: Retrieved from the Library of Congress, https://www.loc.gov/item/fsa1997006101/PP (accessed 8 June 2016)

recently, those catalogs were harder to come by, so most investigators had to rely on more circumstantial evidence. Even then, we might only be able to identify it as a Deere two-row planter but not be sure if it is the No. 999; its sibling, the No. 335; or something else, like one of its successors, the integral Model 246. Like with documents, the best evidence available may have to serve in lieu of absolutely positive identification.[25]

While identifications are helpful, they are only the first part of understanding. The next piece to examine is provenance—the known history of the artifact. With something like Colt revolvers or even tractors, a researcher could contact a corporate archive or consult some books to check a serial number and learn when the item was produced and maybe where it was sold. Since farm implements typically were not produced with serial numbers, we will have little luck with that unless we can tie it to a particular production period using part numbers. Instead, we need to know something about the donor or the owner.

If pieces identified lack strong provenance, that does not mean they are silent in what they can tell a researcher. Particularly in the analysis of farm equipment, we have to examine an implement in great detail to see what information it possesses. That examination usually yields several points but no understanding unless some comparative work is done. Schlebecker pointed out that field modifications are an important piece of understanding how a particular user added to his or her machine so it would accomplish particular functions. To know those modifications, however, we have to compare to other implements—ones of similar type, ones of identical model, or ones in the same area or region. The building of these comparative analyses will eventually yield understandings of both the overall and the specific.[26]

Modifications are the key things to look for on a farm implement. A horse-drawn modified hitch is not unusual—many farmers did not want to buy new equipment when they purchased a tractor; they just modified their old implements. The significance of a tractor-drawn modification is that the piece did make the transition from horses to tractors. If we know from a farm's history, or from other pieces in a farm's implement collection, that there are separate horse-drawn and tractor-drawn implements, this indicates that the farmer did buy new equipment for his tractor. This might suggest a good crop year with abundant funds, or perhaps a "wealthier" farmer—not someone who was rich, per se, but someone who was willing to invest the money for equipment designed especially to work with a tractor, rather than trying to jury-rig a modification. One thing to look for with this kind of modification is whether any of the operating handles for the implement have been modified so the tractor driver could reach back and still manipulate the implement. A No. 999 planter at the Bayer Museum of Agriculture (Lubbock, Texas) does not show any evidence of this, which would suggest this operator either had to stop periodically to adjust things, or s/he had an assistant who could either drive the tractor or ride on the planter while the farmer handled the other task.

When combined with closer study of the properties suggested by Fleming on a wider scale, we can begin to construct a wider knowledge of the role these implements played in the farming culture. This is the third operation of Fleming's four-step analytical process—assessing and placing the object in its original cultural context.[27]

A complete analysis would take dozens of implements and more resources than can be recounted in this short article. Fleming's final analytical process is interpretation. For our purposes, this equates to understanding. Each artifact contributes to a better understanding of original culture, which we can then assess or compare to our current culture. Today's farmers find something like the Deere No. 999 Two-Row Planter a very interesting, but somewhat amusing, piece of equipment. They relate to how it works—today's planters still have some kind of plow or runner to open the soil and large seed boxes with plates in the bottom to regulate the dispensing of seed. In their farms of thousands of acres, though, they cannot imagine how they would replace their eight-row (or more) equipment with a little two-row planter like this, much less how they would deal with all the headaches and hassles of horses, mules, or oxen to draw the equipment.

With the exception of the weather, most of the challenges of farming "back then" are very different from today. Museums and historical societies have the opportunity to educate modern audiences about these changes. The objects in their collections and in other collections in their region hold clues about farmer consumption patterns, about the techniques they used to repair equipment, and about the ways they modified equipment to keep it in the field. Fleming's model, or any one of several other models, can help staff develop a framework to use to discern patterns in the artifact assemblage that they and their peers curate. If they have a better understanding of the objects involved—planters, in this example—then they will be better positioned to explain and interpret the stories that their collections hold.[28]

Collections Care and Management

Most museums and historic sites have farm tools and agricultural machinery in their collections. Museums accepted them from sentimental owners and accessioned them for posterity's sake. The poor condition and slim provenance associated with many of these objects makes them prime targets for deaccessioning. Jettisoning these collections may free up storage space, but removing the tangible evidence of the rural and agricultural past will not solve any other problem. In fact, as the piles of agricultural artifacts shrink, so might the potential to reach visitors. Museums must balance the need to manage limited storage space but still collect and preserve the material evidence needed to interpret a foreign time that is really not so long ago or far away, and that still remains relevant.

The once-common utilitarian objects became problematic artifacts through no fault of their own in a process repeated over and over across the country: The donors wanted to respect their ancestors but did not want to care for the non-glamorous material evidence associated with the physically taxing and monotonous nature of their elders' lives. So the story goes, great-grandpa operated the walking plow while great-grandma processed much of the farm's production. Grandma, in turn, kept all the tools on the farm that she inherited. But grandma's failing health required disposition of the farm and the equipment, old and new alike. As developers purchased the land, and auctioneers hawked the objects that had monetary value, grandchildren gave the local museum what they couldn't bear to throw away. The names of owners may have accompanied the gift, but more often than not, the history of the farm family did not get transferred with the objects. Such reactive collecting resulted in underdocumented collections, liabilities on the bottom line of any museum's spreadsheet.

What should museums and historic sites do? Should staff deaccession the agricultural artifacts in their collections that they deem undocumented, in ill repair, or irrelevant to their museum's mission? Or should they make a renewed effort to think about the history that they tell in ways that can incorporate the agricultural (and the rural) into their story? Deaccessioning will remove redundant and dilapidated items from the collection, but it will not absolve a museum of addressing the topic of agriculture, which relates to just about every history everywhere.

Those with questions about how to manage these objects, from the smallest file to the corn planters and cotton pickers, can turn to their peers for help. A curator should not launch a deaccessioning program targeting all agricultural equipment in disrepair because of limited storage space. Such a broad sweep might eliminate a planter that documents a farmer's modification of the horse-drawn implement for use with a tractor. Identification guides can help you decide what you have, but you might not have time to dedicate to that. Reach out to volunteers who might know, and collectors and agricultural curators and living history farmers who have the knowledge of the equipment to do a quick assessment of relevant objects. If you have an artifact that has no provenance, that is one of many that other museums have in their collections, and that is in poor condition, deaccession it. Follow the protocols advised in *Museum Registration Methods*, 5th Edition.[29]

Ensuring proper care for these objects can overwhelm staff and resources. The size, mechanical complexity, inherent instability, and lack of familiarity with agricultural tools and equipment can make the objects difficult to curate. Storage is expensive, and putting objects up on blocks and closing doors does not translate into preservation of cultural heritage for the public's edification. Almost any artifact can help interpret agriculture, but that does not mean that museums need to keep all objects. They must determine what they have that can tell the stories that their missions commit them to tell.

Care and management of agricultural artifacts force staff to have a well-rounded sense of basic care standards for all materials from paper to wood, from skin to metal. Staff will find it useful to compile a quick guide to environmental standards, marking guidelines, care and handling procedures, and storage needs for materials, that is, wood and metal that make up the bulk of their collections. This should balance best practices with practical modifications that take into account exhibition spaces and storage situations at your institution. For example, a stable RH (relative humidity = proportion of water vapor that the air can hold at a given temperature) and stable temperature reduces stress to historical artifacts. But the range for RH varies depending on the type of object and the nature of the storage facility. Many objects might have the longest life expectancy in an environment with a constant 50 to 60 percent RH and with fluctuations of no more than +/- 5 percent; and a temperature range of 68° to 72°F +/- 2° to 3°F, in twenty-four hours. Few historic houses or barns (or even spaces designed for storage) can reasonably meet these standards. Maintaining those standards can actually put the historic structures at risk. Museums and historic sites ultimately must reduce the risk that an artifact may face by providing secure, clean, monitored storage with reasonable environmental controls. Equipment in outdoor storage areas or areas with no environmental controls must be monitored, cleaned, and maintained regularly (keeping wheels on blocks above dirt level to reduce the potential for moisture migration, and rotating wheels on a schedule).

Considerable debate has occurred about preservation standards for tools and equipment. The most damage results from handling, so for practical purposes, staff should avoid excessive handling. Know where you will put the object before you move it. Carry only one object at a time. Get help to move heavy or cumbersome objects. That said, not using some objects will compromise their integrity. Best practices indicate that equipment intended for use in interpretation should be maintained in running order, and that repair of such equipment extends its working life and its historic provenance.

John T. Schlebecker summed up the challenges that he believed living historical farms would face with objects. He balanced preservation requirements—"above all, no object, tool, implement, or machine [or animal] should show signs of neglect"—with the reality of use—"some original machines may have to be used . . . such machines should be treated with care, and restored and repaired as necessary."[30]

Practical solutions to determining what to use and what not to use resulted in a system of ranking or tiering artifacts. The Henry Ford implemented the system in 1993 to identify the historical significance, rarity, value, and/or significance of individual items in the collection. Then they ranked objects from 1 to 4, with 1 being the most well-preserved and historically significant and 4 being most appropriate for use in exhibits or interpretation. The ranking system guided decisions that staff had to make about appropriate treatment, handling, and management of objects given numerous interpretive options and high demand.[31]

Schlebecker's standards raised another issue that affected collections care and management: "Reproductions should be treated with care even though they are reproductions. Some reproductions, however, have to be considered expendable, such as flails, buckets, and most edged tools. . . . Farming objects should be identified by metal tags or wood stamps because paint wears off quickly on working tools." Debates about why to replicate, how to replicate, how to permanently mark, and what sorts of records to maintain on reproductions eventually coalesced into standard practices in place at various museums including children's museums and living history farms.[32]

Ultimately, staff responsible for artifacts that can help interpret agriculture often have to balance professional standards with interpretive expectations. The best practices depend on knowledge of professional standards balanced against institutional reality. The result must ensure the longevity of a variety of artifacts, be they in storage, on exhibit, or in an active interpretive context. Collections policies and procedures should articulate expectations for care of artifacts in general, and for care of living collections, ranking objects for use, and tracking reproductions in use. The policies and procedures should state the philosophy and practice of deaccession and can outline collections development strategies, too. A collection development plan should start with a scope of collections statement that addresses the collection and its relevance to agriculture interpretation. The plan will itemize the strengths of existing collections, identify areas needing objects, and the strategies to accomplish proactive collecting.

With these basic documents in place, institutions should be prepared to take full advantage of the grain cradles, pitchforks, and tractors to tell the story of agriculture in the house, historic site, or museum that they curate.

Notes

1. Marc Bloch, *The Historian's Craft*, trans. Peter Putnam (New York: Vintage Books, 1953), 66–69. Bloch in his "Introduction" to *French Rural History* waxed eloquent about "invaluable maps . . . handsome objects (mostly of seigneurial origin)," "which lay bare the anatomy of the land" and considered immersion in agrarian antiquities essential because "the pattern of fields is older by far than even the most venerable stones. But . . . these survivals have never been 'ruins'; they are better compared to a composite building of archaic structure, never deserted but constantly remodelled [sic] by each fresh generation of occupiers. . . . Deliberate refusal to notice and investigate these changes is tantamount to a denial of life itself, since all life is change" (xxvi–xxvii, xxix–xxx). Christopher Witmore's comment appeared as part of a dialogue among five scholars noted for their work with material culture. See Leora Auslander et al., "AHR Conversation: Historians and the Study of Material Culture," *American Historical Review* (Dec. 2009): 1,354–404.

2. John T. Schlebecker, "Keeping the Records: Historical Objects," *Agricultural History* (Jan. 1975): 108–10. For more on agricultural historians who advocated for collecting, preserving, and

documenting artifacts, see Debra A. Reid, "Agricultural Artifacts: Early Curators, Their Philosophy and Their Collections," *ALHFAM Proceedings 2010*, 33 (North Bloomfield, OH: ALHFAM, 2011), 30–52.

3. John T. Schlebecker, "The Use of Objects in Historical Research," *Agricultural History* (January 1977): 200–08; reprinted in Thomas J. Schlereth, ed., *Material Culture Studies in America* (Nashville, TN: American Association for State and Local History, 1982), 106–13.

4. Darwin P. Kelsey, "Outdoor Museums and Historical Agriculture," *Agricultural History* (Jan. 1972): 105–28.

5. Schlebecker, "Use of Objects," 200.

6. For example, C. H. Wendel, *Encyclopedia of Antique Tools and Machinery* (Iola, WI: Krause Publications, 2001); C. H. Wendel, *Encyclopedia of American Farm Implements & Antiques* (Iola, WI: Krause Publications, 1997).

7. R. W. Runyan, *Identifying Horse-Drawn Farm Implements* (Lincoln, NE: Authors Choice Press, 2000); Cameron L. Saffell, "An Alternative Means of Field Research: Extending Material Culture Analysis to Farm Implements," *Agricultural History* (2014), 517–37, quote 520.

8. Lynn R. Miller, *Work Horse Handbook*, 2nd ed. (Reedsport, OR: Mill Press, 1981; Davila Art and Books, 2015); Lynn R. Miller, *Horsedrawn Plows and Plowing* (*Small Farmer's Journal*, 2001); and Lynn R. Miller and Kristi Gilman-Miller, *Training Workhorses Training Teamsters* (Sisters, OR: Small Farmer's Journal, 1994).

9. Saffell, 520.

10. Edward C. Kendall documented early plow construction in *John Deere's Steel Plow* (Washington, D.C.: Smithsonian Institution, 1959); available as a Project Gutenburg eBook #34562 (2010), 15–25. Schlebecker, "Research in Agricultural History," 207–10.

11. Henry Glassie, "The Variation of Concepts Within Tradition: Barn Building in Otsego County, New York," *Geoscience and Man* (June 1974): 177–235; Henry Glassie, *Folk Housing in Middle Virginia: A Structural Analysis of Historic Artifacts* (Knoxville: University of Tennessee Press, 1975); Henry Glassie, *Passing the Time in Ballymenone: Culture and History of an Ulster Community* (Philadelphia: University of Pennsylvania Press, 1982); Charles E. Orser, *The Material Basis of the Postbellum Tenant Plantation: Historic Archaeology in the South Carolina Piedmont* (Athens: University of Georgia Press, 1988).

12. Saffell, 518.

13. Emanuel Vocale, interview by Nigel Holman, 15 June 2000, Oral History Program, Tape Three, side A, New Mexico Farm and Ranch Heritage Museum, Las Cruces, NM.

14. Thomas J. Schlereth identified three eras—the Age of Collecting (1876–1948), the Age of Description (1948–1965), and the Age of Analysis (1965–)—and indicated the lasting influences that scholars active in each era had on material culture studies. He also identified and summarized nine approaches. See Schlereth, "Material Culture Studies in America, 1876-1976," *Material Culture Studies*, 40–72. This 1982 article has stood the test of time, but it should not be taken as the last word on the subject. More recent models of study have come from Karen Harvey, ed., *History and Material Culture: A Student's Guide to Approaching Alternative Sources* (New York: Routledge, 2009), particularly the essay by Giorgio Riello, "Things that Shape History: Material Culture and Historical Narratives," 24–46; model scholarship by Laurel Thatcher Ulrich, *The Age of Homespun: Objects and Stories in the Creation of an American Myth* (New York: Alfred A. Knopf, 2001); and Ulrich, "Presidential Address: An American Album, 1857," *American Historical Review* (February 2010): 1–25.

15. Debra A. Reid, "Tangible Agricultural History: An Object's Eye View of the Field," *Agricultural History*, 86, no. 3 (Summer 2012): 57–76.

16. Dwight P. Lanmon, *Evaluating Your Collection: The 14 Points of Connoisseurship* (Winterthur, DE: Henry Francis du Pont Winterthur Museum, 1999). Lanmon expands on Charles Montgomery's principles proposed in "Some Remarks on the Practice and Science of Connoisseurship," *American Walpole Society Notebook* (1961), 7–20; Charles F. Montgomery, "The Connoisseurship of Artifacts," *Material Culture Studies in America*, 143–52.

17. John T. Schlebecker, "Research in Agricultural History at the Smithsonian Institution," *Agricultural History* (July 1966): 207–10.

18. Canned good label, R. J. K. Co., Chicago Reg. 900, Original Antique Label Art, Cerebro, http://www.cerebro.com/ (accessed 7 February 2012); "Skysweep Brooms," R. J. K. Co., Reg. 1931, no. 925, thelabelman.com, http://www.thelabelman.com/ (accessed 7 February 2012); Carolyn Dorf, "Interview with Mr. Robert T. Shaw and Joy Weber of Marissa, IL, Grandchildren of Mr. Ralph L. Shaw," *Randolph County Genealogical Society: The Trails* (December 2011), 27–28; "Sorghum Mill at Steeleville Wye Reminiscent of an Earlier Day," *Chester (Ill.) Herald Tribune*, 26 November 1965.

19. "Sorghum Mill"; Dorf, "Interview."

20. Indiana Cane Growers Association, "Discussion of Chemicals used in Sorghum Making, Among Other Things," *Annual Report of the Indiana State Board of Agriculture*, 40 (Indianapolis: Indiana State Board of Agriculture, 1891): 517–21.

21. Robert C. Williams, "Antique Farm Equipment: Research and Identifying," American Association for State and Local History Technical Leaflet 101, published insert in *History News* 32 (November 1977), 1–2; R. Douglas Hurt, *American Farms: Exploring Their History* (Malabar, FL: Krieger, 1996), 70.

22. E. McClung Fleming, "Artifact Study: A Proposed Model," *Winterthur Portfolio*, 9, no. 1 (January 1974): 153–173; reprinted in Thomas Schlereth, ed., *Material Culture Studies*, 162–73.

23. John Deere, "From Deere & Mansur to John Deere Seeding: Deere Planters Have a History of Innovation," *The Plowshare: News for John Deere Collectors*, 23 (2011): 2. The two companies had always been interrelated—Deere & Mansur founder Charles Deere became Deere & Company president in 1886, and Deere & Mansur products had been sold through Deere & Company outlets. Description of Deere No. 999 Planters based on observations of actual implements and illustrations from trade literature, such as Deere & Company, *Directions and Repair List for John Deere No. 999L Corn Planter* (Moline, IL: Deere & Company, 1939); Deere & Company, *John Deere No. 999 Corn Planter* (Moline, IL: Deere & Company, 1941). Don Macmillan and Russell Jones, *John Deere Tractors and Equipment: Volume 1, 1837–1959*, 2 vols. (St. Joseph, MO: American Society of Agricultural Engineers, 1988), 1:238–39.

24. H. P. Smith and M. H. Byrom, *Calibration of Cotton Planting Mechanisms, Bulletin, No. 526* (College Station, TX: Texas Agricultural Experiment Station, 1936), 13–14; Deere & Company, *The Operation, Care, and Repair of Farm Machinery*, 12th ed. (Moline, IL: John Deere, [1938]), 68–71.

25. C. H. Wendel, *150 Years of International Harvester* (Iola, WI: Krause Publications, 2004), 72–73; MacMillan and Jones, *John Deere Tractors*, 1:238–40.

26. Schlebecker, "Use of Objects," 204.

27. Fleming, "Artifact Study," in Schlereth, 169–72.

28. Ibid., 172–73.

29. Published guides emphasize best practices. The most comprehensive collections care and management guide is Rebecca A. Buck and Jean Allman Gilmore, eds., *Museum Registration Methods*, 5th ed. (Washington, D.C.: The AAM Press, 2010). See also Brent A. Powell, *Collection Care: An Illustrated Handbook for the Care and Handling of Cultural Objects* (Lanman, MD: Rowman

& Littlefield, 2016). Per E. Guldbeck wrote *The Care of Historical Collections: A Conservation Handbook for the Nonspecialist* (American Association for State and Local History, 1972) to serve small historical societies and museums. It reflected practical concerns in an agricultural museum setting (The Farmers' Museum, Inc., of the New York State Historical Society in Cooperstown, New York). For a revised and expanded edition, see A. Bruce MacLeish, *The Care of Antiques and Historical Collections* (American Association for State and Local History, 1985).

30. John T. Schlebecker, "Standards of Excellence for Living Historical Farms and Agricultural Museums," Proceedings of the *1975 ALHFAM Conference and Annual Meeting* 2 (Washington, D.C.: Smithsonian Institution, 1976), 1–6, first quote 4; second quote 5.

31. "Preservation Policy," Henry Ford Museum and Greenfield Village Policy and Procedure Memorandum, No. 25a (March 2001), available at http://www.cool.conservation-us.org/byorg/henryfordmuseum/preservation-policy.html (accessed May 2015). ALHFAM conferences provided opportunities for curators and collections managers to discuss protocols and deliver their models. Deborah Scott and Carl Schlichting (1989); Franz Klingender (1990) discussed tiering at Historic Sites, Parks Canada; and Sarah LeCount coordinated a session on Policies, Procedures, and Case Studies of Collections Tiering (2009). The consensus follows: Tier 1 (permanent collection): research value; datable; provenance; rare, one-of-a-kind, 60 percent original; Tier 2 (permanent collection): datable with provenance; Tier 1 and 2 artifacts are all accessioned, catalogued, and receive care compatible with accreditation standards. Tier 3 (program collection): photographed, inventoried, not catalogued; restored and suitable for active use. See also Trevor Jones, "Go Ahead and Tier Your Collections!" *History News* (Autumn 2014): 14.

32. Schlebecker, "Standards," 4; Bill Reid and Ron Kley, "Replicas, Facsimiles, Analogs, Fakes . . . and Other Stand-Ins for Authentic Historical Artifacts," *ALHFAM Proceedings* 8 (n.p. 1988), 39–40; Bethany Watkins Sugawara, "But They're Not Real!: Rethinking the Use of Props in Historic House Museum Displays," *History News* (Autumn 2003): 20–23.

CHAPTER 7

WE CAN'T EAT GOLD

Agriculture in Early Colorado City, 1858–1867

Carol Kennis Lopez

NOTE: This essay collects evidence about how early settlers to the Central Front Range of the Rocky Mountains turned the lands inhabited by Ute, Southern Cheyenne, Kiowa, Arapaho, and Navajo peoples into wheat fields and market gardens. The research supported interpretation commemorating the 150th anniversary of the start of the Pikes Peak gold rush in 1858. This included programs at Rock Ledge Ranch, formerly White House Ranch, a historic site designated on the National Register of Historic Places. Public institutions such as Rock Ledge provide opportunities for visitors to explore the places where farmers grew the crops that fed the gold miners and the livestock that they and other farmers depended on for food and fiber. She delivered this research at the 2012 conference of the Association for Living History, Farm and Agricultural Museums, and a version of that paper was published in the *Proceedings of the 2012 ALHFAM Conference and Annual Meeting* (2013).

IN MID-NINETEENTH-CENTURY America, most if not all food was slow food, and just about everyone could be considered a locavore. So during the gold rush of 1858–1859, when 100,000 Euro-Americans moved farther west, beyond the food frontier of eastern Kansas and Nebraska territories, one wonders how these people fed themselves. As I studied the Pikes Peak gold rush in preparation for its sesquicentennial (1858–1861 to 2008–2011), our modern concern about where our food comes from influenced my approach. If just about everyone was prospecting for gold, who grew the food?

I wondered how the sudden surge in population affected agriculture in a region that was unfamiliar to thousands of newcomers. Primary sources documented starvation:

> I am within six miles of Bent's Fort, with my face turned towards the Peak. I think we shall get through, but starvation stares us in the face. . . . I have seen some men so near starvation that they could not walk. Some were eating crows. . . . I have seen human bones bleaching on the plains, today. There is great sympathy for the starving emigrants, among those who have anything to give, it is freely done. Some men dig roots to prevent starvation. I think there is no gold at Pikes Peak, and those who staid home acted the wiser part. . . . It is hard parting, with friends on the plains, not knowing but their fate would be starvation.
> —Anonymous, *Kansas Press*, July 11, 1859[1]

My search for secondary sources revealed a paucity of published research on the agricultural history of Colorado. Most of the agricultural history surveys of the United States ignore the pre-railroad Rocky Mountain West, and almost all surveys of American Western history ignore agriculture in Colorado, at least until the founding of the agricultural colony of Greeley, in 1870.[2] It is as though people in the Colorado Territory, be they American Indian or Euro-American, did not eat before the railroads arrived in the 1870s.

The Pikes Peak or Bust gold rush stimulated agriculture in Colorado and northern New Mexico by creating markets; by bringing farmers, seeds, and tools into the area; and by spreading irrigation technology throughout the territory. In fact, agriculture saved the boom town of Colorado City, the primary focus of my research and one of the first towns established in present-day Colorado, from becoming a ghost town when the gold fever died down.

Before we delve into agriculture, it's important to review the changing political geography of the region, because the terms people used in the past conveyed the geopolitics of that time. Prior to 1848 the Arkansas River was the international boundary between the United States and Mexico. Thus, primary documents refer to people living south of the Arkansas River as "Mexicans" or "New Mexicans" regardless of their heritage, Hispanic or otherwise. New Mexico Territory, established in 1850, included what is today the southern part of Colorado. In 1859 Colorado City and Denver were part of the Kansas Territory. Colorado Territory was not established until February 1861, well after the rush began. It was carved out from the four surrounding territories.[3] To avoid confusion because of the shifting boundaries during this period, my references to Colorado and New Mexico territories reflect current boundaries.

The financial panic of 1857 caused such widespread unemployment and economic ruin that the risks of pursuing the rumors of gold in the unsettled Rocky Mountains became worth the risk for people with nothing else to lose. In May of 1858 two groups traveling separately, but nearly at the same time, journeyed into western Kansas Territory to investigate the rumors. One was the William Green Russell party of seventy people from Georgia and the Kansas Territory. The second was the Lawrence party of forty-eight men, two women, and a child from Lawrence, Kansas.

Both parties followed the Santa Fe Trail beyond the ruins of Bent's Fort and then followed the Arkansas River to the base of Pikes Peak. As the two parties worked their way deeper into the mountains, prospecting along the way, they did, indeed, find free gold. When some of the parties returned to Lawrence, Kansas, showing their gold and describing the route, the rush was born.

Soon three main routes to the mountains were advertised:

1. The Santa Fe Trail (or Arkansas Route) from Council Grove, Kansas, to Bent's Fort and then northwest along the Arkansas River and Fountain Creek to the base of Pikes Peak was a trek of seven hundred miles and led to the site of Colorado City. This was the most popular route initially, and certainly the most documented, because traders had followed the Santa Fe Trail since the 1820s.
2. The Platte River Trail to the north from Fort Kearny, Nebraska, to Denver City eventually became the most popular route and followed portions of the Oregon Trail. It was also seven hundred miles long.
3. The Smokey Hills Trail ran from Leavenworth to Denver, and at five hundred miles long, it was the quickest but most deadly trail. It traversed sandy deserts and was the least documented. Along it both people and animals perished.

When the fifty-niners entered Pikes Peak country, they did not arrive in an empty land. Thousands of American Indian people lived there. Multiple bands of Ute, Southern Cheyenne, Kiowa, Arapaho, and Navajo people hunted, traded in, and fought over the region as they had for hundreds of years. There were also a few frontier folk who farmed, traded, and hunted along the Arkansas, Huerfano, and Purgatory Rivers. Some of these people were Hispanic with ancestry extending back to the 1700s. They maintained homes in the San Luis Valley and today's northern New Mexico.

Initially, in the spring of 1859, hundreds of people arrived at the base of Pikes Peak, after following the Arkansas Route. The Peak, which towered over the grassy plains at its base, was a beacon for travelers following the Arkansas River to the diggings. It was the only landmark with a name and the first of Colorado's many mountains visible from the eastern plains. Upon reaching its base, weary travelers discovered that their trip had not ended. The actual gold discoveries lay farther to the west and north among the headwaters of the Arkansas and Platte Rivers.

Thus in 1859, a few unsuccessful prospectors, who decided that instead of prospecting they would "mine the miners," founded a new town, Colorado City. The town, the county seat of the newly formed El Paso County, was platted at the confluence of Fountain and Camp Creeks in August. The site was practically the same area where the Lawrence Party had camped the year before and it lay on the Old Trappers or Taos Trail. This trail connected the Santa Fe Trail, the villages of Taos and Pueblo, and the Colorado Branch of the Overland Trail, in a similar fashion to the way Highways 285 and 260 connect Taos to Pueblo and Interstate 25 connects Pueblo to Fort Collins today. By 1859 these trails were already decades old and well known to the frontier people who made New Mexico their home and to the Ute, Cheyenne, Kiowa, and other Indian people who used them. Present-day maps mark this area as Colorado Springs, a city of over 350,000 people.

In the early years of the rush, the food supply along the routes and in the gold camps was definitely an issue. Newspaper publishers advised migrants to prepare accordingly. On April 23, 1859, the first edition of the *Rocky Mountain News* reported that:

> Every emigrant should bring with him from the States a full set of mining tools and at least three months provisions and clothing, then there need not be this gloomy foreboding and fear of starvation if he should fail to find remunerative employment immediately on his arrival. It is a mistaken idea to expect that supplies can be found in this new country now for fifty or even ten thousand people or that they can be obtained from New Mexico, they must be brought from the States.[4]

Almost immediately food was shipped to Denver and Colorado City from established farms in southern Colorado and northern New Mexico territories. There, farming had been underway for a number of years preceding the rush. Mormon farmers also freighted goods east from Utah.

Denver's *Rocky Mountain News* often announced the arrival of supplies, and so we can track where shipments originated. At least initially, the gold rush created a surge in business for these farmers.[5] Hispanic and Anglo farmers from northern New Mexico, the San Luis Valley, and the Arkansas and Huerfano river valleys brought food to the mining settlements.

Farmers William Kroenig, Joseph B. Doyle, Charley Autobee, and Felipe de Jesus Baca all had farms in this area and helped to feed hungry soldiers at Fort Union in Mora County, New Mexico, and prospectors in Colorado. Kroenig brought pork, cornmeal, potatoes, onions, cabbage, and other winter vegetables into Denver during the winter of 1859 and 1860. In 1860 Felipe Baca, prior to helping establish Trinidad, Colorado, traveled with four wagonloads of corn from Mora County, New Mexico, to the Cherry Creek area near Denver. That same fall Albert Archibald, brother of the famed "Bloomer Girl," Julia Archibald Holmes, worked for William Kroenig near Watrous, New Mexico. Archibald and a companion drove two wagonloads of sauerkraut and onions to market, some three hundred miles north to Denver. Apparently the sauerkraut was not a hit, but they made a profit on the onions.[6]

Joseph B. Doyle, having arrived in the Arkansas Valley in the 1840s, was a particularly successful farmer and merchant. By 1861 his ranch and flour mill on the Huerfano supplied stores in Pueblo, Denver, Colorado City, and Canon City. His shipments also included goods he received via the Santa Fe Trail at La Junta. The *Rocky Mountain News* promoted Doyle & Co. on December 1, 1859, as keepers of an "immense stock . . . including 30,000 pounds of flour, 15,000 pounds of corn meal, and 4,000 pounds of onions." In the same issue, Doyle & Co. advertised that a shipment of "superfine flour, Albuquerque onions, corn meal, oats, [and] corn," in addition to saddles, spurs, and Mexican and American blankets, had arrived from his warehouse in La Junta.[7]

William Kroenig was well known for his farms in both Colorado and New Mexico Territories. In 1859, Thomas Wildman wrote the following in a letter published in the *Kansas Journal*: "In answer to our questions concerning the agricultural resources of that region . . . near the mouth of the Huerfeno [sic.], a Mr. Krengag, [Kroenig] an old Mexican trader, had 500 acres in corn, wheat and barley. This same gentleman has a large flouring mill already in operation, and is now engaged in building a brewery to make lager beer."[8] Interestingly, the Kroenig ranch in Watrous, New Mexico, is known today as the Hashknife Ranch, operated by his great grandson, "Dogie" Jones. The ranch is registered as a New Mexico cultural property.[9]

According to historian Elliott West, these farmers and others sustained the prospectors during the first winter by freighting Taos Lightning (whiskey), corn, beans, wheat, flour, and onions up the eastern side of the Front Range. The mining towns could not become the market those New Mexican merchants sought, however, because the New Mexican suppliers could not offer the magnitude of goods coming from the East.[10]

Guidebooks and town boosters used the promise of agriculture to promote settlement in their locale.[11] On page one of his first edition of the *Rocky Mountain News* published on April 23, 1859, William Byers ran a lengthy editorial under the title "Farming vs. Gold Digging." In it he proclaimed that those who raised stock and produce would get their equal share of the gold dug by others.[12] In his view the country needed farmers.

Even in the earliest days of the rush, garden farming was occurring throughout the Territory and beyond. In a letter of June 28, 1859, Thomas Wildman revealed that he and an acquaintance in Denver "bought some lettuce and green peas and we are going to have a feast this noon, after which I shall start for the mountains. Butter sells here for $1 per pound, consequently we do not indulge in that luxury. Peas are worth 10¢ per quart and lettuce a dime per bunch."[13]

Some early residents apparently came to the Front Range with the intention of farming. In May of 1859, the *Rocky Mountain News* recorded the following under the heading "Local Items":

> A Show for Vegetables.—We recently paid a visit to the garden and farm of J. Smith & Co. on the opposite side of the river from this place. They have enclosed about 40 acres, some ten or twelve of which is already plowed and planted and gives good promise of yielding a heavy crop. We found uncle Jake planting corn but his earlier crops, as peas, onions &c, are up, several inches.
>
> Whilst there we noticed a covered wagon drive up alongside the enclosure, two or three men got out unhitched their team unloaded a plow and in less than half an hour had began turning over the rich black sod, another farm was commenced.[14]

The following year the *Rocky Mountain News* ran a lengthy description of Colorado City. The piece gushed with the vintage optimism of nineteenth-century town boosterism. And why not? The hard times that accompanied the Civil War had not yet taken hold, and the future seemed bright. Colorado City still hoped to be the gateway on the southern avenue into the goldfields. From this piece we gain not only a description of what Colorado City was, but also a glimpse at what it *hoped* to be. Agriculture had a primary role in that vision.

> This growing city is situated immediately eastward of the great Ute pass to the South Park, Tarryall, Blue and head waters of the Arkansas gold fields. The town site contains some twelve hundred odd acres, admirably situated for all the natural advantages of water, wood, coal, and regularity of streets and avenues, parks and cemetery, sunny slopes and grassy hill-sides. The principal streets are 100 feet wide, running east and west, and affording the most admirable locations for thousands of business buildings. . . . Three saw-mills are erecting, or forthcoming, for operations therein.

Under the subheading "Agricultural Advantages," the article continued: "The finest and richest tracts of arable land and pasturage, perhaps to be seen in this country, lie all along for forty miles to the eastward and southeastward of Colorado City. . . ." Exuberantly, the writer predicted that the area "should be able to support an agricultural population of at least fifty to one hundred thousand."[15]

Colorado City did not grow as predicted. Instead, by early 1861 violence on the eastern plains diverted emigrants away from the Arkansas route to the Platte River Trail that led toward Denver. At the same time the Civil War took attention away from the newly formed Colorado Territory. Ultimately it was agriculture that saved Colorado City from becoming just another abandoned gold rush–era ghost town.[16]

Only three days after platting and registering Colorado City, the principal residents commenced establishing a "claim club" on August 15, 1859. This non-governmental organization did not register mining claims, but rather town lots and agricultural claims. Citizen-originated claim clubs were important in the initial years of the gold rush, because the land had not been officially surveyed and offered for sale by the (federal) General Land Office. Settlement in Pikes Peak country had outpaced the government machinery to deal with it. Therefore people claiming land were officially squatters, and the solution to protecting those claims was the creation of extralegal "claim clubs" or "settlers associations."

The primary purpose for establishing the El Paso County Claim Club, then, was to assure that land claims were made and recorded in an orderly fashion until the official governmental bureaucracy was created to deal with them; the claimants wanted their claims to be protected and honored when that time came. So until September of 1861, the El Paso Claim Club served "ex officio as the clerk and recorders office."[17]

In general, the El Paso County Claim Club followed the land claiming procedures as outlined in the Preemption Act of 1841. It allowed the head of a family, a man or a widow over twenty-one years of age, who was a U.S. citizen or an alien who had declared his intention for citizenship, to claim 160 acres from the public domain.[18] Improvements had to be made and the land lived on before he or she could purchase the land from the government for $1.25 per acre.

Nationally, critics complained that the Preemption Act of 1841 (like land policy before it) was a tool for land speculators. The Preemption Act was intended to sell federally owned land, at a set and low price, to individuals. Undoubtedly speculation was occurring in El Paso County as well as elsewhere in the nation. For instance, a curious claim was registered in the Claim Book on October 20, 1861. On this date, fifteen-year-old Irving Howbert (a future county clerk and prominent citizen of Colorado Springs) claimed 160 acres adjacent to his father's claim on Cheyenne Creek (Photo 7.1). The entry reads:

> Irving Howbert claims under the jurisdiction of the El Paso Claim Club one hundred and sixty-acres of land for farming purposes situated on Cheyenne Creek described as follows commencing at the Northwest corner of James Roberts claim thence running North one hundred and sixty rods, thence west one hundred and sixty rods, thence south one hundred and sixty rods, thence east along the north line of Wm Howberts claim to place of beginning. Claim staked and foundation laid. Oct. 21, 1861. Witnessed by Wm Howbert, Irving Howbert. Recorded Oct 22, 1861, MS Beach Recorder, George Bute Dept.[19]

Settlers arrived to claim and purchase public domain land in the Colorado Territory before the surveyors had a chance to establish legal boundaries. This posed a problem, because legal claims first had to be documented by a government surveyor. The General Land Office contracted with surveyors to slowly, incrementally, and precisely mark the township and range lines on public lands in the west. Not all of the land in the area was fully surveyed until some twelve years after it had been occupied, so farmers improved land on their claim without legal assurances that they owned the land.[20]

An example of this peculiarity in land acquisition and transfer is the Camp Creek Valley homestead of Scottish immigrant Walter C. Galloway. Although Galloway arrived in Colorado City after the rush had waned somewhat, his experience is emblematic of others who tried farming in the area. According to El Paso County tax records, Galloway squatted on a 160-acre parcel of land between Camp Creek and the Garden of the Gods from about 1866 until 1871, when he was finally able to legally make a claim in accordance with the Homestead Act of 1862. General Land Office records show that the exterior survey of the township (thirty-six square miles) was accomplished in 1864 and 1869, but the interior subdivisions were not surveyed until May 22, 1871.[21] Thus Galloway, or any other claimant in that area, could not register his homestead claim, and pay his fee to the government until that time. According to an 1868 *Rocky Mountain News* story, Galloway was among others in the area raising buckwheat.[22] After registering his claim, Galloway, although not financially successful, was not idle. He reported in November 1874 that he had constructed a frame house eighteen by twenty-four feet with a plank roof and floor, with two windows and one door. Additionally he dug one-half mile of irrigation ditching and plowed, fenced, and cultivated about three acres, and plowed about ten acres not under fence. Like many would-be homesteaders, rather than staying the required five years, he commuted his claim by paying a cash fee and gaining the title in November 1874. He sold it for $1,400 the next day.[23]

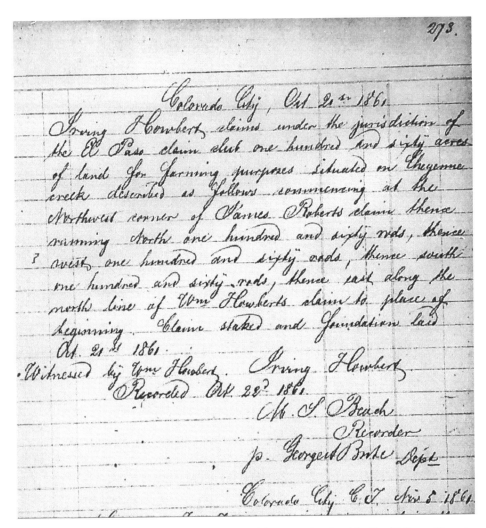

Photo 7.1 The land-claim of fifteen year-old Irving Howbert in the El Paso County Claim Book.

Photograph by Carol Kennis Lopez

Two men who participated in surveying the thousands of acres in the Colorado City area and beyond were A. Z. Sheldon and Robert Finley; both farmed in the area, as well. Sheldon selected land watered by Fountain Creek, and Finley was a neighbor to Galloway in the Camp Creek Valley (Photo 7.2). When they were not surveying for the General Land Office, they surveyed irrigation ditches for their neighboring farmers.[24]

Before surveyors arrived, the Claim Club did its best to describe land claims using metes and bounds. For example, the legal explanation of William Henry Garvin's claim, "for farming purposes," used the gypsum quarry as the benchmark, and geological features (Red Rocks and the Garden of the Gods) as well as another claim as the bounds.

Photo 7.2 The Camp Creek Valley, heavily farmed from 1859, was photographed by William Henry Jackson for the U.S. Geological Survey. The image shows Colorado City in the middle distance and Cheyenne Mountain, a bold promontory-like headland with an elevation of 4,000 feet above the plain. Along its north face, and extending behind it, are Cheyenne and Bear Canyons, extremely wild and rugged. The long white streak running from center to lower right was known as the road to Denver. The board fences and sheds of Chambers Ranch are visible between the ribbon of trees and the foothill near the right edge of the image. The parallel white streaks may have been irrigation ditches with water reflecting the light.

Source: Credit: U.S. Geological Survey, Department of the Interior/USGS, U.S. Geological Survey/photo by William Henry Jackson, taken 1859

The description also mentioned the water source, "Camp Creek," a critical detail in the arid Central Front Range:

> Colorado City Dec 15th 1859
>
> Wm Henry Garvin claims within the jurisdiction of the El Paso Claim Club one hundred & sixty acres of land for farming purposes, described as follows, commencing at a stake on the north east corner of said claim near the north end of the "Gypsum Quarry" so called about two miles north from Colorado City, and running from said stake west 160 rods and immediately across the upper or north end of the "Red Rocks" so called, from thence at right angles running south 160 rods along the west line of the place known and designated as the "Garden of the Gods" from thence at right angles

160 rods east to a point near the north west corner of the claim known as M. S. Beach's claim on "Camp Creek" from thence at right angles in a north line to stake or place of beginning. The said claim taken Dec. 12th/59 and the foundation laid immediately west of the large "Red Rocks" & as near the center of said claim as may be.

    Witnessed by Wm H. Garvin M. S. Beach James Garvin

    Recorded Dec. 15, 1859 H P Burghardt Recorder[25]

Besides the land claimed within the limits of Colorado City, the countryside adjacent to the area's waterways—the Fountain, Cheyenne, Monument, and Camp Creeks—were some of the first spots to be claimed. Initially, however, the need for and the "how to" of irrigation was not a skill that most farmers had when they arrived in the semiarid plains at the base of Pikes Peak. Here they were, in the place also known as the Great American Desert. It must have been daunting to think about harvesting wheat or produce in a place that apparently only grew abundant yucca and prickly pear. Anthony Bott, who became one of the town's principal leaders, remarked, "Few of the early settlers knew anything of irrigation but soon got an idea of it from the Mexicans who came up to this region after the first settlements were made to secure employment."[26] The El Paso County Claim Club book shows that claims were frequently made, abandoned, and claimed by another party, owing probably in part to the ease or difficulty of getting water to the land.[27]

Gradually, however, the early residents became experienced in the proper techniques of irrigation. Successful ditch (or *acequia* as the New Mexicans call it) irrigation had been practiced for decades in the San Luis Valley and northern New Mexico. For some farmers, seeing was believing. For instance, Irving Howbert recalled that:

> The show place of Colorado City at the time of our arrival [1860] was a small tract of land east of town in the valley of the Fountain, that was under cultivation by irrigation, a method of farming unknown to the people of the regions whence most of the gold seekers came. Only recently had it dawned upon any of those who had come to the Rocky Mountains seeking gold, that there might be other industries in the Pike's Peak region besides mining. Few of them had the least idea that the lands of this arid section could be made of any value agriculturally, but those who visited the garden tract and saw corn and all sorts of vegetables growing luxuriantly as a result of irrigation, came away with new ideas as to the possibilities of this country. Already they had discovered that these great plains were admirably adapted to stock raising, and now it was proved that by irrigation methods, they could be made great agriculturally as well.[28]

Irving Howbert arrived at the base of Pikes Peak with his father when he was fourteen years old. For a short time in 1860 they stayed in the mining camp of Hamilton. While there he saw "a procession of forty or fifty burros coming from the south, driven by three Mexicans. Each burro had a sack of flour strapped on its back." In his memoir of this period, Howbert continues with a description of how the grain was threshed in New Mexico at the time:

In eating bread made from this flour an unpleasant quantity of grit was found in it. The explanation as to the source of the grit was, that, there being no threshing machines in New Mexico, the separation of the wheat from the straw had to be done by burros tramping it out, usually on a dirt floor. After this, the wheat was winnowed by hand to remove the chaff, which process served well enough except when little particles of gravel and sand, happened to have worked up out of the floor during the tramping, remained with the grain and were ground up with it in the mill.[29]

The story of another emigrant, Sylvester Buzzard, provides insight into the experience of others who made the trip and eventually settled at the base of Pikes Peak. In May of 1862, twenty-four-year-old Buzzard left his home in Iowa for the adventures of "Pikes Peak or Bust" as he called it. Working his way to Pikes Peak country as a camp cook and general camp laborer, he eventually made his home in Colorado City.

Luckily for Buzzard, his group traveled with eight yoke of oxen and one yoke of cows, so he enjoyed fresh milk all along the route. Once they made it to South Park, the group sold the cows to ranchers for fifty dollars each. This was a tidy sum, which he remembered for many years, illustrating that milk cows were scarce in the gold fields.[30]

Sylvester Buzzard was one of the men who had some farming experience at home and who decided to rely on that skill when his hopes of getting rich quick faltered. His reminiscences provide some of the best details of farming and irrigation in El Paso County in the early 1860s. Buzzard took a break from prospecting by 1863, and he found work in Bachelor Flats, a group of farms along Fountain Creek south of Colorado City. Among the men there, he met a carpenter, sailor, printer and bookbinder, and a photographer. None were farmers, however, and they did not know how to sow grain by hand. So Buzzard took on the job, which kept him busy.

Once Buzzard saw that all of the crops were planted, including potatoes, all hands of Bachelor Flats fell to digging the irrigation ditch surveyed by Sheldon the previous winter. This ditch tapped the Fountain below the mouth of Monument Creek. They built a dam with brush and stone and allowed the beavers to build it up.[31] The head gate they installed allowed them to regulate when water flowed into the ditch. Eventually the men of Bachelor Flats irrigated their crops and grew plenty of wheat and oats.

Buzzard, who was skilled with a handheld cradle scythe, cut the grain (Photo 7.3). Collectively the men hired a farmer from Pueblo who brought up a machine to thresh the grain. He charged between twenty and twenty-five cents per bushel for the service.[32]

In 1862, when Buzzard first arrived in the territory, farmers used a yoke of oxen and some shovels and hoes to accomplish most tasks. "Farming implements were scarce and crude such as a blacksmith might put together," he recalled. Crop yields were low during the early years, as well. Within a short time however, after the practice of irrigation became better applied, the farmers of Bachelor Flats produced more and easily sold their surplus vegetables at high prices to the people in the mining camps.[33]

As Buzzard's story unfolded, he went from being a "hired man" and farming "for shares" (meaning farming another's land and sharing the proceeds), to acquiring eighty

Photo 7.3 This image shows the historic grain harvesting tools common before the 1870s, as well as a twine binder, manufactured after 1902. The seated man holds a sickle, and the standing man wields a grain cradle. A grain rake used to gather loose grain (pre-binder days) leans against the binder. Farmers could buy a variety of reapers starting in the 1840s, but laborers still had to bind the cut grain into sheaves and stack the sheaves in stooks to dry in the fields prior to threshing. By the early 1870s, inventors experimented with binding mechanisms using wire and then twine to reduce labor costs. Binders cut and bound the grain (you can see the canister that held the ball of twine), but laborers still had to stack the sheaves. This binder was manufactured by the Milwaukee Harvester Company (as distinguished by its trade name and the Milwaukee four-leaf clover logo).

Source: Wisconsin Historical Society, Image ID: 59874

acres of his own on Bachelor Flats in 1866. There he raised wheat, oats, corn, a vegetable garden, and chickens. His subtle pride can be heard in his comment:

> From now on I should make my own bargains, pay my own bills, do my own cooking, washing and ironing, milk my own cows. . . . I cut my own grain with the cradle, hired a man to rake and bind it after me and while I was getting supper, milking the cow, feeding the pigs and chickens, the hired man would do the shocking. . . . I would some days cut three acres and when I did, and night had come, I went to bed, went to sleep and never turned over till morning.[34]

Sylvester Buzzard's skill as a reaper of wheat kept him busy. Even after acquiring his own farm and becoming the part-time county assessor in 1867, Buzzard cut George Bute's wheat planted along Camp Creek with his cradle. He got so busy cutting Bute's wheat that he had to hire a mechanical reaper to harvest his own. It was the only machine in the area and belonged to a man in Pueblo who purchased it "somewhere in Yankeydom" in 1864. It was shipped to the Missouri River and hauled from there to Denver by ox teams. It was a "peculiar affair. I never saw one before, nor since like it. There was not a cog wheel in its whole construction. It cut grain and raked it off in very good shape, but when you put it to mowing it was like all other mules, it balked."[35]

By 1862 Colorado City boasted a water-powered flour mill on Fountain creek. Flannigan, Colton, and Whittimore constructed the mill in the fall of 1862, according to Anthony Bott. Farming, Bott said, made such progress by this time that the mill was busy all the time grinding wheat raised in El Paso County.[36] Later two more mills were built along the creek. Milling became a small but important industry in Colorado City. The *Denver Weekly Commonwealth and Republican* of August 20, 1863, related that:

> Our thanks are due the firm of Colton & Co. of Colorado City, for 59 pounds of flour, manufactured from new wheat at their mill in that place. It is a superior article. Colton & Co. are prepared to manufacture from one to one hundred sacks per day. They warrant all their work. They will undoubtedly get the custom of the whole southern country, as there is no other mill in that section nearer than Fred Maxwell's beyond the Raton Mountains.[37]

Farmers in the Pikes Peak region managed many risks. Besides the challenges of aridity, simple equipment, flash floods, and early and late snowstorms, they tried to mitigate the damage done by voracious plagues of grasshoppers. Locusts were a problem in the region from the earliest days of settlement. This hardship is mentioned repeatedly in letters, newspaper articles, and reminiscences of the period. The *Rocky Mountain News* reported on grasshopper infestations as early as 1860. One such report read:

> Grasshoppers. Many of the farms and gardens in this vicinity are suffering severely from the ravages of these insects. They seem to hatch out in certain spots along the valleys of the streams, first appearing as a minute grayish fly, at which time they prey upon cabbage and other tender plants. In a few days they assume grasshopper form, and rapidly advance to the full grown, voracious pest. We think that when they have grown a little larger, they will migrate—at least we earnestly hope so. Should they remain through the summer, they will desolate many farms in situations exposed to their ravages.[38]

Sylvester Buzzard related multiple treatments for the infestations. Some farmers, he said, increased their flocks of chickens and turkeys, others allowed the pests to collect on straw during the night then burned it in the morning, and some farmers shoved the insects into a flowing irrigation ditch. One farmer built a contraption to sweep his fields, scalded bags of the grasshoppers, then fed them to his pigs. The result of this solution, Buzzard said, was that "the swine learned a bad habit, they hopped out of the pen."[39] Just as today, farmers like Sylvester Buzzard needed to maintain their sense of humor when faced with such trials.

Remarkably, the grasshoppers did not arrive with the settlers. When Major Long's expedition entered the region in 1820, Dr. Edwin James and two other men took a side excursion to climb what eventually became known as Pikes Peak. In his official report of the expedition, Dr. James wrote:

> The weather was calm and clear, while we remained on the Peak, but we were surprised to observe the air in every direction filled with such clouds of grasshoppers, as partially to obscure the day. They had been seen in vast numbers about all the higher parts of the mountain, and many had fallen upon the snow and perished. It is perhaps difficult to assign the cause, which induces these insects to ascend to those highly elevated regions of the atmosphere. Possibly they may have undertaken migrations to some remote district, but there appears not the least uniformity in the direction of their movements. They extended upwards from the summit of the mountain, to the utmost limit of vision, and as the sun shone brightly, they could be seen by the glittering of their wings, at a very considerable distance.[40]

The hoppers did not come every year, but the invasion of 1865 was particularly severe, and worse plagues arrived during the 1870s. For some farmers who operated on a thin margin in the best of times, it was the end of their agricultural lifestyle. Molly Dorset Sanford's description captures the heartbreak and the defeat experienced no doubt by many when she wrote:

> We thought ourselves settled for years on the ranch, and today finds us living in Denver. Our crops were just coming up so that the fields looked green in the slanting sunset, when the grasshoppers came, and in a few short hours destroyed the work of weeks, and about all the hopes we had. Of course others have suffered, but this has just about used us up.[41]

Colorado's premier agricultural historian, Alvin Steinel, called this beastie the Rocky Mountain locust, or *Melanoplus spretus*. According to his source, the breeding grounds were in the mountains and the migrations were nearly always eastward and usually in a southeasterly direction. The farmers of the gold rush days would be glad to hear that according to Steinel's source, this pest was extinct by 1926.[42]

As the 1860s continued, agriculture in El Paso County held its own in spite of the adversity so familiar to farmers. Land was inexpensive, market demand in the nearby mining camps and Denver was strong, and with increased irrigation there was, for a time, enough water for all.

Colorado City continued to grow, although slowly, and was eventually annexed to Colorado Springs in 1917. Today most of what was Colorado City has been subdivided and urbanized. No agricultural activity that I know of, besides possible backyard farms, exists in the Cheyenne Creek area. Along the Camp and Fountain Creek corridors, however, there are a few properties that preserve open space and continue the farming and ranching legacy of the area.

The Camp Creek Valley remained agricultural until the suburban housing boom of the 1950s. Today, the city-owned 230-acre Rock Ledge Ranch Historic Site protects the last remaining open space in the valley. Adjacent to the Garden of the Gods Park, the Rock Ledge Ranch preserves several historic structures, including two houses and several agricultural buildings, as well as vestiges of a reservoir and irrigation system begun by Walter Galloway (and possibly others) during the 1860s. The property, now a living history farm and museum, re-creates agricultural activities that took place on the property from the 1860s until the end of the century. A segment of the historic site represents the pre-railroad squatter claim and later homestead of Walter Galloway, who farmed the land beginning sometime around 1866 and who, coincidentally, worked occasionally for surveyor A.Z. Sheldon.[43]

The history of the Rock Ledge Ranch is deeply woven into the fabric of the area's history. Not only did A. Z. Sheldon survey this land for the U.S. Land Office, the aforementioned farmer and surveyor Robert Finley was a nearby neighbor, Irving Howbert's family claimed land adjacent to the property in the late 1860s, and the physical description of the historic site closely resembles that of William Henry Garvin's 1859 claim included above. The Robert Finley house still stands nearby, though the farm is gone and it is surrounded by mid-twentieth-century homes.

Farms and ranches also remain along Fountain Creek between Colorado Springs and Pueblo. Most notably, the Venetucci and Penello Farms, now operated by the Pikes Peak Community Foundation, work to protect the open space, the agricultural traditions of the valley, and the connection between people and their food. Just north of Pueblo, the T-Cross Ranch, operated by the Norris family, continues quality cattle and American quarter horse operations.

Although there were a few successful farms along the Arkansas River prior to the Pikes Peak gold rush, agriculture in the Pikes Peak region did not begin in earnest until the influx of hopeful prospectors in 1859. Those prospectors were advised to bring six months' worth of provisions with them, and many did, but local agriculture was necessary to sustain the growing population, especially when the realization dawned on the greenhorns that six months was not nearly enough time to make a fortune in gold. It also became a primary occupation for many gold seekers who either quickly or eventually traded in their picks and gold pans for plows and hay forks. As a result, the rush stimulated agriculture in early Colorado and New Mexico by creating markets; by attracting farmers, seeds, and tools into the area; and by spreading irrigation expertise throughout the territories. Not-for-profit institutions such as the Rock Ledge Ranch Historic Site preserve portions of some of the best farmland in the area and preserve the skills and stories of the earliest residents who developed it.

Notes

1. As quoted in Mark Gardner, *In the Shadow of Pike's Peak: An Illustrated History of Colorado Springs* (Carlsbad, CA: Heritage Media Corporation, 1999), 25.

2. For a sample of this oversight, see the following: Alan Brinkley, *The Unfinished Nation: A Concise History of the American People* (New York: McGraw Hill, 2006); David Danbom, *Born in the Country: A History of Rural America* (Baltimore, MD: Johns Hopkins University Press, 1995); R. Douglas Hurt, *American Agriculture: A Brief History* (Ames, IA: Iowa State University Press, 1994); John T. Schlebecker, *Whereby We Thrive: A History of American Farming 1607–1972* (Ames: Iowa Sate University Press, 1975); Richard White, *"It's Your Misfortune and None of My Own": A New History of the American West* (Norman: University of Oklahoma Press, 1991). A "modern" online resource, "Growing a Nation: The Story of American Agriculture," describes itself as "an interactive multimedia program that tells the story of American agriculture and its influence on important events and issues in American history," but it does not mention Colorado or the 1859 gold rush in its timeline: http://www.agclassroom.org/gan/index.htm (accessed 8 April 2011).

3. Thomas J. Noel, Paul F. Mahoney, and Richard E. Stevens, *Historical Atlas of Colorado* (Norman: University of Oklahoma Press, 1993), 14.

4. *Rocky Mountain News*, 23 April 1859, 2.

5. Eugene Berwanger, *The Rise of the Centennial State: Colorado Territory, 1861–1876* (Urbana: University of Illinois Press, 2007), 11; Alvin T. Steinel, *History of Agriculture in Colorado* (Fort Collins, CO: State Agricultural College, 1926), 47.

6. See Morris F. Taylor, *Trinidad, Colorado Territory* (Trinidad, CO: Trinidad State Junior College, 1966), 17–18; Paul D. Andrews and Nancy L. Humphry, "*El Patron de Trinidad:* Don Felipe de Jesus Baca," *Colorado Heritage* (Winter 2004): 3; Steinel, 47–48.

7. *Rocky Mountain News*, 1 December 1859, 3.

8. LeRoy Hafen, *Reports from Colorado, the Wildman Letters, 1859–1865: With other related letters and newspaper reports, 1859* (Glendale, CA: Arthur H. Clark, 1961), 181. At the same time, W. M. Pierson had a successful dairy farm on the Huerfano and may have been the first dairy farmer in the territory. His operation milked 100 cows and made butter and cheese for markets in Denver. Steinel, 48.

9. For current information about the family ranch, see http://www.hashkniferanch.net/web%20pix/index.htm (accessed 27 May 2016).

10. Elliott West, *The Contested Plains: Indians, Goldseekers, and the Rush to Colorado* (Lawrence: University Press of Kansas, 1998), 217–18.

11. West, 251.

12. *Rocky Mountain News*, 23 April 1859, 1. See also Steinel, 53.

13. Hafen, *Reports from Colorado, the Wildman Letters, 1859–1865,* 41.

14. *Rocky Mountain News*, 28 May 1859, 3; http://www.coloradohistoricnewspapers.org (accessed 23 March 2011).

15. Colorado City and Pike's Peak Vicinity, *Rocky Mountain News*, 14 March 1860; www.coloradohistoricnewspapers.org (accessed 23 March 2011).

16. Irving Howbert, *Memories of a Lifetime in the Pike's Peak Region* (1925; reprint, Glorieta, NM: Rio Grande Press, 1970), 44. Anthony Bott wrote, "As the town declined, the agricultural and cattle business began to grow" in "Life and Reminiscences of Anthony Bott," Special Collections Department, Pikes Peak Library District, file # CU112, 6.

17. Curt Poulton. *A Historical Geographic Approach to the Study of the Institutionalization of the Doctrine of Prior Appropriation: The Emergence of Appropriative Water Rights in Colorado Springs, Colorado* (PhD thesis, University of Minnesota, 1989), 16–17. Steinel, 38–41.

18. For more information on land policies and surveying, see Wallace Stegner, *Beyond the Hundredth Meridian* (New York: Penguin Books, 1992), 212–13; Benjamin Hibbard, *A History of Public Land Policies* (Madison, WI: University of Wisconsin Press, 1924; 1965). The U.S. Congress passed the Preemption Act of 1841 in its search for a satisfactory land policy. Congress revised it many times and finally repealed it in 1891. The Homestead Act of 1862 closely resembled it.

19. El Paso County Claim Club Book, 273, microfilm in author's collection.

20. United States Department of Interior Bureau of Land Management, Rectangular Survey Index for Township 13 South Range 67 West; survey notes of Section 34, Township 135 Range 67 West; General Land Office, Washington, D.C. Tract Book for Range 67 West, page 36 shows that the exterior of this range was surveyed in 1864 and 1869, but the interior subdivisions were not surveyed until May 22, 1871, when the plat was approved. This particular area happened to include the claim of Walter Galloway, early Colorado City resident. See fn 21 and 23.

21. Ibid. The Continental Congress established the township and range survey system with the Land Ordinance of 1785. It was first applied to sell public lands in the Northwest Territory (the Midwestern United States). After 1814, the U.S. Public Land Survey System crossed the Mississippi River into Arkansas, and became the standard to legally document public lands in the Louisiana Purchase. This facilitated sales that helped finance the national government. Each township was thirty-six square miles, consisting of thirty-six one-square-mile sections. Real estate purchases fit the grid, and aerial views of the landscape look like a giant checkerboard as a consequence.

22. *Rocky Mountain News*, 5 June 1868, 4.

23. We know that Galloway commuted his homestead claim by paying the required $1.25 per acre fee on November 9, 1874, from Certificate No. 1348, General Land Office patent records. Galloway sold his property to Robert M. Chambers on November 10, 1874; Warranty Deed, El Paso County, land records.

24. A.Z. Sheldon Diary. Unpublished manuscript, original in Starsmore Center for Local History, Colorado Springs Pioneers Museum.

25. El Paso County Claim Club book, 49.

26. Bott, 8.

27. Howbert's father abandoned a claim of land east of Monument Creek because of the light flow of water there. Instead he claimed land on Cheyenne Creek. He described that others were doing the same along the "Fountain and its tributaries, wherever water for irrigation purposes could be obtained and brought to the land without too much cost. Within the next year or two a large acreage of land along these streams was brought under cultivation." Howbert, 50–51.

28. Howbert, 49. Irving Howbert was probably referring to H.M. Fosdick, one of the men who started the El Paso County Claim Club and who was also a surveyor. Bott described Fosdick's farm located on the south side of Fountain Creek in the spring of 1860. It was planted "in a small sort of way all sorts of grain and vegetables, and that was the first demonstration as to what the possibilities were in the way of agriculture." Bott, 8.

29. Howbert, 33–34. This wheat may have come from farms in the San Luis Valley. See fn 3.

30. Sylvester M. Buzzard, unpublished manuscript, original in Starsmore Center for Local History, Box: Manuscripts and life reminiscences; File: A-46-59, 1.

31. Remarkably, this area along the two creeks is still on active beaver habitat today, even though it is adjacent to a major power plant and surrounded by the city of Colorado Springs.

32. Buzzard, 9.

33. Buzzard, 35.

34. Buzzard, 24–25. Sources indicate that men could cradle between two to two-and-one-half acres of grain per day. See Leo Rogin, *The Introduction of Farm Machinery in Its Relation to the*

Productivity of Labor in the Agriculture of the United States during the Nineteenth Century (Berkeley, CA: University of California Press, 1931), 127.

35. Buzzard, 26. J. Sanford Rikoon, *Threshing in the Midwest, 1820–1940: A Study of Traditional Culture and Technological Change* (Bloomington, IN: Indiana University Press, 1988); Thomas D. Isern, *Bull Threshers and Bindlestiffs: Harvesting and Threshing on the North American Plains* (Lawrence: University Press of Kansas, 1990).

36. Bott, 6. The date of this mill is not firm. Alvin Steinel, in *History of Agriculture in Colorado*, lists several dates and references to the mill, the earliest being 1860 based on a newspaper reference in the *Canon City Times*, 33.

37. Steinel, 35.

38. *Rocky Mountain News*, 8 June 1861, 3.

39. Buzzard, 21.

40. Maxine Benson, ed, *From Pittsburgh to the Rocky Mountains: Major Stephen Long's Expedition—1819–1820* (Golden, CO: Fulcrum, 1988), 225.

41. Mollie Dorsey Sanford, *Mollie: The Journal of Mollie Dorsey Sanford in Nebraska and Colorado Territories, 1857–1866* (Lincoln, NE: University of Nebraska Press, 1959), 192.

42. Steinel, footnote, 74.

43. Galloway appears in the county tax rolls of 1866 and 1867 and the census of 1870. On July 15, 1874, he was hired by A.Z. Sheldon to work on his well. A.Z. Sheldon Diary, 185. After Galloway sold his claim to Robert M. Chambers, the new owner continued farming and developing the irrigation system, turning the property into one of the most productive farms in El Paso County (Elsie Chambers, unpublished manuscript, Rock Ledge Ranch Historic Site). This property, known as Chambers Ranch, or White House Ranch, was listed on the National Register of Historic Places in 1979. During the 1990s, research documented that the house was not originally painted white, and that the name used during the 1880s was Rock Ledge Ranch. The site's name was changed from White House Ranch to Rock Ledge Ranch in the 1990s. See "About Rock Ledge Ranch," http://rockledgeranch.com/ (accessed 27 May 2016).

CHAPTER 8

CHANGES IN CORN-BELT CROP CULTURE

Iowa, 1945-1972

J. L. Anderson

NOTE: J. L. Anderson analyzes farmers' decisions made after World War II and the ways these helped create the modern Corn-Belt landscape. Farmers owned tractors before the war, but farmers did not use the tractors in ways that transformed their farm life routines before the war. After the war, a combination of factors pushed farmers to use technology in ways that changed every aspect of their lives and businesses in the time span of a generation. When farmers adopted hybrid corn along with synthetic herbicides, pesticides, and fertilizers, they increased yields per acre, and potentially, their profit margin. When farmers adopted machinery to cultivate more acreage faster, they freed themselves from dependency on agricultural laborers. When farmers invested in such technology, they realized that their cost of doing business escalated at pace with their income, exacerbating the cost-price squeeze. Furthermore, the investment in new crop technologies forced them to invest even more in machinery and buildings designed to harvest and dry the bountiful corn crop. The land became too valuable to run hogs or cattle, and industrialized animal husbandry developed. The corn farmers kept their marketable livestock close by but confined in farrowing houses, finishing houses, and feed lots. These changes inform us about what we see flashing by automobile windows on interstates that crisscross the Midwestern Corn Belt. It helps us develop context for discussions about modern agriculture, and it helps us understand the ways that industrial production distances crop cultivation from animal husbandry.

The following excerpts from J. L. Anderson, "From Corn Picker and Crib to Combine and Bin," *Industrializing the Corn Belt: Agriculture, Technology, and*

Environment, 1945–1972 (DeKalb, IL: Northern Illinois University Press, 2009), appear courtesy of Northern Illinois University Press (paragraphs excerpted from pages 169–90). Debra A. Reid selected photographs and wrote captions to help readers envision architectural and landscape features common across the Corn Belt after the mid-twentieth century.

HARVESTING EAR CORN by hand was among the most tedious and time-consuming jobs on the farm. . . . Farmers spent weeks, sometimes months, conducting their harvest. Carl Hamilton grew up during the interwar years and claimed that picking corn by hand was the worst drudgery on the farm. Each ear had to be removed from the stalk and tossed into a wagon. Hand picking was not only a long day of labor, it continued over weeks or months until all of the ears had been gathered from the field. The longer the corn stayed in the field, the more likely it was that some ears would fall off the stalks or the stalks would break in the wind, forcing the pickers to bend over to recover the crop from the ground.[1]

Families hosted itinerant corn pickers during the harvest season to help get the crop into the crib in a timely manner. Unlike regular hired men, who were paid a regular wage for an entire year, corn pickers were paid by the bushel, and the family furnished room and board for the duration of the harvest. Regular hired men did other farmwork when it was raining or too muddy to get into the field. The corn pickers did not. Instead they waited indoors for conditions to improve in the field. Imogene Hamilton dreaded picking season in the age of hand picking, for she would have to deal with "a bunch of corn pickers loafing around the house." Carl Hamilton noted that many of these men performed their work admirably, but "they were not always the kind of fellows you would invite in for Sunday dinner. The extra work of hosting these men as 'house guests' for a few days of nasty weather was not appreciated." Even under the best conditions, feeding pickers and cleaning up after them were onerous additions to the farm women's regular duties. As one Wisconsin woman stated, no one mourned the end of the hand corn-picking era. "And mother mourned it least of all." Two southwestern Iowa women contrasted the new days with the old days of feeding up to seven men three meals a day for weeks on end. Instead of having meals ready before daylight and scrambling to get a pie baked by the late morning, one woman whose family owned a mechanical picker went to town in the morning, helped a neighbor butcher chickens, and fed only one extra man at dinnertime.[2]

The mechanical corn picker was far from perfect, however [and not widely available].[3] Next to the tractor, it was the most complicated piece of machinery on the farm, and there was a lot of work involved in setting it up and operating it both properly and safely. Ray Gribben of Dallas County documented in his diary the amount of work required to prepare the corn picker for operations, as well as the frequency of its problems and his accompanying exasperation. In 1947, he spent half a day just searching for his operator's manual, plus a full day to get the machine in operating order. He began mounting the picker on the tractor on November 3, borrowed a chain hoist on November 4 to get the large sections mounted, and finished mounting the machine on November 6. When the machine was in position on the tractor, Gribben found that some of the husking rolls (that removed husks from the harvested ears) did not work. In Gribben's words, these parts would "take a long time to adjust." Getting a corn picker ready for the field was a process that could take hours, or even days; it was much more complicated and time-consuming than the old work of mounting the bangboard on the wagon and hitching the team of horses[4] (see Photo 8.1).

As farmers grappled with the annual headaches of the corn harvest, they confronted a new and enviable problem, the increase in corn yields. The combination of using hybrid seed corn and applying larger amounts of commercial fertilizer resulted in higher yields per acre. The trend began in the late 1930s and continued during the war years. Corn yields did not increase dramatically each year, but with a slow and steady rate they grew higher in the 1940s and early 1950s than they had been for most of Iowa's

Photo 8.1 Farmer operating a two-row corn picker, 4 December 1926. He is driving a Farmall Regular tractor, mounted with a McCormick-Deering corn picker, both products of the International Harvester Company. The farmer hitched a wooden wagon, with bangboards fixed atop the sides, to the back of the tractor to catch the picked ears. When the wagon filled, a team of horses or another tractor would haul it out of the field. The spacing of the stalks of corn warrants attention because of the spacing between the stalks. This allowed farmers to cultivate along and across the rows. After harvest, farmers turned hogs or cattle into the fenced fields to eat the stalks and nubbins and fertilize the soil as they foraged.

Source: Wisconsin Historical Society, WHS 23649

history. Farmers of the 1920s expected yields from the upper thirties to the low forties [in bushels per acre], while yields in the 1930s varied widely from lows of twenty-eight to thirty bushels per acre during the drought years of 1934 and 1936 to highs in the low fifties in 1939 and 1940. With favorable weather conditions, farmers confronted improved yields and a storage problem that their parents in their wildest dreams would never have anticipated.[5]

When [World War II] ended, it became possible again for farmers to consider building new cribs, in large part because of federal farm policy. In 1942 Congress guaranteed supported prices for many commodities and passed the Steagall Amendment, which provided for the continuation of price supports at wartime levels for two years after the war. This promise gave farmers a degree of security they had never experienced before. Congress extended the provisions of the Steagall Amendment well into the 1950s, thus guaranteeing a degree of predictability in income that allowed farmers to invest in their farmsteads.

In the 1940s and 1950s many Iowa farmers were willing to purchase new corn-storage buildings, and the corncrib-and-granary combination was the ideal. The center driveway ran from gable end to gable end, with rooms on either side of the drive for storage of ear corn and shelled corn. The new cribs, however, differed in two major respects. First, the floor plan of new cribs was often larger than the cribs constructed during the "golden age" of farming from 1900 through the 1910s. (See Photo 8.2.) Modern cribs also included more overhead grain storage, which meant they were often taller than the older cribs. As a writer for *Wallace's Farmer* noted in 1948, there were few "modern" corncribs in the state. The center driveways of the older corncribs were designed for horses and wagons, not trucks. With a few modifications to accommodate tractors and trucks, the old-style crib could be modernized (Photo 8.3).[6]

Farmers who were open to new ideas about what constituted a good permanent crib [and who could afford the investment] could try styles designed by agricultural experts from the private sector or the land-grant colleges. The Quonset building associated with the military during World War II became a feature on many Iowa farms and was used for a variety of purposes, including storage for equipment and grain. In 1952 W. R. Mitchell of Grundy County constructed a Quonset as a granary, complete with a force-air drying system. . . . These cribs [for ear corn] did not become popular, however. The timing of the new buildings coincided with the rise in harvesting shelled corn.[7]

For all the flurry of construction of new and temporary cribs during the 1940s and 1950s, few farmers considered the implications of the new harvesting machines on the market in those years (Photo 8.4). The problem, according to one writer for *Wallace's Farmer* in 1954, was that the old-style crib was not necessarily the best thing for the future. He asked farmers if the old-style crib "will fit your corn harvesting methods and corn storage needs in the 1960s and 70s." By the mid-1950s, farmers had more choices in harvest technology. The picker-sheller was simply a corn picker with a shelling unit attached, but the combine for corn was something new. John Deere introduced the first self-propelled combine adapted for corn in 1955. The combine with corn-harvesting attachment (called the head) enabled farmers to harvest only the corn kernels and leave the cobs in the field.[8]

Photo 8.2 A double corncrib-granary (left), constructed during the "golden age" of agriculture, when farmer income exceeded the cost of production. The Buckley family, near Lowell, Indiana, invested their hard-earned profits into the crib-granary and new dairy barn in 1916. Horse-drawn wagons entered one end of the crib-granary and dumped their loads of ear corn (or grain) into a trough in the floor. The Meyer Elevator system moved ear corn and grain into storage areas, ear corn to the cribs on both sides of the drive-through and grains to the upper story. The closed cupola above the peak of the roof accommodated the conveyor mechanism. Chutes in the floor of the granary reversed the flow when it came time to sell or feed the grains. The Buckley family stored farm machinery and equipment in the sheds attached to the cribs. Location: Buckley Homestead State Park, Lake County Park District, Lowell, Indiana.

Source: Photograph by Debra A. Reid

Farmers who used picker-shellers could expect several advantages over those who used mechanical corn pickers. One of the most important changes was the timing of the harvest. Farmers with picker-shellers could harvest earlier in the season when the corn in the field had a higher moisture content. Harvesting high-moisture corn allowed them to harvest more of the crop. As corn dried in the field, the ears were more likely to drop to the ground beyond the reach of mechanical pickers. The problem of ear drop became a much bigger issue in the 1940s and 1950s as farmers contended with infestations of the European corn borer, which weakened both the stalk itself and the ear shanks holding the ear to the stalk. The longer the corn stayed in the field, the greater the risk that high winds could knock the stalks over or force ears to drop, especially in infested fields. Harvesting

Photo 8.3 Corn crib on farm of G. H. West, an owner-operator near Estherville, Iowa (Emmet County). The implements around the crib indicated the investments that farmers made in tools needed to do specific jobs, from tractors to wagons to corn pickers, elevators, and frames to lift and dump wagons. Equipment from left to right: a wooden dump-wagon in a frame constructed to lift the wagon to dump the load into the trough on the elevator; the elevator situated to dump corn into the cupola at the top of the roof peak, apparently powered by a drive shaft (not visible but covered by a wooden box running between the base of the elevator and the corn crib; another wooden wagon with barge boards, ready for the corn harvest; a single-row corn picker-husker with corn spout, powered by the power-take-off on the John Deere Model D tractor (built 1927–1939) parked at the entrance to the drive through. Farmer West hung shovels, manure forks, scythes, and other tools on the walls of the corn crib. An extension rim that Farmer West would bolt to the side of the wheel to give the tractor more traction when pulling a heavy load (like a corn picker) leans against the fence. A hog in a pen with woven wire fencing, and fuel cans complete the essential elements of a Corn-Belt farm.

Photograph by Russell Lee (1903-1986), Farm Security Administration, December 1936. LC-USF34-010114-D [P&P] LOT 1155, Library of Congress, Washington, D.C.

Photo 8.4 A temporary crib for ear corn that used old telephone or telegraph poles for posts, woven wire for sides, and dimension lumber for the frame to stabilize the structure. The ears, exposed to the elements, deteriorated more rapidly than ears stored in a crib, but the proximity to feedlots provided an advantage to farmers, particularly during bad winters.

Source: Courtesy of Ag Illustrated

machines also created their own losses. Pickers inadvertently shelled some of the kernels off the ear as it moved through the machine and into the wagon that trailed the picker. This problem was worse in dry conditions. Harvesting corn early at high moisture content with a picker-sheller allowed farmers to get more of the crop from the field to the crib.

Purchasing a picker-sheller made financial sense for farmers who wanted to get the most out of their harvest or who harvested many acres of corn. Harold Folkerts of Butler County invested both in a picker-sheller and in drying facilities because his corn yields were so high he would otherwise have had to build new expensive corncribs. Folkerts reasoned that the investment in a new machine would actually save money, since the cost of the picker-sheller and dryer was less than the cost of cribs. Iowa State engineers reached the same conclusion the following year when they recommended that farmers who harvested more than 125 acres of corn could use a picker-sheller for less expense than mechanical picking and storing ear corn. Howard Sparks of Story County was in an ideal situation for converting to a picker-sheller in the early 1950s. He needed to replace a worn-out picker, and his landlord invested in storage bins for shelled corn. Sparks claimed that the harvest was easier and allowed him to reduce harvest losses.[9]

Moving shelled corn rather than ear corn meant there was much less bulk to haul and fewer trips from the field to the storage building, a major advantage during a period of scarce labor (Photo 8.5). It was easier to utilize family labor or part-time help rather than rely on a hired man to do the hauling. Fewer trips also meant less fuel consumption. Iowa State extension specialists calculated that it cost farmers $0.25 per bushel to transport shelled corn compared to $0.32 for ear corn. This savings might seem small, but it becomes significant when multiplied by thousands of bushels. A farmer who harvested 60 acres of corn at fifty bushels to the acre in 1962 might believe that $210.00 of savings was enough to warrant investing in new corn-harvesting technology, but a farmer with 200 acres of corn at fifty bushels to the acre could save approximately $700, roughly 10 percent of the purchase price of a new combine suited for corn harvesting.[10]

The development of the combine to harvest corn in addition to small grains and soybeans was another tool to minimize harvest losses and to harvest earlier. In 1950 agricultural engineers worked to develop the corn head to mount on a self-propelled combine. In 1955 John Deere Company introduced the first corn head on the market, the Number 10. The new corn head could be mounted on self-propelled combines in place of the attachment head for cutting small grains or other seed crops such as soybeans. "Corn combining is here—and here to stay," boasted John Deere advertisers in the summer of 1956. According to the company, farmers who used combines cut their shelled-corn loss by 75 percent and ear-corn loss by 50 percent compared to mechanical pickers."[11]

Harvesting shelled corn also cut costs after the harvest, too, since it was no longer necessary to hire custom shellers to visit their farms periodically and shell the ear corn. Shelling and grinding corn was the best way to prepare it for feeding, since livestock utilized more of the nutritional value of the grain when it was cracked. Shelling was not normally considered a direct cost of harvesting, since farm families incurred shelling costs

Photo 8.5 The photographer composed this photograph to make overt the potential of shelled corn for hog farmers. The picker-sheller, farm trucks, and pigs at the self-feeders all in the frame simultaneously conveyed the utility of a picker-sheller to a feeder-pig operation. Shelled corn went directly from stalk to truck bed to storage bin, ready for grinding into hog feed to feed the self-feeders in the feed lot.

Courtesy of Ag Illustrated

over the course of the year as they depleted feed stocks. It was, however, an avoidable indirect cost that was no longer necessary if farmers harvested shelled corn.

For all the advantages and promotion of picker-shellers and combines, farmers did not rush to adopt this new technology in the second half of the 1950s and the early 1960s. Most farmers simply did not have the number of acres to justify purchasing a combine unless they planned to do extensive custom harvesting. Two Grundy County farmers interviewed at the Farm Progress Show in 1959 estimated that a farmer would "need about 300 acres [of corn] to justify owning one." That same year agricultural engineers estimated an acreage threshold for combine ownership of 200 acres, which suited the needs of only a small minority of Iowa farmers. The discrepancy between the perception of the two men at the Farm Progress Show and the carefully calculated figure of extension experts reveals the gulf between the majority of farmers who could not envision a profitable use for a combine and the minority who could afford to study the acreage threshold. As expected, farmers with large acreages were often the first to purchase combines. Clarence and Lester Wolken of Marshall County began using a combine in the late 1950s to harvest 150 acres of corn. A survey conducted in 1965 indicated that approximately one-third of farmers like the Wolkens, who planted 150 acres or more of corn, would harvest at least part of their crop with a hired or purchased combine. By contrast, only 10 percent of farmers with less than 150 acres of corn that year planned to harvest shelled corn. Most farmers agreed with the Grundy County farmers at the Farm Progress Show—that combine harvesting was impressive but was also someone else's business.[12]

High costs accounted for part of farmers' initial reluctance to purchase combines. Joseph Ludwig's farm records indicate the high capital requirements of making the transition from mechanical corn picker to combine. Ludwig purchased two new corn pickers in the years after World War II, the first in 1946 and the second in 1955. These machines cost $943.23 and $1,300, respectively, making them some of the most expensive machines Ludwig ever purchased for his farm. In 1966, however, he invested $8,600 in his first self-propelled combine for harvesting corn, small grains, and soybeans. While this machine was capable of harvesting a greater variety of crops than his older corn pickers, the expense was more than the cost of a new corn picker and a new small-grain combine put together at 1966 prices. Ludwig's new 1966 machine had more capacity than either a corn picker or a tractor-drawn combine, but it was still a sizable investment when compared to the older technology. . . . Iowa State economists estimated that repairs and depreciation costs totaled approximately 14 percent of the original cost of the machine. Calculated this way, Ludwig's $8,600 combine was actually a $9,804 investment, excluding interest.[13]

The most significant obstacle to harvesting shelled corn with combines or picker-shellers was the problem of how to store the shelled corn. The majority of farmers were equipped to store ear corn, not shelled corn. The writer for *Wallace's Farmer* who asked farmers in 1954 if the old-style crib "will fit your corn harvesting methods and corn storage needs in the 1960s and 70s" addressed an important issue. While the capital outlay for new harvesting equipment was high, it was compounded by the fact that farmers who harvested shelled corn needed expensive new storage buildings and special drying equipment. In the early 1960s new drive-through-style cribs cost as much as $1.25 per bushel [capacity], and metal bins cost approximately $0.35 per bushel. The Gerlach family of Story County built an old-style crib in 1956 but converted it to shelled-corn storage just three years later. As Ralph Gerlach explained, "We had no idea when we built it to hold ear corn that we would switch to using a picker-sheller so soon." Most farmers were trapped with buildings designed for an earlier era. According to Ken Smalley of Johnson County, "farmers already had these cribs and they felt like they had to use them." So farmers continued to use the harvesting machines that matched their infrastructure.[14]

Remodeling old corncribs was one of the most attractive ways to obtain storage for shelled corn throughout the 1950s and 1960s. . . . Harry Wassenaar of Jasper County explained, "Converting our old crib was the cheapest way" to get more storage and convert to harvesting shelled corn. Delmar Van Horn of Greene County was one of the first of many farmers featured in *Wallace's Farmer* who remodeled cribs. Van Horn claimed that he spent $470 in materials to convert his entire four-thousand-bushel ear-corn crib to a building that would store eight thousand bushels of shelled corn. The total cost for new construction, including labor, was approximately twenty-five cents per bushel [capacity]. Clarence Wolken and his son Lester of Marshall County converted a crib in 1958 for approximately seven cents per bushel, by using salvaged lumber and their own labor. In 1959 they hoped to remodel another crib for five cents per bushel for materials. Without salvaged lumber, farmers could expect to spend approximately fifteen cents per bushel for supplies. As long as the labor costs did not exceed ten cents per bushel, remodeling was cheaper than new construction. These kinds of savings made the transition to shelled-corn storage affordable for many farmers.[15]

Modifications of older cribs and farm buildings minimized farmers' expenses, but new grain-storage buildings such as grain bins also became common on farms as more farmers harvested shelled corn. Steel grain bins were distinctive buildings, characterized by their cylindrical shape, conical roof, and corrugated steel siding. Bins adapted for drying often had perforated floors to allow heated air to be forced up through the grain. Unlike corncribs, there was never any intention of holding ear corn in these new-style bins or segregated spaces for ear, shelled, or cracked corn. They were strictly for shelled corn, grain, or soybeans. Although grain bins were on the market in the early 1900s, few farmers had invested in them at that time because most corncribs or granaries included enough capacity for as much grain as farmers produced in the era of mixed farming and corn picking by hand.

Grain bins were structures for industrial agriculture, just as combines were machines for industrial farming. The largest and most highly mechanized farms were the most likely sites for the new grain bins. A 1956 advertisement for the Behlen Manufacturing Company for cribs, bins, and dryers indicated the size of operation in which grain bins could be most successfully utilized. The advertisement featured Cedar County farmer Carl Levsen and his three adult sons who farmed 700 acres, of which they planted 250 acres in corn. They installed eight grain bins with a total capacity of twenty-five thousand bushels and owned seven more thirty-two-hundred-bushel bins that they had not yet assembled. According to the advertisements, Levsen emphasized cutting operating costs and marketing quality products. "We call it industrialization," Levsen and the advertisement copywriters proclaimed, suggesting that contemporary farm operators would have to borrow from the world of business management to survive. The Behlen Company emphasized the role that grain storage could play in industrializing agriculture, and in changing the landscape of the farmstead.[16]

The development that allowed farmers to harvest and store shelled corn was the crop dryer. Farmers who harvested corn at 25–30 percent moisture content needed to reduce the moisture to 13 percent in order to prevent grain from rotting in storage. Drying corn had not been such a problem when farmers harvested corn by hand over the course of weeks, even months. In the 1940s and early 1950s, farmers' desire to get corn out of fields infested by the European corn borer before ears dropped meant they harvested wet corn. Farmers who tried to store wet ear corn experimented with dryers to solve these problems. As soon as farmers used picker-shellers and combines to speed the harvest, drying corn became a necessity. Ray Hayes of Crawford County summed up this viewpoint in 1958, "I picked [ear] corn early last year and dried it. I liked the results," he stated. "Now I'm looking forward to a picker-sheller."[17]

Throughout the 1950s, farmers boasted of the benefits of early picking and drying the crop with portable units called batch dryers. Just before picking season in 1954, a farmer warned that those who did not pick corn early were "likely to have trouble" with dropped ears because of severe European corn borer infestations. Walter Cramer of Wright County used a batch dryer to dry shelled corn before storing it. He harvested with a picker-sheller when his corn tested at 28 percent moisture and then dried "batches of 335 bushels of grain at a time." Merrit Wassom of Sac County declared that his harvest losses were so low after picking early and drying that "There wasn't enough corn left in the field to keep a goose alive.". . . Warm weather in March and April of 1958 and the onset of mold growth in cribs and bins was powerful evidence that renting or purchasing a dryer was necessary to save stored corn.[18]

A new innovation called the continuous-flow dryer was even faster than the batch dryer. This was a portable dryer that continuously moved the grain in the dryer, drying faster than the batch dryer, which simply held the corn in a chamber. . . . This type of dryer was expensive and best suited to farmers who harvested large amounts of shelled corn, since they could keep the combines running without having to wait for a batch to be removed from the dryer. Experts suggested that farmers who harvested more than thirty thousand bushels per year could best utilize this system.[19]

The variety of new techniques, machines, and structures made grain storage and drying more complicated over the course of the 1960s. Just as farmers who dealt with herbicide and insecticide faced an ever more complicated array of products, combinations of products, and restrictions on the use of products, farmers who used dryers found that corn drying also required careful management. They hoped to prevent problems associated with under-drying and over-drying. Mold was the obvious problem with wet corn, but overheating or heating too quickly resulted in cracked grain, which also allowed mold to grow. Corn that was to be sold in the fall needed to be dried to only 15 percent moisture while corn to be stored for a year needed to be 13 percent. Sometimes drying was uneven, which meant that some of the corn might stay too moist and spoil.[20]

Farmers took the initiative in addressing the problem of uneven moisture content in their new-style bins designed for drying. In 1962 Eugene Sukup of Franklin County bought his first grain bin to dry and store shelled corn. He was not satisfied with the results. Sukup found that pockets of grain did not dry properly and were ruined. He designed a system to break up those pockets of grain that were not drying properly using an old coal-stoker auger from a furnace mounted in an electric drill suspended from a chain at the top of the bin. The drill stirred the grain and broke up any pockets that were too moist. Sukup filed for a patent and began to sell his "Easy Stir Auger" to implement dealers and farm-equipment companies. . . . Tests by Iowa State agricultural engineers confirmed what farmers already knew or suspected—that stirring was a fast and effective way to store the highest-quality grain.[21]

Government programs helped farmers change their harvesting and storage practice by providing loans to farmers who stored grain as well as to those who wanted to build storage facilities. Many farmers participated in the Commodity Credit Corporation (CCC) program, which loaned farmers money to keep their crops on the farm until prices rose. The CCC, an agency of the USDA, allowed farmers the option of storing corn in bins or cribs at a low fee in exchange for government loans. A government inspector measured the storage area to determine storage capacity and then sealed the stored crop with a paper label across the door to prevent tampering. If prices advanced above the loan rate, farmers could sell their crop and keep the difference between the two prices. If prices failed to rise above the loan rate, farmers forfeited their crop to the U.S. government and kept the loan payment. Officials from the Production and Marketing Administration (which replaced the Agricultural Adjustment Administration during the Truman administration) provided an incentive for farmers to reseal their corn in on-farm storage. They provided a payment of thirteen cents per bushel for resealing corn in 1953, with fifteen cents per bushel in 1955, figures that amounted to almost half the costs of constructing new grain bins. By the early 1950s, one-fourth of all Iowa farmers wanted to build or buy new corn-storage space, with another 7 percent willing to settle for temporary cribs. Those farmers who planned to build new storage space had a special incentive to construct modern storage facilities that included grain dryers.[22]

Corncribs or bins for drying could be constructed with loans from the Agricultural Stabilization and Conservation Service, with a loan amount of up to 80 percent of the cost of construction. These programs continued into the 1960s. In 1965 construction loans for bins were available at 4 percent interest for five years, with a one-year grace period before the loan was classified as delinquent. The government even sold surplus CCC-owned grain bins to farmers. . . . Rules for the 1967 and 1968 programs allowed individual farmers to borrow up to twenty-five thousand dollars to construct storage and drying facilities, although loans of over ten thousand dollars required a real-estate mortgage. Joseph Ludwig of Winneshiek County utilized this program to help him finance new bin construction in the late 1960s.[23]

Combines, drying equipment, and structures for shelled-corn storage were much more expensive than pickers and cribs, but more farmers were using the combine on more acres by the early 1970s. The claims made for the big combines by promoters and farmers were true. Farmers could harvest earlier to minimize losses in the field, a critical consideration when they spent increasing sums of money on the chemical cocktail of fertilizer, herbicide, and insecticide. They invested their labor and the costs of fuel, machinery, and seed to get their most important crop in the ground and then helped the crop reach maturity by applying chemical fertilizer and pesticides. A growing number of farmers viewed high harvest costs as necessary to justify the other expenses of making a crop. They needed to reduce harvest losses, to harvest early, and to do so with the least amount of labor, which made increased investment a strategy to minimize risk.

Notes

1. Carl Hamilton, *In No Time at All* (Ames: Iowa State University Press, 1974), 78–84.

2. Hamilton, 82–83. *Wallace's Farmer* articles Beth Wilcoxson, "We'll Take Machines," 20 October 1956, quote 65, and "Thru Picking by Thanksgiving?" 16 November 1946.

3. Allan G. Bogue, "Changes in Mechanical and Plant Technology: The Corn Belt, 1910–1940," *Journal of Economic History* 43 (March 1983): 1–25; Thomas Burnell Colbert, "Iowa Farmers and Mechanical Corn Pickers, 1900–1952," *Agricultural History*, 74 (Spring 2000), 531; M.N. Beeler, "What Users Say about Their Corn Pickers," *Farm Implement News*, 21 September 1939, quote 32; Sid Dix, "The Arrival of the Corn Picker," *Farm Implement News*, 7 January 1943 (cartoon).

4. Ray L. Gribben Diary, State Historical Society of Iowa, Iowa City, 3, 4, and 6 November 1948.

5. Annual corn yields are included in the annual and later biennial editions of the *Iowa Year Book of Agriculture* and are also accessible on the website https://www.nass.usda.gov/Statistics_by_State/Iowa/ (accessed 4 June 2016).

6. "How Many Buildings Are Modern?" *Wallace's Farmer*, 7 August 1948.

7. For changes in corn-crib construction, see J.L. Anderson, *Industrializing the Corn Belt: Agriculture, Technology, and Environment, 1945–1972* (DeKalb, IL: Northern Illinois University Press, 2009), 172–75; 218n8–n12 and 219n13.

8. "When You Build Corn Storage," *Wallace's Farmer*, 17 July 1954.

9. "What They Say on Picker-Shellers," *Wallace's Farmer*, 5 September 1953, quote 24; Floyd L. Herum and Kenneth K. Barnes, "What's the Best Way to Harvest Corn?" *Iowa Farm Science*, 9 (July 1954), quote; Sherwood Searle and Vernon Schneider, "Here's Why We Like Field Shelling," *Successful Farming* (October 1953), quote 46. See also C.H. Van Vlack and Hobart Beresford, "The Picker-Sheller: Its Advantages and Disadvantages," *Iowa Farm Science* 8 (July 1953).

10. "How Will You Harvest Corn?" *Wallace's Farmer*, 15 September 1962.

11. The following articles from *Agricultural Engineering* describe the technical development of the corn head: L. W. Hurlbut, "More Efficient Corn Harvesting," "Laboratory Studies of Corn Combining," C. S. Morrison, "Attachments for Combining Corn," all in *Agricultural Engineering*, 36 (December 1955). John Deere 45 Combine and Corn Attachment advertisement, *Wallace's Farmer*, 4 August 1956.

12. *Wallace's Farmer* articles "Pick Corn When You're Ready," 15 August 1959, quote 13; Jim Rutter, "Field Shell Your Corn?" 5 September 1959, "A Sign of the Times—Combining Corn,"

3 October 1964, quote 45a; and Norman West, "Which Way to Harvest Corn?" 14 August 1971, quote 97.

13. Joseph Ludwig Papers, Special Collections, Parks Library, Iowa State University, Ames, Iowa. [Anderson, 179]; Monte Sesker, "What It Costs to Own a Combine," *Wallace's Farmer*, 14 September 1968.

14. *Wallace's Farmer* articles "When You Build Corn Storage," 17 July 1954; Dick Hagen, "Remodeled Cribs Can Double Your Storage," 3 October 1959, quote 54–55; "Twice as Much Corn in the Crib," 1 October 1960, quote 47; Marsha and Ken Smalley, interview by author, 21 June 2004, Iowa City, Iowa, tape recording.

15. *Wallace's Farmer* articles "Converting Cribs to Shelled Corn Storage," 2 September 1961, quote 45; "Store Shelled Corn in Remodeled Cribs," 2 August 1958, quote 42–43; "Field Shell: Pick Corn When You're Ready," 15 August 1959, quote 13; and "Convert Corn Crib to Shelled Corn Bin?" 17 August 1963; Frank C. Beeson, "Lined Cribs Make Shelled-Corn Storage," *Successful Farming* (October 1959).

16. Behlen Manufacturing Company advertisement, *Wallace's Farmer*, 21 July 1956.

17. "Put Dry Corn in Your Cribs," *Wallace's Farmer*, 20 September 1958.

18. *Wallace's Farmer* articles Dave Bryant, "Harvest Corn Early!" 4 September 1954, quote; "Use Picker-Sheller and Dryer?" 17 September 1955; "Put Dry Corn in Your Cribs," 20 September 1958, quote; "Stop Wet Corn Spoilage Losses," 15 March 1958; and "Emergency Corn Drying," 5 April 1958. *Farmers' Manual of Crop Drying* (Agricultural Development Division of the Lennox Furnace Company, n.d.), Dale O. Hull Papers, Special Collections, Parks Library, Iowa State University, Ames, Iowa.

19. *Wallace's Farmer* articles "Timely Tips," 22 August 1970; Frank Holdmeyer, "Bin Dryers . . . Portable Batch . . . Continuous Flow," 12 August 1971; "Boosting Profits with High-Moisture Corn," *Pioneer Corn Service Bulletin* (n.d., circa 1965), 5; Hull Papers; Norman West, "Match Your Dryer System to Harvest Rate," *Wallace's Farmer*, 28 August 1971.

20. Monte Sesker, "Tips for Better Dryer Operation," *Wallace's Farmer*, 28 September 1968. A good example of the growing sophistication of grain storage and drying can be seen in *Planning Grain-Feed Handling for Livestock and Cash-Grain Farms, MWPS-13* (Ames, IA: Midwest Plan Service and Iowa State University, 1968), Records of the Midwest Plan Service.

21. Sukup advertisement, *Farm Industry News* (February 2003); "Stirring Devices Will Speed Grain Drying," *Wallace's Farmer*, 23 September 1967.

22. *Wallace's Farmer* articles "Many Will Get New Cribs, Bins," 1 August 1953; and "Need More Corn Storage," 6 August 1955.

23. "A Federal Loan Helped Build This," *Iowa Farm and Home Register*, 2 May 1954; *Wallace's Farmer* articles "To Make Loans on Grain Dryers," 5 November 1949; "Government Grain Bins for Sale," 6 February 1965; "Loans for Bins and Dryers," 26 August 1967; and "Low Cost Loans for Grain Storage," 28 July 1968.

CHAPTER 9

A CURATOR'S LEGACY

William S. Pretzer

NOTE: Bill Pretzer wrote this article as a tribute to his colleague Peter Cousins, and as a testimony to the art of collecting. Cousins applied a humanities-centric agenda to collecting technological innovation. This sort of proactive collecting philosophy contrasts with reactive collecting, which often occurs due to limited time, knowledge, or pressures from factors beyond anyone's control. Cousins came close to acting in desperation in his effort to secure one of two 1933 experimental machines, rather than the 1950 Ben Pearson Rust Cotton Picker, the thirty-fourth manufactured. Fate intervened when the Ben Pearson Company warehouse scrapped the two 1933 pickers that Cousins had considered early in his research quest. Only a herculean effort eventually got the object to The Henry Ford. This article tells an inspirational story, but an intimidating one, as well. Adopting the humanist agenda to collect and preserve agriculture takes effort, but with planning, patience, and timely action, some dreams will come true. The objects do not have to be as big as a cotton picker to warrant the effort. Significance and provenance should drive the collection plans.

The article was originally published in *History News*, 51, no. 2 (Spring 1996), 24–28. It appears here with permission from the American Association for State and Local History. This version preserves Pretzer's narrative but adds notes (compiled by Debra A. Reid) to help readers learn more about the published materials that Cousins collected, and to learn more about how others have interpreted the story of the inventors and the corporation that manufactured the cotton picker.

I WANT TO TELL you a story about three men and an artifact. The story says a lot, perhaps, about the meaning of objects and how they can connect us to each other. Maybe it's about why museum people care about objects.

The main characters in this story are an inventor, a man who bought and used his invention, and the curator who acquired it for a museum. The artifact is a mechanical cotton picker nicknamed "Grandma." The story spans decades, each chapter taking twenty to twenty-five years to unfold.

No one knows where and when Peter Cousin first came upon the story of John Rust and his mechanical wet-spindle cotton picker. Maybe he read it in his copy of James Street's 1957 book, *The New Revolution in the Cotton Economy*.[1] Maybe he encountered the story in one of the hundreds of other books that Peter kept in his museum office. Or perhaps he found it in one of the doubtless dozens of articles he read on his customary Friday "reading day" at the University of Michigan.

Whatever the inspiration, Peter Cousins, curator of agriculture at Henry Ford Museum and Greenfield Village (today, The Henry Ford), did not hesitate when the time came in 1975 to acquire key artifacts for interpreting twentieth-century American agriculture.

In July 1975, Peter wrote to the Ben Pearson Manufacturing Co. of Pine Bluff, Arkansas, asking for assistance in acquiring a revolutionary machine—a self-propelled, mechanical cotton picker. He knew that the Pearson Company was a pioneer manufacturer of cotton pickers and going directly to the original source was simply his curatorial instinct. Of course, he could have gone to International Harvester or John Deere, better known and more successful manufacturers of agricultural equipment. Both companies had experimented with barbed-spindle cotton pickers during World War II, but those were major corporations working with large research and development units in addition to national marketing and distribution systems. The Pearson Company produced a picker based on a different technology and with an unusual, but for Peter, a more meaningful lineage.

The Story of the Invention

Before World War II, the Pearson Company was known for archery equipment rather than for agricultural machinery. In 1949, it began manufacturing cotton pickers in an effort to diversify its manufacturing operations. The company did not, however, develop its own mechanical cotton picker. In April 1949, the company purchased the rights to the wet-spindle picker developed by John and Mack Rust. The Rust picker already had a long and highly publicized history.

Born in 1892, John D. Rust was the son of a small-scale cotton farmer in Texas.[2] Orphaned when he was sixteen, he worked for years picking cotton as a migrant farm worker. His brother, Mack, was just eight when their parents died and he, too, spent time as an itinerant worker. Together, the young men fantasized about inventing a machine that would relieve them and others of the backbreaking work of picking cotton by hand.

In 1924, with only some correspondence school training in automotive engineering and mechanical drawing, John Rust began to work in earnest on his cotton picking invention. Initially, he was frustrated by finding that he could use barbed spindles to remove cotton from the plant, but then could not efficiently remove the cotton from the spindle.

In 1927, he drew on his own boyhood memories as the inspiration for the most distinctive element of his picker: a wet spindle without barbs. Rust recalled how, when picking cotton wet from the morning dew, the cotton fibers would stick to his fingers. He later wrote: "I jumped out of bed, found some absorbent cotton and a nail for testing. I licked the nail and twirled it in the cotton and found, that it would work."[3] Later, he reaffirmed his intuition and experience when he recalled that his grandmother would wet the spindle on her spinning wheel in order to get the first strands of cotton to adhere.

He was able to attract only small investors and the support of his brother and sister in Weatherford, Texas, and it took Rust years to develop a fully manufacturable and marketable machine. He obtained his first patent in 1928. During 1930–1931 he lived in a cooperative community in Louisiana while developing "the first [machine], as far as I know, ever to harvest a bale of cotton in a day." By 1933, Rust had developed a machine that could pick five bales a day and had formed a corporation to produce the pickers (Photo 9.1).

Rust's machine worked, but acquiring the needed capital was not going to be easy. Farmers lacked either the resources to afford the machine or the trust that it would work in yearly operation. And no one, most particularly John and Mack Rust, was sanguine about the impact that the mechanization of cotton picking would have on the social structure of the South.

Rust recognized that the mechanization of cotton picking would not only relieve men and women of hard labor but would also result in the loss of their means of living. He knew this machine could drive hundreds of thousands of small farmers—men like

Photo 9.1 John (right) and Mack Rust stand next to a 1932 version of their wet-spindle cotton picker. From *A Pictorial History of the Development of the Ben Pearson Rust Cotton Picker*, Pine Bluff, Arkansas, c. 1963.

Source: From the collections of The Henry Ford Museum, Dearborn, Michigan

his own father—from their farms. It would destroy the livelihoods of millions of migrant farm workers.[4]

In a *Business Week* article about the Rust picker (September 5, 1936), it was estimated that seven of the nine million workers in the cotton-producing states would be unemployed. *Time* magazine (March 23, 1936) quotes John Rust as saying: "Thrown on the market in the manner of past inventions, it would mean, in the share-cropped country, that 75 percent of the population would be thrown out of employment. We are not willing that this should happen."

So he and Mack set about trying to envision alternative futures. They proposed leasing—not selling—his invention only to farmers who promised to maintain minimum wages, abolish child labor, and accept agricultural labor unions. He and Mack agreed that their wages as owners of the manufacturing company would never exceed ten times the wages of their lowest paid employees. They went so far as to establish a nonprofit foundation that owned the patent rights and would channel profits from the invention into providing relief and educational funds for displaced workers. John Rust considered himself a socialist and was intent on having his invention benefit, not harm, the largest number of people possible.

All of this planning was for naught, however. After working twenty-five years, Rust still had not secured enough capital to mass-produce his machine. In 1949, the Pearson Company stepped in.[5]

The Story of the Curator

No wonder Peter—who campaigned fiercely for liberal Democrats—was enthralled with this story! Scholars already knew its basic contours. Peter wanted to bring it to a wider public in order to ponder its implications: Why don't more inventors consider all the effects of their inventions?

Having done his homework, Peter addressed a 1975 letter to the president of the Pearson Company, Gerry D. Powell. Within a week of receiving Peter's letter, Powell fired off a note to an agricultural equipment representative in Fresno, California: "Note attached letter—thinking of your friend and his 1950 model, reckon he'd want to see it put in a museum?"

Within a couple of weeks, Peter received a letter from Powell noting that they had two experimental machines built by John Rust in 1933. He also got a letter from Allan Jones, a cotton farmer in Porterville, California, who owned the thirty-fourth Rust cotton picker produced by the Pearson Company in 1950, the first year of production. Jones was retiring the machine after twenty-six picking seasons. A few phone calls and a letter or two later, an antique agricultural equipment appraiser recommended by Peter was traveling from Kansas to California to appraise the cotton picker (Photo 9.2).

Negotiations moved along, but Jones decided that tax implications would not allow him to finalize the donation. The donor of an International Harvester cotton picker to the Smithsonian Institution was claiming a $250,000 deduction and a lawsuit was brewing between the IRS and the donor. Since Jones's machine was the only one left from that initial year's production, he valued it at $500,000 and wanted assurances that he could

Photo 9.2 Farmer Allan Jones posed with his Rust cotton picker in about 1975, the year he retired it from active service.

Source: From the collections of The Henry Ford, Dearborn, Michigan

Photo 9.3 Peter Cousins climbs onto "Grandma" in early 1995.

Source: From the collections of The Henry Ford, Dearborn, Michigan.

deduct that amount as a charitable donation. Peter was called as an expert witness in the Smithsonian matter, but he could not guarantee Jones his deduction.

In late October 1975, Allan Jones's wife, Fannie, passed away and inheriting her estate only increased his tax concerns. In addition, his very personal loss made him reluctant to part with any more of his past. He never signed the museum acquisition form and asked that no further action be taken about his initial offer. Here the matter was to rest for years.

Peter was patient but not passive. He continued his research, corresponding with the president of the John Rust Foundation and the director of the West Tennessee Historical Society. On that oily photocopy paper common in the 1970s, he preserved dozens of articles and essays, ranging in date from 1933 to 1975, from sources such as *The Southern Workman, Agricultural Engineering, Business Week, Survey Graphic, Fortune, Reader's Digest, Time, Harper's*, and the *West Tennessee Historical Papers*.[6]

In 1979 Peter attempted to borrow the picker for a special display. Jones was amenable as long as the museum made all the arrangements and paid all the bills. If only he could get it to Michigan, surely Jones would not want to go to the trouble of taking it back, reasoned Peter. A memo to Peter from the museum registrar, Robert Springer, speaks volumes about a museum's culture of camaraderie amidst challenge.

Re: Your mechanical zoo piece. I had the pleasure of speaking with "Harvey" of Diamond Transportation Systems today. He gave me a figure based on the cotton picker being of legal height and width and less than 30,000 lbs. . . . $3,000—Wow! Maybe you should have Randy [Mason, curator of transportation] try his hand at cross-country cotton-picker road rallying!

The picker did not leave California that year. The opportunity to include the Rust picker in the renovation of the agricultural exhibits had passed, so had the bicentennial, and the 1979 special display. Peter was frustrated but moved on to other things.

He moved on particularly to the creation of the Firestone Farm in Greenfield Village. This was to become a working twelve-acre farm with the original 1880s house and barn from Columbiana County, Ohio, where tire magnate and Ford-confidant Harvey Firestone was born. Peter led the acquisition process, the research, the siting and construction, the acquisition of equipment and livestock, and finally, the creation of programs, activities, and a continuing staff commitment to authenticity, accuracy, and the power of living history.

In 1985, Peter, and a few colleagues he preferred to call friends, brought to life a living historical farm. As he had anticipated years before, that farm "disarms even the most astute viewer into relaxing his critical faculties and believing for the moment that he is experiencing the past as it actually was."

Then, in September 1991, Allan Jones suddenly called Peter. He wanted to discuss the museum's interest in the cotton picker he called "Grandma." You bet Peter was interested! He was also more than a bit wary. He talked to the museum's Collection Committee about pursuing such an old idea. He traded phone calls with Jones at all hours of the day and night, as often at home as at the office.

Another year passed. Jones, retired and getting on in years, was no longer so concerned about the tax implications. He was concerned that the human side of the story, how peoples' lives were changed by the cotton picker, would be lost if no one preserved the artifact and captured the stories. Peter assured him that the museum was "most interested in finding a way to capture and preserve the stories of peoples' lives associated with the history of cotton production in California."

Then came the letter.

March 26, 1993

Dear Mr. Cousins:

Thank you for having the patience and concern to help me to decide, and to have the patience to wait until the time seemed right to give "Grandma" the credit she deserves in history. The Lord can be thanked for giving me two talented children, Ruby A. Cuevas and James E. Jones, and time for them to grow up and help me put the items together that I'm donating to the museum.

Sincerely,

Allan Jones

P.S.—The coffee will be hot when you arrive. O.K.

Letter in hand, Peter wrote an atypically long, five-page memo to the Collections Committee detailing the history of negotiations and providing a succinct but passionate history of the Rusts' invention. Drawing on details from the original sources in his office, he reconstructed the biography of John Rust, "unusual as an inventor who feared his invention" and offered "the richness of the stories" as his rationale for acquiring the artifact.

He received approval to acquire the machine and the funds to go to California to interview the donor. By this time, however, Peter had been diagnosed with lung cancer. His doctors forbade him to travel. Between bouts of radiation and chemotherapy, he simply didn't have the energy to fly to California.

He did write a letter to Gerry Powell at Ben Pearson inquiring about the two 1933 experimental pickers. Powell's anguished response nearly broke Peter's heart. After sitting in the storage yard for more than forty years, the machines had been sold for scrap less than a month earlier!

So, Peter began digging deeper into the story of "Grandma." If the Rusts had not been able to influence the future of the Southern Cotton Belt in the 1930s, what had in fact happened when their mechanical cotton picker was introduced in California in the 1950s? Jones sent videotapes of family activities and copies of his stepdaughter's school papers on the family's history and the history of cotton growing in California. Peter listened to him discuss his new interest, the health and economic benefits of growing black-eyed peas. Slowly, Peter recognized that donating "Grandma" was just part of a larger story that Jones had to tell. Peter listened.

The Story of the Invention's User

Jones was his own historian, interpreting California's transformation in the twentieth century. With his teenaged stepdaughter, Ruby A. Cuevas, he gathered together his own reminiscences and interviews with others to document the history of cotton production, especially the role of the Rust picker in mechanizing the cotton fields. He attributed the exponential growth of California's cotton industry in the 1930s and 1940s to the many migrants who came from cotton-growing regions and naturally carried their traditions with them. It was a theme in agricultural history that resonated with Peter's earlier publications, including *Hog Plow and Sith: Cultural Aspects of Early Agricultural Technology.*[7]

Jones had been born on a chicken ranch in California in 1919. His own parents had been migrants from Missouri. He was old enough to remember the Dust Bowl of the 1930s and proud to say that he was already in California to watch the influx:

> The migrants came here, they adapted, sang their cowboy music, and they had a language of their own. These people survived, but in a different state. They became known as "Okies," "Texans," and "Arkies."

He attributed the strength of California's people to their diverse backgrounds:

> Today, second and third generations live here in the San Joaquin Valley; they are the backbone of America—they weathered the storm. They knew tough times, they raised tough children, and they knew how to survive.

Jones acknowledged just how much he owed to the migrants.

> I learned "Country Music" from the migrants. I quickly learned cowboy songs on the harmonica and guitar. The vegetable varieties in our garden increased, blackeye peas, mulagan stew, succatash, and many different ways to serve them.
>
> They proved this to me, "If you are willing, there is a way," and in spite of all their misfortunes they succeeded.
>
> As final proof that my life definitely changed, I married a migrant from Oklahoma in 1937, married a migrant from Texas in 1940, and married again in 1976 to my present wife—a migrant from Mexico.

Like John Rust, who studied the history of cotton production and wanted to shape its future, Allan Jones understood the history of his people and wanted to influence their future by acknowledging their past. He was also quite ill himself and desperately wanted to speak face-to-face with Peter, the man to whom he was entrusting his legacy.

In March 1995, Peter ignored his doctors and summoned enough strength to fly to Fresno and then drive to Porterville, tape recorder in hand. He stayed in the small trailer next to the Jones's farmhouse and sat for hours in the kitchen, drinking hot coffee, listening to reminiscences of cotton growers, gin operators, and equipment dealers.

He heard how Jones and other growers suffered from a lack of hand labor during World War II and had to employ German POWs to pick cotton. He learned how Jones vowed to buy the first available cotton picker after a late picking in 1948 drove his prices down.

He heard how the farmers from miles around, most of them friends, gathered at Jones's farm in 1950 to see the first demonstration. And how they all left, embarrassed for their friend, when the machine tore up a whole row of cotton plants.

He recorded the machinery dealer's description of how Jones's experience led him to make several improvements adopted by the Pearson Company: an override clutch, double instead of single sprocket chains, dry graphite rather than oil for lubrication. The dealer even acknowledged that the company manufactured pickers with a stripper bar (to remove cotton from the spindles) that Jones designed. This documented a modern example of "bottom up" evolutionary technological change that Peter had written about earlier in his career.

Ever the historian looking for how people coped with change, Peter was sensitive to stories of Americans who were skeptical of "progress" and new technology. He pointedly asked one farmer to repeat the story of how farm workers, fearful for their jobs, drove iron stakes into the ground in fields where the mechanical pickers were first used. There wasn't an era or movement of American Luddites, or machine breakers, but Peter was capturing one more example of machine breaking in America.

Peter was tickled to read that Kirkpatrick Sale mentions the Rusts, but not the spindle-smashing iron stakes, in his book, *Rebels against the Future*. And he ruefully agreed with Sales's conclusion that "the spindle-picker was in the saddle, riding even its inventor."[8]

Peter heard the farmers and gin operators confirm that the Rust picker produced cleaner, finer cotton than did competing machines using barbed spindles. He also learned that farmers had to spray defoliants to remove leaves from plants before using the barbed-spindle machines. The Rust machine, they said, required no such environmentally threatening measures. If the defoliants are banned, the Rust wet-spindle picker may make a comeback.

So why hadn't the Rust machine been more popular in California? It was an accident of history. In 1951 a tractor-trailer rig filled with fuel plowed into the Pearson warehouse, destroying it and all the replacement parts in a memorable conflagration. For several years, the company could not readily sell or service machines in the region. The market was soon dominated by International Harvester and John Deere. All of Jones's friends agreed that the Rust picker would have been preferred had the warehouse not burned.

A Story Preserved

Peter had begun twenty years earlier with the story of John Rust and his cotton picker. The socialist inventor born in 1892, the family farmer born in 1919, and the museum curator born in 1941 all shared an interest in how people's lives were changed by the mechanical cotton picker. Around "Grandma," Peter was assembling a narrative that moved far beyond the confines of the artifact.

Maybe that's it. Maybe this is about how a curator's work habits and empathy with a donor intertwined with his intellectual curiosity and political commitment to construct the meanings of an artifact.

When the Ben Pearson Rust Cotton Picker No. 34[9] was delivered to the museum in January 1995, Peter climbed up onto "Grandma" to have his photograph taken, practically hugging the machine, not merely standing next to it.

It was a great story. I wish you could have heard Peter tell it. But he died last July [1995], just four months after sitting down with Allan Jones in the farmhouse kitchen.[10]

Notes

1. James H. Street, *The New Revolution in the Cotton Economy: Mechanization and Its Consequences* (Chapel Hill: University of North Carolina Press, 1957).

2. Donald Holley, "John Daniel Rust (1892–1954)," *Encyclopedia of Arkansas History and Culture*, updated 29 December 2010, http://www.encyclopediaofarkansas.net/encyclopedia/entry-detail.aspx?entryID=2272 (accessed 28 May 2016).

3. *The Literary Digest*, 1936; John Rust, "The Origin and Development of the Cotton Picker," *West Tennessee Historical Society Papers*, 7 (1953): 38–56. The Rust story, complete with photographs, a timeline, and a bibliography, is available at "John and Mack Rust: Cotton Picker Inventors," https://johnandmack.wordpress.com/timeline/ (accessed 28 May 2016).

4. Donald Holley documents the transformation in *The Second Great Emancipation: The Mechanical Cotton Picker, Black Migration, and How They Changed the Modern South* (Fayetteville: University of Arkansas Press, 2000).

5. Corporate lawyers negotiated conflicts between the John Rust Company and Ben Pearson, Inc. A 1954 decision in *Ben Pearson, Inc. v. John Rust Co.*, 268 S.W.2d 893 (1954) determined that Pearson owed Rust more royalties; decision available at http://law.justia.com/cases/arkansas/supreme-court/1954/5-340-0.html (accessed 28 May 2016). Another case indicates the shared goals of the Company and inventors not wanting to be pawns in a mechanization takeover of cotton fields. See a case on appeal, *Modern Farm Service, Inc., v. Ben Pearson, Inc.*, 308 F.2d 18 (1962), available at http://openjurist.org/308/f2d/18/modern-farm-service-inc-v-ben-pearson-inc (accessed 28 May 2016).

6. For examples of the published primary sources that Peter tracked down to document perceptions of the Rust brothers and their invention at the time of its development and initial marketing, see Oliver Carlson, "The Revolution in Cotton," *American Mercury*, 34 (September 1935): 129–36; Robert Kenneth Straus, "Enter the Cotton Picker: The Story of the Rust Brothers' Invention," *Harper's*, 173 (September 1936): 386–95; and "Mr. Little Ol' Rust," *Fortune*, 46 (December 1952): 150–52, 198–205.

7. Peter Cousins, *Hog Plow and Sith: Cultural Aspects of Early Agricultural Technology* (Dearborn, MI: Greenfield Village and Henry Ford Museum, 1973).

8. Kirkpatrick Sale, *Rebels against the Future, The Luddites and Their War on the Industrial Revolution: Lessons for the Computer Age* (Reading, MA: Addison-Wesley Publishing, 1995).

9. Two images of the "Self-Propelled Cotton Picker, 1950" (object ID: 75.133.1), one taken outside (THF92255) and the other on exhibit at The Henry Ford (THF151663): https://www.thehenryford.org/collections-and-research/digital-collections/artifact/250111/ (accessed 28 May 2016).

10. Peter H. Cousins Jr. was curator of agriculture at Henry Ford Museum and Greenfield Village in Dearborn, Michigan, from 1969 until his death from cancer in 1995. Educated at Columbia University and the Universities of Virginia and California, Cousins worked at the Oakland Museum before joining the staff of The Henry Ford. He was a past president of the Association for Living Historical Farms and Agricultural Museums. In his memory, The Henry Ford dedicated the fields of Firestone Farm as "Peter's Fields" and created the Peter Prize, "to be awarded to a staff member who demonstrates attention to historical authenticity and accuracy based on solid research and scholarship, as well as adherence to the highest professional and ethical standards."

PART 3

THEMATIC STUDIES TO INFORM LOCALIZED AGRICULTURAL INTERPRETATION

CHAPTER 10

ROADS AND BRIDGES IN RURAL AGRICULTURAL INTERPRETATION

Cameron L. Saffell and Debra A. Reid

NOTE: Most of us take roads and bridges for granted unless construction slows us down, but if you ever have driven behind a slow-moving tractor, you know that farmers own the roadways just as much as commuters do. In their origins, roadways and bridges represented the collective effort of local, state, and national governments to construct an infrastructure that linked farms to markets, commodities to processors, and consumables to the general public. This essay provides an overview of roads and bridges during the era of the Good Roads Movement of the late nineteenth and early twentieth century. It shares three examples from three distinct regions of the United States (New Jersey, New Mexico, and Maryland) that indicate how a common cause (farm-to-market transport) and a consistent product (steel truss bridges sold in kits) led to rapid expansion of rural roads. It incorporates the ways that special interest groups influenced rural landscapes including roads and bridges. Lastly, this paper documents the ways that different preservation-minded organizations have documented, repurposed, and relocated bridges and preserved heritage roadways as important components of rural historic landscapes. The most successful projects take time and money, but also depend on well-meaning individuals who can see the landscape from the same vantage point as the horseman driving the team. Farmers may not agree with the preservationists, because they still need their roads to serve their needs, which often involves commodity shipments in milk tanks and tractor-trailers.

MOST HISTORIC homes and farm museums concentrate their interpretation on the site itself—who lived there, what did they grow, what equipment did they use? Some will extend the interpretation to the commercial aspects of agriculture—growing crops, raising livestock, and selling butter, eggs, and other products in nearby towns. But one of the most often overlooked items is the landscape in between—the critical importance of roads and bridges to farmers and ranchers between rural and urban areas. There may not be any historic vestiges left—like an old bridge or remnants of the old highway—but their modern descendants are there. Roads and bridges actually figure prominently into the process, but they are omitted from most interpretation.

The earliest roads in the United States were the turnpike routes, often chartered by state governments or Congress to private companies for construction as toll roads. Congress also authorized several military routes, like the Natchez Trace and the Jackson Military Road, that were built by the U.S. Army to facilitate troop and supply movements. The development of overland roads paralleled the introduction of canals and railroads in the nineteenth century. For local travel, though, roads followed boundaries between farms or the lands least suited for agriculture, and thus were often winding, poorly located, and difficult to travel. As the Great Plains and Western states developed, counties declared all section lines reserved for public roads, which helped the situation initially. The period between 1850 and 1900 has been called the "dark age of the rural road," but it saw over 1.5 million miles of such country roads built.[1]

Rural transportation was always very rugged, but the Good Roads Movement starting in the 1880s to 1890s raised the profile of the discussions about the importance of roads to agriculture. In 1903, a speaker at the National Good Roads Convention said, "Whatever makes for the agricultural prosperity and development of the country aids every other industry in the land."[2] In 1912, the Office of Public Roads explained why farmers needed improved roads: "The business of farming is essentially dependent on the condition of country roads, for whatever is not produced on the farm must be hauled to the farm, and many crops of the farm must be hauled away to the railroad station and local markets."[3] With such strong statements connecting agriculture with roads, it should come as little surprise that from its formation in 1893 until 1939, the Bureau of Public Roads—forerunner of today's Federal Highway Administration—was part of the U.S. Department of Agriculture.[4]

The move was also logical, because the country's rural roads had been built and maintained largely by farmers. With transportation needs increasing, they were looking for help with this enormous task. One farmer told the audience at the 1903 National Good Roads Convention that: "After a century of loyal support in this direction [the farmer] is knocking at the doors of the State and the Nation, asking if they will not appropriate money to be used to help him improve the highway from his home to the town."[5]

Backers of the Good Roads Movement offered several arguments as to how better roads benefited agriculture. "The speed of transportation from farm to the unloading point is essential. . . . Where bad roads prevail, farmers are forced to move their crops, not when the market price is favorable, but when the roads are favorable." A poor road also meant that a farmer had to hire on extra help or equipment or make several trips that could be markedly reduced if he could transport over a good road. A good, level road also reduced the wear and tear on horses, harnesses, wagons—and later farm trucks. Having access to good roads meant land values increased because of being near that road. Supporters also said that when a rural road was improved, the farmers living along it tended to improve the appearance of their homes and outbuildings—lest they be embarrassed when everyone comes driving past.[6]

Of course, the benefits went beyond the farm. A good road "is the common property of everybody; it is shared by all; it is needed by all; it benefits all." For example, the Postal Service wanted better roads to further the relatively recent introduction of Rural Free Delivery of mail and packages. This was becoming an increasingly important part of American society, as the popularity of Sears Roebuck and Montgomery Ward soared—particularly in large rural expanses like New Mexico and the American West. No longer did consumers have to go to town or the local rail station to get the newest conveniences of living; it was delivered right to their door. Advocates of Good Roads, particularly in the West and Midwest, argued that with better roads, numerous one-room schools could be consolidated into a single, larger facility centralized in a community. Not only did this increase what could be done in teaching, but the consolidated school became a gathering place for public events of all kinds—entertainment, short courses, political rallies, lectures, and farm meetings. Further, casual travel and tourism by automobile was on the rise. Better roads and special routes like Route 66 had more Americans traveling the countryside.[7]

Though it was slow in developing, the Good Roads Movement did spur the eventual establishment of road networks across the country. The Federal Aid Road Act of 1916 (also called the Bankhead-Shackleford Act) provided the first matching federal funds to support construction and maintenance of primary roads—the network that became the U.S. Highway System in 1926. States supplemented this with support for local roads—often routes with importance to farming, ranching, and rural life. Texas, for example, established a separate class of roads called the Farm-to-Market Road (or Ranch-to-Market Road in sparse rural areas of southwest Texas).[8] By the late twentieth century, roads were almost taken for granted, and their origins with and importance to agriculture were largely forgotten.

The Green Bridge: A Case Study

After the turn of the century, the New Mexico Farm and Ranch Heritage Museum had a unique opportunity to bring attention to these forgotten historic landscapes. The forty-seven-acre museum is divided in half by the Tortugas Arroyo, which will run wild with water after any rainstorm in the area. When it first opened in 1996, a sidewalk cut down the banks to cross the wash, but Museum officials recognized that this was a potential safety hazard in the event of a sudden storm. The long-term solution was to put in a bridge to allow for safe passage at any time.

Many people associate large steel truss bridges with late-nineteenth- and early-twentieth-century America. They are a feature of not only the development of road systems, but also the expansion of railroads, which are yet another reflection of agriculture. (Remember, the long cattle drive routes from Texas to the Great Plains ended at large railheads where "beef on the hoof" could be shipped to slaughterhouses in Chicago and the Midwest.) A steel truss bridge to cross a wash, a creek, or a river was critical to moving products from the farm to the city. If the banks were too steep—or even worse, if the river was flooding—then the farmer's perishable products sat on the sideline waiting for conditions to improve before he could sell it.

Like many Great Plains and Western states, New Mexico has dozens of examples of steel truss bridges that are representative of this story. The Farm and Ranch Heritage Museum had a unique opportunity to meet a physical need while collecting and restoring one of these bridges and making it a centerpiece of its interpretation of rural transportation in New Mexico agriculture.

Although the New Mexico legislature established a Territorial Roads Commission in 1909 and a new State Highway Commission after statehood in 1912, the development of roads, particularly those outside of towns in rural areas, were an often-neglected responsibility borne by local county governments and municipalities.[9] The population was widely scattered and tax revenues were low, meaning there was little funding to work on road or bridge construction. Like other states, New Mexico imposed a mandatory work requirement. Through state statute, all able-bodied men between twenty-one and sixty years old were required to perform between two and five days' labor on local roads annually—or pay the county road supervisor $1 per day so he could hire someone else. By the 1920s counties could establish a "road fund" funded through taxes, but as late as 1938 a taxpayer could elect to provide his labor to the road supervisor in lieu of paying the road tax.[10]

Local residents also had to fund the building of bridges. With very limited funds available in both regular revenues and the road funds, most governments early on built only simple, timber-beam bridges. Citizens, however, could get one hundred "voters and tax payers" to sign a petition to create a special tax levy for bridge projects. This started a process that could result in a more substantial iron bridge being completed. This was how the residents of Chaves County, New Mexico, went about getting their first steel truss bridge built.[11]

A taxpayer petition in 1899 launched an effort to construct a bridge across the Pecos River east of Roswell. This bridge would physically connect Roswell with the Eastern New Mexico communities of Tatum and Lovington (over seventy miles away), the new oil fields, and the smaller settlements, farms, and ranches of the countryside with the largest urban community and market in the region.[12] In October 1901, the Chaves County commissioners reviewed fifteen possible bridge plans submitted by five companies, all of which were commercial bridge firms from the Midwest and New York. After "long prayerful consideration of the various bids," the commissioners selected Plan No. 2 of the Midland Bridge Company at a final cost of $11,008.[13]

The *Roswell Record* commented on the project and the award:

> The bridge has long been needed and the board has won for itself an immortal crown
> by the placing of the contract for a bridge of this class, which will last as long as the

hills and solve forever the troubles of those who are making the wilderness bloom over beyond the treacherous Pecos.

Considering the grade of the structure the price is very reasonable indeed, and the board is to be congratulated upon its course.[14]

The Pecos River Bridge was a three-span Pratt through-truss bridge with pinned connections (Photo 10.1), a wood deck of 3-by-12-inch lumber, and an overall length of 438 feet. This style of bridge was popular in the late nineteenth and early twentieth centuries because of its lightweight steel and ease of assembly.[15] In July 1902, the construction was completed, and commissioners and editors of both local newspapers rode three miles out from town to review their new structure. Both papers lavished praise upon both the bridge and the politicians. The *Roswell Register* reported:

> The party examined the bridge carefully, and so far as they could see, it proved to be a splendid piece of work, and was greatly admired by all. . . . The bridge will be a great convenience to a large number of people, who many a time, have had to camp on the river bank for hours or days, until a flood would subside so that they could cross, or run the risk, as many have done, of drowning, in attempting to cross before the water had gone down enough to make the attempt safe.[16]

The Pecos River Bridge survived several flood events over the years. It was the only structure in the region not washed out in the 1919 floods. In 1937 the Pecos River was reportedly three to five miles wide, as waters of the nearby Rio Hondo and Spring Rivers swept through the community of Roswell. One nearby resident recalls seeing water all over the valley, with the Pecos River Bridge sticking up in the middle of it all. None of the floodwaters came over the top, he recalls, but it completely covered the road leading to the bridge on both sides.[17]

Photo 10.1 Looking east at the Pecos River Bridge with two buggies of unidentified sightseers in a photograph probably taken in the early 1900s. "Pecos River Bridge–Roswell, NM," accession #2193.

Source: Courtesy of the Historical Society for Southeast New Mexico

The floods of 1937 marked the beginning of the end for the Pecos River Bridge. In August 1939, the old road was effectively replaced with the opening of the new, federally funded U.S. Highway 380, which ran directly east from Roswell to Tatum. The new road completed the first fully oiled highway from Roswell to the Texas state line and trimmed 4.4 miles from the route in the area closest to Roswell.[18] The old Pecos River Bridge and road were not maintained, so in 1943 Chaves County commissioners decided to "sell" the bridge to the State Highway Department if it would dismantle the three spans and give one back to the county in lieu of payment.[19]

Starting in the 1930s, the New Mexico Highway Department had systematically begun improving roads and bridges on its main highway systems, as it did with U.S. Highway 380 near Roswell. Rather than scrap old steel truss bridges, though, the state recycled them through federal New Deal projects to improve the state's secondary and farm-to-market roads. Thus, many bridges were relocated to small county roads. This was a common practice of the New Mexico State Highway Department until about 1950 that "exemplifies the versatility of truss bridges and the practice used by the Highway Department of moving them from place to place as conditions change."[20]

The State Highway Department reconstructed the central span of the 1902 Pecos River Bridge some forty-six miles west to Lincoln County Road A-4 across the Rio Hondo near its intersection with U.S. Highway 70. This provided better access to ranch lands south of the river in southeastern Lincoln County. The structure was repainted, leading locals to call it the Green Bridge. Local residents recall the folks mostly using the bridge were local ranchers in their pickup trucks and big eighteen-wheelers moving cattle in and out of grazing areas in southeastern Lincoln County. The bridge continued in operation until the late 1980s, when it was determined that it was a historic structure that should be bypassed and replaced.[21]

One contributing report to that decision was the 1987 New Mexico Historic Bridge Survey, which identified the Green Bridge as one of the first "engineered" bridges in the state. It was labeled as the oldest documented steel-truss bridge in New Mexico and the state's second-oldest highway bridge of any type. In a subsequent National Register nomination, the bridge was identified as "historically significant for its long association with highway transportation in New Mexico dating to the territorial period." The structure was also listed on the State Register of Cultural Properties in 1997.[22]

In the early 1990s, shortly after the Rio Hondo Bridge at Picacho was taken off the system, the Lincoln County Board of Commissioners offered to donate the bridge to the recently created New Mexico Farm and Ranch Heritage Museum. The Museum elected to pass on the offer at the time, since all the efforts were focused on designing and building the main facility. The idea was resurrected in the early 2000s when Museum staff instituted a new investigation into the feasibility, cost, and appropriateness of acquiring the bridge for the Museum. The general finding was that it fit the criteria for a bridge to cross the Tortugas Arroyo at approximately the same cost to restore as to engineer and build a new structure from scratch. Further, with its history and use in rural New Mexico, it was felt that the bridge would be an excellent means to open a dialogue on the role and importance of transportation in New Mexico farming and ranching.

Due to the bridge's historic status on the State Register, the Museum fully cleaned and restored it during its relocation with a priority emphasis of maintaining the structure's high degree of historic integrity. The structure was dismantled and moved based on the 1943 relocation blueprints, replacing the deteriorated wood deck and several critical steel components that were rusted beyond safe use. After work was completed in 2007, the Museum successfully pursued a listing on the National Register of Historic Places, based on not just its being a prime example of pre-statehood bridge development and later policies to relocate and reuse steel truss bridges on rural secondary roads, but also on its critical importance and significance as part of road and transportation networks to the farming, ranching, and rural life of New Mexico.[23]

Today the Green Bridge (Photo 10.2) is the centerpiece of the Farm and Ranch Heritage Museum's interpretation of roads and transportation. The Pratt Through-Truss is described and interpreted as a typical example of early steel truss bridges in New Mexico and of how the State Highway Department would reuse these structures at other locations on smaller secondary, rural roads. No longer primarily a vehicular bridge, the Green Bridge serves as the principal pedestrian connector across the Tortugas Arroyo to permit visitors to cross from the Bruce King Building to the barns, fields, outbuildings, and exterior exhibits of the museum's "South 20"—a passive reminder of the connection between urban and agricultural areas in New Mexico and throughout the United States.

Photo 10.2 The Historic Green Bridge across the Tortugas Arroyo adjacent to the main interpretive center at the New Mexico Farm and Ranch Heritage Museum.

Source: Courtesy of the New Mexico Farm and Ranch Heritage Museum

Farm-to-Market-to-Documentation

The state of New Mexico proactively managed bridges on its farm-to-market and county roads. Relocating bridges made sense in a place geographically remote from the manufacturers of metal truss bridges and crisscrossed by dry arroyos or small creeks and rivers that needed bridges. The state worked with counties to relocate bridges during the 1930s and 1940s that had outlived their usefulness in their original locations. This helped preserve physical evidence of engineering landmarks that solved rural transportation problems. The cooperative arrangements between local and state government facilitated stewardship of farm-to-market roadways through relocation. The Green Bridge at the New Mexico Farm and Ranch Heritage Museum documents this pattern of adaptive reuse.

Metal bridges like the Green Bridge were the most common form built in the rural United States between the 1850s and the 1920s. Many of them incorporated Pratt or Warren designs, patented in 1844 and 1848, respectively. These incorporated vertical and horizontal elements, joints connected with either pins or rivets, and one of three standard truss configurations (through truss, pony truss, or deck).[24] A few variations existed, but anyone interested in developing their visual literacy of rural landscapes can become proficient at identification fairly quickly. All it takes is an identification guide, mastery of the vocabulary, and a bit of practice. Then consistency in design and execution becomes evident. Such visual literacy can make these vestiges of rural economic development more obvious to the modern eye.

Metal bridges provided an invaluable tool to Good Roads advocates. While bridges required government investment, private companies could provide the required engineering from an array of wrought standardized parts and sizes; some bridge manufacturing companies even had catalogs from which county or state government officials could select something to meet their needs. Bridge companies then customized the design to the site, prefabricated sections, and packaged the parts to specification based on the orders. Local contractors could then assemble and install the bridge and its components.

The lucrative business prompted steel magnates to integrate bridge construction into their operations. J. P. Morgan and Company organized the American Bridge Company (ABC) in 1900 by consolidating several companies. Then Andrew Carnegie's U.S. Steel Corporation acquired ABC's corporate stock in 1901. The ABC bought other independent bridge construction companies after 1900. Most states have inventories of the historic bridges, documenting as many details as possible, including names of construction companies and contractors. Details about a state's bridges provide invaluable detail for safety and security concerns of state highway administration or departments of transportation, and can also facilitate resource stewardship.[25]

The U.S. Congress mandated a nationwide survey of public bridges after a tragic bridge collapse in 1967. The survey documented the condition of bridges so as to help identify older structures that needed replacement but also to identify historic bridges that should be designated as examples of historic engineering or that should be repaired and retained in use. Standardized data collected at the local and state levels has resulted in a National Bridge Inventory with millions of entries documenting all bridges on public roads at least twenty feet long. The inventory data conforms to the National Bridge Inspection Standards of 1971 and includes data collected starting in 1983. The enabling legislation required evidence of structural integrity and performance data as well as evidence of historical significance and context. Thus, the Federal Highway Administration provides information about legislation supporting bridge preservation, advises on preservation treatments, and identifies examples of partnerships formed to preserve bridges and strategies to accomplish the goals. For example, the 2012 report, *Communicating the Value of Preservation: A Playbook* prepared for the National Cooperative Highway Research Program, can help special interest groups, local governments, and preservation organizations lobby for bridge and road preservation.[26]

A Bridge in Rural Maryland

The Harmony Road Bridge in Frederick County, Maryland, installed in 1918 to cross Little Catoctin Creek, provides a good example of the importance of accurate documentation of historic roads and bridges in order to support preservation. The Lackawanna Steel Plant in Buffalo, New York, constructed standardized parts used in the Harmony Road Bridge. Frederick County officials ordered a single-span, Pratt pony truss bridge with pinned connections. The company that manufactured the Harmony Road Bridge is unknown, but as was typical, the local contractor, M. D. Porman, was a general contractor who did not normally engage in bridge-building projects. It took many hands to make the bridge that spanned Little Catoctin Creek. It resulted from the collective labor of steel-mill workers, bridge engineers, corporate executives, experts in bridge construction, laborers from the farming community who helped build the piers, local government approval, taxpayers' dollars, Good Roads advocates, and farmers' demands for better market access.[27]

The person who prepared the Historic American Engineering Report (HAER) on Harmony Road Bridge, Elizabeth Jo Lampl, described the countryside through which Harmony Road passed as "rural and picturesque, although Harmony Road is fairly heavily traveled." The bridge's local significance rested on "its role in expanding the agricultural economy of Frederick County by connecting remote farm roads with more well-traversed thoroughfares," which included the Baltimore National Pike. The HAER report, however, focused on the Harmony Road Bridge's significance as an engineered solution to a problem. The HAER documentation emphasized parts, construction details, and steel and bridge corporation history, not the significance of the bridge to farmers and rural residents in Frederick County, Maryland. The photographs, however, indicate the bridge's rural setting, at least in June 1996, when Walter Smalling photographed the site (Photo 10.3).[28]

The Harmony Road crossed Little Catoctin Creek just south of the Baltimore National Pike (U.S. Route 40 in Maryland). Farm families could access this early interstate highway, authorized by the U.S. Congress in 1811, from both directions on the road. Paul Daniel Marriott, in his *Guide to Historic Roads*, indicated that the State of Maryland "identified three eras of significance for the National Road within its boundaries: Heyday of the National Road (1810–1850), Agriculture and Trade (1850–1910) and Revival of the National Road (1910–1960)." The Harmony Road had significance to

Photo 10.3 The Harmony Road wended through Valecreek Farm, visible in the background, looking northwest from the Little Catoctin Creek.

Source: "Harmony Road Bridge (Bridge No. F16-24) HAER No. MD-120," photographer: Walter Smalling, June 1996. Historic American Engineering Survey, Library of Congress, Washington, D.C.

the first two eras, and the 134-feet-long single-span Pratt through-truss bridge confirmed the investment that county officials made to ensure ease of transport in an area adjacent to a major market route. Decisions to rebuild bridges to facilitate local transport ensured market access to locals and contributed to the National Road's economic role.[29]

A more complete interpretation of the bridge would indicate the relationship between the urban and industrial and the rural and agricultural. Farmers paid taxes. In fact, in rural counties with the majority of the population dispersed on farms or in towns with fewer than 2,500 people, farm owners accounted for a significant percentage of a county's property-tax and road-tax revenue. This translated into influence, especially when farmers had effective lobbyist groups. Farmers, owners and tenants alike, had more economic stability during the early twentieth century because, for a few years, they earned more from the sale of the commodities they produced than they spent on production. This era, described as the "Golden Age," coincided with early-twentieth-century Progressive Reform, a period when government responded to special interest lobbying and regulated producers to protect consumer health. Dairy farmers had to comply with state and municipal milk laws that required farmers to improve their milking barns, test their cattle for bovine tuberculosis, and construct hygienic milk storage sheds. Farmers in turn agitated for higher prices of milk per hundredweight and market access via macadamized roads and bridges that could hold the trucks that hauled the full milk and cream cans from the farms to the dairies and creameries.

Many special interests cooperated to secure bridges for rural roads. Many would benefit, including dairy farmers, owners of creameries and dairies, owners of truck farms and market gardens, and commuters in Frederick County, Maryland. They expected quick replacement of a washed-out bridge. The histories that omit the agricultural part of the story do not tell the whole story.

Preserving these structures requires as many individuals, government agencies, and special interest groups as it took to construct them. Sometimes the alliances pay off, as in the case of the Green Bridge, and sometimes not, as in the case of the Harmony Road Bridge. The plan in the 1990s to remove the bridge to Thurmont, Maryland, "for use as pedestrian bridge across Hunting Creek" did not work out. The bridge was "structurally insufficient for its vehicular load." Those agitating for bridge replacement outmaneuvered those hoping to preserve it, and the bridge was replaced.

Farm-to-Market-to-Preservation: Heritage Trails and a Living History Farm in New Jersey

Farmers across the nation hauled milk, meat, grains, fruits, and vegetables to local markets and railway hubs. New Jersey farmers had two major urban destinations for their produce, including the largest city in the nation, New York City, but also Philadelphia. The combination of farmers wanting markets and consumers wanting inexpensive and quality food created significant public interest in roads and bridges.

Some of the oldest rural roads systems that benefited from state funding exist in New Jersey. In 1891, that state became the first in the nation to pass a State Aid Highway Act. It authorized appropriation of state funds to county government to support construction and improvement of rural roadways. Initially the New Jersey State Board of Agriculture administered the funds, but in 1894 state legislators created the Commission of Public Roads. The U.S. Congress, concurrently, established the Office of Road Inquiry within the U.S. Department of Agriculture (renamed the Office of Public Roads in 1905, then the Bureau of Public Roads in 1918). The Office of Road Inquiry provided technical expertise, answered questions, and disseminated news and information to similar commissions nationwide[30] (Photo 10.4).

Sometimes discerning the connections between farmers and roadways requires adopting the viewpoint of farmers who relied on draft animals to haul their loads. This reliance on horses in harness began during the agricultural revolution of the mid-nineteenth century as mechanization replaced stoop laborers and draft horses or mules became the more common power source for this equipment and for hauling wagons, rather than carts, to market. The use of draft horses to haul wagons to market continued throughout the Good Roads Movement, even as farmers bought automobiles and farm trucks in increasing numbers during the 1910s. Photographs provide a glimpse of the farmers'

Photo 10.4 This "old country road" in Far Hills, New Jersey, depicts the condition of a dirt-road surface, circa 1900, one factor that fueled the Good Roads Movement in New Jersey. The image shows four children standing in the front yard of a house, but within the road's right-of-way. The road seems to have a low-grade ascent until it levels off, then rises more steeply in its approach to the simple-span stone bridge (evident in the distance).

Source: Image: LC-D4-11529 [P&P], Library of Congress, Washington, D.C.

perspective. For example, most of us might not perceive the grade of the "old country road" in Far Hills, New Jersey, as evidence of practical road construction in a rural and agricultural context. Why? Because most of us are not trained to look at roadways from the seat of a loaded wagon or from the footpath next to the near ox. But we should look again with an informed eye. Pete Watson of Howell Living History Farm tells a story of what his friend Halsey told him. Halsey was a horseman who called levels on a steady upward ascent "thank you ma'ams." As Pete explained: "These were places where the road leveled off, climbed, leveled off, climbed, etc., to help farmers get loaded wagons up and down hills without a lot of braking or having the horses hold back the load with their britchen."[31]

Construction and improvement continued through the New Deal of the 1930s as roadways became part of state-level relief and recovery initiatives. Automobiles and trucks did not need "thank you ma'ams." Men employed on Works Progress Administration, Civilian Conservation Corps, and Resettlement Administration programs regraded and straightened roads. The economic significance of this work went far beyond the wages they earned. The smoother surfaces made travel to local attractions easier, and this sustained other projects such as local tourism development, and it put more money in farmers' pockets as travelers stopped at roadside markets to buy fruits and vegetables.

Concerned residents and proactive government officials in rural places experiencing rapid development tried to control the pace of change. One large-scale strategy involved U.S. Congressional classification as a reserve area in keeping with the National Parks and Recreation Act of 1978. More than one million acres in southern New Jersey, the Pine Barrens Area, became the first national reserve in 1978. The designation emphasized the natural resources as influential on human occupation over millennia: "Acres of pine-oak forest, extensive surface and ground water resources of high quality, and a wide diversity of rare plant and animal species, provides significant ecological, natural, cultural, recreational, educational, agricultural, and public health benefits." Legislation required formation of a planning committee of fifteen members, some of whom had to "represent economic activities such as agriculture in the area."[32]

In 1988, ten years after the national designation of the Pinelands Reserve, the state of New Jersey, in partnership with the National Park Service, designated the New Jersey Coastal Heritage Trail Route. The route traversed natural areas and rural communities on the way to coastal tourist destinations. Other areas proved themselves eligible for designation as historic sites or historic districts. The National Park Service issued its first *Guidelines for Evaluating and Documenting Rural Historic Landscapes* in 1989, partially in response to the groundswell of interest and partially to provide support to communities and states seeking such designation to manage natural and cultural resources. The *Guidelines* defined a rural historic landscape "as a geographical area that historically has been used by people, or shaped or modified by human activity, occupancy, or intervention, and that possesses a significant concentration, linkage, or continuity of areas of land use, vegetation, buildings and structures, roads and waterways, and natural features." The *Guidelines* listed eleven characteristics and elements to consider when documenting each. The characteristics included land use and activities; boundary demarcations; buildings, structures, and objects; cultural traditions; and patterns of spatial organization, among other things. Roads were listed as a feature of "circulation networks" along with paths, streams, or canals, highways, railways, and waterways. Directions suggested doing the following to document "circulation networks":

- Describe the principal forms of transportation and circulation routes that facilitate travel within the landscape and connect the landscape with its larger region.
- Name, date, and describe principal or significant examples.
- Identify principal roadways and other transportation routes, by name, type, and location, and classify as contributing or noncontributing.[33]

Those seeking protection for rural heritage areas, including roadways and bridges, buildings, archaeological sites, and all features and characteristics deemed worthy of consideration have resources to consult that can hasten the documentation process. For example, the National Bridge Inventory consolidated standard information. State-level surveys collected additional information on historic bridges as a proactive step to comply with Section 106 of the National Historic Preservation Act of 1966. Between 1991 and 1994, the State of New Jersey completed a Historic Bridge Survey that inventoried all state and county bridges built before 1946 and evaluated them in relation to National Register criteria. The New Jersey survey also included histories of transportation in each county, and in the state. These became useful in writing context statements to designate National Register sites and districts and to nominate bridges for Historic American Engineering Record status.[34]

Other features contributing to rural landscapes, in addition to bridges, became the focus of preservationists. Roadside stands contributed to the designation of heritage areas, including the New Jersey Coastal Heritage Trail Route. During the early 1990s, the Historic American Buildings Survey documented one such market stand operated by Kenneth and Ruth Camp during the summer of 1992. Kenneth's father, Hise Camp, began a stand on the Big Oaks farm as early as the 1920s. The stand provided a local sales point for truck farmers such as Camp who sought additional outlets for vegetables grown for the Philadelphia market[35] (Photo 10.5).

Photo 10.5 Camp's Big Oaks Farm Market, South Delsea Drive (State Route 47), Port Elizabeth, Cumberland County, New Jersey. This view of the roadside stand, looking southwest, shows details of the stand, market baskets with vegetables, and pallets covered in pumpkins and squash. A tractor in the field pulls a low-sided wagon used to haul produce. Customers could also purchase soda from a Pepsi cooler.

Source: Photograph by David Ames, October 1990. HABS NJ,6-PTELIZ,1—2, Historic American Building Survey, Library of Congress, Washington, D.C.

Threats to rural roads and roadside features came from many directions. A regional project to document "high risk rural roads" in Delaware Valley counties in Pennsylvania and New Jersey justified its work not on the basis of reducing threats to historic integrity, but because of the need to reduce traffic fatalities.[36] Local preservationists found themselves arguing for preserving rural roadways as circulation networks in opposition to reports that designated roads as high risk for commuter safety. In 2010, Paul Daniel Marriott, an expert in historic road preservation and management, argued that "State Historic Preservation Offices (SHPOs) across the nation have had difficulty defining and defending historic roads in the face of overwhelming political, social, and judicial pressures predicated on highway safety and efficiency."[37]

Those seeking to preserve bridges faced similar challenges—arguing against those who lobbied for safety and efficiency. Local officials had to balance the need for bridges to carry twenty-first-century loads with the passion that preservationists expressed about saving historic bridges. Relocation projects offered options to salvaging restricted-load bridges, but projects with historically significant bridges suited to well-documented sites for relocation may fail if a bridge lacks structural integrity.

Sometimes public property includes historic roadways and bridges worth interpreting. The Howell Living History Farm, a property of the Mercer County Park District since 1974, included several rural landscape features, including Moore Creek and the bridge crossing it on Hunter Road. The New Jersey Historic Bridge Survey described the Moore Creek Bridge as a "pin-connected Pratt half-hip span on the grounds of Howell farm in Hopewell." It had suffered irreparable damage in 1982, but the Survey still described it as "distinguished for . . . completeness of setting and integrity of original design."[38] The condition of the bridge gives farm visitors the opportunity to see the bridge from a unique vantage point—atop a loaded farm wagon looking at it from the level of the creek ford. The popular driving tour includes other historic rural landscape features including the "thank you ma'ams" on Hunter Road. Visitors on the driving tour have a fine view of the stone abutments that Samuel H. Chatten constructed in 1889. But Howell Farm interprets the 1890s–1910s, a period noted for farmer politicking and special interest groups agitating for reform. True to the form of New Jersey farmers during the early years of the Good Roads Movement and the Golden Age of agriculture, Howell Farm staff support relocation of another Pratt through-truss bridge over Moore Creek.

Incorporating farmers' opinions about rural roads and bridges fits the site's interpretive agenda perfectly. When not wearing his farmer's hat, site administrator Pete Watson of Howell Living History Farm has been involved with a project to replace the compromised bridge with another historically significant bridge already dismantled and waiting for relocation. Developing the partnerships took years, and success is not yet guaranteed. The bridge identified for relocation, the Bear Tavern Road Bridge over Jacobs Creek, was built by the King Iron Bridge and Manufacturing Company, Cleveland, Ohio, in 1882.[39] In 2009, officials closed the structurally deficient but historic Bear Tavern Road Bridge, in the Bear Tavern Road/Jacob's Creek Crossing Rural Historic District, designated in 2011. Later that same year, Hurricane Irene damaged the bridge even more, but local residents rallied to try to save it. This prompted officials to remove the historic iron-truss bridge and replace it. They also budgeted to store the structure before relocating it to a historic site. This increased the cost of the multimillion-dollar project and left those who had opposed its removal only partially assuaged. Watson looked forward to installing the iron-truss bridge on the Howell farm grounds. He "dreamed" of the bridge's potential. Watson testified before the freeholder board that the Jacobs Creek Bridge "would marry perfectly with the Pleasant Valley Historic District and that its addition would create one more 'wonderful place to interpret the history of Mercer County.'"[40]

The efforts made to preserve bridges and rural roadways indicate that rural landscape preservation requires collective effort. It takes a team of people to make such projects successful. That team needs to include a local or state government agency, a local preservation agency, public or private not-for-profit institutions, and a need to fill. The bridge that survives can continue as a pedestrian or light-load bridge. The bridge can also provide a primary document for students studying mathematics, physics, and engineering. What loads can a Pratt truss bridge carry? How do you do the math? Can this bridge hold a person? Can it hold a single horse and buggy? Can it hold a two-horse hitch and wagon full of hay? Does the road have a grade that makes hauling a full load easy or hard? What do engineers need to do to solve the problems? Can it hold a steam engine? Can it hold an eighteen-wheeler? A bridge can become the evidence to support a study of politics in rural and agricultural contexts, and an example of cooperation. That seems a good way to put historic Pratt steel-truss bridges and the associated roadways in three states to work.

Notes

1. U.S. Department of Transportation Federal Highway Administration, *America's Highways, 1776–1976: A History of the Federal-Aid Program* (Washington, D.C.: Government Printing Office, 1977), 8–37.

2. J. B. Killebrew, "Improvement of Our Highways," in *Proceedings of the National Good Roads Convention Held at St. Louis, Mo., April 27 to 29, 1903*, U.S. Department of Agriculture, Office of Public Roads Inquiries, *Bulletin 26* (Washington, D.C.: Government Printing Office, 1903) [hereafter cited as *Proceedings of the National Good Roads Convention*], 25.

3. Office of Public Roads, *Benefits of Improved Roads*, U.S. Department of Agriculture, *Farmers' Bulletin 505* (Washington, D.C.: Government Printing Office, 1912), 12.

4. The agency originated as the Office of Road Inquiry (Office of Public Roads Inquiries) when USDA Secretary J. Sterling Morton implemented provisions in the Agricultural Appropriation Act of 1893, and was renamed Office of Public Roads in 1905. It became the Bureau of Public Roads in 1918. In 1939, as part of a broader governmental reorganization, the Bureau was renamed the Public Roads Administration and moved from the USDA to the Federal Works Agency (FWA). Federal Highway Administration, *America's Highways*, 44, 142. When the FWA was eliminated in 1949, the Public Roads Administration became the Bureau of Public Roads again, a division of the U.S. Department of Commerce. In 1966, the U.S. Congress established the U.S. Department of Transportation, and in 1967, the Federal Highway Administration assumed the functions of the Bureau of Public Roads.

5. R. H. Kern, "The Farmers' Right to Recognition," in *Proceedings of the National Good Roads Convention*, 32.

6. Office of Public Roads, *Benefits of Improved Roads*, 11–16, 19–20.

7. Killebrew, "Improvement of Our Highways," 28; Office of Public Roads, *Benefits of Improved Roads*, 16–19.

8. Federal Highway Administration, *America's Highways*, 86–87; Bruce E. Seely, *Building the American Highway System: Engineers as Policy Makers* (Philadelphia: Temple University Press, 1987), 70–80, 158–60; Paul Burka, "The Farm-to-Market Road," *Texas Monthly*, 11(4) (April 1983): 134. Eventually, under terms of the Federal-Aid Highway Act of 1936, limited federal funding was also made available to counties for designated and state-approved secondary roads; Seely, 159.

9. Steven R. Rae, Joseph E. King, and Donald R. Abbe, *New Mexico Historic Bridge Survey* (Santa Fe: New Mexico State Highway and Transportation Department, 1987), 8–9.

10. *Public Roads of New Mexico: Mileage and Expenditures in 1904*, USDA Office of Public Roads, *Circular No. 52* (Washington, D.C.: Government Printing Office, 1904); William H. Courtright, comp., *New Mexico Statutes Annotated for 1929* (Denver, CO: W. H. Courtright Publishing Co., 1929).

11. Idem.; *New Mexico Historic Bridge Survey*, 7.

12. Chaves County Commissioners Proceedings, 3 July 1899 (Volume A, 247), County Clerk's Office, Chaves County Courthouse, Roswell, NM (hereafter cited as Chaves County Proceedings).

13. Chaves County Proceedings, 7–8 October 1901 (Volume A, 354–55).

14. "Pecos River Bridge," *Roswell Record*, 11 October 1901.

15. "Rio Hondo Bridge at Picacho," National Register of Historic Places Registration Form, 1996, as found in the Historic Preservation Division files, State of New Mexico (hereafter cited as 1996 National Register Nomination); "Pecos River Bridge," *Roswell Record*, 11 October 1901; "Bridge No. 1487," New Mexico State Highway Commission, Plan & Profile of Proposed State Highway Project No. 753(1) [4 November 1943], 6, as found in Records Control Unit, New Mexico State Highway and Transportation Department, Santa Fe, NM.

16. "Pecos River Bridge," *Roswell Register*, 25 July 1902.

17. Herbert Yeo Papers, Rio Grande Historical Collections, New Mexico State University; "Adj. Gen. Charlton Makes This Estimate After Survey Sunday," *Roswell Record*, 31 May 1937; Morgan Nelson, personal recollections to Cameron Saffell, 8 April 2001.

18. The dedication of the new 1,500-foot-long bridge—at that time, the longest in the state—was a major community event that had extensive local media coverage. *Roswell Morning Dispatch*, 20 August 1939; and *Roswell Daily Record*, 14–27 August 1939.

19. Chaves County Road Board, 7 June 1943, in Chaves County Proceedings, Volume D, 551.

20. Descriptive narrative, 1996 National Register Nomination; Historic Bridge Survey, 38–39.

21. Descriptive narrative, 1996 National Register Nomination; personal recollections told to Cameron Saffell and Dave Harkness of the N.M. Farm and Ranch Heritage Museum during their general research, 2000–01.

22. Historic Bridge Survey, 26 and 86, which identified the structure as the Rio Hondo Bridge at Picacho, named for the nearby community and to distinguish it from a different steel truss bridge a few miles away near Tinnie; 1996 National Register Nomination.

23. "Green Bridge," National Register of Historic Places Registration Form, 21 August 2008, as found in National Register Digital Assets, National Park Service Focus Digital Asset Management System: narrative at http://npgallery.nps.gov/pdfhost/docs/nrhp/text/08000791.pdf and photographs at http://npgallery.nps.gov/pdfhost/docs/nrhp/photos/08000791.pdf (accessed 28 December 2015).

24. T. Allan Comp and Donald Jackson, *Bridge Truss Types: A Guide to Dating and Identifying*, American Association for State and Local History, *Technical Leaflet 95*, packaged with *History*

News, 32, no. 5 (May 1977), n.p. [2, 3, 6]; Milo Ketchum, *Design of Highway Bridges of Steel, Timber, and Concrete*, 2nd ed. (New York: McGraw-Hill, Co., 1920), 103.

25. Victory Darnell, *A Directory of American Bridge-Building Companies, 1840–1900*. Occasional Publication No. 4 (Washington, D.C.: Society for Industrial Archeology, 1984); Dixie Legler and Carol Highsmith, *Historic Bridges of Maryland* (Crownsville: Maryland Historical Trust Press, 2002); Newcomer Road Pratt Half-Hip Truss Bridge over Beaver Creek, near Roxbury, Washington County (MHT-WA-II-475); Maryland Historical Trust Inventory Form for State Historic Site Survey, Summer 1979; and "The Pratt Truss," 72–73, available at https://www.roads.maryland.gov/OPPEN/V-Pratt.pdf (accessed 5 June 2016).

26. National Bridge Inventory Database, Federal Highway Administration, available at http://www.fhwa.dot.gov/bridge/nbi.cfm (accessed 4 June 2016). For a brief overview of the NBID, and an example of how structural engineers used 14.3 million inspection entries collected between 1983 and 2006 to document patterns of bridge damage, see Waseem Dekelbab, Adel Al-Wazeer, and Bobby Harris, "History Lessons from the National Bridge Inventory," *Public Roads*, 71, no. 5 (May–June 2008): 30–36; available at http://www.fhwa.dot.gov/publications/publicroads/08may/05.cfm (accessed 4 June 2016). The agencies supporting research and historic bridge preservation can be overwhelming. For example, the National Cooperative Highway Research Program (NCHRP) began in 1962, when the American Association of State Highway and Transportation Officials launched a program, in cooperation with the Federal Highway Administration of the U.S. Department of Transportation, to perform objective research. The Transportation Research Board of the National Academies administers the NCHRP. Joe Crossett et al., *Communicating the Value of Preservation: A Playbook*, NCHRP Report 742 (Washington, D.C.: Transportation Research Board of the National Academies, 2012), available at http://onlinepubs.trb.org/onlinepubs/nchrp/nchrp_rpt_742.pdf (accessed 4 June 2016).

27. Comp and Jackson, [6]; Elizabeth Jo Lampl, "Harmony Road Bridge (Bridge No. F16-24) HAER No. MD-120," spanning Little Catoctin Creek, Myersville vicinity, Frederick County, Maryland, Historic American Engineering Record, National Park Service, report available at https://cdn.loc.gov/master/pnp/habshaer/md/md1400/md1462/data/md1462data.pdf (accessed 29 May 2016); photographs available at https://www.loc.gov/item/md1462/ (accessed 29 May 2016).

28. Lampl, first quote 2; second quote 3–4.

29. Paul Daniel Marriott, *Preservation Office Guide to Historic Roads: Clarifying Preservation Goals for State Historic Preservation Offices Establishing Preservation Expectations for State Transportation Departments* (Washington, D.C.: Historic Preservation Office, June 2010), available at http://www.historicroads.org/documents/GUIDE.pdf (accessed 4 June 2016), 23n2; Lampl, 4. For more on road preservation, see Mary E. McCahon et al., *Design and Management of Historic Roads*, NCHRP Web-Only Document, 189 (n.p.: National Cooperative Highway Research Program, 2012), available at http://onlinepubs.trb.org/onlinepubs/nchrp/nchrp_W189.pdf (accessed 4 June 2016).

30. Marriott, 37. Richard F. Weingroff, "Federal Aid Road Act of 1916: Building the Foundation," *Public Roads*, 60, no. 1 (Summer 1996), available at http://www.fhwa.dot.gov/publications/publicroads/96summer/p96su2.cfm (accessed 4 June 2016).

31. E-mail, Pete Watson to Debra A. Reid, 5 June 2016. In the author's collection.

32. *State of New Jersey Pinelands Commission, National Parks and Recreation Act of 1978*, Sec. 471i(a)1, Pine Barrens Area, New Jersey (Lisbon, NJ: Pinelands Commission, 1998), 2, 4, available at http://www.nj.gov/pinelands/reserve/NR_act_1978_502_16.pdf (accessed 6 June 2016).

33. Linda Flint McClelland et al., "Guidelines for Evaluating and Documenting Rural Historic Landscapes," *National Register Bulletin*, no. 30 (1989, revised 1999), n.p., available at https://

www.nps.gov/nr/publications/bulletins/nrb30/ (accessed 5 June 2016). The guidelines stressed the need to provide context for the features, and the need to document their relationship to each other. The National Park Service demarcated characteristics that "should be located on sketch maps accompanying National Register forms" with an asterisk. Bold is in the original.

34. *New Jersey Historic Bridge Survey* (September 1994), available at http://www.state.nj.us/transportation/works/environment/pdf/Survey_Doc.pdf (accessed 5 June 2016), 4–5, 11–23.

35. Kimberly R. Sebold, historian, David Ames, photographer, Camp's Big Oaks Market, Historic American Buildings Survey, HABS No. NJ-997 (Summer 1990), available at http://cdn.loc.gov/master/pnp/habshaer/nj/nj1200/nj1283/data/nj1283data.pdf (accessed 4 June 2016).

36. *The High Risk Rural Roads Program in the Delaware Valley*, Publication 10070 (Philadelphia, PA: Delaware Valley Regional Planning Commission, 2011), available at http://www.dvrpc.org/reports/10070.pdf (accessed 5 June 2016).

37. Marriott, *Preservation Office Guide to Historic Roads*, 3–4; McCahon et al., *Design and Management of Historic Roads*.

38. *New Jersey Historic Bridge Survey*, 182. Larry Kidder, *Farming Pleasant Valley: 250 Years of Life in Rural Hopewell Township, New Jersey* (n.p.: self-published, 2014), 167–77.

39. *New Jersey Historic Bridge Survey*, 60.

40. "Bear Tavern Road/Jacob's Creek Crossing Rural Historic District Registration Form," entered 11 November 2011, available at https://www.nps.gov/nr/feature/weekly_features/2011/BearTavernRoad_JacobsCreekCrossingHD.pdf (accessed 30 May 2016); "Hughes presents 'minimized' plan for Jacobs Creek bridge to freeholders," press release, Mercer County, New Jersey (22 September 2011), available at http://nj.gov/counties/mercer/news/releases/approved/110922.html (accessed 30 May 2016); Brendan McGrath, "Bear Tavern Bridge Opens after Closely Watched 5-Year Replacement Project," *The Times of Trenton* (9 September 2014), available at http://www.nj.com/mercer/index.ssf/2014/09/bear_tavern_bridge_opens_after_closely_watched_5-year_replacement_project.html (accessed 30 May 2016).

CHAPTER 11

HORSES, HARNESS, AND TRANSPORT

Informing Interdisciplinary Interpretation

Barbara Corson, VMD

NOTE: Barbara Corson, a doctor of veterinary medicine, has influenced the ways that people at living history farms understand the tools and equipment with which they work. She has accomplished this because of her attention to detail and her enthusiasm for learning. She has presented at numerous conferences of the Association for Living History, Farm and Agricultural Museums (ALHFAM), and her illustrated articles are must-reads, whether a person is starting a career or needing a reboot. The following consolidates two articles: "Putting the Cart before the Horse: An Overview of Horse-Drawn Vehicle Design," *Proceedings of 2006 ALHFAM Conference and Annual Meeting* (2007), and "Harness the Horses, and Get Up, Ye Horsemen," *Proceedings of the 2015 ALHFAM Conference and Annual Meeting* (2016), 64–71. This revision shifts the delivery a bit to better meet the needs of museums and historic sites seeking to interpret the humanities, biology, physics, and technology of agriculture.

Photographs provide opportunities for you to practice identification of features that Barbara Corson explains in her narrative. She wrote the captions for these photographs, so after you practice, check the captions to see how you did.

T HE EFFORT to learn about horses, harness, and vehicles is worthwhile, whether you are focused on understanding and preserving the past, or interested in a sustainable future.[1] Like other agrarian kinetifacts,[2] the lore of horses, harness, and horse-drawn vehicles warrants documentation and study. Fewer and fewer people with knowledge and skills share in the task. If more don't join in, the knowledge and skills are at risk of being lost.

Horses and mules outnumbered oxen historically, but horses, mules, and oxen coexisted, and oxen suited certain farming landscapes more than horses. Horses and mules could be ridden or harnessed, so they had the advantage over oxen to satisfy the need for transportation. Oxen, however, had a niche, providing slow and steady draft. By the end of World War II, tractors eliminated the need for draft stock on farms. The U.S. Census no longer counted workhorses after 1950. Some people continued to use horses and other draft stock for farmwork, and to keep horses for riding, carriage driving, or other businesses and hobbies. Living history farms and open-air museums helped preserve traditions, and publications such as *Small Farmer's Journal* and Lynn R. Miller's *Work Horse Handbook* (1981) provide high-caliber how-to advice.

Artifacts in many forms attest to the predominance of horses. Every museum or historic site holds tangible evidence in the form of letters, diaries, census data, photographs and artwork, literature and poetry, and three-dimensional artifacts such as harness and horse-drawn vehicles. Mules and mule skinners, and oxen, yokes, and carts warrant comparable study. The overview provided in this chapter will help you interpret exceptions to the norm, too, such as the photograph depicting a cow pulling a plow, or a goat pulling a small wagon.

This paper provides an overview of harness, hitches, and vehicles that will increase your understanding of historic collections. It takes a form-and-function approach to help you recognize combinations of horse, harness, and horse-drawn vehicles appropriate to a given task. The draft horses hauling the beer wagon from the brewery have a different harness than the pony hauling the cart in a downtown parade. Everything is suited to the task. The most common horse, the dual-purpose animal trained to drive, ride, and cultivate, was not suited to haul the beer wagon or the pony cart. Horses and associated artifacts also provide avenues to interpret livestock in the city, and by extension, interpret agriculture in the city.

The subjects of harness and horse-drawn vehicles interest me but also confuse me. Even after buying (and even reading!) many books on carriages, and trying to memorize pages of terminology, I was (am) still confused, in part because there is a large amount of information, and in part because the references sometimes contradict each other. I have organized the material and categorized it to make it easier to recall and to understand. The memorization of terminology comes naturally after understanding some basic facts about fitting harness to horse anatomy and fitting the carriage to the horse, too.

Horse and Automobile Analogies

Most of us are familiar with automobiles—so familiar, in fact, that we tend to forget that automobile terms often derive from horse-drawn carriage terminology. Today the average person might laugh when they hear a person say, "I'm teaching my horse to drive." The verb "drive," meaning "to urge onward and direct the course of," as of an animal drawing a vehicle, is as old as c. 900 and first articulated in Old English (according to the *Oxford English Dictionary*). We have been "driving" cars only for a bit more than one hundred years. In many languages, the verb "to drive" has its roots in words originally meaning "to follow animals," as in "driving game." Since you follow the horse when riding in a carriage, it was natural to apply the verb "drive" to this form of transportation. Other words—*car, cab, truck, van, bus*—all applied to horse-drawn vehicles long before the combustion engine appeared. Because of our familiarity with automobiles, I have adopted the horse–automobile metaphor to describe parts of a carriage.

This quote from *Audels Automobile Guide with Questions, Answers, and Illustrations for Owners, Operators, and Repairmen* (1915) helps us launch our exploration:

> No hard and fast rules can be laid down regarding the skills required in the driver of an automobile. As a general rule of thumb: the man who is a first class horseman will make a first class automobile driver because he will show the same understanding, consideration and mercy for his motor car that he would show his horse.

The engine of a horse-drawn vehicle, is, of course, the horse (or horses). The number of horses (the horsepower) needed to move a vehicle provided a way to classify horse-drawn vehicles. Although people have been designing vehicles based on the strength of horses for millennia, the term *horsepower* as a standardized unit of power did not come into use until the beginning of the nineteenth century. The Scotsman James Watt is credited with first defining *horsepower* as a measure of work done per unit of time. After careful observations of horses at work on sweeps, he calculated (with apparent accuracy) that a horse can move 22,000 foot-pounds of coal per minute. Then, for some reason, he increased this carefully calculated amount by 50 percent to arrive at the seemingly arbitrary amount of 33,000 foot pounds per minute, which is the current definition of one horsepower. In other words, the average horse does not reliably produce one horsepower. Such are the complexities of physics, biology, and semantics.

Visitors to historic sites often ask: "How much can a horse pull?" The answer to that, of course, starts out, "it depends . . ." It depends on the type of vehicle (wheeled versus sliding), the road surface (ice versus mud), how far you're going (sixty miles or twelve feet), the weather conditions (65 degrees and low humidity versus Mississippi in August), etc. For wheeled vehicles, the American Driving Society offers some rules of thumb:

- In excellent conditions: (i.e., level and firm road surface, pleasant weather conditions) pulling capacity = horse's weight x 1.25, i.e., if the horse weighs 1,000 pounds, then the cart and its contents can weigh 1,250 pounds and the horse will be able to pull it.
- In average conditions: (i.e., road surface varies slightly, some hills, less-than-perfect weather) pulling capacity = horse's weight.
- In bad conditions: (i.e., soft ground, mud or unpacked snow, hilly ground, heat, humidity or severe cold, wind, etc.) pulling capacity = horse's weight x 0.75 or less.

These are useful rules of thumb for today's drivers—but it would be a mistake, I believe, to think that these guidelines were followed uniformly in the past.

Harness Function

I consider the harness equivalent to the "transmission" of the horse-drawn vehicle, because the harness connects the horsepower to the workload. Horses need to be harnessed so their strength can move and control the load. I explain it like this: "Humans and primates move things using their hands, elephants use their trunks, and many animals pick up things in their mouths, but horses need to be harnessed to use their strength to pull loads."

To be technically correct, horses don't really pull things, they push. In its simplest form, a horse harness consists of something to push against (i.e., a collar) and something to connect the collar to the load (i.e., the traces). The rest of the harness either connects the collar to the load and/or keeps the collar in place.

In theory, all anyone needed historically (or today) to drag a plow or a log on level ground is a horse with a collar and traces. The harness needs more parts when the surface varies in grade, or is slippery, or steep, or when the load is raised on wheels, or when the load must be pushed back as well as forward. Added harness parts allow the animal's strength to slow or stop the load. These parts include a harness saddle, britchen, shafts, or tongue to help the horse turn, stop, and back up the load. Pairing horses affects the harness, too, requiring a team or pair harness to connect the horses to the load and to each other.

The study of harness design complements the study of harness function. There are many factors that influence harness design, beginning with the laws of physics (e.g., friction and inertia) and biology (horse anatomy and physiology). Other factors include materials available to a given culture (wood, rawhide, leather, bronze, iron, stainless steel, etc.); the type of terrain being navigated (flat, marshy, mountainous, rocky, etc.); and the type of load (wheeled, dragging, or sliding). Considering all the variables, it is no surprise that different cultures have developed different harness systems. And considering the universality of the laws of physics and biology, it's no surprise that there are commonalities.

The first type of harness (using the word loosely) is the neck yoke[3]—an ancient piece of technology that works well on cattle because of their anatomy and physiology. Cattle generally have a horizontal neck carriage, and the shoulders are located slightly farther back on the torso than those of a horse. The bovine anatomy creates a good seat for the wooden neck yoke, especially when the animals are worked in pairs.

The first-known horse harness systems include a yoke held in place with straps around the neck and body. A horse pulling an Assyrian chariot has such a harness, as depicted in a seventh-century B.C.E. bas-relief on display at the Louvre in Paris, France. Such horse yokes do not work on horses as they do on cattle, because horses tend to have a more upright neck carriage and a firm crest, and the shoulders are located farther forward, overlying the withers (i.e., the first thoracic vertebrae). Equine anatomy doesn't create a good seat for a neck yoke, and ancient horses were limited in the amount of work they could do wearing a neck yoke.

The breast-collar or breast band harness was (and is) an improvement over a neck yoke, but still did not allow a horse to use its full strength. With a breast band, the forces of pushing into the harness are focused on a fairly small area of the chest. And the horse's shoulder anatomy decrees that the "point of draft" (the most efficient and comfortable place for the horse to push against) is located approximately at the neck of the scapula (or shoulder blade). On most horses, this area is located a few inches higher than the chest, buried in the neck, and therefore out of reach for a breast band. Instead, the breast band has to be positioned below the point of draft, either over the point of the shoulder or in front of the upper arm bone. This is inefficient at best and can actually be painful and damaging for the horse. Other problems arise when using a breast band. When pulling a heavy load, the breast band deforms and constricts the horse's shoulders and chest. Also, if the breast collar is used to pull an object on the ground, the line of force passes below the horse's center of gravity, which decreases the efficiency, and the downward angle of the trace tends to displace the breast band downward.

These failings of the breast collar harness help explain why horses were not much used for agricultural power or other "heavy draft" work (in Europe) until the neck collar was developed. The equine shoulder and neck do form a good seat for a neck collar, developed around 800 C.E. The neck collar consists of a system of firm padding, usually made of leather and/or cloth, combined with rigid pieces of metal and/or wood called hames. The neck collar accommodates the needs of the horse as a draft animal in several ways:

1. It has a wide surface area against which the horse can put all its force without discomfort,
2. If the collar is designed and fitted correctly, the line of draft (the line taken by the traces from the collar to the load) will pass through the horse's center of gravity, increasing the amount of work the horse can comfortably do, and
3. The rigid hames made of wood and/or metal prevent the traces from pulling the collar out of shape. (An out-of-shape collar impinges on the horse's anatomy, in the same way that an out-of-shape shoe would impinge on your foot.) The hames of an Anglo-American collar are connected top and bottom with leather hame straps. Their purpose is not to adjust collar size, but to keep the hames firmly seated on the collar.

The fit of the collar relates to "point of draft." Every horse has its own point of draft based on its anatomy. For most horses, this point is located on the shoulder blade near the actual shoulder joint. To locate this point from the outside (that is, without dissecting the horse), first find the "line of the shoulder," or shoulder angle, which runs from the withers to the point of the shoulder. Then divide the line into imaginary thirds. The anatomic point of draft is usually at or near the junction of the lower and middle third.

Every collar also has a "point of draft," which is a well-padded and reinforced area designed to withstand the pressure and friction of the trace. Of course, each hame also has a point of draft, easily identified as the point where the trace attaches. For correct fit, these three points of draft (anatomic, collar, and hame) must overlie each other.

Table 11.1 Basic Harness Comparison

	BREAST COLLAR (rests on the horse's chest)	NECK COLLAR (encircles the horse's neck)
Chronology	Is ancient in design	Developed in Europe during the early Middle Ages
Form	Consists of a strap across the horse's lower chest	Consists of rigid wooden or metal hames with leather padding resting on the shoulders
Function	Best suited for relatively light loads and a high point of attachment, like a two-wheeled cart or a sleigh	Best when the load is much more than half the weight of the horse; for coaches, carriages, hilly areas, longer rides; agricultural work; forestry and freight hauling
Positive Characteristics	Is easy to make and fit ("one size fits all")	Provides a larger surface area for the horse to push against Does not compress the horse's chest
Negative Consequences	Provides only a small surface area for the horse to push against Compresses the horse's chest if the load is heavy	Construction requires specialized equipment (particularly if leather) Different size horses require different size neck collars (individual fitting is ideal) Collar requires padding that conforms to the horse's neck The hame needs to fit the collar and the horse's neck so the hames and collar fit together snugly

In a perfect world, horses would always have perfect conformation and harnesses would always fit. As we know, this is not a perfect world. Whether you look at old images or modern photographs, you will see frequent examples of imperfect horse conformation and imperfect harness fit.

Returning to the automobile analogies, another part of the "transmission" is the singletree (also known as, swingletree, whiffletree). The singletree is a bar of wood that is attached to the load (for our purposes, the vehicle) by a central pivot point. The traces attach to the ends of the singletree. When the horse moves its shoulders, the singletree swivels and this smooths the transfer of energy from the horse's shoulders to the vehicle. This feature was invented sometime in the Middle Ages and is used not only for agricultural work but also on a majority of wheeled vehicles, with a few exceptions.

One such exception: During the nineteenth century, it became fashionable to hitch teams using a fixed bar called a "splinter bar" on the carriage to attach the traces, or to be more precise, the traces were attached to upright cylinders called "roller bolts," which, in turn, were mounted on the splinter bar. This made for tighter control of carriage movements (less slop and wiggle than using singletrees), but it was also harder on the horses' shoulders. Roller bolts can still be seen on carriages designed for use in town, where tighter control during stopping, starting, and turning is an advantage, and where shorter trips and flatter roads are the norm.

Cultural distinction exists. An English cart harness does not use a singletree. Instead, the collar and other harness parts attach directly to the shafts, which have specialized fittings that facilitate the connections. In Scandinavia (Norway and Sweden), a similar method is used for all types of driving, and the harness attaches via slotted or bracketed shafts directly to carts, wagons, sleds, and even agricultural and logging implements. When pulling a heavy two-wheeled cart, the shafts may bear considerable weight, especially going downhill or braking. So a heavy cart harness includes a cart saddle to distribute the weight, and a Scandinavian harness includes a rigid saddlebow called the høvre.

The body is the part of the vehicle that supports and confines the load, whether the load is rocks or human passengers. The body is probably the most distinctive part of the carriage, and this is the part of the carriage that was made by the "carriage maker." Other specialists—that is, wheelwrights, upholsters, shaft-makers—made other parts of the carriage. In the horse-drawn era, a carriage maker was an essential part of the community. The majority of carriage shops dealt locally and made carriages that fulfilled a local need. This is one factor that has contributed to the large and confusing array of names for types of carriages. What was called a Victoria in one town might have been called a Mylord in another location.

Some carriage makers developed a national or even international reputation, and today, some carriages are still known by the name of their maker. A good example is the Brewster Carriage Company, originally established in New Haven, Connecticut, in 1810. Andrew Jackson and Martin Van Buren both owned carriages made by Brewster. Because the Brewster Company kept careful records of carriages they made, including serial numbers, Brewsters are very collectible today.[4]

The undercarriage, or running gear of an automobile or a carriage, is the interface and connection between the body and the ground. This part includes many subparts, including the axle(s), springs, and the wheels (or runners). In a four-wheeled vehicle with an articulating front axle, the undercarriage includes the fifth wheel, and the various perches, bolsters, hounds, futchells, and swaybars. An understanding of the undercarriage is not essential to an enjoyment of driving (either automobiles or horse-drawn vehicles), but since vehicles can be classified based on details of undercarriage design, it's perhaps worth investing a little effort in learning the basics.

Axle(s)—Wheeled vehicles can be classified based on the number of axles they have: two or four. Axles can be made of wood or metal. Metal axles can often be dated with some accuracy based on their design or imprint from the factory where they were made. Vehicles with wooden axles can be harder to date, since they may be hand-made on the farm using undatable techniques.

Wheels—This is a whole discussion in its own right, really. To increase my understanding of carriages, I have merely skimmed the surface of "wheelology." Wheels make it easier to move things. Something large and/or heavy sliding along the ground generates a lot of friction. When wheels are used, most of the friction occurs at the axle. A big wheel with a small axle minimizes friction per distance covered, and lubricating the axle reduces friction even more. Wheels also, in effect, reduce the size of obstacles. The larger the wheel, the smaller the relative size of the "bump." This helps explain why "primitive" carts (in South America, for example) use huge wheels.

There are difficulties with wheels, of course. Making a strong, light wheel is a technological challenge, and unless you have roads, it's probably not worth it. Roads and wheels evolve together. The other component that seems to have been necessary for the development of the wheel is some form of draft animal. The Aztecs had wheeled toys, but lacking draft animals, they never developed wheeled transport.

A well-made wheel is dished to better withstand the horizontal force that the axle places on the hub when the road surface is uneven. To be strong, a dished wheel must also be angled, so that as the spokes rotate under the hub, they become vertical. These are just some of the factors that contribute to making wheel-wrighting a science as well as an art.

Since ancient times, wheels have had tires. The first tires were metal. Iron or steel tires on wooden spoked wheels were standard in Europe and America from the fourteenth through the nineteenth centuries. Goodyear's invention of the vulcanization process around 1840 made rubber tires a possibility. The first rubber tires on carriages were solid. Pneumatic tires were patented around 1880. Whether solid or pneumatic, rubber tires of the correct hardness or density are great "horse savers"; they even out irregularities in the road surface without contributing significantly to friction. They also make for a quieter and smoother ride for the passengers.

Steering Mechanism—Turning a two-wheeled cart is easy. The shafts provide leverage to turn the body, and one wheel simply travels farther than the other. Turning a four-wheeled vehicle is more complicated, especially if the wheel base is of any length. If the vehicle has no "articulating axle" (in which one axle pivots under the body of the carriage), the only way to turn is to skid the rear wheels laterally, using levers and/or jacks. Since the articulating axle is thought to have been invented sometime in the last millennium before the Common Era, it's small wonder that four-wheeled vehicles were barely known in ancient times. Vehicles on straight, parallel runners have similar problem with steering. On ice or packed snow, sleds and sleighs skid laterally to turn, but if you get into deeper, firmer snow, lateral skidding is difficult and you are likely to get "up sot" as related in the song "Jingle Bells." (*"The horse was lean and lank. Misfortune seemed his lot. He got us in a drifted bank and then we were up sot."*)

Articulating Axle—Definitions for the various terms for the parts of the undercarriage can be confusing and references sometimes conflict. Here is my current working understanding of some of the terms. The hounds and bolsters support the body of a four-wheeled wagon and also elevate it over the axle, giving more space for the wheels to turn underneath. Hounds are longitudinal supports; the bolsters are transverse supports. The futchells are transverse members that form a socket for the shafts of a two-wheeled vehicle, or the tongue/pole of a four-wheeled vehicle. Swaybars are diagonal wooden members that attach between the futchells and the pole and that help strengthen the foregear when turning. The axle turns under the forward bolster on a pivot point called the kingpin. In many carriages, the weight of the forepart of the carriage is supported during its turn by the fifth wheel. The perch is a longitudinal member of wood or iron that joins the front and rear axle; this term usually applies to coaches and carriages, while the term *hound* is used for wagons. (My reference for these definitions is the Guild of Model Wheelwrights in Edinburg, Scotland, to whom I send my thanks as well as my apologies if I still don't have it quite right!)

As an aside: For me, the complexities of undercarriage terminology illustrate the usefulness of thinking about carriages based on form and function. Even if you aren't sure of the exact definition of a given carriage term, if you have an understanding of some of the basics of design (i.e., the purpose of a given structure), you can still have an intelligent conversation on the subject.

The articulating axle by itself solves some of the problems of turning a four-wheeled vehicle, but not all. If the wheels are outside of the vehicle body, turning the axle means the wheel rims will intersect with the vehicle. At best, this means you have a very limited turning radius; at worst, it can damage the carriage or even upset it. An early (Renaissance through eighteenth century) solution to the problem was to use smaller wheels on the front axle. Some vehicles had very small wheels, which allow for sharp turns but make small irregularities into big obstacles, impeding forward progress. A later solution was to design the carriage body with a "cut under" that (as the name suggests) allows the wheels to travel under the carriage.

Brakes—In an automobile, brakes are a distinct entity, but for horse-drawn vehicles, brakes are more of a general concept: Brakes are whatever helps you control the vehicle's forward (or backward) movement. For a stone boat sliding on dirt or grass, friction provides the only brake you need. In a light wheeled vehicle, or a vehicle sliding on ice or packed snow, the horse and harness can provide the brakes, often by way of the shafts (or pole/tongue) and the breeching assembly. Some carts use a "false britchen," which is basically a strap between the shafts behind the horse. When the horse stops, the breeching stops, then the shafts stop, and so the cart or sleigh has to stop, too.

Heavier vehicles (anything that weighs more than the horse) need additional brakes. Those brakes can take various forms, including drags, brake "shoes," and eventually, hydraulic disk brakes.

As a "side bar": A six-horse team can use all six horses going uphill, but going downhill will only have two horses' worth of braking power, because only the "wheel horses" are harnessed to the rigid pole or tongue. In various travel accounts, you can read about the coach or wagon stopping at the top of a downhill stretch of road to engage the brakes in various ways, e.g., placing a stout pole through the spokes of the rear wheels to lock them.

Springs—Primitive vehicles had no springs, and needless to say, did not provide a very comfortable ride even at slow speeds. There is a funny and graphic paragraph in Harriet Beecher Stowe's book *Uncle Tom's Cabin* that describes how the passengers in a coach are tossed about during an average outing. An early method of producing an "easy carriage" was to suspend the vehicle over the wheels on leather straps. This practice has been associated with the Hungarian city of Kotse, or Kocs (spelled various ways), and this was apparently the origin of the word *coach* (English) and *Kutsche* (German). During the sixteenth and seventeenth centuries, a "coach" was a suspended, covered vehicle, while a "chariot" was an uncovered and rigid vehicle (ref. *A History of Carriages*, by Lt. Col. Paul H. Downing, *The Carriage Journal*, vol. 1, no. 4).

The first metal springs are documented in the later half of the seventeenth century (1669), and metal springs in the shape of Whip or S springs were common by the eighteenth century. C-springs were in use from around 1790 to the early twentieth century.

The engine, transmission, body, and undercarriage are the most basic and fundamental parts that I try to keep in mind when looking at a carriage and relating form to function. You can continue the metaphor with analysis of the accelerator (whip), glove box, spares kit, horn, fenders, dashboard, etc., if you're so inclined.

Another way of learning about carriages is to look at the factors that influence their design. The comedian Gallagher once asked, "Have you ever wondered what chairs would look like if your knees bent the other way?" You might ask a similar question about carriages, such as, "What would carriages look like if there were no horses and instead, there were one-thousand-pound rodents that we used for draft?"—making the point that a primary reason carriages are built the way they are is because horses are built the way *they* are.

There are significant differences between horses and other draft animals, like cattle, camels, reindeer, and dogs. Here is a short list:

- Horses are (generally speaking) more reactive and less stoic than cattle.
- Horses are faster than cattle. The average ox walks at about two miles per hour, even when feeling frisky. The average horse (if there is such a creature) walks at about four miles an hour and can trot steadily at twelve miles per hour if the road or other surface allows.
- Horses tend to use momentum when moving. For example, when trying to start a heavy load, or when starting up a steep hill, or when stuck in mud or snow, they often make sudden lunging movements. Sudden lunging movements tend to break things more often than the slow deliberate movements of oxen.
- Compared to cattle, which have thick skin loosely attached to the underlying tissues, horses have a relatively thin skin that is fixed tightly to the underlying muscle. This means that something rubbing against a horse's skin is very likely to create friction and make a sore.
- The shape of the equine neck, chest, and shoulders does not provide a natural seat for a yoke (primitive technology), but they do provide a natural seat for a collar (more complicated technology).

These differences help explain why oxen are used preferentially for heavy draft over horses in primitive agrarian settings. With their stoic natures and low-gear, "tractor"-type power, oxen are well suited to rough terrain and heavy loads. Ancient cultures, including the Assyrians, Greeks, and Celts, used horses for light draft (chariots), packing, and riding, until technology favored the construction of roads and the developments of lighter, stronger vehicles and harnessing systems. In Western Europe, carriages were still relatively heavy and clumsy in the sixteenth century and horse-drawn transport between population centers was limited. The "carriage age" in Western culture was the latter half of the nineteenth century, when carriage-building, harness-making, and road-building technology reached a kind of common zenith.

Physics—In addition to friction, which was briefly mentioned above, many other principles of physics apply to carriage design. (This may help explain the small number of people who are interested in carriage design!) To mention a few:

- Gravity: Heavy loads demand heavy construction. Moving heavy objects like rocks begs a design that minimizes lifting, hence the design of stone boats, and of dump carts (off-loading rocks or manure is hard work unless you have a dump cart).
- Leverage: In a two-wheeled cart, the axle and wheels, carriage body, shafts, and horse are a lever system. The force pushing down on the horse's back can be changed by the location and amount of the weight behind the axle. A good example of this principle is the Hansom cab, which was well balanced when the driver took his seat behind the cab. The Norwegian Karjol (cariole) is another example. In this vehicle, the driver's seat is placed on the long, flexible shafts and the horse consequently bears much of the driver's weight—unless the "gate boy" takes his place behind the driver. In the absence of the gate boy, the humane driver would place a bag of shot or similar heavy material in the second seat as a counterweight.
- Centripetal force: Carriages that are top-heavy tend to fall over when turning corners. This did not stop people from designing tall carts in the nineteenth century, including one called "the Suicide," in which the driver sat about four feet from the ground and the groom sat about three feet higher.
- Entropy: All things in the universe tend to a state of decay or randomness, and carriages are no exception. Parts that tend to wear out fastest are those in contact with the damp ground (wheels or runners) or parts that are subject to high friction. Some things cause more problems by breaking than others when they break. In a two-wheeled cart, decay in a shaft or a wheel is potentially life-threatening for the driver and passengers.

Another factor that undeniably influences carriage design is fashion. Some vehicles were seemingly designed, not in response to the above factors, but rather *in spite* of them! Baroque coaches come to mind.

There are many other factors that influence the design of carriages, including the type of load to be moved, the distance of travel, the speed required, the road surface (or lack of one), and the materials available to the builder. These numerous factors translate into numerous designs.

Classifying Vehicles

Faced with any large group of diverse objects, humans naturally try to organize, group, and classify the objects. This is true whether the objects are books, species, politicians, or vehicles. There are quite a few "taxonomy" systems for classifying carriages, based on characteristics such as:

- Number of horses (single-horse vehicles versus multiples)
- Style (formal, pleasure, or sporting vehicles)
- Driver (owner-driven versus coachman-driven)
- Age (antique versus modern)

For me, the system that makes the most sense is the "form and function" classification system. In my version of this system, vehicles are classified depending on the:

- Type of load (freight or people)
- Weight of load (heavy or light)
- Intended distance (short versus long)
- Ground/road conditions (good roads versus not)

The beauty of this system is that you can, to some extent, approach the vehicle from either the "form" side or the "function" side of the equation. In other words, if you know the vehicle's function, you can deduce a lot about its form, and conversely, if you know the vehicle's form, you can deduce the function. At the risk of overstating the obvious, I offer an example or two.

Conestoga wagon: The function is to carry heavy freight for relatively long distances over bad roads. The well-known form is a result of these requirements and the availability of plentiful materials (wood, iron, etc.) and a high degree of craftsmanship.

The slipe: The function of this primitive Irish "vehicle" was to carry heavy objects (like peat) over poor or nonexistent roads. The form is a result of limited materials and technology available to the builder. Only relatively short, slow hauls were practical with this type of vehicle.

The phaeton: Usually defined as a four-wheeled vehicle for two people, this is a light carriage designed for getting around town while having a pleasant time and showing off a little.

The Concord coach is also a four-wheeled vehicle for transporting people, but the similarities end there. The Concord coach is a heavy vehicle designed for carrying multiple people (paying customers) some distance between towns over fairly rough roads.

A Short List of Vehicles and Definitions

Finally, I have arbitrarily selected a handful of carriages out of the hundreds that appear in museum collections' carriage identification guides.[5] I tried to select examples that would show something of the great variety in horse-drawn vehicle design. Hopefully something in the list will pique your interest, conform with examples in your collection, and encourage you to learn more and share what you learn. Space (and time) limitations prevent the inclusion of illustrations, but these can be found in the referenced texts.

Dray—A dray can be two- or four-wheeled. They were usually commercial vehicles, and are considered to be the heaviest of the general purpose freight vehicles. Used for deliveries around town, they characteristically had a stake body, with the wheels located underneath so that the load (planks, pipes) could project. They were used into the twentieth century. Incidentally, the word *dray* is related to the words *draw*, *drag*, and *draught*. The term *dray-horse* dates to the early 1700s; the earliest-known use of the term *dray-man* (one whose work is hauling by dray) was in the late 1500s.

Omnibus—A four-wheeled vehicle with longitudinal bench seats designed for carrying paying passengers (most commonly around ten people, but sometimes more) around town. These vehicles were ubiquitous in American and European cities in the late nineteenth century. According to some references, Nantes, France, may have been the first city to have a "bus" route, in 1826. The largest omnibus on record was built in New York, in 1875, and reportedly carried 120 passengers. It was thirty-six feet long and designed to be pulled by ten horses. It is not clear that it was ever actually used: It would certainly have been difficult to maneuver in the streets and alleys of New York City.

Landau—A light, elegant four-wheeled carriage on springs with two bench seats so four people could sit facing each other. The vehicle has a folding top over each seat and is usually driven by a coachman. This is a luxury vehicle that offers maximum visibility of the occupants, so it is popular for parades.

Gig—The name originally meant "a light, quick action" as in "gigging for eels." This is a good example of how definitions of carriage terms can vary depending on time period and reference cited. Some authorities define a *gig* as a two-wheeled cart for a single horse and a fixed seat for two people. By this definition, shays (chaises), meadow brooks, and village carts would all be types of gigs. Other references add the criterion that the seat must be above the shafts for the vehicle to be a "real" gig, or state that "the gig is more formal than the meadowbrook." Some references include the curricle, which is a two-wheeled cart for two people pulled by two horses, as a type of gig. Even under the strictest of definitions, there are many different types of gigs based on the type of springs (Dennett gig), the designer (Stanhope gig), or the intended use (park gig).

Booby Hut—This is basically a coach body on sleigh runners. A coach, in turn, is a vehicle with a closed body (including doors) and at least two transverse bench seats. For a beautiful picture of a booby hut, see the catalog of the Carriage Collection by the Museums at Stony Brook.

Break—The term *break* originally referred to a heavy (sturdy) vehicle with a high seat for breaking horses. The term came to be applied to other vehicles with heavy builds and similar high seats.

Buckboard—Originally a springless American vehicle common in "mountainous areas" or at least areas where ash trees grew. The floor was made of long, springy planks of ash wood mounted directly on the axles. Later types had separate springs. This is another good example of how definitions change with time.

Buggies—A large class of American vehicles that have four wheels, can carry two or more passengers, with a body that sits on springs. Most buggies had tops, and the shape of the box or body determined its name.

Cutter—A two-person sleigh. The American Albany cutter has curving sides; the Portland cutter was/is more common and has straight sides.

Sulky—A one-horse, one-passenger, two-wheeled vehicle. The name refers to the presumed sulky nature of the sole passenger. Also called a "selfish" in period literature, the definition could technically apply to a riding chair, but the sulky is a nineteenth-century vehicle and the riding chair is an eighteenth-century one.

Governess Cart—Designed to be pulled by a single pony, these two-wheeled vehicles had seats arranged in a backward-facing U. The driver (governess) had to drive facing sideways, so that she could keep one eye on her pony and the other on her human charges.

Wagonette—A four-wheeled vehicle that is defined (at least in part) by its seating arrangements: that is, a transverse bench seat for the driver and one passenger, and two longitudinal bench seats behind, facing each other. The passengers enter through an opening in the back.

Photo 11.1 Unlike Thoroughbred racing ("the sport of kings"), harness racing has long been considered a sport in which every man—or woman!—could take part. Currier and Ives did not necessarily treat the female competitors fairly, depicting them as aggressive and cloddish. But did Currier and Ives get the harness right for the job? Currier & Ives. *The Old Mare—The Best Horse*. New York: Published by Currier & Ives, c. 1881. Chromolithograph.

Source: Retrieved from the Library of Congress, https://www.loc.gov/item/2001700363 (accessed 30 May 2016)

Photo 11.2   Collars and traces are all that is needed for these horses to pull the street cart forward. This simple harness does not provide a means for the horses' strength to turn or stop the load, but in this case, the rails provide the steering and the human operator is in charge of the brakes. Note: It appears that one horse (the one being offered something in a bucket) appears to be lame in the right front leg. Normal horses often rest one hind leg but never a front; this posture is called "pointing," and it is uniformly a sign of pain in the pointed leg. The horse's ears also indicate (in the opinion of the author, a VMD) that he is depressed or uncomfortable. Lame horses that were nonetheless working must have been an everyday sight in the pre-petroleum era. *Horse car, New York, 1908.* 1908. Image.

Source: Retrieved from the Library of Congress, https://www.loc.gov/item/2006689803 (accessed 30 May 2016)

Photo 11.3 Four horses pull a sled with articulated front runners that allow turning. The two "wheel horses" are hitched on either side of the tongue, or pole. These horses can use their weight and strength to turn or stop the sled. Note that their harness includes a britchen. The lead team (in front) can only provide forward power because nothing rigid attaches them to the weight. This team has no britchen and only trace-carriers. Although we can't see the horse's feet in detail, we can assume that they are "sharp shod," meaning that their horseshoes have calks, or studs, that prevent them from slipping. All the power in the world won't help you if you can't get traction! *Horses pulling U.S. Mail Sled* [Nome, Alaska, between 1900 and 1927]. Image.

Source: Retrieved from the Library of Congress, https://www.loc.gov/item/99614288 (accessed 30 May 2016)

Photo 11.4 This horse is wearing a breast-collar that appears to be correctly fitted and lying above the point of the shoulder. The harness has no britchen, so the shafts acting on the girth provide the only means of stopping the vehicle. This is not a problem in the flat show-ring with a light load, but it may explain the fact that the shafts are sticking out in front of the horse's shoulders farther than the optimum. The vehicle is a four-wheeled carriage, which (lacking a cut-under) would have a relatively large turning radius. *Horse Show, 1921*. National Photo Company Collection. Image.

Source: Retrieved from the Library of Congress, https://www.loc.gov/item/npc2007004117 (accessed 30 May 2016)

Photo 11.5 Although this picture is labeled "horse and wagon," the animal is definitely a mule. It is wearing a cart harness, which, by definition, includes a wooden saddle padded with leather and cloth. A chain holds the shafts up and—because it runs in a wooden trough, or channel, over the animal's back—it can also help in moving the cart forward and in stopping it. The primary force of draft comes from the neck collar, through the "fore trace," which attaches to the staple on the shaft. A britchen, or breeching, is present, although it appears to be so loose that the cart would run into the animal before the britchen would engage. There are two girths: a tight one that holds the harness saddle in place, and a loose one, which functions to keep the cart and shafts from pivoting over backward if the load is unbalanced behind the axles. Russell Lee, photographer. *Horse and Wagon, Taylor, Texas*. Oct. 1939. Image.

Source: Retrieved from the Library of Congress, https://www.loc.gov/item/fsa1997027428/PP (accessed 30 May 2016)

Notes

1. Animal power is sustainable agriculture: A key concept in sustainable agriculture is independence from petroleum and other nonrenewable energy. Draft animals, of course, have been a source of renewable power for more than ten thousand years. In my opinion, there are many good reasons to use them in the future, and it has nothing to do with nostalgia.

2. *Kinetifact*: I don't remember where I first heard or read this word, but I have adopted it and assigned a definition: "an historic skill worthy of preservation," just as I've assigned the word *artifact* a definition: "an historic object worthy of preservation."

3. Like many words, *yoke* can have several meanings. Here it is used in its oldest sense and refers to the system of harnessing cattle in which the cross piece rests on the neck just in front of the withers. But note that the term *neck yoke* also appears in horse harnesses, usually referring to the cross piece at the forward end of the tongue or pole. The word *harness*, on the other hand, is a

younger word (from the fourteenth century) and stems from old Norse words meaning (roughly) "relating to the army." In the fourteenth century, apparently, *harness* meant the armor and other trappings of a knight or mounted warrior. The first definition of the word *harness* in the modern *Merriam-Webster Dictionary* is: "the trappings of a draft animal other than the yoke."

4. New Haven, Connecticut, *Business News Journal*, 26 February 2001; The Carriage Association of America.

5. The American Driving Society: http://www.americandrivingsociety.org; Donald Berkebile, *American Carriages, Sleighs, Sulkies, and Carts* (New York: Dover Pictorial Archives, 1977); *Carriage Terminology: A Historical Dictionary* (Washington, D.C.: Smithsonian Institute, 1978); Carriage Association of America: http://www.caaonline.com; Museums at Stony Brook, *The Carriage Collection*, 2001; Sallie Walrond, *Looking at Carriages* (J. A. Allen & Co., 1981; 2nd rev. ed., 1999); and *The Encyclopedia of Carriage Driving* (J. A. Allen & Co., 1996; updated 1999).

CHAPTER 12

LIVESTOCK IN AGRICULTURAL INTERPRETATION

Jonathan D. Kuester and Debra A. Reid

NOTE: Interpretation of agriculture remains only partially complete unless an awareness of livestock informs the interpretation. The following reflects historic precedent to rationalize interpretation of livestock (and relevant crops). Museums do not have to have living animals, or acres of crops, to interpret agriculture, but a more nuanced understanding of the historic context of crop and stock production can affect the ways that staff interpret those subjects. For those institutions in a position to support acquisition of heritage breeds and seeds, this article provides an overview of the things that staff should consider as they debate whether or not to add heritage livestock or plants to their interpretation. This decision should not be taken lightly. Livestock can become a lightning rod for public comment on farm animal conditions. Museums must recognize this and strategize responses based on established standards and museum-specific policies and procedures before issues arrive. Farmers at living history farms compiled the ALHFAM Information Sheet, "Livestock Care in Museums," to identify topics essential to consider when developing policies and procedures. ALHFAM (the Association for Living History, Farm and Agricultural Museums) has other resources, and provides workshops and conference sessions for those wishing to learn more. Because museums are educational institutions, additional useful information can be found in the *Guide for the Care and Use of Agricultural Animals in Research and Teaching* (hereafter the FASS Ag Guide), prepared by the Federation of Animal Science Societies.

This chapter began as two separate articles, one by Debra A. Reid, "Livestock and Living History: A Discussion on Professional Standards," *Midwest Open Air Museums Magazine*, 27, no. 2 (2006): 4–13; and one by Jonathan D. Kuester, "Livestock

Need Living History, Too," *Midwest Open Air Museums Magazine*, 27, no. 2 (2006), 9–12. Both were reprinted in a special issue featuring articles on research and interpretation of livestock in museums: *Midwest Open Air Museums Magazine*, 32, nos. 1 & 2 (2011). For this submission, Reid composed everything before "Livestock Need Living History," and Kuester composed everything thereafter.

W HAT ROLE can or should livestock play in agriculture interpretation? Obviously, livestock represent one of the two main approaches to agriculture, either growing crops or tending livestock. And livestock (like humans) remain dependent on the crops grown for feed. Changes in agricultural practices affect the care and feeding of both livestock and humans. Understanding these symbiotic relationships can inform the general public in ways that talking about one or the other cannot. For instance, museums and historic sites can focus on intensive animal husbandry as practiced for centuries in Europe and as transplanted to the British North American and French North American colonies. Population pressures, the need for manure, and the climate prompted farmers to limit the range of livestock to pastures and paddocks and stalls. The manure fertilized the fields, which in turn produced grain crops and hay crops to fatten the stock. Humans stabled the stock, spread the manure, harvested the crops, fed the livestock, and in turn consumed the meat. Secondary scholarship on these intensive practices can inform staff in museums and historic sites as they work on exhibits relevant to the time period and geographic area. A team of scholars documented *Robert Cole's World* in colonial Maryland, as farm families tried to stabilize their local subsistence while cultivating commodities for export to England. Brian Donahue documented early agricultural practices in Concord, Massachusetts, in *The Great Meadow*. He explained that the farmers practiced sustainable methods using hay meadows, pastures, tilled acres, orchards, and woodlots. Steven Stoll described a comparable relationship between people, livestock, and local cultural ecosystems in *Larding the Lean Earth*.[1]

The intensive animal husbandry system meant that land held value because of its productive potential, not because of its pastureland potential. The value of soil—meaning the potential of the soil to produce crops—affected soil use. Places with naturally flat land, timely rainfall, and fertile soils became, over time, the location of both monoculture and confinement operations because of the symbiotic relationship of livestock to crops. Humans instigated this transformation. J. L. Anderson's *Industrializing the Corn Belt* offers the most artifact-sensitive interpretation of the process by which soil became more valuable to till than to pasture.[2]

This chapter addresses the ways that interpreting livestock can inform public understanding of agriculture, today and historically. The interpretation does not have to include real livestock. It just needs to help the public comprehend the ecosystem required to sustain livestock in a particular time and a particular place. Some institutions might decide that the time is right to add barnyard fowl and a period-appropriate coop to their interpretive programming. How should they proceed? What factors should they consider to ensure humane care within a historic context? This chapter addresses concerns that museums and historic sites staff must address when they decide to use living animals as the basis for the interpretation. It discusses factors to consider when developing policies and procedures and operating standards. It also includes examples of different scales of livestock inclusion at historic sites and museums, and it includes suggestions about where to find more information.

Anyone interested in becoming more informed about livestock has numerous resources to consult. Namely, the organizations that support the interpretation of agriculture in historic context, ALHFAM, and its regional affiliate, the Midwest Open Air Museums Coordinating Council, offer workshops at regional and annual conferences, and institutional members willing to coordinate staff exchanges to facilitate professional development of livestock in museums and historic sites. Organizations such as Tillers International, near Kalamazoo, Michigan, likewise offer formal training programs in oxen and draft-horse husbandry and use. Publications by ALHFAM and MOMCC and the *Small Farmer's Journal* provide "how-to" advice. You do not have to invest in livestock to interpret them, but be aware of the resources that can inform you of the complex world in which domesticated animals lived.

Agriculture and Living History

The mode of interpretation affects the policies and procedures that the museums should consider to ensure that they can address public interest and manage public concerns. An early explanation of living history and agriculture interpretation indicated the centrality of crops and livestock to the practice. In 1972, John T. Schlebecker, agricultural historian at the Smithsonian Institution and advocate of living historical farms, and coauthor Gale E. Peterson (Schlebecker's graduate assistant at the time), began their *Living Historical Farms Handbook* with this definition: "On living historical farms men farm as they once did during some specific time in the past. The farms have tools and equipment like those once used, and they raise the same types of livestock and plants used during the specified era. The operations are carried on in the presence of visitors."[3] Schlebecker's advocacy for living history and agriculture interpretation helped launch the formation of the Association for Living Historical Farms and Agricultural Museums during the 1970 meeting of the Agricultural History Society. A cohort of agricultural economists, land-grant faculty, USDA employees, and state-level public officials looked to ALHFAM and to Schlebecker for the standardization in vocabulary that they needed to sustain the museums they curated and the historic sites and farmsteads that they knew people were preserving and interpreting.

Schlebecker's definition became the benchmark that colleagues referred to regularly. In 1974, Darwin Kelsey, Old Sturbridge Village agricultural historian at the time, built on it when he identified different scales of operation. In 1975 Edward L. Hawes, then a history professor at Sangamon State University (also known as the University of Illinois–Springfield) and director of the Clayville Rural Life Center, built on Kelsey's idea that living history farms varied in scale and elaborated that they adopted different degrees of abstraction, all dependent on historically appropriate environments, breeds, and seeds.

Hawes believed that the iconic living history farms, ones that interpreted the operations of a particular person at a particular time, had great potential for understanding symbiotic relationships between humans and their environments. But founders also developed representative living history farms that depicted typical farms in certain regions or of certain eras. Regardless of the approach, Hawes believed that the farms should show complete historic processes. "The land area [is] sown in different crops and the livestock will be in relative proportion. . . . The grains [will yield] . . . needed fodder, food and marketing. The farm will have crops and livestock which have the appropriate yields. . . . The farming systems and the environmental systems are accurately scaled. As such the farm setting can be used for serious research purposes."[4] According to Hawes, living history farms could convey to the general public concepts about ecosystems critical to survival but no longer familiar to the visitors. To do so, proper amounts or relative proportions of land, crops, and livestock proved vital to accurate interpretation.

Hawes recounted that, as early as the 1960s, advocates of living history farms believed that living collections, specifically "historically validated seed and plant stock, the old breeds of livestock," had to be acquired and used and systematically replaced in keeping with historic processes.[5] Already, in 1975, Darwin Kelsey had worked to backbreed chickens and sheep at Old Sturbridge Village to attain more historically accurate types of carcasses and fleece weights. The research proved rigorous and involved forensic science, with zooarchaeologists comparing contemporary skeletons to archaeological findings. Hawes and Kelsey and others argued that backbreeding for phenotype was less important than the associated goal of preserving genotype. They advocated for minor breed conservation, as initiated in Britain with the Rare Breeds Farm Parks, and in the United States through the American Minor Breeds Conservancy, now the Livestock Conservancy. Hawes noted that "'North Americans may well find the resources of living historical farms of importance in survival in the future."[6]

Little had changed ten years later, when Bill Reid, then assistant director of Old Sturbridge Village, described the acquisition of historic livestock for Firestone Farm at The Henry Ford in Dearborn, Michigan. Through a combination of purchase and genotype backbreeding, staff secured appropriate cows, chickens, hogs, and sheep to populate the relocated birthplace of Harvey Firestone. The project served as a model of research, restoration, and public interpretation from 1985 into the 1990s.[7]

Almost thirty years after ALHFAM's formation, some farmers at living history farms found themselves the targets of animal rights activists. Concerned citizens picketed and protested some institutions so aggressively that it compromised the educational nature of the livestock programs. ALHFAM's farm members wanted to ensure that museums with livestock could justify the authentic farm environments they had worked so hard to document and re-create. This included lots that became muddy when it rained and dusty when it did not rain; flies buzzing around visitors in the barnyard, and seasonal butchering programs. In 1999 the ALHFAM farmers proposed guidelines to help museums and historic sites draft policies and procedures for livestock care and management.[8]

Obviously, the definition hardly matters if the museum fails to engage an audience. When museums clearly articulate the significance of their livestock in relation to accomplishing their educational mission, they will be better positioned to defend the expenditures on livestock and staff, and better able to tie those interpretive tools to meaningful programming.

Problems and Potential

It takes a lot of time, money, expertise, knowledge of local ordinances, flexible staff, and physical resources in the form of buildings and grounds to accomplish the ideal living history farm complete with heritage stock. Advocates of living history farms during the 1970s realized that not all institutions had the resources to collect, preserve, and interpret all stock, from chickens to cattle. They advocated for livestock exchange to help distribute appropriate stock as widely as possible. But it seemed easier to justify the purchase and retention of oxen and draft horses. Public interest in livestock remained high, and that interest outweighed concerns about actual costs of livestock programs. In fact, the interest in stock outpaced resources and forced compromise on everything from inappropriate stock to inauthentic fencing. Having animals sometimes trumped the need to ensure historic context.

Hawes wrote about the problems in 1975. He identified lack of money and lack of awareness of "sophisticated techniques of analysis" as critical challenges to living history farm development. He allowed that "backbreeding is costly," and he urged sites to avoid going to the same source for livestock, or regional variation would be lost.[9] Normal hours of operation, eight to nine per day, likewise challenged farm staff to create accurate visual representations even if resources and research supported such development. Finding trained staff and retaining them proved challenging, as well. Traditional animal care practices often did not survive the progressive reforms legislated during the early 1900s. Few sites interpreted early-twentieth-century agriculture, and sites often had to work around evidence of "modern" farming to emphasize "frontier" farming. Hawes believed that experimental research conducted as interpretive programming could help staff discover the traditions, but time and money had to be allocated to support such efforts. He believed that if living history farm staff clearly identified their missions, and determined their scale of operation, they could allocate their resources wisely and still develop quality programs to depict a representative, or typical, farm of a given region or era, or a particular farm associated with a person or specific event.

Other museums cared about living animals. Zoo staff responsible for domestic animal exhibits shared concerns with living historical farm advocates committed to improving living collection curation. In 1983, Wendy Engler, senior keeper of domestic stock at the Woodland Park Zoological Gardens in Seattle, Washington, shared findings from a survey she conducted of one hundred institutions that managed and interpreted livestock. This included historic farms and ranches in Canada and the United States. Fifty-eight responded, and one-half of them milked, while nearly two-thirds processed agricultural products, sheared sheep, and plowed or did similar work with stock. Just over 55 percent gave wagon and sleigh rides. These activities formed critical parts of their interpretive and educational programming. Nearly three-quarters of all respondents expressed an interest in conserving historic and rare stock breeds. Yet, they indicated that "old fashioned" fencing proved ineffective in containing animals, and that they had trouble finding farriers and historically appropriate equipment. Furthermore, about one-fifth of the respondents believed that old traditional farming methods were "too slow for staff" and others critiqued the public for assuming "that the farm is a 'petting zoo.'"[10]

As staff realize more appropriate ways of doing things, they also can learn about efficiency related to historic stock-raising practices. This is part of the process of site and staff maturation. It can also contribute to sustainability and stewardship movements. In 1984, Tom Woods shared the results of experimental archaeology conducted at Oliver Kelley Farm in Minnesota. The staff matched photographs of the site with a poultry house plan from the *Register of Rural Affairs* (1859). They reconstructed the structure, complete with double walls, straw insulation, and two large, south-facing windows. The solar energy heated the structure during the day, kept the hens from suffering frostbite, and provided needed sunlight for hens not inclined to lay eggs without adequate light.

So much can be learned from animal-centered research and interpretation. Museum and historic site staff, however, have to do so much on a daily basis to keep their institutions open to the public that research and experimental archaeology often takes a backseat to more pressing concerns. Furthermore, professional standards and best practices demand high levels of care and interpretation. Certainly there are legitimate reasons to minimize compromises or avoid them entirely.

Public Concern and Professional Standards and Best Practices

The general public has expressed outrage at the treatment of livestock for nearly two hundred years. The Royal Society for the Prevention of Cruelty to Animals began in 1824 in London and the Society for the Prevention of Cruelty to Animals began in 1866 in New York City. These urban-based organizations argued for humane treatment of draft horses especially.[11] The focus on health and welfare of animals shifted from the city as the place of abuse to farms during the 1960s. Ruth Harrison's book, *Animal Machines*, with a foreword by Rachel Carson, criticized intensive poultry farming and livestock operations in Great Britain, equating confinement as inhumane and cruel.[12]

The public outcry that followed the release of *Animal Machines* led to the appointment of a committee, chaired by F. W. Rogers Brambell, a distinguished professor of zoology at the University College of North Wales. In 1965, Brambell's committee presented a "Report of the Technical Committee to Enquire into the Welfare of Animals Kept under Intensive Livestock Husbandry Systems." The report stated that animals should have the freedom "to stand up, lie down, turn around, groom themselves and stretch their limbs." These minimum expectations became known as "Brambell's Five Freedoms." A memorial to Brambell concludes with a statement about its significance from the perspective of his career: "It was of the utmost importance and pride to him that his report was both unanimous and strong in its recommendations. He was very much committed to seeing that intensive systems were run on humane lines and he did not hesitate to condemn those systems he felt were inherently inhumane."[13]

The Farm Animal Welfare Council developed as an independent research organization that collected data on farm animal health and welfare and proposed policy to the United Kingdom Government. A 1979 press release announcing the Council's formation, elaborated a bit on Brambell's Five Freedoms:

1. Freedom from thirst, hunger, or malnutrition
2. Appropriate comfort and shelter
3. Prevention, or rapid diagnosis and treatment, for injury and disease
4. Freedom to display most normal patterns of behaviour
5. Freedom from fear[14]

In somewhat modified form, these Five Freedoms established the basis for international standards of livestock production. Governmental organizations such as the Food and Agricultural Organization and non-governmental organizations such as the Humane Society International keep these standards at the heart of their policies or advocacy. For example, president and CEO of the Humane Society of the United States, Wayne Pacelle, addressed farm animals and their treatment in *The Humane Economy*. He conceptualized this economy as a product of human ingenuity and human virtue, a combination that can lead to "a better world for us and for animals, too."[15] Under his leadership, the Humane Society has emphasized human responsibility for ensuring adequate care and treatment of animals as a part of the food supply. Thus, the Five Freedoms established a yardstick by which to measure the humane treatment of agricultural livestock. It does not equate animal welfare with animal rights, nor does it accept that animals are sentient beings.

In what way do the original Five Freedoms of animal welfare—"to stand up, lie down, turn around, groom themselves and stretch their limbs"—influence animal care policies and procedures? That's hard to say. John Schlebecker advocated for professionalization and standards of excellence from ALHFAM's beginning. In 1975 he addressed ALHFAM members as their past president and urged them to adopt standards of accreditation constructed around ALHFAM's articles of incorporation, namely, encouraging research, publication, and training in historic agricultural practices and developing a genetic pool of endangered agricultural plants and animals. ALHFAM members abandoned the idea of accrediting institutional members, but a subcommittee was appointed, and it worked diligently with the American Association of Museums (AAM) to ensure that living history farms and open-air museums could meet AAM accreditation standards, and to apply other appropriate standards. ALHFAM founders may have been aware of Brambell's Five Freedoms and the international response to them, given the roles that many played in land-grant university education and national agencies such as the National Park Service. But no national standards existed in the United States to guide farm animal care. Instead, during the 1980s, a consortium of administrators of research and educational institutions drafted the *Guide for the Care and Use of Agricultural Animals in Research and Teaching*, first issued in 1988, revised in 1999, and published in a third edition in 2010.[16]

ALHFAM makes available guidelines, written by living history farm staff, that help living history farms and agricultural museums develop their own policies. The Midwest

Open Air Museums Coordinating Council, ALHFAM's Midwestern regional affiliate, took a different approach, drafting a "Statement of Professional Conduct" that MOMCC members approved in November 2004. As its rationale, the preamble indicated that "the MOMCC strives to honor and promote the public's trust by issuing this statement to guide professional and ethical conduct." The Statement reinforced the mission of MOMCC as stated in its Articles of Incorporation: to support living history and open-air museums.[17]

The MOMCC Statement of Professional Conduct serves as a yardstick that individuals can use to conduct their business and justify institutional resource allocations essential to achieve and maintain high standards in all areas of operation, including historic livestock. Its adoption coincided with the AAM's effort to streamline accreditation. In December 2004 AAM addressed two core questions:

1) How well does the museum achieve its stated mission and goals?
2) How well does the museum's performance meet standards and best practices as they are generally understood in the museum field, as appropriate to its circumstances?

The AAM staff recognized the MOMCC Statement as a document that could help define the circumstances under which living history farms and open-air museums operate.

Stewardship: Livestock as Collections

How does MOMCC's Statement of Professional Conduct relate to best practices in livestock care at living history farms and open-air museums? Livestock have always been considered a living collection, fundamental to living history farm and open-air museum interpretation. Ed Hawes indicated that living history farm development "necessitate[d] different approaches to collection formation than those of the traditional museum," including new methods of control and registration. Building the living collection required collaboration between "researchers and interpreters, maintenance people and historic farmers."[18]

John T. Schlebecker indicated that living history farms should have all of the appropriate livestock and crops and "have no inappropriate animals or plants." The farm should have complete and accessible seed and breed records, and the cataloguing system for the livestock should include breed lines, sources of foundation stock, and probable sources for replacement.[19] The stock should be permanently marked (branded, tattooed, or ear notched).[20] From a record-keeping perspective, livestock should be treated as artifacts, documented in ways that confirm title transfer, provenance, pedigree, physical location, and condition. These records form the basis for physical and intellectual control of livestock, just as they allow staff to control artifacts. The best livestock management policies and procedures in living history farms rationalize the detail of record keeping required to manage their livestock. The best also reference professional guidelines such as those adhered to by zoos, veterinary associations, research and education institutions, and heritage breed associations. Taking these steps can sustain the living history farm's credibility with the public that they exist to serve.[21]

Collecting stock has become somewhat easier over the decades. Organizations such as the Livestock Conservancy or the Society for the Preservation of Poultry Antiquities focus on breed preservation in partnership with interested farmers and living history farms. They have made heritage breeds more accessible to museums, thus negating the argument that a specific breed is difficult, if not impossible, to procure. Living history farms and open-air museums may find it easier to acquire heritage varieties as a result, but caring for them remains challenging.

The MOMCC Statement of Professional Conduct becomes a tool that museums and historic sites interested in interpreting livestock (and crops) can use to support their rationale and gain institutional support. The MOMCC Statement indicates that living history museums have a range of collections, from the traditional inanimate artifact to the living or animate flora and fauna necessary to make a site vibrant. The Statement indicated that MOMCC members should recognize best practices in the care and management of both inanimate and living artifacts, be sensitive to their origins, and recognize their intrinsic worth. Then, the staff can put both types of artifacts to work in helping them further their institution's mission to create intellectually provocative and historically honest interpretation.[22]

For example, Conner Prairie collected a pair of rare Randall Lineback steers in late 2005, one red and one blue. By doing so, Conner Prairie advocated genotype preservation, even if neither steer can reproduce, and increased the diversity in the types of ox breeds that visitors to historic farms may encounter. Conner Prairie explained the rationale in its newsletters. This helped members understand historic terms critical to the historically accurate use of the steers, specifically basic work commands—*gee, haw, get up*, and *whoa*. Public relations focused on the steers, and the reporting included language that appealed to all ages. Photographs appeared in membership newsletters and calendars of events, and naming the steers became a contest that culminated on April 16, 2006. Through the purchase, Conner Prairie indicated its commitment to backbreeding efforts, and the institution helped spread interest in heritage breed preservation and livestock care and maintenance.

Livestock lend context on which museums and historic sites can build interpretation. This applies to living animals as well as animals long gone but still visible in photographs or represented in other artifacts such as harnesses or carriages. The most complete interpretation must put livestock into its appropriate context. They must be interpreted honestly, within legal and ethical parameters. They must be well documented, as must be their surroundings, including fencing, pastures, barns and sheds, and accoutrements such as harnesses, milk pails, and troughs. And their influence on educational experiences must be documented.

Steps to take to accomplish this include recognizing living history farms and zoos as places to go to learn more about domesticated animals. These provide some of the few opportunities for all of us to learn about traditional agriculture. Organized school programs and weeklong youth camps allow children and adults some sustained interaction with livestock and opportunities to be responsible for their care. Such experiences can help youth learn about historic practices as well as contemporary issues in agriculture.

The participants can become more knowledgeable citizens as a result, cognizant of the need for biodiversity and sustainable agriculture, and perhaps advocates for livestock in living history in the future. Such experiences can also provide staff of museums and historic sites without livestock the opportunities to learn about the livestock associated with artifacts, such as harnesses used on animals similar to those in the living history museum or zoo.

Livestock Need Living History, Too

Living history farms flourished between the 1970s and 1990s. The fever pitch of development that began during the bicentennial era inspired many professionals to take Ed Hawes's advice that a site's greatest potential lay in developing full-scale agriculture within a specific time and place. Many sites launched into this idea wholeheartedly during the 1970s and, while few accomplished it, many persisted with the goal of full-scale farming. At the time, increasing visitation was not a high priority, because visitation seemed steady. Neither was improving visitor interaction given a high priority, because staff believed that depth of knowledge and accuracy were the key components of effective interpreter/visitor interaction. Many sites invested heavily in the most complete interpretation possible, with appropriate stock and large fields to maintain. This created problems.

One problem that arose was that full-scale agriculture inevitably resulted in a separation between the interpreter and the public. This separation occurred in many ways, not the least of which was separation by distance. The physical distance between the interpreter and the public has a direct impact on the quality of the interpretation. A man using historic livestock, particularly draft animals, to plow the middle of a forty-acre field, hundreds of yards from the public, serves as an iconic symbol only. The interpreter and his draft animals have little opportunity to directly provoke the visitor; they cannot engage the visitor directly or inspire them to consider alternatives. Time spent working with stock instead of working with the public may create an even bigger separation than distance. Any museum that attempts to interpret an accurate number of livestock paired with accurate housing and breeding practices will inevitably require more staff to devote more time to livestock care. Staff may be forced to work hours outside of normal visitation times. An increase in staff hours outside of the public eye in every case equals decreased visitor interaction.

Andy Baker, who learned historic farming at Old Sturbridge Village during the 1980s and now directs Lake Farm Park, explained another flaw in the full-scale ideal. He explained how "side projects" can distance interpreters from the public even as they engage in the epitome of process-based, accurate historic interpretation. In a consultation he completed during the late 1990s, Baker used an example of a haying program he had set up one summer, in which they were attempting to bring in a year's worth of hay without mechanized equipment. Well into the summer, the crew worked mowing farther and farther away from the public eye. Everything went fine from an experimental standpoint, but no one ever saw it. At one point, Andy turned around on a wagon and realized that all of his most skilled interpreters were in a field where no one saw them. One can assume that their normal positions had been filled by less-skilled interpreters or left vacant. Not only was the public not seeing what they were doing, but they weren't getting the normal level of interpretation anywhere else.

Such experiences have helped convince many veteran living history farm staff that farming to scale may not be as important to maintaining accuracy as once believed. While one may agree with maintaining the accuracy of the environment, compromises can be made that encourage complete depictions of farming without jeopardizing visitor interaction or a site's financial stability. Volkening Heritage Farm, administered by the Schaumburg Park District in Schaumburg, Illinois, offers a great example of how this can be done. For the past decade, Volkening staff have maintained four cows on a farm that would have averaged about thirteen. While this is far from an accurate-sized herd, it enables them to sustain a quality breeding and milking program. To a public that has rarely seen a cow, four seems like a lot, and the number allows interpreters a comparative tool to provoke a response for the visitors (Photo 12.1). Fewer cattle require less pasture, generate less manure, and do not eat as much purchased feed, thus representing a relative

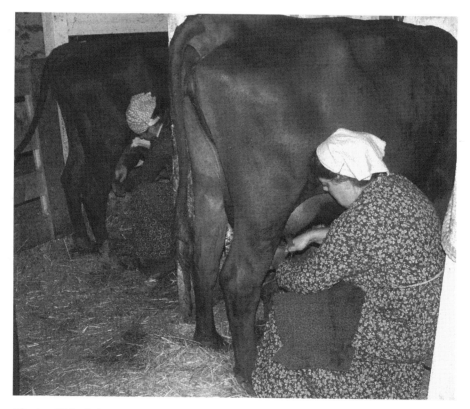

Photo 12.1 Interpreters Monique Inglot and Shari Rosenquist milking the cows at Volkening Farm. Site-specific research should yield evidence about what roles women, men, children, or all contributed to milking, processing, and marketing the commodity.

Source: Photograph by Peter Noll; courtesy of Volkening Heritage Farm, Schaumburg Park District

savings to the site. At the same time, the stock require relatively less care, which means that interpreters can spend more time working with each animal, leading to better training for the staff, the stock, and the visitors. Because of this, the livestock in question lead a more accurate life through a full cycle of breeding, calving, milking, and eventually slaughter. This leads us to our next point.

The role livestock play in living history interpretation needs serious analysis. There is a direct connection between the behavior of the animal and its programmatic impact. You cannot have a discussion about livestock without someone pointing out that you have to take the time to work the animals. This is often stated, but rarely understood. Livestock in general serve to fill some interpretive objectives just by being there. Contemporaries in the environmental education field often state that people will always come to a farm because it has the animals. What is not understood by many even in the living history and open-air museum field is that, by themselves, livestock only fill the iconic image role. They are just like the farmer in the middle of the field whom no one can talk to. It is only through their interaction with humans that they become more than a lawn ornament (Photo 12.2).

Photo 12.2 The horse is hitched to a burr mill to grind corn. The horse walks around, hitched to the machine, which cracks kernels as they pass through the burr. The two interpreters, Chuck Henry and Dick Ruffolo, and the horse work together often and understand each other.

Source: Courtesy of Volkening Heritage Farm, Schaumburg Park District

Livestock at living history sites can be more than lawn ornaments, or props, only if the animal is well trained and in good practice. To be very blunt, oxen that do not plow have no more place on an 1840s farm than a broken-down tractor. During the 1840s, farmers would not have kept them but would have instead completed the cycle by butchering them for tallow and hide. Livestock that are ill-trained and out of practice are anachronistic to working farms, much as twentieth-century equipment is on a nineteenth-century farm. Both are misrepresentations of the past, and such misrepresentative practices can lead to a skewed view of history.

One segment of *Frontier House* (2002), the PBS docudrama set on the plains of Montana that attempted to interpret 1883 frontier experiences, comes to mind as an example of how ill-trained staff and livestock can create false impressions about past knowledge, skills, and challenges. The segment featured participants attempting to plow their gardens. The commentator announced to viewers that because of the dangerous nature of plowing, the head wrangler and nineteenth-century livestock expert would have to help them. The experiment proved a total failure, and the participants resorted to shovels and hoes to work the prairie soil. The fact is that the experiment failed because of a lack of three elements needed to plow efficiently. First, it was painfully clear to any living history farm interpreter that the participants had no experience plowing and were receiving little instruction from their handlers. Second, the team of horses brought to plow had obviously never plowed before and were ill trained and out of practice for the job. Third, the plow was insufficient for the job of breaking heavy sod and thus, even with a well-trained team and a practiced driver, it was not going to do a good job. Real Montana pioneers would have had a lifetime of experience directing a plow, or at least a knowledgeable neighbor to do the directing for them, and their livestock would likewise know how to pull the plow. They also knew of implements designed specifically for the job of sodbusting. What the viewer perceived as an impossible task was, in fact, carried out on a daily basis for nearly one hundred years with great success. The real shame is that any number of historic farms are still demonstrating this skill today and would have been more than happy to show how it was done.

This example illustrates the major point: Without proper knowledge of what the animals are capable of it is all too easy for sites to dismiss the potential livestock hold for interpretation at living history farms. If site administration does not direct staff to put effort into animals, there is no reason to expend the resources to retain livestock. Livestock must be used, and used accurately, to be considered legitimate at living history farms. They must be part of a complete cycle, beginning with conception through birth, maturation, fattening, and use, and be used accurately, to be considered legitimate at living history farms. If all phases of an animal's life are not viewed as integral to living history interpretation, then the animal loses its importance and cannot be justified.

All too often, livestock at sites are left to their own devices and become lackadaisical and ill-tempered due to SLD (sedentary livestock disorder). I believe this perception of livestock as sedentary causes some sites to decide to get rid of large livestock. While it is true that it takes more staff time and money to actually use livestock than to just keep them alive, the extra cost can be deferred by an increase in visitor experience. When administrators face the need to justify the cost of the livestock, they have trouble supporting financial expenditures to keep sedentary livestock, also known as lawn ornaments or props. Yet, as a site decides to deaccession large livestock, it may also identify other livestock as "easily funded while sedentary" and retain them. Such stock, often pigs, chickens, even sheep, can be used effectively, but only if incorporated into a complete cycle through butchering, breeding, or shearing programs. More time and effort put into the livestock program could support more reasonable justification for the animals though increased visitor interaction. Livestock can be indispensable to living history, but making them indispensable requires a combination of institutional commitment and staff expertise.

Notes

1. Lois Green Carr, Russell R. Menard, and Lorena S. Walsh, *Robert Cole's World: Agriculture and Society in Early Maryland* (Chapel Hill: University of North Carolina Press, 1991); Brian Donahue, *The Great Meadow: Farmers and the Land in Colonial Concord* (New Haven, CT: Yale University Press, 2004); Steven Stoll, *Larding the Lean Earth: Soil and Society in Nineteenth-Century America* (New York: Hill and Wang, 2002).

2. J. L. Anderson, *Industrializing the Corn Belt: Agriculture, Technology, and Environment, 1945–1972* (DeKalb: Northern Illinois University Press, 2009).

3. John T. Schlebecker and Gale E. Peterson, *Living Historical Farms Handbook* (Smithsonian Institution, 1972). For a more recent version of a handbook to guide living history farm creation and stewardship, see Debra A. Reid, "Starting a Living History Farm," *Midwest Open Air Museums Magazine*, 33, nos. 2 and 3 (2012): 8–17. The Association for Living History, Farms, and Agricultural Museums offers access to electronic reprints of articles published in the ALHFAM *Bulletin* and the ALHFAM *Proceedings of the Annual Conferences* online for members using the ALHFAM Skills and Knowledge Database (also known as ASK ALHFAM).

4. Darwin P. Kelsey, "Historical Farms as Models of the Past," *Proceedings of the 1974 ALHFAM Conference and Annual Meeting*, Vol. 1 (Washington, D.C.: Smithsonian Institution, 1975), 33–38, reprinted in Jay Anderson. *A Living History Reader* (Nashville, TN: American Association for State and Local History, 1991), 73–78; Edward L. Hawes, "The Living Historical Farm in North America: New Directions in Research and Interpretation," *Proceedings of the 1975 ALFHAM Conference and Annual Meeting*, 2 (Washington, D.C.: Smithsonian Institution, 1976), 41–60, especially 45, reprinted in Jay Anderson, *A Living History Reader* (Nashville, TN: American Association for State and Local History, 1991), 79–97.

5. Hawes, 49.

6. Hawes, 51.

7. William Reid, "Breeding for Authenticity: The Firestone Farm Livestock Program," *Henry Ford Museum & Greenfield Village Herald*, 14, no. 2 (1985), reprinted in the *Midwest Open Air Museums Magazine*, 8, no. 3 (Fall 1987), 10–15; and reprinted in a special issue of the *Midwest Open Air Museums Magazine*, 32, nos. 1 and 2 (2011): 21–25.

8. "Livestock Care in Museums," ALHFAM.org. The Livestock Conservancy, formerly the American Minor Breeds Conservancy, organized in 1977, exists "to protect endangered livestock and poultry breeds from extinction." It serves as an information point for anyone interested in participating in the process, from farmers to donors. Examples of the thought process that should precede the acquisition of living animals in museums has been published in ALHFAM and MOMCC publications since the formation of both organizations. Consult ALHFAM's Livestock

in Museums Information Sheet, the special issue of the *Midwest Open Air Museums Magazine* 32, nos. 1 and 2 (2011), and the ASK ALHFAM feature at ALHFAM.org for more information.

9. Hawes, 54.

10. Wendy Engler, "Living with Livestock: A Primer on Livestock Program Planning and Implementation," and "Livestock Management and Interpretation Survey, June 1983, Summary (Appendix)," *Proceedings of the 1983 ALHFAM Conference and Annual Meeting*, 7 (1984), 121.

11. Antony Brown, *Who Cares for Animals?: 150 Years of the RSPCA* (London: William Heine-mann, Ltd., 1974); Brian Harrison, "Animals and the State in Nineteenth-Century England," *English Historical Review* (October 1973): 786–820.

12. Ruth Harrison, *Animal Machines: The New Factory Farming Industry*, foreword by Rachel Carson (London: Vincent Stuart Pub., 1964); reissued with new contributions (Boston, MA: CABI, 2013); Karen Sayer, "Animal Machines: The Public Response to Intensification in Great Britain, c. 1960–c. 1973," *Agricultural History*, 87, no. 4 (September 2013): 473–501.

13. For a biography of Brambell, see J. S., "Memoir: F.W. Rogers Brambell (1901–1970)," *Journal of Reproduction and Fertility*, 27 (1971): 1–3, available at http://www.reproduction-online .org/content/27/1/NP.full.pdf (accessed 1 June 2016).

14. Press Notice, Farm Animal Welfare Council (5 December 1979), Surrey, England, http://webarchive.nationalarchives.gov.uk/20121007104210/http://www.fawc.org.uk/pdf/ fivefreedoms1979.pdf (accessed 31 May 2016).

15. Wayne Pacelle, *The Humane Economy: How Innovators and Enlightened Consumers Are Transforming the Lives of Animals* (New York: William Morrow/HarperCollins, 2016).

16. The American Association of Museums changed its name to the American Alliance of Museums in 2012. *Guide for the Care and Use of Agricultural Animals in Research and Teaching, 3rd ed.* (Champaign, IL: Federation for Animal Science Societies, Inc., 2010) appears at http://www. fass.org/docs/agguide3rd/Ag_Guide_3rd_ed.pdf (accessed 7 June 2016).

17. "Statement of Professional Conduct," approved by the MOMCC membership November 2004, *Midwest Open Air Museums Magazine*, 15, nos. 2 and 3 (2004): 69–71.

18. Hawes, 49.

19. Schlebecker, 4.

20. Schlebecker, 5.

21. ALHFAM's "Livestock Care in Museums" identifies points to consider and proposes an outline of a farm management plan, available at http://alhfam.org/resources/Documents/PIGS/ livestock_care-06.pdf (accessed 1 June 2016). *ALHFAM's FARM Professional Interest Group (PIG)* prepared this during the 1990s to provide guidance about the care of living animals in a museum setting. Members of the FARM PIG revised and reformatted it on June 12, 2006. ALHFAM's webmaster reformatted "Livestock Care in Museums," FARM PIG Info Sheet #2, in January 2009, FASS Ag Guide, 3rd ed. (2010).

22. "Statement of Professional Conduct," *Midwest Open Air Museums Magazine*, 15, 70.

CHAPTER 13

SEX, DRUGS, AND GMOs

Interpreting Modern Agriculture

THE MAJORITY of Americans live in urban and suburban locations, farthest removed, physically, from row-crop production or free-range or confinement livestock operations. Some might ask why an urban or suburban institution should expend limited and valuable resources to learn about modern agriculture. In response, consider the reality of an uninformed majority relying more and more on a shrinking minority of farmers as the source of commodities processed into fiber, fuel, and food. And consider the chasm that exists between producers and consumers and the ways tempers flare when genetic modification, synthetic chemicals, organic production, and farm policy become the topics of conversation. People care. Museums and historic sites can offer platforms to bridge the distance between perceptions, opinion, and reality.

Everyone has a stake in agriculture, and the stake involves more than a reliance on the food commodities that farmers around the world produce. Today this stake involves diverse consumables. The Economic Research Service of the U.S. Department of Agriculture (USDA) reported in 2014 that farm production contributed 1 percent ($177.2 billion) to U.S. Gross Domestic Product (GDP). But the ERS claimed that "the overall contribution of the agriculture sector to GDP is larger than [1 percent] because sectors related to agriculture—forestry and fishing; food, beverages, and tobacco products; textiles, apparel, and leather products; and food service and drinking places—all relied on agricultural inputs." More accurately, agriculture and agriculture-related industries contributed 4.8 percent of the U.S. GDP in 2014 ($835 billion).[1]

You might think that 4.8 percent of the U.S. GDP is not significant, but that segment of the nation's economy affects all our lives, because we all consume those items. Our investment in food (meat and dairy products, fruits and vegetables, baked goods and beverages) helps employ 14 percent of all employees in manufacturing industries.

The average American invests 12.6 percent of total household expenditures on food. Adding other consumables derived from agricultural commodities increases the outlay to nearly 25 percent. These items include apparel (3.3 percent) made from cotton, wool, silk, linen, ramie, and other animal- and plant-based fibers; entertainment and alcoholic beverages (6 percent); transportation costs, including corn- or soybean-derived ethanol as a gasoline additive (a fraction of 17 percent); and even tobacco (included in "other" expenditures totaling 3.3 percent).[2] Medical marijuana products and services will only increase agriculture's contribution to the GDP.

How can learning about agriculture help us wrestle with modern issues? It takes self-confidence to launch into conversations about topics that can be controversial, and the public becomes richer for it, as Julie Rose has documented in *Interpreting Difficult History at Museums and Historic Sites*.[3] The commitment to educate the public by engaging them in dialogue accrues value as participants learn about healthy dialogue, conflict resolution, and respect for multiple perspectives.

Agritourism Destinations

A neutral place to start might involve reaching out to farmers in cities who grow food close to the people who consume it. Urban agriculture remains viable as permaculture advocates plant porch and yard gardens, and other green advocates install intensive hydroponics and aquaponics operations. Aeroponics and hydroponics allow farmers to grow crops without soil, while aquaponics allows farmers to grow fish in tanks instead of oceans or ponds. These techniques helped solve problems caused by limited acreage, and individuals can practice the techniques and wield some control over their food supply.

Talking with urban farmers makes obvious the variety of philosophies that inform different responses to the challenge of raising crops and livestock. Proponents of sustainable agriculture link crop cultivation and animal husbandry to healthy ways of living. They practice permaculture—taking inspiration from natural environments as the basis for human spaces. Advocates of permaculture design eco-friendly and sustainable farms. Growing plants in gray water and in microclimates seems at odds with permaculture, and more in keeping with extractive monoculture or confinement operations.

Farmers in the countryside practice similar extremes, ranging from "farming" through membership in a local CSA to massive robotic milking parlors. Grasping the diversity may require field trips to farms that will welcome tourists for a day, if not for the season, so visitors can learn by seeing and doing. Agritourism destinations exist across the nation, offering a variety of hands-on experiences, formal educational programs, and even interpretive exhibits. Farmers at living history farms perform the same service, as do curators at zoos that have domestic livestock as part of the exhibit.

Fair Oaks Farms provides a good example of extreme agritourism. The public can learn about the dairy industry, pigs, and crops in one place, and can return often, given ease of access to the facility. The tourist destination in Fair Oaks, Indiana, generates so much traffic that it has its own interstate exit. Visitors can take a cow-bus tour around the entire facility, through the free-stall dairy barns, past the trench silos, and into the birthing barn, where they can watch a calf being born (an average of three to four calves are born every hour). They can watch a whole rotation of the seventy-two-cow robotic milking platform that operates twenty-four hours a day, seven days a week, 365 days a year. This all costs money, but that does not seem to discourage people who realize that Fair Oaks Farms provides a rare opportunity to tour the inner workings of industrial-scale livestock and crop production.

Fair Oaks Farms has interactive exhibits in the Pork Education Center and in the WinField Crop Adventure. Each emphasizes the science of agriculture and promotes the agriculture industry. These resources help introduce modern agriculture to the 99 percent of the U.S. population who depend on the other 1 percent of the population who work in dairy production.

Some agritourism attractions, such as Eckert's Farm near Belleville, Illinois, take extra steps to put the consumer experience into context. The corporate website provides pre-visit information that orients customers to the history of the Eckert family and the family farm.[4] Grandparents reminisce to their grandkids about their experiences with similar technology. Children play in the "Fun Corral." Teachers book school tours. Foodies can sign up for special classes. Customers buy quality meats, vegetables, preserves, seasonal fruits, and baked goods (rhubarb pie!) fresh from the oven all year round; or they can pick their own fruit of the season. Families make the market-orchard their destination, and pay dearly for the full experience, but they still have a lot to learn about the modern business of agriculture. Customers may not realize that Eckert's is not organic, because customers do not make the connection between pretty fruit and non-organic practices. Eckert's may not have a policy for preserving its agricultural artifacts in perpetuity. Regardless, the family that runs the business that sells the rhubarb pie that tastes just like Mama used to make obviously cares about their farm's past. It has a business plan that takes public engagement with agriculture, if not education about modern agriculture, seriously.

Museums and historic sites can take a lesson from agribusinesses that incorporate history into marketing strategies. First, operations like Eckert's put people into the crop cycle. Second, personal experience with agriculture matters (and they expect the personal touch to help customers justify the expense for the experience). Third, the popularity of pick-your-own fruit orchards indicates that a sizeable proportion of the population wants more hands-on experiences. Fourth, agritourism lures customers to return for more. Hosting a tour of area agricultural attractions and adding a humanities context might be just the inspiration it takes to gain the public trust and start a conversation about museum-specific experiences that continue the lessons.

Imagine the potential if a group of sites dedicated to interpreting agriculture in close proximity ally in the effort. The CALHF Club of Chicago, an informal meeting of representatives from Chicago-area living history farms, offers an opportunity to explore agricultural history as practiced in the shadow of "Nature's Metropolis," as William Cronon called Chicago.[5] Touring these sites could take the form of a Staff Ride, part of the required curriculum of Reserve Officers' Training Corps (ROTC) and of advanced military training delivered to active-duty officers. On a Staff Ride, students travel to a battle location, walk the site, explore the landscape, and gain insights into factors that affected the outcome. A Farm Ride could feature sites with well-documented agricultural histories that provide unique opportunities to study original artifacts (from complete environments to the garden hoe) and that interpret the complexity of agricultural practices at a given time.

Oral Histories: Listening to Farmers Tell Their Stories

If talking with practicing farmers is not practical, then turning to oral histories might offer the next best option. Many museums, historical societies, and libraries have oral history collections that feature local farmers telling their personal stories. If no collections exist, establish a protocol for documenting contemporary agriculture, complete your basic research, contract your informants, write standard permission forms, draft your questions, contact the farm and farm business operators, and start recording. Numerous "how-to" books can help you get started.[6]

Oral histories that result from carefully planned interviews document philosophies of farming, the mind-set and attitudes of the farmer, and the methodology essential to the business. These become essential ingredients in exhibits and programs that introduce the public to current practice. Farmers may talk about how to plow and how to plant or how to follow the signs of the moon and anticipate the vagaries of the weather without reliance on meteorologists. Farmers may describe their strategies for managing forces beyond their control, specifically cash flow and credit (money), commodity markets, and financial management through complex business practices. They may share the good, the bad, and the ugly sides of farming.

Three examples of successful oral history projects suffice. The stories document routines of farm life otherwise not documented, as well as tension and conflict in three different regions of the United States. The stories provide the farmers' and laborers' perspectives on the outside forces that affected their business—the legislation, the markets, and the lack of money being the three most often itemized as being beyond the farmers' control.

The Illinois State Museum developed the Audio-Video Barn in cooperation with four educational institutions and one business that specialized in oral and video histories. It received a National Leadership Grant from the Institute of Museum and Library Services, which partially funded the two-year project, "Oral History of Agriculture in Illinois." The project included numerous tasks. It collected and made available interviews conducted during the 1950s through the 1990s and housed in the archives of the four partner institutions. It facilitated conversations about the history of agriculture in the state and identification of topics warranting further study. It funded staff to systematically collect oral interviews of individuals involved in agriculture across the state, and to design a website to provide access to these virtual collections. The public can now access more than 130 oral interviews, audio/video-recorded, with transcripts, via the Audio-Video Barn website [http://avbarn.museum.state.il.us/]. The project received the 2010 Elizabeth B. Mason Major Project Award from the Oral History Association.[7]

The Bracero History Archive (Bracero Oral History Project), University of Texas at El Paso [http://braceroarchive.org/], documented an even more elusive and controversial history, that of millions of agricultural laborers who worked in more than half of all states in the United States between 1942 and 1965. The project involved staff at institutions dedicated to collecting and preserving stories of national significance headquartered at the Institute of Oral History at the University of Texas–El Paso, and including the Center for the Study of Race and Ethnicity at Brown University, the Smithsonian Institution's National Museum of American History, and the Center for History and New Media at George Mason University in Virginia. The unique aspect of the project involved research across national borders. Interviewers traveled to villages in Mexico to interview former Braceros or relatives of Braceros. The virtual collection, Bracero History Archive, provides access to 3,169 items, including 702 oral histories, supplemented with images and other documents. A collaborative research grant from the National Endowment for the Humanities provided partial funding. The archive received the 2010 Public History Project Award from the National Council on Public History.[8]

The Bracero History Archive provides data that can help other institutions plan and implement comparable projects. These include several "How to . . ." tutorials delivered as PowerPoint slides with narration via YouTube ["Conducting an Oral History Interview" and "Scanning and Photographing Objects for Addition to the Archive"]. The site provides permission forms used in the project and required to allow public dissemination of the interviews. The archive also includes lists of questions tailored for former Braceros or former border control police so they really could tell it like it was. Other "How to . . ." instructions can help teachers make the most of the materials provided, and students learn how to turn the resources on the site into evidence to support their research.

The third example, "Breaking New Ground: A History of African American Farm Owners since the Civil War" [http://sohp.org/2013/10/29/breaking-new-ground-now-online/], grew out of the work of two agricultural historians, Adrienne Petty and Mark Schultz. They followed the model established by the Bracero History Archive, secured funding from a collaborative research grant of the National Endowment for the Humanities. This supported a thirty-six-month project that involved training students at several universities to collect the memories of African American farmers across the South, from Maryland to Oklahoma. The three hundred interviews with black farm owners and their families that resulted are available through the Southern Oral History Project [http://dc.lib.unc.edu/cdm/landingpage/collection/sohp].[9]

Public access to these products means that museum and historic site staff can incorporate them into virtual exhibits, three-dimensional exhibits, and programming on site, and even consider them as a basis for developing museum theater and other living history programming.

Interpreting Modern Agriculture

Interpreting current issues in agriculture might start with an organized tour of existing attractions, with an eye toward adding humanities dimensions to their programming. It could continue with a discussion series featuring multiple points of view on a hotly debated topic related to agriculture—tobacco and smoking, for instance, or even more polarizing, medical marijuana. The series could feature changing ordinances about smoking and questions about the safety of e-cigarette technology, while debates about legalizing marijuana might provide an avenue to develop a series of programs along the topic of "Growing Addictions: Then and Now." Items from your collection such as photographs of smokers, or advertisements published in periodicals or graphic art in the form of an ashtray printed with a local business's logo provide the link between your institutional mission and the series topic. You might launch a discussion on the politics of a pack of cigarettes from the time when tobacco became a commodity in Virginia Colony after 1607. You could continue with a program on marijuana and hemp as crops with a long list of uses but a misunderstood association that allowed powerful lobbyists to convince the U.S. Congress to tax heavily starting in 1937. Developing any series that puts past and present agriculture into a coherent package will take a lot of homework, but that is true of any topic curated at your museum or historic site. It's time to get started.

Survey participants in these programs. Brainstorm additional ideas based on their interests. Survey your collections to identify what you have to support relevant programming. Identify artifacts needed to make your collections more representative of agriculture in your area. Partner with local collectors to help you expand your range. For example, you might be one of dozens of museums, historic sites, living history farms, and open-air museums that interpret pre-industrial farming, and the stoop labor required to make a living on the farm. Hundreds more interpret the first agricultural revolution of the mid-nineteenth century when horse-drawn machinery rapidly reduced or replaced human laborers in certain crop cultures (especially planting, cultivating, and harvesting of wheat and other grain crops). Museums collected tractors and equipment from the second agricultural revolution of the early twentieth century, but much less attention has been paid to larger machinery, and few museums collect farm machinery produced since the 1950s. Instead, antique tractor collectors and antique machinery clubs have accumulated impressive collections of iconic artifacts mass-produced during the post–World War II production revolution—the John Deere combine with interchangeable headers, for instance. Farmers could invest in one combine, and use it to harvest both grains, soybeans, and shelled corn by simply changing headers on the machine. Farmers would spend more than one-third of a million dollars for one combine, and at least twenty thousand more for each header by the early twenty-first century.

Other machines that revolutionized agriculture during the mid-twentieth century have been identified as Historic Agricultural Engineering Landmarks. For instance, the Smithsonian Institution acquired "Old Red," the first commercial spindle cotton picker, in 1970, along with the Farmall tractor on which the picker was originally mounted. The machine was one of four mechanical pickers that operated in the western San Joaquin Valley during the 1943 harvest season. It replaced human cotton pickers and permanently changed the human dimension of farming across the Cotton Belt. "Old Red" was designated a Historic Agricultural Engineering Landmark by the American Society of Agricultural and Biological Engineers on October 20, 1978.[10] The Henry Ford collections include other artifacts that symbolize changes in agricultural engineering and science that made traditional planting and harvesting practices obsolete, specifically a

1979 no-till planter by Deere and Company, and a tomato harvester produced in 1969 by the Ford Motor Company. Both technologies became practical only after considerable scientific research that reduced cultivation requirements through the use of herbicides and liquid fertilizers, and the perfection of durable tomatoes through selective breeding.[11]

The second and third agricultural revolutions remain within the living memory of Americans, and thus, artifacts donated to collections have a higher likelihood of being accompanied by provenance—the gold standard for museum collecting. That said, few museums have risen to the challenge. Why? Because museums worry about the cost of storing and maintaining the massive artifacts, because every object in storage amounts to a liability on the balance sheet. Museum staff also worry that the association of large artifacts with large-scale production, synthetic chemical applications, genetic modification, and rural depopulation will be controversial and could alienate donors. The object's interpretive potential must warrant the fiduciary risk.

Proactive collecting can help you manage the risk. It might be impossible to collect a confinement hog operation, but you might collect a creep feeder used by hog farmers in their barns, and you could collect their stories and document their operations in photographs.[12] Nothing takes the place of the tangible artifact, but reason has to prevail in the process of documenting and preserving with an eye toward interpretation.

You can use a series of programs to test your plan to document topics relevant to your mission and audience. For instance, *A Pig's Point of View: Then and Now*, would allow you to slowly introduce the idea of local livestock production by starting with a yearlong reading circle focused on pigs in literature from E. B. White's *Charlotte's Web* to George Orwell's *Animal Farm*. You could reach out to teachers in local schools to see whether they would be interested in an interdisciplinary research project to document examples of pig farming in your area, then and now. This could include modern open-range hog-farming compliant with certified organic and slow-food locavore standards, or confinement operations that meet sanitation and environmental standards. The students could identify local pig farmers and feed store operators, and they could be part of a panel that would include their perspectives on how hog farming has changed in your town over time (Photo 13.1). In addition to the farmers at the table, quotes could come from letters, diaries, published animal husbandry manuals, and prescriptive literature from U.S. Department of Agricultural resources, all readily available in local archives or through digitized collections at the Library of Congress, through local university research libraries, and through the Core Historical Literature of Agriculture at Cornell University.

Another rich resource to learn about modern agriculture in your county and state can include an exploration of records documenting centennial farms. Every state has a centennial farm program, and most have a sesquicentennial and many a bicentennial program, too. Agencies overseeing the programs include state departments of agriculture, state Farm Bureau offices, and state historical or preservation societies, among others. The people who operate farms so designated supported their applications with evidence that confirmed that the farm has remained in continuous operation within the same family for at least one hundred years or more. The program files contain rich resources that document the attitudes of farmers at the time of the application. Yes, the person who

Photo 13.1 Hogs in a feedlot, confined to a model hog-finishing operation with concrete pad and self-feeders. An auger moves the feed from the Purina Chows truck to the self-feeders. The feed consists of ground corn and nutritional supplements that corporations marketed and animal science experts promoted as protection for feed lot hogs. The low-level antibiotic doses prevented contraction and spread of infectious diseases while in close quarters.

Source: Courtesy of Ag Illustrated

completed the information provides evidence of the farm's history, but the descriptions of that heritage indicate the mind-set of the farmers of our times, not of the past. The centennial-farm-program archives include invaluable evidence about agricultural practices over time, and they convey the importance that modern farm operators place in public recognition of their efforts. Farmers self-identify by posting the "Centennial Farm" sign in a prominent location on their driveways. With the permission of farmers, you could develop a driving tour aided with a phone app for the public to explore the landscape around them. Searching the state databases, consulting published directories of the farms, and finding their physical location on the landscape can help you identify members of farm families who can talk about what it takes to survive in agriculture in your area.

Other national projects document rural and farm landscapes. Four warrant mention, and the materials in these repositories are publically available via web-based databases. The National Register of Historic Places, the Historic American Buildings Survey, Historic American Engineering Record, and the National Historic Landmarks each contain valuable evidence of farms and farm businesses. Barn Again is a good example of a private initiative, but a popular one that features farmers' efforts to save their historic-built environment. Numerous resources exist to help you put your agricultural heritage into local context today.

Notes

1. "Ag and Food Sectors and the Economy," Economic Research Service, U.S. Department of Agriculture, http://ers.usda.gov/data-products/ag-and-food-statistics-charting-the-essentials/ag-and-food-sectors-and-the-economy.aspx (updated 17 February 2016).

2. Based on the 2013 U.S. Census Survey of Manufacturers and U.S. Bureau of Labor Statistics, Consumer Expenditure Survey, 2014. For charts and summaries, see "Ag and Food Sectors and the Economy," http://ers.usda.gov/data-products/ag-and-food-statistics-charting-the-essentials/ag-and-food-sectors-and-the-economy.aspx (updated 17 February 2016).

3. Julia Rose, *Interpreting Difficult History at Museums and Historic Sites* (Lanham, MD: Rowman & Littlefield, 2016).

4. Three Eckert farms in Millstadt and one Eckert's farm in Belleville appear in the St. Clair County listings in the Illinois Centennial Farms database (Millstadt farms began in 1836, 1838, and 1892; and the Belleville farm in 1879). Illinois Centennial Farms, www.agr.state.il.us/marketing/centfarms/ (accessed 21 May 2016). Yet, "About Us," www.Eckerts.com, does not identify the Millstadt farm or the Eckert's headquarters as having a Centennial Farm designation.

5. William Cronon, *Nature's Metropolis: Chicago and the Great West* (New York: W. W. Norton & Co., 1991).

6. For example, see Valerie Raleigh Yow, *Recording Oral History: A Guide for the Humanities and Social Sciences*, 3rd ed. (Lanham, MD: Rowman & Littlefield, 2014).

7. Robert E. Warren et al., "Restoring the Human Voice to Oral History: The Audio-Video Barn Website," *Oral History Review*, 40, no. 1 (Winter/Spring 2013): 107–25.

8. Mireya Loza, "From Ephemeral to Enduring: The Politics of Recording and Exhibiting Bracero Memory," *The Public Historian*, 38, no. 2 (May 2016): 23–41. For the collection, see "The Bracero History Archive" [http://www.braceroarchive.org] and for the Smithsonian traveling exhibition, see "Bittersweet Harvest: The Bracero Program, 1946–1964," [http://americanhistory.si.edu/exhibitions/bittersweet-harvest-bracero-program-1942-1964].

9. Mark R. Schultz, "Conversations with Farmers: Oral History for Agricultural Historians," *Agricultural History*, 90, no. 1 (Winter 2016): 51–69.

10. See the American Society of Agricultural and Biological Engineers (ASABE) Historic Agricultural Engineering Landmark, http://www.asabe.org/awards-landmarks/asabe-historic-landmarks.aspx (accessed 22 August 2016).

11. FMC Tomato Harvester, 1969, THF151662; and Deere and Company No-Till Planter 7000, 1979, THF151661, both on display at The Henry Ford, Dearborn, Michigan.

12. Debra A. Reid, "Creeps, Feeders, and Creep Feeders," *Agricultural History*, 92, no. 2 (Spring 2018), forthcoming, a special issue featuring papers presented at the 2015 conference, Artifacts in Agraria, sponsored by the University of Guelph, Canada.

PART 4

DEVELOPING
INTERPRETATION

CHAPTER 14

INTERPRETING AGRICULTURE

A Multi-Step Sequential Process

T HE DAILY routines required to raise crops and tend to livestock dictated the rhythms of life for a majority of the nation's population until 1870, when the proportion of those living on farms dropped below half of the total national population. The nation remained predominately rural until 1920. Many in the city, and in the country, continued to keep livestock, raise crops, and follow the rhythm of agricultural seasons. Others worked in industries that manufactured and marketed agricultural products. Over one hundred years, however, the knowledge of and association with agriculture has disappeared. Today, interpreting what was once common starts with an introduction to a foreign topic.

This chapter provides some examples of ways that interpreters can learn about agriculture in the past by studying the evidence that still survives. It seems appropriate to start by revisiting the six principles that Freeman Tilden proposed in his 1957 book, *Interpreting Our Heritage*:

1) Any interpretation that does not somehow relate what is being displayed or described to something within the personality or experience of the visitor will be sterile.
2) Information, as such, is not interpretation. Interpretation is revelation based on information. But they are entirely different things. However, all interpretation includes information.
3) Interpretation is an art, which combines many arts, whether the materials presented are scientific, historical, or architectural. Any art is in some degree teachable.
4) The chief aim of interpretation is not instruction, but provocation.
5) Interpretation should aim to present a whole rather than a part, and must address itself to the whole man rather than any phase.

6) Interpretation addressed to children (say, up to the age of twelve) should not be a dilution of the presentation to adults, but should follow a fundamentally different approach. To be at its best it will require a separate program.[1]

What would Tilden say about interpreting agriculture? The humanist approach ("interpretation is an art") is the best approach to analyze the scientific, historical, and architectural evidence of agriculture, broadly defined. This multidisciplinary evidence becomes the basis for interpretation that relates to the audience, provokes them to think, and is age-appropriate and intellectually rigorous.

A Warm-Up

Historical thinking requires us to assess historic evidence for its own sake, as an expression of its time and not ours. Thus, interpreting agriculture involves a certain degree of sensitivity training. You can test your degree of acclimatization by looking at Photo 14.1 and then answering the following questions: What do you see when you look at this photograph? Do you see cold animals? Do you see a barnyard during winter, full of animals well-fed, not jockeying for position at the feed trough? If you selected the well-fed animals, congratulations. You have taken a major step toward thinking historically about agriculture.

Photo 14.1 Livestock in a feedlot in the snow.

Courtesy of Ag Illustrated

Study Tours

You can reinforce the process of historical thinking by taking staff away from the familiar and asking them to identify the evidence of agriculture at other museums and sites. Many historic sites preserve farms, ranches, and plantations, some still productive and others as showplaces. The following examples represent the breadth of possibilities, across time, culture, and spanning the United States from New Jersey to Oregon.

Johnston Farm and Indian Agency interprets two thousand years of human land use on a 250-acre historic site in Piqua, Ohio. Surviving structures include a house, barn, springhouse, cider house, and part of the Miami and Erie Canal, all constructed between 1808 and 1835.[2] Farmington preserves eighteen acres of a 550-acre hemp plantation near Louisville, Kentucky, owned by John Speed and cultivated by dozens of slaves. The brick home dates to 1816. Today the grounds feature formal gardens.[3] Hunter's Home, completed in 1845 by Virginia merchant George M. Murrell, documents the antebellum lifestyle of an elite Cherokee family in the Indian Territory. Surviving structures that supported domestic agricultural processing include a root cellar, smokehouse, and springhouse.[4] Freewoods Farm interprets the experiences of families that exercised their new liberty after the Civil War by buying land and building communities. Burgess, in Horry County, South Carolina, began as one of these unincorporated freedmen communities, built by formerly enslaved men and women from large rice plantations in the Low Country. The forty-acre living history site, opened in 2001, interprets this unique agricultural area situated in a tidal marsh (now a wetland preserve). Programming features routines of African American farm life between 1865 and 1900, rural community formation, and twentieth-century rural education as delivered in Rosenwald Schools.[5] Paulsdale, a 6.5-acre site in New Jersey, preserves the birthplace of a prominent woman suffrage and women's rights advocate. It is all that remains of the 173.4-acre diversified farm that included barns, a hog house, a chicken house and laying coops, a granary, and equipment sheds.[6] Dorris Ranch interprets the first commercial filbert orchard in the United States, begun in 1892.[7] Cantigny Park documents the gentleman's farm operated by a newspaper owner and his first wife. She kept pure-bred Guernsey cattle and he kept polo ponies between 1915 and 1939. Today the suburban site features the historic house, formal gardens, and a twenty-seven-hole golf course.[8]

Each of these historic sites anchored a farm (or ranch or orchard or plantation). Families (free and enslaved) farmed them during the nineteenth and twentieth centuries. Most are listed on the National Register of Historic Places.[9] Some have also been designated National Historic Landmarks.[10] Private and public organizations, including not-for-profit foundations and friends groups, county park districts, and state historical societies, administer them. These six sites, and tens of thousands more just like them all across North America, have the potential to serve as outdoor classrooms for history lessons on the topic of agriculture.

The written descriptions about the sites hint at the existence of diversified agriculture. Surviving material evidence on the sites—smokehouses, springhouses, creameries, and root cellars—provide tangible proof that people on the property raised hogs, milked cows, planted orchards, and tended gardens at the least. These activities helped them feed themselves. Surviving material evidence also confirms the cultivation of commodities such as rice, sugarcane, hemp, and cereal grains, all produced for market consumption. Few descriptions mention the role of agricultural markets historically, even though phrases such as "first commercial filbert orchard" or "thriving 550-acre hemp plantation" indicated that markets motivated these farmers and planters.

The public values museums and historic sites as places to learn about the past.[11] Many historic houses and sites, however, began as showplaces built by those who "raced, gendered, faithed, and classed" agricultural policies, practices, and groups in the past (to borrow words that Brewster used in her critique of Agriculture in the Classroom).[12] The palatial homes at sites such as Farmington and Hunter's Home indicate how lucrative agriculture could be, but the most complete story must incorporate lessons that laborers on the farms, not just the owners, can tell us. This involves adding other evidence to the narratives. Laborers viewed the farms from other places. The vantage point from outbuildings, farm fields, and backyards can offer valuable and underutilized vantage points to public interpretation. Interpreters can see this better when exploring other sites, and then they can rethink places more familiar to them. Taking a different vantage point can make the interpretation more inclusive and more informative.

Staff can also critique the techniques utilized at sites. At least four of these examples offer guided tours that explain building use and provide a sense of the farm's landscape and operation. Several have living history programming seasonally or during special events. These include multisensory experiences such as a canal boat ride, syrup making, or crop harvesting. One conveys information about agricultural buildings using historical quotes from letters written by the farm family. Acreage on another remains a source of revenue for the property, still growing the historic crop. One hosts a seasonal farmers' market, and one has plans to market local produce. Only one, the filbert ranch, retains a working farm that visitors can access on walking trails. In general, however, these museums and historic sites underinterpret their agricultural histories. The backyards and barnyards serve as walkways from parking lot to house or exhibit building. Rarely do they serve as the site for conversations about agricultural practices, but many have taken steps to expand the topic by paying more attention to the historic ecosystem, seasonal rhythms, domestic labor demands, market relationships, and human stories documented at the site.

Many museums and historic sites have a lot in common with these representative examples. The agriculture of the past, often long ago abandoned and replaced with formal gardens or suburban lawns, tends not to drive site interpretation. Or the interpretation stops with process and does not move beyond to help visitors grasp the social and cultural context for the process, or its significance for understanding agriculture as practiced at a time and in a place.

Museums, on the other hand, seem to incorporate agricultural productivity into their exhibits. It is difficult to ignore the business (farming) that most people in most places before the 1920s did, and just as difficult to ignore the work that they performed (agriculture). Add to this the fact that collections donated to museums include the material evidence of that business and the tasks performed, and most museums have the artifacts

Photo 14.2 Three mannequins representing three generations of Plateau Indian women from the Warm Springs Reservation gathering roots. The exhibition, *By Hand through Memory*, opened at the High Desert Museum, Bend, Oregon, in 1999, with the goal of telling a different story of the ways that Plateau Indians managed change over two hundred years.

Source: Photograph by Debra A. Reid, 29 September, 2012

to tell the story in static exhibits (Photo 14.2). Thinking about how to address these opportunities at other sites can inspire staff to think about the possibilities at their own places of employment.

The Multi-Step Process

Managing the process of awareness building, research, and interpretive planning can follow a multi-step process that has a sequence. It takes time but is essential for museums and sites to be more proactive about collecting, preserving, and conveying the complexity of agriculture in the past in ways that intellectually engage visitors. The following summarizes the steps in the process of planning agricultural interpretation:

1. What agricultural topics interest your constituents, broadly defined? Talk to visitors, prioritize topics, review the list, refine the list, and commit to exploration.
2. Identify relevant secondary sources. What do secondary sources (articles and monographs) tell you about agriculture as practiced at the place that your museum or historic site interprets and over time (not just at the time of your site's significance)? Develop a working knowledge that allows you to find connections between local and regional agriculture and the interests of your constituents.

3. Conduct site-specific research. What primary evidence exists to document agriculture as practiced at your site and in your region at a particular time in the past? What does the archival data tell you about the people and the practices? The policy and the science? The changes over time and the consequences of those changes? The more you know, the better the questions you can ask. Keep asking questions!

4. What material culture existed historically? How does your collection compare to the items identified in the sources and used in your location over time? Collections should be broadly defined to include tangible and intangible evidence. This means that a comprehensive review should include buildings and landscapes, as well as tools and equipment, surviving customs, and living plants and animals used in the place and at a particular time.

5. Refine collections as needed. Create a collections development plan to guide the process of refining what you need to interpret agricultural topics.

6. Based on your secondary reading and primary research, what agriculture topics warrant the investment of time and money to interpret? What disciplines can inform the process? Identify specific programs, exhibits, events, and other forms of intellectual engagement with goals, artifacts, discipline-specific activities, and formal assessment. Present the programs, assess, and refine.

7. Draft an Interpreting Agriculture Plan that includes a historic overview, current context, and resources to help you accomplish the goals.

8. Planning should continue with brainstorming about a variety of minds-on programming that engages visitors of all ages and is evidence rich. Engage constituents in review and refinement. Collect summative evaluation data, evaluate it, and apply it when planning future programs or exhibits. While the visitors go about their business, you, invigorated by what you know and inquisitive about what more you can learn, identify a new project, return to step one, and begin the process anew. And the visitors will return for more.

Exercise in Agricultural Chronology

If we wonder why we should care, Jonathan Kuester, historic farm supervisor at Volkening Living History Farm in Schaumburg, Illinois, shared a sobering perspective on the extent to which people fail to understand agriculture. His conversations with visitors at Volkening and with attendees at programs off-site have led him to conclude that the plow and the draft horse seem to be ingrained in the American psyche. "[Plowing] is the number-one job that adults associate draft horses with, even though few of them could identify a plow and even fewer know what [a plow] actually does. Ten years ago children also associated plowing with horses. . . . We recently did a program with the Cook County Farm Bureau, and I was shocked to find that more than half of the kids we saw (all inner-city youth) thought that American farmers were still using horses for field work [today]. These children are so removed from agriculture that they have lost 'tractor' from their vocabulary."[13] What role does myth play in this? Or race? Or gender? Does an emphasis on the topic of slavery and sharecropping leave students thinking that no options existed in agriculture other than walking behind a plow pulled by a horse (or a mule)?

How do we overcome these real barriers to engaging audiences? The process involves starting with the present and documenting the "now" before moving to the history. This requires reversing the traditional approach to studying history—starting with the past and moving to the present. Instead, lessons can start at the peak of their knowledge, their present, and convey information about farming today, relevant to their place. Then lessons can excavate down through numerous chronological levels. Each level has value in the learning process, because each level holds new information, and warrants full exploration. As people move from the top (what they can see) to the base of the pyramid (the historic and prehistoric past, unseen, possibly romanticized or inconceivable, but authentic), they gain the context to understand changes that make what they see very different from what "original" land stewards or "first" farm owners cultivated in the past (Figure 14.1).

This reverse-chronological approach can start the process of undermining misconceptions of agriculture, often based in romanticized notions of independent landowning family farmers. Instead, constituents can start by sharing the reality of agriculture that they either know about, or can see around them. Understanding agriculture in the present can help people grasp the complicated relationships that existed historically between economic and political philosophies (mercantilism, capitalism, communism, and democracy) and public policy that favored farm owners and exploited laborers.

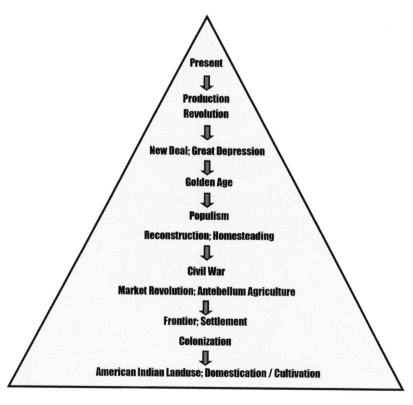

Present
⬇
Production Revolution
⬇
New Deal; Great Depression
⬇
Golden Age
⬇
Populism
⬇
Reconstruction; Homesteading
⬇
Civil War
Market Revolution; Antebellum Agriculture
⬇
Frontier; Settlement
Colonization
⬇
American Indian Landuse; Domestication / Cultivation

Figure 14.1 Thinking backward, from present to past agricultural practices, can help novices put their knowledge of agriculture into a chronology that starts at the peak (the present) and moves down through many layers of change to the first farmers—American Indians.

Source: Created by Debra A. Reid, 8 May 2016

The Big Picture

Interpreting agriculture can start with local, personal stories, but the local and the personal gain significance when put in the context of regional, state, national, and global topics. Interpretive training can include reading circles. Staff can discuss secondary sources, identify relevant topics, and start connecting the scholarship to local history and public interests.

The staff can discuss themes such as labor, markets, money and banking, agricultural technologies, the environment, ethnicity, race, policies, and the myth and romance of the agrarianism. Being more informed about agricultural history can help staff develop more balanced, accurate, and authentic stories and present less romanticized information. Furthermore, being more informed about agriculture in general can enrich process-focused interpretation.

Exercise in Interpreting Documents: Primary Source Analysis

Interpretive staff can also practice primary source analysis to become more informed, both about evidence and about details. As an exercise in source analysis, read the following letter from a young man who relocated from Maine to central Illinois in 1849, to his friend back in Lisbon, Maine. Test your recall of basic facts through the quiz at the end (yes—there is a test!), and then think about ways that a primary source such as this can contribute to interpretation in more than one location.[14]

> Letter
> From Chas. [Charles] D. Sufkin, Shelbyville, Illinois, to Henry Thompson, Lisbon, Maine, January 7, 1850.
> Shelbyville Ills. Jany 17th 1850.
> 9 O'Clock P.M.
> [the following single line is a note written along the left side of the first page]
> I fear I have worried you but when I commence writing I never know when to stop
> Friend Henry
>
> I was much gratified to learn, by the reception of your very welcome letter that you had not, in my case, verified the old adage, "Out of sight, out of mind", and, I am happy to take this opportunity to assure you that I consider a friend, too precious to be neglected even if our "interests do clash" which in our case is impossible;
>
> I sleep at the store tonight, as the streets are almost impassable on account of the mud, and having just finished my days work, I will steal a few moments from "Natures Sweet Restorer" and devote them to you in a (sleepy) account of my progress in this land of Suckers[.]
>
> You have, no doubt, learned from, Henry, the particulars of my journey hither. & let it suffice, that I consider it well worth my time & money, as certainly, the time was the most pleasantly spent of any three weeks I ever passed. Since my arrival here

I have been so busily engaged that I have had no time to learn much of the country, but from what I have seen, I have been much pleased. In many respects I consider it far superior
[page break]
to the "Land of Steady habits" but in many others vastly inferior. A man can get a living here with one half the labor which he must exert there, but many things which are enjoyed there are here, not known, but the time is not far off I think when the different section of this "great country" will be more on a level, and the blessings of the free schools and other New England privaliges will be more widely diffused.

The region about here is, as yet, quite sparsely settled but is rapidly filling up. Our Town is very small, perhaps about the size of <u>Little river Vill</u>, but the county for 20 miles round depend upon it for goods, and a great amount of goods are sold here; The principal business of the country is raising stock, ie, cattle horses and hogs, the latter especially, which are driven to Chicago, & St Louis, and sold for cash[.] One man left here a short time since with 3000 hogs, all in one drive; Immense quantities of Pork are slaughtered here and made into Bacon which is the only manner of putting it up here[.] It would be a losing business for a New England farm to raise pork to sell at 1.50 & 2.00 per cent but here there is no trouble or expense scarcely in <u>making</u> it. (The suckers speak of <u>making</u> pork & <u>raising</u> children) as they can do nothing else with the great crops of corn they raise, which is only worth 10 & 12 1/2 cents per Bushel, but this probably does not interest you[.]
[page break]
I would like to look in upon the Brunswick people occasionally, to see what they are doing, but I dint know when I shall have that pleasure[.] You are there frequently no doubt, and so just please keep me posted up on all things of interest that occurs in the old place, and give me the record, if you think is with your while to continue a correspondence with so tedious a person as myself[.]

Poor B. seems to be doomed to conflagrations since I left I was very sorry to learn that Cushing had met with another misfortune, but presume he was fully insured. ——Henry I suppose still continues dealing out pork & [unreadable] at the old place I have not heard from him since the letter [unreadable] yours, I sent him one the day before I recd that I shall write again as soon as possible. Where is Thomas this winter? give my regards to him and ask him to write me[.] I suppose you are enjoying fun sleighing now and the bells are jingling merrily. we have no snow of any consequence here, and people do not prepare for sleighing. once in a great while there is slight fall of snow which is said to last a week, sometimes, but not often. we have had this winter two days of sleighing, and it is snowing now on top of about 8 inches of clear fat mud[.] How did Newells' Singing School come out? And what has become of the Association? Is there any dancing going on this season, down east? I attended a ball here [canceled "three"] night before last and had a "special time" - my paper wont allow or I would attempt a [unreadable] description of
[Page break]
it, but fear I could not do justice to the subject —————

Give my regards to Mrs Hall, Emma & Caroline and all others who may take any interest in such an individual

as, your sincere friend

Chas. D. Sufkin

[mailed to]

Mr. Henry H. Thompson

Little River P.O.

Lisbon, Maine

Take the quiz to see how well you recall details of the letter. (See the footnote for the answer key.)[15]

1. TRUE/FALSE: Sufkin tells Henry that a man can make a living in Illinois ("this Land of Suckers") with half the labor he expends in New England (the "Land of Steady Habits").

2. What does Sufkin's comparison of Illinois and New England imply about Illinois? (Pick three.)
   a. That Illinois did not compare favorably to Maine because it did not have "free" schools (i.e., schools funded through property tax on free-holders).
   b. That business was good in Shelbyville because the small town served the population in a twenty-mile area.
   c. Shelbyville residents must have eaten a *lot* of bacon while residents of Maine ate different pork products.
   d. Sufkin did not like Illinois and told his friend Henry to send money so he could get a train ticket and return home.
   e. Sufkin thought the Illinois winters were much worse than those in Maine, much colder, and with no social outlets to pass the time.

3. Sufkin says that farmers near Shelbyville make their living doing which one of the following?
   a. Selling corn in Chicago and St. Louis markets.
   b. Selling hogs for $1.50 to $2 per 100 weight (per cent) in Chicago and St. Louis, raised on cheap corn (10 to 12½ cents per bushel).
   c. selling wheat raised on the Shelbyville prairie to grain elevators in Chicago.

Sufkin told Henry that "This probably does not interest you." Why? Henry might not be a farmer or he might not care about the stock economy (markets for cattle, horses, and hogs) that drove agriculture in the Shelbyville area in early 1850. Sufkin understood the farming economy in New England, and he might have known that the corn-hog economy in Illinois had no comparison back in the "land of steady habits." In addition to the details of stock droving, and hog and corn production, the letter indicates that differences existed between agricultural practices in Illinois and those in old farming communities in Maine. Additional research into published U.S. Bureau of the Census reports can document production of hogs (and corn or other associated products) for states and counties over the years (from 1840 to the present). Study of manuscript returns prepared by census enumerators offer additional details that can help you document production farm by farm.[16]

Exercise in Visual Literacy

Engage interpreters in exercises that push them to apply their growing understanding of agriculture and increased skills in historical thinking. Share artwork or photographs relevant to your museum or site, provide reference material (visual dictionaries and collectors guides), and have them identify the details. For example, a photograph of farmers at an open-air market can help interpreters overcome numerous assumptions and develop techniques to engage visitors in the process, too.

Urban markets existed only because of farmers' commitments to production agriculture. Truck farmers grew large amounts of fruits and vegetables, and shipped their produce to market for wholesalers to purchase. Market gardeners grew vegetables and fruits for sale directly to customers. Truck farmers and market gardeners found market outlets in urban environments. Public markets, identified on Sanborn Maps, for insurance purposes, usually existed close to city centers. Farmers of all races participated in these markets (Photo 14.3).[17]

Identify all components of the image. Look at it in minute detail. A digital image available at Shorpy.com allows you to enlarge the image and hone in on the details. Be specific about the evidence of agriculture (i.e., the horse, harness, cart, corn in husks, types of melons). Be specific about the people, their attire, and their occupation at the moment the photographer stopped. Itemize the evidence that might lead some to think that the market was dirty (i.e., horse manure on the street, flies on the crops), and find as many examples of evidence that might lead some to think about the economic opportunity, even the prosperity of the market gardeners. Conclude the exercise by having staff "interpret" the image and then discuss the ways this can inform their interpretation of the museum or site.

Exercise in Reading Objects

Tim Grove questioned the standard interpretation of Eli Whitney's cotton gin in *A Grizzly in the Mail*. He explains the steps he took to revise interpretation of that object by collecting information about other machines that removed seeds from cotton. He talked to people who used the machine, and revised interpretation at the National Museum of American History in the process.[18] The exercise began by questioning common interpretations of an iconic machine, and by exploring objects in detail.

Thomas J. Schlereth surveyed approaches to material culture analysis as practiced since 1876. He itemized nine approaches:

1. "Art history" tends to concentrate on high-quality or expressive objects and their makers. Art history analysts emphasize the ways that a culture in one place and time imprints its values on objects and how changes in style can represent culture shifts.

Photo 14.3 Sixth Street Market in Richmond, Virginia, with watermelons, squash, musk melons, and ear corn (probably sweet corn) displayed on the brick street pavement, farmers hawking their produce, and a horse standing in harness, still hitched to the cart. 1908. Detroit Publishing Company.

Source: Courtesy of Shorpy.com

2. The "symbolist perspective" considers selected objects as symbols or material manifestations of myth.
3. The "cultural historical orientation" seeks to combine scant object and textual evidence into a reconstruction of a culture in a specific time and place. Archaeological excavations often generate the evidence scholars use to re-create the culture. The work up until the 1980s concentrated on rural places.
4. The "environmentalist preoccupation" emphasizes rural and folk topics, using buildings and landscape features as artifacts.
5. The "functionalist rationale" seeks to explain the relationship between humans and their environment, particularly the interrelationships between the folk (often the maker), the technology they use, and the environment in which they use it. Each aspect of a cultural action (expression, organizations, networks) has a role or performs a function.
6. The "structuralist view," as Schlereth explains it, hinges on the assumption that "all cultural systems should be treated as languages and, as such, can be systematically analyzed as to their structure."

7. The "behavioralistic concept" shifts the intent of object analysis from understanding the artifact to comprehending the goals, tastes, or agendas of individual makers or users.

8. The "national character focus" takes the opposite approach, that objects can convey the goals, tastes, or agendas of a culture group of national scale. Scholars often seek material evidence of attributes associated with a nation, and as Schlereth explains, examples of this approach have tried to show "how pragmatic, vernacular, and progressive forces of democracy have shaped and been shaped by American things."

9. The "social history paradigm" seeks objects representative of the nonliterate masses, objects not usually elevated to exceptional levels by collection in museums or by identification with a maker or user.[18]

Exercises in reading material culture can start with an object in the collection that relates to themes significant to the site, and that has good provenance. It is best to start with the known. Have staff identify materials and manufacturing techniques. They should look closely for evidence of wear and repair. This leads them to describe the decoration or finish on the object. What proportion does the object have; does it "feel" balanced? Could a farmer use it to accomplish a task? If not, what causes it to be out of balance, or potentially not useful? What function did the object serve? How was it used? After reading the object in detail, then staff can move to context. Who donated the artifact? Did that person use it, or collect it? Last, the staff can brainstorm about ways the artifact can inform interpretation at the site—both the history of the site, but also as evidence of the process of collection and preservation.

This process can be repeated over and over again, with staff and with visitors. The goal is to encourage people to recognize artifacts as valuable bits of historic evidence. Individually, they may carry personal stories; collectively, they help to explain human responses to agricultural challenges.

Two case studies provide additional examples of interpreting agriculture. One features the Magoffin State Historic Site, a house museum in a modern urban environment that once sat in the heart of an orchard in fledgling El Paso. Cameron L. Saffell summarizes agricultural topics that inform interpretation at the site administered by the Texas Historical Commission. The other example features an exhibit that orients visitors to the agricultural businesses as the basis for philanthropy. An exhibit about Cyrus McCormick's widow, Nettie, and her support of Tusculum College, curated by undergraduate students enrolled in the college's museum studies program, and guided by their professor, Peter M. Noll, provides an example.

Interpreting Agriculture provides a road map that museums and historic sites can use to develop humanities-focused interpretation. The setting of the museum or historic site should not limit the possibilities. Rural, small town, suburban, and urban institutions all can develop meaningful exhibits and programs. The interpretation that results can help visitors gain perspective about human-animal-crop-environment symbioses over time. Partnering with agricultural processing industries, local farms, and living history farms and agricultural museums can help you accomplish your goals. The stakes are high.

Proactive planning can help you document local agriculture philosophies and practices in your areas and cultivate partnerships that will help you interpret agriculture, then and now. Doing so will expand your institution's visibility and its critical role in launching conversations about complicated and essential topics.

Notes

1. Freeman Tilden, *Interpreting Our Heritage*, 4th ed. (Chapel Hill: The University of North Carolina Press, 2008).

2. Johnston Farm and Indian Agency. The 250-acre historic site in Piqua, Ohio, includes evidence of prehistoric occupations, early national-era farming practices, agricultural processing, and regional transportation networks. Surviving structures include a house, barn, springhouse, and cider house, all constructed between 1808 and 1828, and a remnant of the Miami and Erie Canal constructed during the mid-1830s. John Johnston worked for the U.S. government as an Indian agent in the Northwest Territory. He and his family moved to the Piqua, Ohio, property in 1811. He operated a gentleman's farm, and served as Indian agent to several Indian nations in the area from 1812 to 1829. The Ohio History Connection owns the site, and the Johnston Farm Friends Council operates it. See "Johnston Farm and Indian Agency," http://www.johnstonfarmohio.com/ (accessed 7 January 2016).

3. Farmington: This site began as a 550-acre hemp plantation owned by John Speed, who also owned sixty to seventy slaves in Jefferson County, Kentucky. The brick home, completed in 1816 and listed on the National Register of Historic Places, is owned and operated by Historic Homes Foundation, Inc. Site promotion features the elegant house, formal gardens, and a seasonal farmers' market to attract visitors. See http://farmingtonhistoricplantation.org/ (accessed 9 January 2016). Significance of the property focuses on the connections between Speed family members and Thomas Jefferson, and the similarity of Farmington's layout to Jefferson's architectural designs. "Farmington," National Register of Historic Places Inventory-Nomination Form, 18 October 1972, http://focus.nps.gov/nrhp/GetAsset?assetID=7ee19462-0912-48fc-a1b1-854f6b0ff712 (accessed 16 January 2016), and "Farmington (Speed House)," Louisville, Jefferson County, KY, Survey (photographs, measured drawings, written historical and descriptive data), Historic American Buildings Survey, National Park Service, U.S. Department of the Interior, 1934 and 1979. From Prints and Photographs Division, Library of Congress (HABS KY-24); http://www.loc.gov/item/ky0155/ [accessed 17 January 17 2016].

4. George M. Murrell Home: Once the headquarters of an antebellum stock farm built around 1845 by a Virginian in the new Cherokee Nation, Indian Territory, it was home to a merchant and his family including his first wife, Minerva, and his second wife, Amanda Ross, nieces of John Ross, principal chief of the Cherokee Nation. The historic house is operated by the Oklahoma Historical Society and is located in Park Hill, Oklahoma. It is listed on the National Register of Historic Places and is a National Historic Landmark. See http://www.okhistory.org/sites/georgemurrell.php (accessed 6 January 2016); "Murrell House, Hunter's Home," National Register of Historic Places Inventory-Nomination Form, 11 November 1973, http://focus.nps.gov/pdfhost/docs/nrhp/text/70000530.pdf (accessed 7 January 2016).

5. Freewoods Farms, operated by Freewoods Foundation, opened in 2001 in Burgess (near Myrtle Beach), South Carolina. For a history of the culture constructed by enslaved people on Low Country rice plantations, see Philip D. Morgan, *Slave Counterpoint: Black Culture in the Eighteenth-Century Chesapeake and Lowcountry* (Chapel Hill: University of North Carolina Press, 1998). For an overview of Black farm community formation, see Debra A. Reid and Evan P. Bennett, eds., *Beyond Forty Acres and a Mule: African American Farm-Owning Families since*

Reconstruction (Gainesville: University of Florida Press, 2012). For a case study of freedmen communities in a very different agricultural zone, East Texas, see Thad Sitton and James H. Conrad, *Freedom Colonies: Independent Black Texans in the Time of Jim Crow* (Austin: University of Texas Press, 2005). For a history of Rosenwald Schools and their significance, see Mary S. Hoffschwelle, *The Rosenwald Schools of the American South* (Gainesville: University Press of Florida, 2006).

6. Paulsdale: Alice Stokes Paul, suffragist and advocate for equal rights, was born and lived on the farm in Mount Laurel Township, New Jersey, between 1885 and 1920. The six-and-one-half-acre site includes a brick farmhouse constructed before 1849, and an icehouse, the only surviving structures of a 173.4-acre diversified farmstead that included a horse and cow barn, calf sheds, a hog house, a chicken house and coops, and storage buildings including a granary and equipment sheds. The site is a National Historic Landmark and was also listed on the National Register of Historic Sites in 1988. It serves as headquarters of the Alice Paul Institute. See http://www.alicepaul.org/ (accessed 7 January 2016); "Alice Paul House"; "Paulsdale," National Register Inventory-Nomination Form, 5 July 1989, http://focus.nps.gov/pdfhost/docs/nrhp/text/89000774.pdf (accessed 7 January 2016).

7. Dorris Ranch: The first commercial filbert orchard in the United States operated between 1892 and 1936, listed on the National Register of Historic Places, and operated by the Willamalane Park and Recreation District, Springfield, Oregon. The historic site is a working farm (and public park). An orchard manager maintains the 9,250 filbert trees on seventy-five acres and markets nuts from those trees. See http://willamalane.org/park/dorris-ranch/ (accessed 6 January 2016); "Dorris Ranch," National Register of Historic Places Registration Form, 22 June 1988, http://focus.nps.gov/pdfhost/docs/nrhp/text/88000724.pdf (accessed 7 January 2016).

8. Cantigny Park: Robert R. "Colonel" McCormick owned and operated the *Chicago Tribune*, a major daily newspaper founded by his grandfather, Joseph Medill. McCormick edited the *Tribune* from 1910 to his death in 1955, and he co-owned the *Tribune*'s radio station, WGN ("World's Greatest Newspaper"). These media served rural populations and reported on agricultural topics. Robert lived in the house Medill built in 1896, on a farm estate in the western Chicago suburb of Wheaton, Illinois. Robert's first wife, Amy Irwin Adams McCormick (?–1939), operated a purebred Guernsey dairy herd at the farm between the 1910s and 1939, when she died. The *Tribune* reported on activities at the experimental farm starting in 1934. The historic site, Cantigny Park, bears little resemblance to the gentleman's farm during the early twentieth century. Today it includes the historic house, the First Division Museum, and formal gardens designed in 1967. See http://cantigny.org/museums/robert-r-mccormick-museum (accessed 6 January 2016).

9. NPS Focus, National Register Information System Database, http://focus.nps.gov/nrhp/ (accessed 6 January 2016).

10. National Historic Landmarks Program, http://www.nps.gov/nhl/ (accessed 7 January 2016).

11. Roy Rosenzweig and David Thelen. *The Presence of the Past: Popular Uses of History in American Life* (New York: Columbia University Press, 1998).

12. Cori Brewster, "Toward a Critical Agricultural Literacy," in *Reclaiming the Rural: Essays on Literacy, Rhetoric, and Pedagogy*, edited by Kim Donehower, et.al. (Carbondale: Southern Illinois University Press, 2012), 34–51.

13. E-mail, Jonathan Kuester to Debra A. Reid, 6 June 2016.

14. Used with permission of the collector, Brent Wielt, Decatur, Illinois. Transcribed and printed in *The Homestead Prairie Astounder*, 19, no. 3 (March 2008), a publication of the Macon County Conservation District, Decatur, Illinois. Note: All spelling and grammar appears as in the original; comments added by the editors of the *Astounder* appear in brackets. What would it take for a drover to keep three thousand hogs on the road between Shelbyville and St. Louis or Chicago in January 1850? R. Lee Slider explained some of this in his commentary, "Oink, Being

Some Comments upon Herding Pigs in Early Shelby County," *The Homestead Prairie Astounder* [Macon County Conservation District (MCCD) in Decatur, Illinois], 19, no. 3 (March 2008):

Once rounded up, the herd, if large, was usually divided up into smaller units of two hundred to three hundred hogs each which made driving them easier along the trails and roads of the time. They would move the units in sections each with several men on horseback as well as a number on foot to control the moving body. Depending on circumstances hog herds could travel around seven to eight miles a day. At night the herds would be sequestered in rented fields adjoining the road or at a cabin or tavern with herd pens that catered to drovers. . . . Sometimes a man in a wagon loaded with corn led the herd throwing out a few ears at a time to entice the lead hogs along.

15. Answer Key:

1. TRUE
2. Sufkin implies that people don't have to work as hard in Illinois to make a living, but the rest of the letter indicates that the costs are less great, so people do not have to work as much to earn enough to afford the things they want in life. Obviously the sales values of hogs and corn is not high, but the cost of living is a lot less in Illinois. The quality of life, however, is not as good (no free schools or other cultured events, such as singing schools, apparently). Specifically:
   a. Illinois did not compare favorably to Maine, because it did not have "free" schools (i.e., schools funded through property tax on free-holders).
   b. Business was good in Shelbyville, because the small town served the population in a twenty-mile area.
   c. Shelbyville residents must have eaten a LOT of bacon, and residents of Maine ate different pork products.
3. Selling hogs for $1.50 to $2 per 100 weight (per cent) in Chicago or St. Louis, raised on cheap corn (10 to 12½ cents per bushel).

16. Electronic access via open source or proprietary websites have made census research much quicker. Use FamilySearch.org for free, Ancestry.com for a fee—both are indispensable in documenting people in specific places. Ancestry.com now has live-text searchable agricultural census returns for farmers in the United States in 1870 and 1880, slave schedule returns for 1860, and population census returns to 1930. Enumerators hired to collect population census data proceeded along roadways, stopping house by house along the route. Enumeration districts were clearly described, so census takers knew what territory they had to cover. These descriptions of the Population Census Enumeration Districts, included on a different microfilm reel of your state's census returns, warrant consultation. Then you can outline the enumeration districts and plot the location of selected individuals and sites on the county plat map, which you can secure at the local courthouse or on facsimile copies of historic Sanborn Maps, produced for fire insurance purposes starting in 1867, and available at your local library and via the World Wide Web. ProQuest Information and Learning has digitized 660,000 of these maps; inquire at your local public or academic library about access. The large-scale maps include footprints of each building, the construction materials, the location of windows and doors, and the function of structures on a property (both residential and commercial) in cities, towns, and neighborhoods across the United States. For additional information, consult http://sanborn.umi.com/.

17. The Sixth Street Market, located on North Sixth Street, was three blocks from Capitol Square. See Sanborn Fire Insurance Map, Richmond, Independent Cities, Virginia, digitized and available at the Library of Congress.

18. Tim Grove, *A Grizzly in the Mail and Other Adventures in American History* (Lincoln: University of Nebraska Press, 2014).

19. Thomas J. Schlereth, "Material Culture Studies in America, 1876–1976," *Material Culture Studies in America* (Nashville, TN: American Association for State and Local History, 1982), 40–72.

CHAPTER 15

CASE STUDY: INTERPRETING RURAL LIFE IN EL PASO

Cameron L. Saffell

THE MAGOFFIN HOME State Historic Site has a unique challenge when it comes to interpreting rural life in El Paso. The site includes a nineteen-room adobe hacienda built in the 1870s by Joseph Magoffin, pioneer resident and city booster, and his wife, Octavia. Joseph inherited over 1,200 acres of land from the Rio Grande to the foothills of the Franklin Mountains from his father after the American Civil War. Their home, on the eastern outskirts of town, was surrounded by dozens of acres of orchards and small gardens that produced apples, peaches, corn, and other fruits and vegetables (Photo 15.1). Early newspaper articles describe the Magoffins' "rural domicile" and mention the quality of the fruits and vegetables that it produced, all irrigated by an old Spanish-style acequia that ran through the property.[1] Although Joseph was involved in several businesses and political offices, he maintained his horses, milk cows, and livestock on his small homestead even as the city expanded around him and enveloped the site over the following four decades.[2]

Today's visitors have a hard time envisioning the rural character of the Magoffin Home of the late nineteenth century. The site is now part of downtown El Paso. The central business district with its skyscrapers begins only six blocks away. An affordable senior housing complex surrounds the Home on three sides, anchored by a nine-story building right behind the historic site. Though it sits in one of El Paso's earliest upscale residential neighborhoods of late Victorian period–style homes, that character has disappeared as century-old homes were subdivided into apartments and the area has become run-down with all the problems of urban downtowns—the homeless, drugs, and more. The Magoffin Home grounds itself is now reduced to only 1.5 acres, with a visitors' center in a restored residential building across the street.[3] Envisioning

Photo 15.1 Detail: Augustus Koch, *Bird's Eye View of El Paso*. The orchards surrounding the Magoffin Home are easily identified running between Magoffin and San Antonio Streets on the east side of town. The Magoffin Home, built ca. 1877, is shown as a large ell structure with an outbuilding in the back. Joseph Magoffin later connected the two parts, creating an enclosed courtyard, which is what visitors see today. Detail from Augustus Koch, *Bird's Eye View of El Paso, El Paso County Texas*, 1886, lithograph, 20 x 30 in. Private collection.

Source: Reproduced from Texas Bird's Eye Views website, Amon Carter Museum, http://www.birdseyeviews .org/zoom.php?city=El%20Paso&year=1886 (accessed 2 June 2016). Public Domain

this as a rural homestead with a working orchard on the outskirts of El Paso is very difficult—particularly since the outskirts of town are now literally more than a dozen miles away.

Interpreting the rural origins is one goal of the State Historic Site's current interpretive plans. Only one aspect has been easy—the architecture. Adobe structures are relatively rare today in El Paso, even though it was the dominant building method until the railroads arrived—with their array of brick and lumber building materials—in the 1880s. Only a few public adobe buildings survive, the rest being small private residences scattered in hidden areas of the oldest neighborhoods of the city and county. Visitors are fascinated seeing walls that are two to three and a half feet thick and learning how the adobe bricks were made on-site and dried in the desert sun. The walls were plastered with lime and whitewashed, with some of the exterior surfaces decoratively scored to give the appearance of large blocks of stone.[4] The "look" of the building—and its stark contrast to the remaining historic homes and the senior housing projects surrounding it—does much to transport visitors back to an earlier time in history.

The next interpretive challenge is the lack of agricultural artifacts and context—particularly in the remaining acreage of the site. The old stables and barn were long ago converted into enclosed rooms, and the henhouse was removed, along with the corrals. The last mounds of dirt across the back of the property marking the acequia that irrigated everything disappeared when the senior housing project was built. Rather than interpret early agriculture, former site managers installed a Certified Texas Wildscape featuring 90 percent Chihuahuan desert cacti and plants. The grounds more closely resemble a manicured city park than its rural agricultural origins.[5]

In 2011–2012 the Magoffin Home underwent a major restoration and preservation project that included significant repairs to both the building and grounds. The grounds had to be regraded so water would drain away from the adobe brick walls instead of towards them; this offered an opportunity to transform the grounds—albeit it with several challenges. The site had to meet modern urban drainage regulations with retention ponds and other features that Joseph Magoffin would never have conceived of; the changes needed to reflect the historic integrity and different uses of the property over time; and they had to balance a myriad of interpretive desires, landscape management needs, and spaces for rentals and special events.[6]

Site Manager Leslie Bergloff, the team from the Texas Historical Commission, and their project architect studied the problem. They worked to minimize the footprints of the retention ponds while trying to open up new areas where agriculture and rural life could be interpreted. They removed the desert garden and planted two small orchard trees and a new garden. Certain aspects of the previous historic landscape had to be retained—like the grass and plantings along the front walkway, but the edges were redressed for a new mission. It does not convey the size of the original homestead with acres and acres of orchards, but the look is there—with enough plantings to convey the interpretation of a rural property offered by the site's tour guides.[7]

With the physical dimensions addressed, the final step was to bring in some period artifacts. Historic records describe the Magoffin Home with a couple of carriages and a farm wagon or two, but those artifacts disappeared decades ago. A few hand tools that would have been used to prune rosebushes, trim the trees, or carry harvested fruit in baskets complete the transformation.[8]

The Magoffin Home's current downtown surroundings make it difficult for visitors to imagine the important agricultural history that took place along the Rio Grande on small farms and properties just like the Magoffins'. However, changes to the site landscape and a directed emphasis in the interpretation will take those visitors back to the origins of the family and help transform what they think about agriculture and rural life in early El Paso.

Notes

1. Cameron L. Saffell, "Historical Evolution of Land Ownership from James Wiley Magoffin to Joseph Magoffin and the Glasgows," Magoffin Home State Historic Site Docent Paper (December 2010), 12–20; "River and Valley," *El Paso Times*, 2 May 1888; "Joseph Magoffin," *El Paso Times*, August 1887, as found in Joseph Magoffin Vertical File, El Paso Public Library; "Locals," *El Paso Lone Star*, 24 June 1885.

2. Joseph Magoffin Glasgow, interview by Sarah E. John, June–October 1982, Institute of Oral History, Interview no. 605, University of Texas at El Paso (hereafter Glasgow Oral History), 11, 27–29.

3. Martin Davenport, "Magoffin Historic District," National Register of Historic Places Registration Form, SBR Draft available at http://www.thc.state.tx.us/public/upload/preserve/national_register/draft_nominations/El%20Paso,%20Magoffin%20HD%20NR%20SBR%20Draft.pdf (accessed 2 June 2016), 5–8, 22.

4. Carol Bossert and Robert West, *Master Interpretive Plan, Magoffin Home State Historic Site* (Austin: Texas Historical Commission, 2009), 43–45; Texas Parks & Wildlife Department, *Preservation Plan and Program for Magoffin Home State Historic Site* (Austin: The Agency, 1977), a-44–a-49.

5. Glasgow Oral History, 10, 28–29; Sanborn Map Company, *El Paso, El Paso County, Texas, Sheet 21* [map] (New York: Sanborn Map Company, July 1905); *Master Interpretive Plan for the Magoffin Home*, 9.

6. Rick Hassler, "Party Like It's 1875: Magoffin Home to Re-Open," *El Paso, Inc.* [newspaper], 22 April 2012.

7. Leslie Bergloff, personal communications to author, 2011–2012.

8. Bossert and West, *Master Interpretive Plan*, 54; Leslie Bergloff, personal communications to author, 2011–2016.

CHAPTER 16

CASE STUDY: AN EXHIBIT

Reaper: Nettie Fowler McCormick and the Machine That Built Tusculum College

Peter M. Noll

TUSCULUM COLLEGE sits beneath ancient oaks within the long shadows of the Appalachian Mountains of eastern Tennessee. Throughout its early history, the college consisted of a single two-story brick building. In late 1883, four recent graduates of the college, then attending a Presbyterian seminary in Cincinnati, traveled to Chicago to meet with Reverend Dr. Willis Craig, the pastor at the Presbyterian church attended by the family of Cyrus McCormick and his wife, Nettie Fowler McCormick. The four men invited Dr. Craig to speak at Tusculum's commencement exercise at the conclusion of the academic year. After Cyrus McCormick's death in the spring of 1884, it was Craig who suggested that the recently widowed Nettie Fowler McCormick consider the small college as an object of her philanthropy. Later that year, the executors of the McCormick estate donated $7,000 to build McCormick Hall. Over the next three decades, Nettie Fowler McCormick established a relationship with the college's administration and provided the financial support to build five additional structures on campus.

Today, the college honors the legacy of Nettie Fowler McCormick with an annual day of service known in the community as "Nettie Day." Students, staff, and faculty spend one day working in the community, and the volunteer groups are a conspicuous presence in their brightly colored "Nettie Day" T-shirts. The McCormick name is known across campus, and the legacy of the family's beneficence is captured permanently in the bricks and mortar of building façades across campus. Within the campus community, knowledge of Nettie Fowler McCormick is broad, but not deep. It was this problem that students in a Museum Exhibits course attempted to remedy through an exhibit entitled *Reaper: Nettie Fowler McCormick and the Machine That Built Tusculum College*, installed in the President Andrew Johnson Museum and Library on campus.

Students conceived the exhibit as an opportunity to explore the social context in which Cyrus and Nettie McCormick acquired the fortune that ultimately facilitated the growth of Tusculum College at the turn of the twentieth century. They researched and planned the exhibit during the fall semester of 2013. Then, in January of 2014, they completed the production phase of the exhibit during an immersive three-and-one-half-week-long course. Their plan included documenting the business activity of the McCormick Company, which built agricultural machinery, including harvesting equipment. Their findings indicated the ways that the company changed the working lives of millions of residents across the Americas (not just in Chicago, Illinois) during the nineteenth century, and of students at Tusculum College since 1884.[1] Sterling Evans's award-winning study, *Bound in Twine: The History and Ecology of the Henequen-Wheat Complex for Mexico and the American and Canadian Plains, 1880–1950*,[2] provided a basic interpretive structure for student research. The Wisconsin Historical Society's online archive of McCormick Company documents and artifacts also enriched their research.

Students began the exhibit process by researching themes and producing individual research papers. The themes included nineteenth-century gender and philanthropy with an emphasis on Nettie Fowler McCormick's philanthropic ventures. But it also included several agricultural topics that explained the source of the McCormick fortune and the not-always-overt connections between agricultural production, technological innovation, labor systems, global politics, and local philanthropy. These topics included:

- Harvest technology and McCormick innovations
- The social implications of farm mechanization in the nineteenth-century United States
- The origin and evolution of McCormick businesses and major competitors
- McCormick, industrial production in Chicago, and the nineteenth-century labor movement
- Connections between the U.S. Government, the agricultural economy, and gunboat diplomacy in Latin America
- The complicity of the McCormick Company in exploitive labor systems in Central America that ensured the production of raw materials essential to McCormick business interests, and
- The effects of farm mechanization on the American environment.

Students distilled their research into seminar papers, then into exhibit label copy. They identified historic images (Photo 16.1). They designed interpretive panels that carried the narrative thrust, and installed the finished product.

The Tennessee Association of Museums recognized the exhibit *Reaper: Nettie Fowler McCormick and the Machine That Built Tusculum College* with an Award of Excellence in May 2015.[3] Reviewers were impressed not only by the quality of the exhibit work, but

Photo 16.1 Tusculum College students layer a historic photograph of Cyrus and Nellie McCormick in the exhibit *Reaping.*

Source: Photograph courtesy of Peter Noll

also by the breadth of the topic and its ability to connect local stories to broader historical themes.

By exploring the machines that the McCormick Company manufactured, students were able to show museum visitors a much larger history. Students demonstrated that the picturesque campus they inhabited was much more than the product of a singular act of philanthropy. It was in a very real sense the product of factory workers in Chicago, of farm families on the American and Canadian plains, and the forced labor of indigenous peoples on the Henequen plantations of the Mexican Yucatan. Students, and museum visitors, learned that the Tusculum College history is an agricultural history.

Notes

1. McCormick Hall was actually built in 1887.
2. Sterling Evans, *Bound in Twine: The History and Ecology of the Henequen-Wheat Complex for Mexico and the American and Canadian Plains, 1880–1950* (College Station, TX: Texas A&M University Press, 2007).
3. "Tusculum College Museums Win Two State Awards" (7 May 2015), available at http://www3.tusculum.edu/for/news/2015/tusculum-college-museums-win-two-state-awards/ (accessed 13 August 2016).

CONCLUSION

I T IS REALLY difficult to avoid the topic of agriculture when interpreting almost any topic at museums and historic sites. The process starts with a commitment to learn more about farming, about plants and animals, about diverse philosophies and business approaches. Agriculture incorporates so many different topics and disciplines that it can overwhelm the most dedicated. Public interest can provide a place to start, but the long-term process needs to keep artifacts and archival documents at the center of exhibits and programs that help the public grasp the human dimension of agriculture. These items provide evidence of a nation's history, accumulated through local, personal stories that convey diverse perspectives, attitudes, philosophies, and cultural practices.

Interpreting Agriculture is not designed to tell you what you need to know about the place that you interpret. Instead, it provides a rationale for launching a planning process that will help you identify what is distinctly local, unique to your place and time, and engaging to your constituents. *Interpreting Agriculture* should help you gain confidence enough to start to talk with the public about their interests, develop a research plan that will generate information about agriculture as practiced at your site at a given time in the past, and use that as the basis for reviewing collections and coordinating public programs and exhibits. This approach should apply to any site, be it a farmhouse in Tennessee, a fish farm in Mississippi, or a gentlewoman's farm in the shadow of the city. This process will take time, especially because much remains to be learned about the personal experiences of farm families. These gaping holes represent opportunities rather than barriers to learning about agriculture.

Objects can help fill in the gaps, but understanding artifacts requires time and intellectual investment. Not everything in a collection warrants full attention. Curators who manage agricultural collections prioritize objects based on their integrity and relevance to the mission of the museum or site. Developing a comprehensive list of agricultural objects in your collection, correctly identified, is well worth the effort. Objects low on the integrity list become the first objects to deaccession. Deaccessioning frees storage space that you can then fill with objects needed to tell your agricultural story better. The research reports that result become the foundation for developing proactive collection development plans.

An interpretive plan should provide an overview of agriculture—past and present—but it should also address the ways that the museum founders perceived agriculture. The first part requires research into primary and secondary sources and a standard research report, but the second part depends on the institutional history, biographies of founders, articles of incorporation, and the collections as evidence. The archives and artifacts that patrons donated might tell more about the agricultural past that they sought to preserve than the history that the farm families lived. Understanding what donors of agricultural artifacts thought about those artifacts will help you discern the biases in your collections and will help you utilize the objects to tell these stories.

Interpreting Agriculture provides justification to dedicate limited resources to researching, collecting, and interpreting a topic that encompasses nothing less than the entire nation's history, one humanized local story at a time. These stories can inform a public very distant from the fields that feed and clothe them, about a topic too important to ignore.

APPENDIX

LINKS TO USEFUL INFORMATION

NOTE: Readers can access the complete files at http://ALHFAM.org.

Part I: Professional Organizations Supporting the Study of Agricultural and Rural History

(in alphabetical order)

Agricultural History Society (AHS): founded in 1919. http://aghistorysociety.org/.

American Association for State and Local History (AASLH): founded in 1940. http://aaslh.org.

International Association of Agricultural Museums (*Association Internationale des Musées d'Agriculture*) (AIMA): founded in 1966. http://agriculturalmuseums.org/.

Association for Living History, Farm and Agricultural Museums (ALHFAM): founded in 1970. http://alhfam.org/.

Midwest Open-Air Museum Coordinating Council (MOMCC): founded in 1978. http://momcc.org.

Rural Sociology Society (RSS): founded in 1937. http://www.ruralsociology.org

Rural Women's Studies Association (RWSA): founded in 1998. http://www.ohio.edu/cas/history/institutes-associations/rwsa.

Vernacular Architecture Forum (VAF): founded in 1979. http://www.vafweb.org/.

Part II: Selected Advocates of Agricultural Education and Potential for Partnering

The National Council for Agricultural Education (The Council) describes agricultural education as "a systematic program of instruction available to students desiring to learn about the science, business, and technology of plant and animal production and/or about the environmental and natural resources systems." In 1981, National Agriculture in the Classroom was launched through a partnership between the U.S. Department of Agriculture, and state departments of agriculture and state Farm Bureau offices. In 1988, the National Research Council (NRC) defined an agriculturally literate person as a person who "understand[s] the food and fiber system and this would include its history and its current economic, social and environmental significance to all Americans" [http://www.agclassroom.org/]. Numerous organizations support education in agriculture and preservation of farmsteads and landscapes. This list explains the goals of selected organizations and the services they provide.

Part III: Selected Readings in Agricultural History: A Bibliographic Essay

This bibliographic essay is organized by themes in agricultural history (i.e., politics and policy, markets, land, labor, technology, crop and stock cultures, and international relations). It starts with an introduction to national surveys of agricultural history that can help you get a sense of social and cultural patterns of rural and farm life, and economic and policy issues. It provides information about resources to help you locate published primary sources (scientific treatises, for instance, produced in the 1800s) that can help you learn period-specific scientific terms and opinions of a time. It includes brief overviews of major trends in U.S. agricultural history (i.e., formation of land-grant colleges, dryland farming, New Deal agricultural policy, wartime policy, and the Farm Crisis of the early 1980s, to name a few). This reference list will help you identify studies to launch reading circles and begin the process of documenting agricultural history relevant to your site.

Part IV: Timeline: National Policy and Agrarian Legislation

This timeline includes national policy and legislation affected by agrarianism, that is, legislation that favored farmers. The timeline includes events that affected policy or that reacted to legislation. The content reflects three realities: 1) farmers took direct action when government policy did not favor their interests, as the cases of organized protests or outright violence during the 1670s, 1780s, 1870s, 1930s, and 1970s indicate; 2) most policy favored farmers or at least responded to farmer interests; 3) not all farmers received support in the form of proactive legislation. Poor and minority farmers did not fare well. This affirms that agriculture is an industry that is too big to fail. That was the case when the majority of the population had a direct connection to farmers, and it is just as true now as the majority of people depend upon a shrinking number of farmers for food and fiber.

Part V: Livestock Care in Museums, updated in 2016, Association for Living History, Farm and Agricultural Museums. ALHFAM.org

This outline is intended as a guideline that museums and historic sites can use to develop livestock management policies and procedures unique to each museum and reflecting its mission and resources. The approval and input of the institution's governing body and of livestock health professionals will lend credibility to, and increase public confidence in, a museum's livestock program. For additional information, contact the chair of ALHFAM's FARM Professional Interest Group.

INDEX

Page references for figures are *italicized*

beverages, 3, 33, 37, 144, 162, 203–4, 218; alcohol, 64, 107, 204; beer, 7, 22, 26, 72, *73*, 107, 170; milk, x , 9, *13*, 14, 37, 39n4, 43, 51, 66, 113, 158–9, 231

bias, 62, 78, 240

Big Oaks Farm Market, New Jersey, 162, *162*, 167n35

biology, xv, 67, 169, 171–2; biodiversity, 196; DNA, 36, 86; biological sciences, 7, 33, 63; genetic diversity, 32, 34

blacksmiths/blacksmithing, 31, 46, 54n16, 113

Blight, David, *Race and Reunion*, 42, 54n6

Bloch, Marc, 86; *French Rural History*, 99n1; *The Historian's Craft*, 99n1

Bogue, Allan G., 65; "Changes in Mechanical and Plant Technology," 134n3; *From Prairie to Corn Belt*, 65–66, 81n17

Bott, Anthony, 112, 115, 119n16

boyd, danah, *It's Complicated*, 33

Bracero History Archive, 206–7, 211n8; border control police, 207

Bracero Oral History Project, 206–7, 211n8

Bradley, Douglas, 74, *77*

Braeutigam Orchards, Illinois, 10, 15n17

Brambell, F. W. Rogers, 192–93; Five Freedoms, 192–93; "Report of the Technical Committee to Enquire into the Welfare of Animals Kept under Intensive Livestock Husbandry Systems," 192

Breck family, 55n21

Brewster, Cori, 36–7, 78, 218; "Toward a Critical Agricultural Literacy," 40n17, 229n12

bridges, 149–59, 161–64; American Bridge Company, 156; Bear Tavern Road Bridge, 163; construction, 152, 152–53, 156–57, 159; costs, 152–54; "engineered," 154; firms, 152, 156–7, 163; funding, 152; Green Bridge, 151–56, *155*, 159; Harmony Road Bridge, 157–59; highway bridge, 154; historic, 154, 156–57, 161–64; Historic American Engineering Record, 162; improving, 154; iron bridge, 152, 163–64; Jacobs Creek Bridge, 163–64; King Iron Bridge and Manufacturing Company, 163; and local contractors, 156–57; manufacturers, 152, 156–57, 163; Midland Bridge Company, 152; Moore Creek Bridge, 163; National Bridge Inspection Standards of 1971, 157; National Bridge Inventory, 157, 161; National Bridge Inventory Database, 166n26; New Jersey Historic Bridge Survey, 162–63, 167n34; New Mexico Historic Bridge Survey, 154; Pecos River Bridge, 153–54, *153*; pedestrian, 69, 155, 159, 164; Pratt design, 153, 155–57, 163–64; preserving, 154–57, 159, 162–64; relocating, 149, 152, 154–56, 159, 163–64; repairing, 155–56, 158; restoring, 152, 154–55; Rio Hondo Bridge, 154, 165n22; and rust, 155; steel truss bridges, 149, 151–67, *160, 168*, 163–64; stone, 160, 163; survey of public bridges, 156; timber-beam bridges, 152

Brossard, Dominique, 33, 39n8; and Nisbet, Mathew, "Deference to Scientific Authority among a Low Information Public," 39n8

Brown, John, 71, 83n34

Buck, Rebecca A., and Gilmore, Jean Allman, eds., *Museum Registration Methods*, 98, 101n29

Buckley Homestead State Park, Indiana, *125*

Burlend, Rebecca, 81nn20–21; *A True Picture of Emigration*, 66–67, 81n20

Bushnell, Reverend Horace, 42–43

Buzzard, Sylvester, 113–16, 119n30

California, 30, 70, 140, 142–45; cotton industry, 144–45; Davis, 38n2; Fresno, 140, 144; Porterville, 140, 144; San Joaquin Valley, 144, 208; Winters, 31, 38n2

Camp family, 162

Canada, 101n31, 191, 237

canals, 150, 161; Miami and Erie Canal, 217; boatrides, 179, 218

The Cannery Farm, California, 38n2

Cantigny Park, Illinois, 217, 229n8; First Division Museum, 229n8

Carter, Sarah Ann, "A Hand Plow," 27n16, 44, 47, 54n14

Casper, Scott E., *Sarah Johnson's Mount Vernon*, 25, 54n12; "Out of Mount Vernon's Shadow," 27n10

Cass, Lewis, *13*

catalogs, 86; bridges, 156; horticultural, 6, 86; parts, 94–5

cattle, 69–71, 81n20, 83n33, 117, 118n16, 121, *123*, 154, 158, 172, 178, 191, 197, 223–24; beef production, 62, 64; calves/calving, xiii, 66, 198, 205, 229; cattle drives, 152; cattle ranges, 35; cow-bus tour, 204; cows, x, xiii, xiv, *13*, 14, 30, 39n4, 43 51, 64, 66, 113–14, 170, 190, 197, *197, 216*, 218, 231; Guernsey, 217, 229n8; Mrs. O'Leary's, 72; neck yokes, 172, 178, 185n3

CCC. *See* Commodity Credit Corporation

census, 8–9, 67, 82n22, 120n43, 170, 224–25; enumerators, 230n15; records/data, 62, 67, 170, 230n15; U.S. Agricultural census, 9, 64, 67; U.S. Census Bureau, 8, 15n9, 224. *See also* population demographics

Center for Land-Based Learning, California, 31, 38n2

Chambers Ranch, Colorado, *111*, 120n43

Chambers, Robert M., 119n23, 120n43

Chatten, Samuel H., 163

chemicals, 15n21, 18, 63, 92, 134; sprayer, 22; synthetic, 203, 209

Chenhall, Robert G., 87; *Nomenclature 4.0*, 87

Chicago, Illinois, xiv , 3, 24, 66, 72–73, *76*, 91, 152, 205, 223–24, 229n8, 229nn13–14, 235–37; CALHF Club of Chicago, 205; Chicago Department of Aviation, 6; Chicago High School for Agricultural Sciences, 7; Chicago O'Hare International Airport, 5, *6*; fire, 72; Hyde Park, 6; Lincoln Park Zoo, 14n1; O'Hare Urban Garden, 6; stockyards, 6; Union Stockyards, 6; the Yards and Back of the Yards, 6

children, 6, 7, 19, 21, 23, 31, 35–37, 38n2, 38n3, 68, 70–71, 83n34, 99, 104, 140, 143–44, *160*, 205, 220, 223; on the farm, 10, 13, 43, 50, 64–65, 67; games, 19, 37, 85–86; as museum audiences, x, 195,

black-eyed peas, 143, 144; bread, 113; buckwheat, 109; cabbage, 106, 115; deserts, 7; flour, 106–7, 112–13, 115; fruit, xiv, 3, 5, 7, 49, 72, 74, 159, 161, 203, 205, 225, 231, 233; grains, 12, 48, 50–51, 66, 68–70, 72, 112–13, 113–14, *114*, 115, 124, *125*, 128, 132–33, 159, 188, 190, 208, 218; grapevines, 22; lettuce, 107; meat, 6, 9, 10, 21, 23, 30, 32, 62, 64, 66, 106, 159, 188, 203, 205; melons, *162*, 225, 226; mutton, 22; oats, 12, 39n4, 51, 61, 68, 106, 113–14; onions, 106, 107; peaches, 74, 231; peas, 12, 94, 107; porridge, 30, 83n34; potatoes, *4*, 37, 71, 86–87, 106, 113; pumpkins, *162*, 225, 226; rhubarb pie, 205; rye, 68; sauerkraut, 106; soybeans, 12, 33, 35, 63, 128, 130–31, 208; squash, *162*, 225, 226; succotash, 144; sugar, 66, 82n32; sugarcane, 218; tomatoes, x, 74, 209; vegetables, xiv, *6*, 7, 19, 21, 24, 31–32, 49, 71–72, 74, 85–86, 106–7, 112, 113–14, 119n28, 144, 159, 161–62, *162*, 203, 205, 225, 231; wheat, 35, 39n4, 50–51, 61, 66, 68, 103, 107, 112, 113–15, 119n29, 208, 224; yellow string beans, 91

Ford, Henry, 49–50, 64; dealers, 49; Ford Motor Company, 209. *See also* The Henry Ford

forests: forest preserve districts, 3, 68; forestry, 201; logging equipment, 175; lumber, *127*, 131, 153, 232; wood products and woodlots, 32, 34, 48, 51, *127*, 172, 188

Fosdick, H. M., 119n28

fowl: chickens, ix, x, 3, 21, 71, 114–15, 122, 144, 190–2, 200, 217; ducks, 21, 71; eggs, x , 9, 30, 32, 150, 192; fowl, 66, 69, 188; geese, 21, 71, 132; peasants, 21; poultry, 20–21, 67–68, 70, 192, 192, 200n8; rooster, 22; Society for the Preservation of Poultry Antiquities, 195; turkeys, 14, 71, 115

Fowler, David, 70, 82n27, 82n29

France: Louvre, Paris, 172; Nantes, 181

Freedom's Frontier National Heritage Area, Kansas, 36

Freewoods Farm, South Carolina, 217, 228n5; Freewoods Foundation, 228n5

Froedtert Bros Grain & Malting Co., *74*

fuel, 33, 35, 64, 80n10, 185n1, 204; bio/ethanol, 203, 204; consumption/costs, 128, 134; fuel cans, *126*; gas stations, 64, 67; oil fields, 152; oil for lubrication, 145, 176; petroleum, 32, 185n1; rig filled with, 145; solar energy, 192

Funk, Isaac, 65, 81n17

furniture, 6, 23, 27n10, 68, 70, 86, 178; bedroom suites, 43; beds, 21, 114, 139; bed warmer, 44; chairs, 43–44; milking stool, *13*, 14; reflector oven, 44; refrigerator, 37; sideboards, 43; snow shoes, 44; tables, 43

Future Farmers of America, 7

FWA. *See* Federal Works Agency

Gaines, Earnest J., 25; *The Autobiography of Miss Jane Pittman*, 25; *A Gathering of Old Men*, 25; *A Lesson before Dying*, 25

Galloway, Walter C., 109–10, 117, 119n20, 119n23, 120n43

gardens, 19, 20–21, 32–33, 48, 70–73, 107, 112, 114–15, 144, 199, 204, 206, 218, 231–33; aquaponics, 204; backyard, x, 117, 204; botanical, 18; desert garden, 233; flower, 6; formal, 68, 217–18; garden centers, 18; garden plots, 72; gardening programs, 19–20; hydroponics, 204; market, 9, 24, 31, 38n3, 74, 103, 159, 225; Master Gardeners, 18, 21, 27n13; vegetable, 114, 231; vertical aeroponics, 5, *6*, 204; Victory Gardens, 78

Garvin, William Henry, 110–12, 117

GDP. *See* U.S. Gross Domestic Product

genealogical research, 77; Ancestry.com, 77, 82n22, 230n15; family histories, 50, 62, 209–10; FamilySearch.org, 230n15; graveyards, 79

General Land Office (U.S.), 108–10, 117

General Artemas Ward House Museum, Shrewsbury, Massachusetts, 44–46, 54n14, 55n21. *See also* Ward family

geography, xv, 35, 50, 104, 156, 160–61, 171–72; deserts, 105, *219*, 233; Great American Desert, 112; Great Plains, 150, 152; hills, xiv 2, 50, 105, 153, 160, 171, 231; oceans, 204; plains, 104–5, 108, *111*, 112, 150, 152, 199, 237; prairies, 35, 66, 224; terrace, 86; terrain, 105, 171–72, 174, 178–79, 181, 188; topography, 11, 46; wetlands, 19, 217

geology/geologists, xv, 43, 110

George M. Murrell Home, Oklahoma, 70–71, 82n26, 83n33, 228n4, 217–18, 228n4

Gerlach, Ralph, 131

Germany: Berlin, 49; German language, 178; German POWs, 144

Glaspell, Susan, "A Jury of Her Peers," 23

Glassie, Henry, 89; *Folk Housing in Middle Virginia*, 100n11; *Passing the Time in Ballymenone*, 100n11; "The Variation of Concepts within Tradition," 100n11

Glover, Townend, 48

gold, 103–5, 108, 113; camps, 105–6, 112–13, 116; Hamilton camp, 112, 113; miners, 103; prospecting/ prospectors, 105, 105–7, 112–13, 117. *See also* Pikes Peak

Golden Age, 50, 63–64, 124, *125*, 158, 163, *221*

Goodyear, 176

government, 71, 108, 158, 159; county commissioners, 152–54; county, 150, 152, 156, 157–59, 162; inspectors, 133; local, 149, 156–57, 163–64, 191; multi-level cooperation, 156, 159, 161, 163–64; municipal, 152, 158; national, 149–51; public officials, 48, 156, 159, 161, 163; state, 149–52, 156, 159, 158, 160–62, 164, 189

government regulation, 32, 33, 132, 158, 206, 208, 233; business regulation, 11. *See also* policy and government legislation

grass, 19, 233; prairie grasses, 35

Green Revolution, 92

Gribben, Ray, 122–23

Grove, Tim, 225; *A Grizzly in the Mail*, 225, 230n17

Guide for the Care and Use of Agricultural Animals in Research and Teaching, 187, 193, 201n16

guns, 25; Colt revolvers, 95

horse harness collars, 172–75, 178, *183–85*; Anglo-American collar, 173; Assyrian, 172; breast-collar, 173–74, *184*; neck collar, 173–74, *185*; padding, 173–74

horse harness parts, 172–75: britchen and false britchen, xiv, 160, 172, 177, *184*, *185*; cart saddle, 175; hames, 173, 174; harness saddle, 172, *185*; saddlebow (høvre), 175; Scandinavian harness, 175; shafts, 172, 175–77, 179, 181, *184–85*; tongue, 172, 177; traces, 172–75, *183*, *184*, *185*

horsepower, defined, 171

horses, xiv, 7, 36, 64, 66, 68–72, *73*, 88–89, 91, 96, 107, *123*, 124, *125*, 149, 151, *153*, 169–85, *198*, 199, 221, 223–25, *226*, 231; anatomy and physiology, 172–75, 178, *183*, *184*; anatomy/fitting harnesses, 170, 172–75; and beer wagons, *73*, 170; biology, 172; clubs, 39n4; common horse, 170; compared to oxen and cattle, 170, 172, 178; draft, xiv, 39n4, 43, 50, *51*, 89, 96, 97, 123, 159, 164, 170, 173, 189, 191–92, 220; dray, 181; as engine, 171, 178; and farrier, 87, *184*, 192; and friction and inertia, 172–73, 176–79; girths, *185*; horse pulling capacity, 171–72, 178–79; horsehair, 6; lame, 173, 175, 178, *183*; and horseshoes, 87, *184*, 192; and loads, 172–75, 178–82, *183–85*; and physics, 172–79, *185*; polo ponies, 217; ponies, 170, 182; racing, *182*; riding, 71, 153, 170, 179; and roads, xiv, 151, 160, 163–64, 175–82; saddles, 106, *185*; speed, 178–79; spurs, 106, *185*; trip lengths, 174–75, 179–82; "wheel horses" and braking, 177, *184*; whip, 178; workhorses, 170. *See also* driving

Horses pulling U.S. Mail Sled, *184*

horticulture, 17–18, 27n2

households: china, 6, 21; cooking utensils, 21–22; cook stove, 88; dishware, 6, 21; domestic work, 114, 122, 218; domestic tools, 43–44; 86; ironing, 114; iron pan, 66; majolica, 7; pitcher, 85; room and board, 122; "Skysweep Broom," 9; tea-cups, 66; washing, 114

Howbert, Irving, 109, *110*, 112–13, 117, 119n28; *Memories of a Lifetime in the Pike's Peak Region*, 118n16

Howbert, William, 109, 112, 119n27

Howell Living History Farm, New Jersey, xiv, 160, 163–64

Huerfano River, 105–7, 118n8

humanist point of view, xiv, 8, 14, 18, 25–26, 29, 81n15, 169, 205, 207–9, 216, 222, 227, 239–40

humanities, 7, 8, 18, 35, 50, 137, 169, 205, 207–8, 227; National Endowment for the Humanities, 207

Hungary, 48; Budapest, 49; Kotse/Kocs, 178

Hunter's Home. *See* George M. Murrell Home

hunting, 26, 105; eels, 181; frogs, 86–87; hunter-gatherers, ix; trapping, 87

Hurt, R. Douglas, 67; *American Agriculture*, 61–62, 15n20, 118n2; *American Farms*, 67, 82n23, 101n21; *American Farm Tools*, 56n28

identification, form-and-function approach, 41, 46, 87–88, 90–91, 93, 95–96, 170, 172 , 174, 177–78, 180, *185*, 226–27, 230

Illinois, 10, 47, 64, 66, 71–72, 81n15, 81n17, 222, 224; Belleville, xiv, 5, 10; Caledonia, xiv; Cook County Farm Bureau, 220; Cook County, 220; Cutler, 91–92; Decatur, 229n13; Greene County, 39n5; Greenville, 10; Rockford, 62; Rockwood, 91–92; Schaumburg, 197, 220; Schaumburg Park District, 197; Shelbyville, 222–24, 229nn13–14; South Holland, 24; Steeleville, 91–92; Union County, 62–63; Wheaton, 229n8; White Hall, 31, 39n5; Winnebago County, 62. *See also* Bogue, Allan G.; Braeutigam Orchards; Cantigny Park; Chicago; Clayville Rural Life Center; Eckert's; Illinois State Museum; Meyer, Carrie A.; Midway Village and Museum Center; oral histories; Volkening Heritage Farm

Illinois State Museum, 206; Audio-Video Barn, 206; "Oral History of Agriculture in Illinois," 206

Indiana: Fair Oaks, xiv, 204–5; Lowell, *125*. *See also* Buckley Homestead State Park; Conner Prairie; and Fair Oaks Farms

industrialization, 35, 42, 158, 215, 236; growth, 49; industrialists, 35, 46, 140, 142, 145, 156; industrial revolution, 47, 50, 56n28; steel magnates, 156

Inglot, Monique, *197*

insects, 190, 225, *226*; grasshoppers, plagues of, 115–16; insecticides, 93, 132, 134; locusts, plagues of, 115–16; *Melanoplus spretus*, 116

insurance, 223, 225, 230n15; crop and liability, 9; Federal Insurance Contributions Act, 34

International Association of Agricultural Museums (*Association Internationale des Musées d'Agriculture*) (AIMA), 241

International Harvester Company, 72, *77*, *123*, 138, 145; International Harvester Building, *73*; International Harvester's Tractor Works, 73, *76*; planters, 94

international trade and aid, 12, 23, 88; international relations, 62, 104, 242, 39n4; gunboat diplomacy, 236

Iowa, 64, 66, 72, 113, 122, 123–24, 130, 133; Butler County, 128; Cedar County, 131; Crawford County, 132; Dallas County, 122; Estherville, 126; Franklin County, 133; Greene County, 131; Grundy County, 124, 130; Jasper County, *95*, 131; Johnson County, 131; Marshall County, 130–31; Poweshiek County, 71, 83n35; Sac County, 132; state economists, 130; state engineers, 128, 133; state extension specialists, 128 Story County, 128; Winneshiek County, 133; Wright County, 132

irrigation. *See* water

Jackson, Adam, 20

Jackson, Wes, 23, 28n17

Jackson, William Henry, *111*

James, Dr. Edwin, 116

Jefferson, Thomas, 11, 44, 228n3; "The description of a mould-board of the least resistance, and of the easiest and most certain construction," 54n16; Monticello, 55n16

John Brown Farm State Historic Site, New York, 83n34

112, 121, 128, 142, 150, 169–85, 187–200, 204–5, 209, 215, *216*, 223, 231, 242; antibiotic-free meat, 32; branding, 194; butchering, 32, 66, 122, 190, 199–200; confinement approach, 9, 13–14, 18, 63, 188, 192, 203–4, 209, *210*; farrowing houses, 121, *127*, *129*; finishing houses, feed lots, 121, *127*, *129*; feed sacks, xiv; free-range, 9, 32, 203; finishing houses, 121, *127*, *129*; grass fed, 32; at historic sites and living history farms, 187–200; open-range, 13–14; paddocks and stalls, 188; *Planning Grain-Feed Handling for Livestock and Cash-Grain Farms*, 135n20; sedentary livestock disorder, 199; slaughter of, 6, 152, 198, 223; stock shows, 48; urban, ix, 5–6, 72, 170; varieties of, xv, 6, 23, 48, 70, 191, 195, 217. *See also* animals

living history farms/sites, xiv, 1–3, *4*, 7, 8, 20, 34 38, 42, 49, *51*, 53, 54nn12–13, 57n37, 71, 79, 87, 97, 99, 103, 117, 142, 159–60, 163, 169–70, 187–91, 193–200, 204–5, 207–8, 217–18, 220, 227, 241, 243; challenges, 187–92, 195–200; and fencing, 191–92, 195; interpreters, xiv, 20, 29, 71, 98, 137, 187, 196–200, *197*, *198*; and research projects, 190–94, 196–97, *197*; staffing, 7, 190–94, 196–200

lobbying, 163,193, 208; farm lobby, 11–13; farmers as interest group or lobby/power, 11–12, 31, 34, 36, 64, 158–59; special interest groups, 157, 159, 163

Lopez, Carol Kennis, "We Can't Eat Gold," 103–20

Louisiana, 25, 71, 139; Baton Rouge, 25; Bayonne, 25; Cherie Quarters, 25; cooperative community, 139; Louisiana Division of Historic Preservation, 25; Louisiana State University, 25; New Roads, 25

Lowenthal, David, "Memory," 41–42, 44–46, 54n1, 75, 77

Ludwig, Joseph, 130, 133

Lyell, Charles, 43–44

machinery xiv, 5, 7, 8, 9, 12, 88, 93, 97–98, 115, 121–25, *125*, 128, 130–34, 208, 225, 236–37; antique machinery clubs, 208, 39n4; breaking, 145; experimental machines, 137–40, 143, 145; Handy Buncher, *4*

Magoffin Home State Historic Site, 227, 231–33, *232*; Master Interpretive Plan, 234n4

Magoffin, Joseph, 231, *232*, 233

Maine, 49, 222–24, 230n14; Hinckley, 19; Lisbon, 222–24; Little river Vill, 223; *Maine Beautiful*, 49. *See also* L. C. Bates Museum

Mandell, Nikki, 52; "Thinking Like a Historian Chart," 52, *53*

manufacturers/manufacturing, 12, 63–4; 72, 93, *114*, 115 131, 133, 137–38, 139–40, 142–43, 145, 156–57, 163, 175, 203, 208, 215, 227

manure, 5–6 , 17–18, 23, 34, 66, 179, 188, 197, 225, *226*; manure forks, 86–87, *126*

maps, 22, 62, 68, 80n9, 82n28, 86, 99n1, 106, 167n33; Michigan County Histories and Atlases Digitization Project, 62; Missouri Historical Maps and Atlases Project, 62; plat books/platting, 62, 105, 108; Sanborn Maps, 225, 230n15, 234n5

Marcoot Jersey Creamery, 10; Artisan and Farmstead Cheeses, 15n19

marketing. *See* advertising

markets, 8, 23, 30, 50, 62–63, 66–67, 69, 71, 88, 104, 106–7, 112–13, 116–17, 124, 150, 152, 159, 188, 206, 218, 222, 224, *226*, 242; farmers' markets, 7, 24, 218; free 12, 33; hay, 72; history, 62; infrastructure linking farmers to markets, 149–64; market revolution, 62; niche, x; open-air market, 225, *226*; prices, 32, 63–64, 66, 71, 107, 113, 124, 133, 144, 150, 159, 223–24, 230n14; public, 225; regulations, 10, 12, 31; roadside markets and stands, 161–63, *162*; St. Louis (Missouri) Farm Market, 15n5

Marriott, Paul Daniel, 163; *Preservation Office Guide to Historic Roads*, 166n29; *Guide to Historic Roads*, 157

Maryland, 149, 156–59, 188, 207; Baltimore, 157; Frederick County, 157–59; Hunting Creek, Thurmont, 159; Little Catoctin Creek, Frederick County, 157, *158*. *See also* Hampton National Historic Site; Valecreek Farm

Maschhoffs, 9–10

Massachusetts, 44, 46–47; Boston, 68–69; Concord, 188; Lowell, 56n22; Massachusetts Bay Colony, 47; Old Coast Road, 68; Quincy, 68; Plymouth, 68; Plymouth Colony, 46; Springfield, 83n34. *See also* Adams National Historic Park; General Artemas Ward House Museum; Old House at Peacefield; Old Sturbridge Village

material culture, 85, 91–93, 99n1, 100n14, 220, 225–27; approaches to, 225–27; art history, 225; behavioralistic concept, 227; cultural historical orientation, 226; environmentalist preoccupation, 226; functionalist rationale, 226; national character focus, 227; social history paradigm, 227; structuralist view, 226; symbolist perspective, 226

mathematics, xv, 164; as curriculum element, 7, 15n8, 35

McCabe, Betsy, "Portraying Historical Agriculture through Public History," 20, 27n7

McCormick Company, 236–37; documents, 236; McCormick Works "Garden Project," Chicago, 72–73, *75*; McCormick-Deering corn picker, *123*; McCormick-International Harvester Collection, 80n8

McCormick, Amy Irwin Adams, 229n8

McCormick, Cyrus, 227, 235–36, *237*

McCormick, Nettie Fowler, 227, 235–37, *237*

McCormick, Robert R. "Colonel," 229n8

McGraw, Seamus, 31; *Betting the Farm on a Drought*, 39n5

mechanic shops/mechanics, 46, 64, 67

media, x, 15n21, 23, 72, 91, 94, 165n18, 206–07, 209; ABCNews.com, 32, 39n6; coverage, 33; digital age, 74–75, 77; Google, 91; Internet, x, 26, 91, 94; mobile app, 8, 22, 211; social media, 19, 78; tape recorder, 144; telephones, 140; video, 22, 143; websites, 28n18, 206–7, 211, 225, 230n15, 241; YouTube, 207. *See also* movies, theater, films, and television; radio

memory/memorializing, 41–42, 44–45, 53, 74–76, 89, 144; commemorations, 77; Pikes Peak gold rush sesquicentennial, 103; U.S. Bicentennial, 78, 142, 196. *See also* farm programs

merchants, 106–7, 217

Mexico/Mexicans, 104, 112, 144; and Braceros research, 207; Henequen plantations, 237; Indigenous peoples of the Yucatan, 237

Meyer, Carrie A., 62–64; "The Farm Debut of the Gasoline Engine," 80n8; *Days on the Family Farm*, 80n6; *Founding Farmers*, 81n15

Michigan, 31; Dearborn, 49, 190; Kalamazoo, xiv, 189; Kalamazoo Nature Center, 39n4; Michigan County Histories and Atlases Digitization Project, 62

Midway Village and Museum Center, Illinois, 81n15

Midwest Open Air Museums Coordinating Council (MOMCC), 2, 189, 193–95, 200n8, 201n17, 241; *Midwest Open Air Museums Magazine*, 2, 56n27, 200n7; "Statement of Professional Conduct," 194–95. *See also* Association for Living History, Farms and Agricultural Museums

migrants, 30; "Arkies," 144; Euro-American, 103–4, 106, 108–9, 113; "Okies," 144; Swiss, ix; Texans, 144

military, 42, 70–71, 124, 186n3, 205; generals, 44, 71; militia, 47; Reserve Officers' Training Corps, 205; troops, 106, 150; U.S. Army, 70–71, 150

Miller, Lynn R., 88; *Work Horse Handbook*, 88, 100n8, 170; *Horsedrawn Plows and Plowing*, 88, 100n8

mills, 70; burr mill, *198*; flour mill, 106–7, 113, 115, 120n36; saw-mills, 108; sorghum mill, 91–92

Milwaukee Harvester Company, *114*

Milwaukee, Wisconsin, *73*; Hay Market, *74*

minerals, 85–86; graphite, 145; marl, 86. *See also* gold; stone

mining, 62, 112; claims, 108; coal, 108, 171; gypsum quarry, 110–11; tools, 106; towns, 107. *See also* Pikes Peak

Minnesota, 192; Oliver Kelley Farm, 192; Wells Fargo Family Farm, 14n1

Mississippi, 82n28, 171, 239; Madison County, 70

Missouri, 144; Missouri Historical Maps and Atlases Project, 62; St. Louis, 39n5, 223–24, 229nn13–14

Missouri River, 115

Mitchell, W. R., 124

MOMCC. *See* Midwest Open Air Museums Coordinating Council

Monsanto, 9, 14, 15n21

Mount Vernon, Virginia, 20–21, 25, 43, 54n12; Mount Vernon Ladies Association, 44

movies, theater, films, and television: 23–26, 74; *Field of Dreams*, 25; *Finding the Story: Confronting the Past*, 20; *Frontier House* (PBS series) 199; *The Natural*, 25; productions, 20, 27; *So Big*, 24; theater as curriculum element, 7, 15n8, 35. *See also* media; radio

mules, 64, 70–71, 89, 96, 115, 159, 170, *185*, 221; burros, 112–13; mule skinners, 170; mule trains, 71

Murrell, Amanda Ross, 70–71, 228n4

Murrell, Emily L., 70–71, 82n28

Murrell, George Michael, 70–71, 82n28, 82n32, 217

Murrell, John William, 70, 82n32

Murrell Home. *See* George M. Murrell Home; Ross-Murrell family

Museum of Science and Industry, Illinois, 3

museum programming, xv, 22–24, 26, 29, 31, 71, 78–79, 81n15, 98–99, 117, 191, 196–98, 207, 209, 211, 218, 232–33, 239; children/youth, 19, 20, 23, 31, 38n2, 38n3, 195, 204–05, 216; exhibit research and design, 8; film series, 23–24; planning, 6–8, 18, 21, 26n1, 34, 52, 61, 65, 68, 78, 89, 99, 137, 142, 187–88, 205, 207–8, 211, 216, 219–20, 227–28, 239–40; reading circles and discussion series, 23–25, 207–9, 222, 242; *Topic Talks*, 20; tours, 211, 218; types of, 8, 49, 78, 79, 88, 152, 188, 191, 195–200, 205–6, 209, 215, 218, 220. *See also* public interest

museums, x, xiv, xvii, 3, 7, 10, 14, 18–9, 21–2, 26, 29–31, 34–35, 41–42, 48–49, 53, 78, 86–90, 97–8, 137, 140, 142, 150, 169–71, 187–90, 195–96, 203–6, 217–18, 227, 239–40, 243; as agriculture interpreter, x, xiii, 26, 29–30, 34, 49, 52, 61, 74, 76–79, 82n33, 88–89, 96–99, 142, 152, 158, 163–64, 170, 188, 190–91, 196–200, 203, 205–9, 215–28, 231–33, 240; authentic/tangible and hands–on experiences therein, x, 3, 31, 34, 38, 38n3, 79, 98, 142, 187–92, 194–200, 203–4, 205, 218, 221, 231–33; challenges of, 30, 52, 98, 142, 187, 191–92, 195–8, 209, 221–22, 231–33; collecting and managing collections, 5, 30, 31, 34, 35, 38, 42–43, 45, 48–50, 53, 57n37, 68, 79, 88, 97–99, 99n2, 102n31, 137–46, 152, 154, 175, 190–91, 194–200, 206, 208–9, 218–20, 227, 239–40; Collection Committee, 81n15, 142, 143; and controversy and conflict, xv, 11, 22, 30–34, 35–36, 42, 47, 63–64, 78–79, 187, 190, 192–94, 203–4, 206–9; curators, 1–3, 5, 7, 42, 45, 48–49, 54, 63, 72, 86, 88, 90, 97, 102n31, 137–38, 142, 145, 146n10, 204, 239; deaccessioning, 97–99, 199–200, 239; European and world agricultural museums, 48–9; farmers as resource for museums, xiv, 7–8, 140, 142–45, 204–6, 209, 211, 225, 227; founders, 240; history, 3, 53; interpretation revision, 225; Interpreting Agriculture Plan, 220; and livestock acquisition, 187–91, 194–97, 200n3, 200n8, 201n21, 243; and livestock importance, 187–8, 194; and local history, 7, 30, 79, 209, 211, 219, 231–33, 239–40; media outlets, 78; open-air, xiv, 2, 35, 46, 49, 54n13, 57n37, 142, 170, 190–95, 198, 208, 241; registrars, 142; renovation, 142, 233; reproductions, 43, 99; reverse-chronological approach, 221; staff, xiv, 5, 7, 21, 30, 46–47, 52, 68, 78–79, 96–99, 142, 146n10, 154, 163, 187–200, 205–9, 217–19, 222, 225, 227; storage, 97–99, 209, 239; as trusted source of information, x, 41, 53, 74–79, 190, 192–94, 203, 218; underinterpreting, 218; visitor interaction, xv, 7, 57n37, 68, 154, 196–200, 204, 208, 215–16, 218–20, 225, 227–28, 231–33, 239–40. *See also* historic houses/sites

museum studies program, 227; museum exhibits course, 236

myths, 42–43, 44, 45, 49, 63, 72, 130, 220, 222, 226; of independent farmer, 11, 43, 48–50, 61–62, 221–22

8, 88, 170, 189, 206–7; how-to exhibitions, 48; identification/collectors guides, 156, 165n24, 180, 225; newsletters, 195. *See also* newspapers

public health and safety, 32, 151, 153, 155–59, 161, 163–64, 208; consumer health, 7, 11, 12, 19, 143, 158

public interest, xv, 33, 68, 89; in agricultural topics, 3, 5, 10, 14, 18, 20–23, 27, 30, 32, 34, 42, 48–50, 57n37, 61, 63, 74–79; 88, 90, 189, 191, 205, 208, 209, 219–20, 222, 239

public records, 50, 78; archival research, 67–68, 78, 86, 89–90; city directories, 67; land records, 67; tax records, 6, 109, 120n43

Purina Chows, *210*

Quaker Oats, 12
Quonset buildings, 124

race, 37–38, 40n18, 218, 220, 222, 225; Center for the Study of Race and Ethnicity, 207; Creole, 25; ethnicity, 67, 104–7, 222; minorities, 242; race relations, 20–21, 24–26, 30, 62, 70; racial categories, 18, 30, 34, 36–38; racism, 11, 15, 25; segregation, 25; tokenism, 36. *See also* class

radio, 23; WGN radio station, 229n8

railroads, 104, 150–52, 161, 224, 232; hubs, 152, 159; stations, 151; steam engines, 164; tracks, *73*

ranches, 35, 106–7, 116–17, 144, 151–52, 154–55, 191, 217–18; ranchers, 113, 150, 154; ranch houses, 30

Randolph, Wayne, 51; "The Bar Share Plow in Virginia," 54n16

Reconstruction, *221*

Reid, Debra A., 27n15, 82n27, 122, 166n31, 187–88, 229n12; "Agricultural Artifacts," 56n31, 100n2; "Creeps, Feeders, and Creep Feeders," 212n12; "Livestock and Living History," 187–88; "McCormick-IHC Collection, Wisconsin Historical Society, Madison, Wisconsin," 80n8; "Starting a Living History Farm," 200n3; "Tangible Agricultural History," 85, 90, 100n15; and Bennett, Evan P., eds., *Beyond Forty Acres and a Mule*, 27n10; 83n36; and Kuester, Jonathan D., "Livestock in Agricultural Interpretation," 187–201; and Saffell, Cameron L., "Roads and Bridges in Rural Agricultural Interpretation," 149–67

Reid, William (Bill), 190; "Breeding for Authenticity," 200n7

religion, 37–38, 218; churches, 25; Mormon, 106; Old Testament, 47, 50; pastor, 235; Presbyterian, 235; values, 33–34

Riney-Kehrberg, Pamela, *The Routledge History of Rural America*, 62

Rio Grande, 231, 233

Rio Hondo, 153–54

River Lake Plantation, Louisiana, 25; Friends of Cherie Quarters, 25

rivers, 152, 156; arroyos, 156; creeks, 152, 156, 163; ponds, 19, 204; streams, 161. *See also* canals

R. J. K. Company, 91

roads, 68–69, 121, 149–64, *160*, 176, 181, 222, *226*; *America's Highways, 1776–1976*, 164n1; Bankhead–Shackleford Act, 151; building, 150–52, 159–60, 163, 165n8, 179; Bureau of Public Roads/Federal Highway Administration, 150–51, 157, 164n4, 166n26; Commission of Public Roads, 159; commissions, 152; county road supervisor, 152; farm to market transport, 8, 42, 149–51, 154–60; Federal Aid Road Act of 1916, 151; Federal-Aid Highway Act of 1936, 165n8; federally funded, 154; Good Roads Movement, 149–51, 156–57, 159, *160*, 163; *The High Risk Rural Roads Program in the Delaware Valley*, 167n36; highways, 91, 105–6, 150–52, 154–57, 159, 161, 163, 204; historic roadways, 149, 157, 163; and impacting horses, harness, and vehicles, xiv, 160, *160*, 163–64, 171–72, 174–78, 180–82; improving, 150–51, 154, 159–60, 163; and local travel, 150–51, 159–61; locations, 150; maintaining, 150–52, 159–60, 163, 165n8, 179; military routes, 150; National Cooperative Highway Research Program, 157, 166n26; National Good Roads Convention, 150; National Roads, 157–58; Office of Public Roads, 150, 159, 164nn3–4; Office of Road Inquiry, 159; oiled highway, 154; preserving, 157, 163–64; primary roads, 151; road funds, 152; roadside holding pens, 69, 230n13; roadways, xiv, 8, 22, 38, 42, 68–69, *111*, 150; rural roads, 68–9, *111*, 149–52, 154–56, 159–60, 163; section line, 150; State Aid Highway Act, 159; state highway administrations and departments of transportation, 156; toll, 150; U.S. Highway System, 151. *See also* heritage trails and areas; roads, named

Robert Cole's World, 188

Rock Ledge Ranch Historic Site, Colorado, 103, 117

Rocky Mountain News, 106–7, 109, 115

Rocky Mountains, 103–4, 112

Rogin, Leo, 50; *The Introduction of Farm Machinery in Its Relation to the Productivity of Labor in the Agriculture of the United States during the Nineteenth Century*, 56n28, 119n34

Roosenberg, Dick, 39n4

Roosevelt, Theodore, 35

Rose, Julie, *Interpreting Difficult History at Museums and Historic Sites*, 21, 27n11, 204

Rosenberg, Gabriel, 65; *The 4-H Harvest*, 81n14

Rosenquist, Shari, *197*

Rosenzweig, Roy, 74, 77; and Thelen, David, *The Presence of the Past*, 83n37, 229n11

Ross-Murrell family; 70–71; Murrell, Minerva Ross 70, 82n28; Ross, Chief John 70–71, 228n4; Ross, Lewis, 70; Ross, Robert Bruce, 83n33. *See also* Murrell family

rubber, 176

Ruffolo, Dick, *198*

Ruggles, S. B., 66, 81n18

Runyan, W. R., *Identifying Horse-Drawn Farm Implements*, 88, 100n7

rural life, 9, 12, 14, 18–19, 24–5, 35, 38, 42–43, 49–50, 54, 61–65, 68, 149–64, 203, 211, 215, 226–27, 242;

African American communities, 20–21, 24–26, 207, 217, 228n5; communities, 38n4151, 153, 161, 203, 217, 224, 231–33; culture, 10, 22, 23–25, 31–33; poverty, 62

Rural Lit R.A.L.L.Y., 24, 28n18

Russell, William Green, 104–5

Rust, John D., 138–39, *139*, 140, 143–44, 146nn5–6; "The Origin and Development of the Cotton Picker," 146n3; John Rust Foundation, 142. *See also* Ben Pearson Company

Rust, Mack, 138–40, *139*

Saffell, Cameron L., 88, 227, 165n21; "An Alternative Means of Field Research," 100n7; "Case Study: Interpreting Rural Life in El Paso," 231–34; "Historical Evolution of Land Ownership from James Wiley Magoffin to Joseph Magoffin and the Glasgows," 234n1; and Reid, Debra A., "Roads and Bridges in Rural Agricultural Interpretation," 149–67

Sale, Kirkpatrick, 145; *Rebels against the Future*, 145, 146n8

Santa Fe Trail, 105, 106, 108

Schlebecker, John T., 86–87, 89, 91, 95, 98–99, 189, 193–94; *Agricultural Implements and Machines in the Collection of the National Museum of History and Technology*, 55n21; "Keeping the Records," 99n2; and Peterson, Gale E., *Living Historical Farms Handbook*, 189, 200n3; "Research in Agricultural History at the Smithsonian Institution," 101n17; "Standards of Excellence for Living Historical Farms and Agricultural Museums," 2, 102n30; "The Use of Objects in Historical Research," 100n3; *Whereby We Thrive*, 118n2

Schlereth, Thomas J., 225–27, 100n14; edited, *Material Culture Studies in America*, 100n3; "Material Culture Studies in America, 1876–1976," 100n14, 230n18

Schlichting, Carl, 102n31

schools, 7, 25, 35, 72, 143, 151, 195, 206, 209, 223–24; consolidated, 151; correspondence, 138; education, 64, 161, 207, 217, 241–42; lunch programs, 37; milk programs, 37; Newell's Singing School, 223; Rosenwald Schools, 217, 229n5; social studies, as curriculum element, 35; STEALTH (science, technology, engineering, art, literature, theater, history, economics, environment, and politics), 7–8, 15n8; STEAM (science, technology, engineering, art, and mathematics), 7; STEM (science, technology, engineering, and mathematics), 7, 15n8, 35; tours, 205; teachers, 74–75, 205, 207, 209

Schultz, Mark R., 207; "Conversations with Farmers," 212n9

science: agricultural science/scientists, 7, 23, 33, 47–8; as curriculum element, 7, 15n8, 35; and farming, x, 14, 18, 23, 35, 205, 208–9, 215–16, 220, 242; forensic, 190; and technology in farming xiv, 10–11, 18, 33–36, 43–44, 46–48, 50, 62–65, 73, 79, 89, 92, 96, 104, 113–15, 121, 124–25, *125*, 128, 130–34, 137–40, 144–45, 169, 172–85, 205, 208–9, 222, 225–26, 236, 242

Sears Roebuck, 23, 151

Sebold, Kimberly R., 167n35

secondary sources, 61–3, 73, 78, 79n1, 104, 188, 219–20, 222, 240, 242

settlement associations. *See* claim clubs

settlers, 109, 116

sharecroppers/sharecropping, 5, 11, 73, 89, 140, 220

Shaw family, 91–92

Sheldon, A. Z., 110, 113, 117, 120n43

Sinclair, Upton, *The Jungle*, 6, 24

Skansen, open-air museum in Stockholm, 49, 57n37

slavery, 5; 11–12, 20–21, 25–26, 27n9, 27n10, 27n12, 30, 36, 43–44, 67, 70–71, 82n28, 82n33, 217, 220, 228n3, 228n5; and abolitionists, 71; Fugitive Slave Law, 71; slave schedules, 230n15

Slining, Jim, xvii, 46–47, 54n10, 54n13, 54n16, 56n22, 56n24

Smalley, Ken, 131; and Marsha Smalley, 135n14

Small Farmer's Journal, 170, 189

Smithsonian Institution, 2–3, 14n2, 86, 88, 142, 189, 207–8; *American Enterprise*, 3, 14n2; *Dig It*, 3; National Museum of American History, 207, 225

Smokey Hills Trail, 105

sociology, 35, 61, 62; sociocultural identity, 33

soil, 3, 10–11, 13, 17–19, 23, 25, 46, 47–48, 50, *51*, 86, 88, 93–94, 96, 107, 113, *123*, 188, 199, 204; "philosopher's soil," 17–18

sorghum, 91–92, 94; "Discussion of Chemicals used in Sorghum Making," 101n20; M. L. Shaw Pure Country Sorghum, *92*; sorghum can, 85, 91–2, *92*; "Sorghum Mill at Steeleville Wye Reminiscent of an Earlier Day," 101n18

South Carolina: Burgess, 217, 228n5; Myrtle Beach, 228n5

Southern Oral History Project, 207; "Breaking New Ground," 207

Sparks, Howard, 128

Speed, John, 217, 228n3

Staffell, Cameron L., "An Alternative Means of Field Research," 85

state departments of agriculture, 35, 209, 242

Steinel, Alvin T., 116; *History of Agriculture in Colorado*, 118n5, 120n36

stereotypes, 30, 34–35, 37

Stoll, Steven, *Larding the Lean Earth*, 18, 27n3, 188, 200n1

stone, 69, 86, 90–91, 99n1, 113, *160*, 163, 177, 179, 233; boats, 177, 179

stores, 52, 222, 224; bakery, 5; confectionary shop, ix; feed, 67, 209; green grocers, 24, 72; grocery, 42; mercantile, 70; rural supply, 9

Stowe, Harriet Beecher, 177; *Uncle Tom's Cabin*, 177

straw, 71, 113, 115, 192

Street, James H., *The New Revolution in the Cotton Economy*, 138, 146n1

Sufkin, Chas. (Charles) D. 222–24, 230n14

Sukup, Eugene, 133

Sweden, 175; Stockholm, 49; Skansen, 49, 57n37

swords, 47, 50

visual literacy, 5, 38, 90, 156, 225
Vocale, Emanuel, 89, 100n13
Volkening Heritage Farm, Illinois, 22, 197, 220

Wallace's Farmer, 124, 130, 131, 134n2, 134n6, 134nn8–12, 135nn13–23
Walrond, Sallie, *Looking at Carriages*, 186n5; *The Encyclopedia of Carriage Driving*, 186n5
Ward family, 44, 47. *See also* General Artemas Ward House Museum
Washburn-Norlands Living History Center, 79
Washington: Seattle, 191; Woodland Park Zoological Gardens, 14n1, 191
Washington, George, 20, 44; *The Diaries of George Washington* (eds. Jackson and Twohig), 54n15
Wassom, Merrit, 132
water, 11, 72, 86, 104, 108, 109–12, 113, 116–17, 119n27, 120n43, 161, 204; dams, 113; humidity, 98; irrigation ditches, 109–10, *111*, 112, 116, 231, 233; moisture retention, 93; retention ponds, 233; run-off, 50; water power, 115; waterways, 112, 161. *See also* canals; rivers
Watson, Pete, xiv, 160, 163–64, 166n31
weather, 9, 23, 32, 72, 96, 116, 124, *127*, 128, 132, 171, 190, 206, 222, 223; climate, 11, 31–32, 35, 112, 115, 188, 223–24, 233, 242; droughts, 32, 124; flooding, 115, 151–54, 156; humidity, 98, 171; Hurricane Irene, 163; microclimates, 204; National Oceanic and Atmospheric Administration, 32; snow, 115–16, 171, 176–78, *216*, 223; storms, 51, 151; and vehicles, 171; winds, 122, 125
Wells, Marcella, Butler, Barbara, and Koke, Judith, *Interpretive Planning for Museums*, 15n6, 27n1
Wendel, C. [Charles] H., 88; *150 Years of International Harvester*, 101n25; *Encyclopedia of American Farm Implements & Antiques*, 100n6; *Encyclopedia of Antique Tools and Machinery*, 100n6

West, Elliott, 107; *The Contested Plains*, 118n10
West, G. H., *126*
wheels, 88, 94, 115
White House Ranch, Colorado, 103, 117
Whitney, Eli, 225
Whitney, Mrs. George, 69, *69*
Wilder, Laura Ingalls, 45
Wildman, Thomas, 107
William Green Russell party, 104–5
Williams, Elizabeth Dumville, 71
Williams, John W., 71–72
Williams, Margaret Emily, 72, 83n35
Wilson, John S., 67; "We've Got Thousands of These!" 82n24
Wineburg, Sam, *Historical Thinking and Other Unnatural Acts*, 52, 57n41
wire, *127*; barbed and woven, 9
Wisconsin, *73–74*, *114*, 122; Wisconsin Agricultural Society, 36; Wisconsin Historical Society, 80n8, 236. *See also* Milwaukee, Wisconsin
Witmore, Christopher, 86, 99n1
women, 10, 20, 23–24, 30, 36, 45, 67–68, 70–71, *75*, 91, 97, 104, 108, 122, 139–40, *182*, *197*, 217, 235–36, 239; gender, 18, 33, 34, 37–38, 51, 61–62, 64, 67, 70, 152, 189, 218, 220, 236; suffrage, 217
World War II, 73, 121, 124, 130, 138, 144, 170, 208

Yow, Valerie Raleigh, *Recording Oral History*, 211n6

zoos, 3, 14n1, 191–92, 194–96, 204; Lincoln Park Zee, Illinois, 14n1; Minnesota Zoo, 14n1; Phoenix Zoo, Arizona, 14n1; Woodland Park Zoological Gardens, Washington, 14n1, 191; zooarchaeologists, 190; zoology, xv, 192

ABOUT THE AUTHORS

J. L. Anderson, associate professor of history, Mount Royal University, Calgary, Canada, is active in the Agricultural History Society and serves on the board of Heritage Park Historical Village in Calgary. His books include *Industrializing the Corn Belt: Agriculture, Technology, and Environment, 1945–1972* (2009) and *Pigs in America: A Narrative History* (forthcoming). He coedited *The Great National Struggle in the Heart of the Union: Midwestern Perspectives on the Civil War Era* (2013) with Ginette Aley, and edited *The Rural Midwest since World War II* (2014). He has published articles in *Technology and Culture, Agricultural History,* and the *Annals of Iowa.*

Barbara Corson is a retired veterinary pathologist and registered nurse, as well as a lifelong devotee of the agrarian lifestyle. She is currently the farmer at Colonial Pennsylvania Plantation, a nonprofit educational historic farm in Media, Pennsylvania. There she devotes her time to caring for the farmland, crops, and animals while developing programs that engage people in learning about agrarian skills.

Tom Kelleher is a historian and curator of mechanical arts, and works as a historically costumed interpreter at Old Sturbridge Village, a living history museum in Massachusetts. He regularly lectures, demonstrates historic crafts, performs character presentations, and teaches at museums and historical societies around the country. At this writing Kelleher serves as president of the Association for Living History, Farm and Agricultural Museums. He holds a master's degree in history from the University of Connecticut and is also a registered nurse. His writings on technology and history have been published in several journals, books, and popular magazines, including *Early American Life.*

Carol Kennis Lopez earned a BA in American history with a specialization in public history from Colorado State University, and an MA in American history from the University of Colorado at Colorado Springs. For more than twenty-five years Lopez has created experiential and traditional learning opportunities about the history of the American West at the Rock Ledge Ranch Historic Site, the Colorado Springs Pioneers Museum, and the Albuquerque Museum's historic property Casa San Ysidro: The Gutiérrez/Minge House. She is active in professional organizations supporting and promoting excellence in museum education, historical research, preservation, and management.

Jonathan D. Kuester has worked in living history for more than half of his life. A native of Indiana, he began interpreting agriculture at Conner Prairie during the mid-1990s and continued as director of farm operations at Historic Brattonsville in South Carolina. In 2001 he relocated to the Chicago-area living history farms (CALHF) and worked at Volkening Heritage Farm (Schaumburg Park District) and then at Primrose Farm (St. Charles Park District) before assuming his current position as farm manager of Volkening Heritage Farm. He has served as president of the Midwest Open Air Museums Coordinating Council and as cochair of the FARM professional interest group of ALHFAM (the Association for Living History, Farm and Agricultural Museums). Kuester is the author of a variety of articles on historic farm management and livestock care published in the *Midwest Open Air Museums Magazine* and the ALHFAM *Bulletin* and ALHFAM *Proceedings*. He is an advocate for the care and use of livestock in living museums and a willing participant in the living history experiment.

Peter M. Noll is assistant professor of public history and museum studies at Tusculum College in Greeneville, Tennessee. He holds a PhD in agricultural history and rural studies from Iowa State University and an MA in historical administration from Eastern Illinois University. His work in the classroom is profoundly influenced by several years of professional experience working in agricultural and open-air museums.

William S. Pretzer has been a research historian at the National Museum of American History and Winterthur Museum, a curator and educator at Henry Ford Museum & Greenfield Village (now The Henry Ford), and a professor and museum director at Central Michigan University. Currently, he is the senior history curator at the Smithsonian's National Museum of African American History and Culture. He has produced exhibitions, publications, and programs on industrial, social, and political history. He received his BA from Stanford University and his PhD from Northern Illinois University.

Debra A. Reid grew up on a farm in the hills of southern Illinois. She is curator of agriculture and the environment at The Henry Ford. Between 1999 and 2016 she taught in the Department of History at Eastern Illinois University and since 2005, in the College of Agricultural, Consumer, and Environmental Sciences at the University of Illinois in Champaign–Urbana. She has served as president of the Association for Living History, Farm and Agricultural Museums (2013–2015), as first vice-president of the International Association of Agricultural Museums (2011–present), and has been on the board of the Agricultural History Society (2011–2014). She was inducted as a fellow of the Agricultural History Society in 2015. Her publications include *Reaping a Greater Harvest:*

African Americans, the Extension Service, and Rural Reform in Jim Crow Texas (2007) and *Beyond Forty Acres and a Mule: African American Landowning Families since Reconstruction* (2012), coedited with Evan P. Bennett.

Cameron L. Saffell is assistant professor of museum science and curator of history at the Museum of Texas Tech University and is a historian of the nineteenth- and twentieth-century American Southwest. He has researched, written, and exhibited extensively on agricultural and rural topics in the region, including cotton farming and material culture, transportation, regional art, and the early development of El Paso, Texas.